Karnali under Stress

Livelihood Strategies and Seasonal Rhythms in a Changing Nepal Himalaya

BARRY C. BISHOP
National Geographic Society

University of Chicago
Geography Research Paper nos. 228-229
1990

Library of Congress Cataloging-in-Publication Data

Bishop, Barry C.
    Karnali under stress : livelihood strategies and seasonal rhythms in a changing Nepal
Himalaya / Barry C. Bishop.
        p.   cm.   — (Geography research paper : no. 228-229)
    Includes bibliographical references.
    ISBN 0-89065-135-3 :
    1. Karnali Zone (Nepal) — Economic conditions. 2. Karnali Zone (Nepal) —
Social conditions. 3. Karnali Zone (Nepal) — Politics and government. 4. Anthro-
geography — Nepal — Karnali Zone. I. Title. II. Series: Geography research
paper (Chicago, Ill.) ; no. 228-229.
    HC425.Z7K373   1990
    330.95496—dc20
                                                                    89-20206
                                                                        CIP

Geography Research Papers are available from:

The University of Chicago
Committee on Geographical Studies
5828 South University Avenue
Chicago, Illinois 60637-1583

Frontispiece. Karnali physiography

Karnali
under Stress

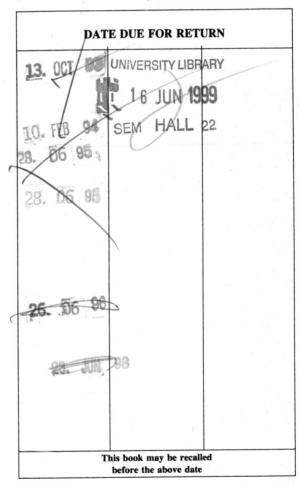

To Lila, Tara, and Brent
—through whose eyes came clarity

Gãthi Na Muthi Bhad Bhad Uthi
"Cut your coat according to the cloth."
—Jumla proverb

Contents

Figures

Tables

Acknowledgments

The first moon landing occurred while I was engaged in my Karnali fieldwork. Upon hearing the news, many villagers sought me out not only to express their awe at the feat but to learn more about an event that was at once a technological and a human triumph. They took particular interest in the fact that the distance from earth to its satellite is equivalent to some 450 round trips by tortuous trail between Jumla and Kathmandu. In the time that has elapsed between that event and the appearance of this monograph my hardy friends from western Nepal could have trekked almost halfway to that orb around which their lives are so inexorably entwined. That is, if they had had the needed life support.

In the course of my earthbound, real, and protracted studies, such support was forthcoming from a wide spectrum of family and friends, scholars and colleagues, institutions and organizations. I am thankful for this opportunity to express to them in writing my heartfelt gratitude. Although so many are not specially named here, they, and the valuable roles they played, are not forgotten.

At the National Geographic Society, Melvin M. Payne gave me initial encouragement to embark on the project. The Department of Geography at the University of Chicago provided stimulating interaction with faculty and fellow students and furnished both a special intellectual atmosphere and a valuable foundation during the preparatory phase of my program. I especially appreciate the guidance given by Marvin W. Mikesell, a mentor mindful of how important "hearing the bells" during foreign field investigations is to understanding.

Subsequently, a number of other scholars and associates, here at home and abroad, willingly shared with me their experience and perspective through lively discussion and constructive criticism of my work. Among those to whom I extend my thanks are Jayaraj Acharya, Dor Bahadur Bista, James Clarkson, Gabriel Campbell, James Fisher, Robert Fleming, Jr., Melvyn Goldstein, Douglas Heck, Carter Ide, Jack Ives, Corneille Jest, Melvin Marcus, Charles McDougal, Barney Nietschmann, Frances Nitzberg, Richard Palmieri, Bhim Prasad Shrestha, Mary Slusser, Mervin Stevens, and Harald Uhlig.

Material support for my work came from a variety of sources and in various forms. During the preparatory period at the University of Chicago I was assisted by a Salisbury Fellowship from the Department of Geography and by an Arctic Institute of North America Fellowship. The field research project itself was supported by grants from the National Science Foundation (GS-2037, 3-5659-XX-1777) and the National Geographic Society through its Committee for Research and Exploration. In addition, a USAID/Nepal contract enabled me to hire four enumerators and thus add an economic flow study of Jumla bazaar to my investigations.

Special thanks to the International Harvester Company and Airstream, Inc., both for the loan of a Travelall and travel-trailer and for the infusion of supplementary travel funds that permitted my family to accompany me to Nepal. Moreover, the mode of travel that this logistical support afforded—an extended overland trip from Rotterdam to Kathmandu—allowed us to visit regions of Turkey, Iran, and Afghanistan that presented multidimensional cultural-ecological problems similar to the ones I addressed in western Nepal. In addition, Miss Gladys Snider, an indomitable trekker and generous lady, also helped assure that the field program was a family operation. While we were away, Lillian and Ralph Mueller and Margaret and Jim Beyersdorfer kept the home fires burning in many ways, both in Bethesda and in Cincinnati. Upon our return from Nepal, partial funding for the processing and analysis of field materials and the writing of the report was provided by the National Geographic Society.

In Nepal T. N. Upreti and Prayag Raj Sharma were most helpful in providing me affiliation with the Research Council of Tribhuvan University. Harka Bahadur Gurung, then vice-chairman of the National Planning Commission, was instrumental in facilitating my work with all appropriate ministries of His Majesty's Government, from whom I received the utmost cooperation.

Indra Narayan Manandar, Ramchandra Lal Shresta, and Ang Tsering Sherpa were not only able and energetic field assistants but amiable and close companions during the field investigations. So too were Donnu, Kancha, Lakpa, and Pasang, the Sherpas who handled our logistics. Those remarkable mountaineers endured, with typical grace and humor, the repetition and monotony of extended fieldwork that precluded the excitement of grappling with ice and rock.

Other friends also helped make the stay in Karnali enjoyable for my family and me. John Nystuen and his family spent six weeks of a sabbatical leave with us, during which he allowed himself to be put to work collecting data. And when Carol Laise and Ellsworth Bunker visited us in December 1969, they brought a complete Christmas feast, which even included some of Boris Lissanevitch's "poor man's" paté. On the few occasions that my work took us back to Kathmandu, Claire and Stan Brooks or Libby and Rick Richardson graciously furnished us a home away from home, our Airstream trailer having been released for use on road-building projects in southern Nepal.

In the final analysis, however, it was the resilient people of Karnali themselves who were responsible for making this period of fieldwork such a memorable experience. Once they had accepted my family and me as neighbors, they shared their struggles, aspirations, and frustrations with often surprising openness and candor. Through them we learned much about their dichotomously rich heritage and meager resources, and in the process much about ourselves as well.

During the final, postfield phase of the project, Christine Gailey and April Putman were of great help to me in reducing portions of the field data. On two occasions my parents and Mary Ann and Mel Marcus provided me with cloistered environments in which to write. Emily Stimson voluntarily typed with precision the drafts of my manuscript at a speed inversely proportional to my output. Sayre Rodman supplied his darkroom expertise for the initial printing of some of the photographs taken by my wife and me that are included in this volume. Michael Garrett made the press-ready prints. Derwin Bell drew the shaded-relief base maps and the block diagram that appear in this volume, and Donald Carrick rendered the final cartography and line work with adroit and creative computer skills. Winfield Swanson attacked the index compilation with tenacity and expertise. Lastly, editor Carol Saller managed to keep her sense of humor throughout the long and laborious process of bringing all the elements of the book together. I deeply appreciate her unflagging attention to detail—it shows.

I am especially grateful to Gilbert M. Grosvenor for his generosity, and his attendant patience, in permitting me long leaves from the National Geographic Society to work on this monograph.

Finally, it is to my family that I am most indebted. My wife, Lila, and our children, Tara and Brent, gave me unstinted support throughout the entire project. They shared with me the delights of the field and problems of reverse culture shock upon our return home. They also tolerated with remarkable equanimity—if with some incredulity—the vagaries and vicissitudes I displayed while writing. When, in frustration, I would voice the Jumla proverb "If I go home, my wife is mute; if I go the cowshed, the roof leaks; there is no happiness for an unfortunate person," Lila would calmly counter, "Fed-up persons find stone even in their yogurt." During this period of stress and considerable family sacrifice, she managed our home and a full-time teaching profession with unshakable cheerfulness and efficiency.

This monograph is as much Lila's and the children's as it is mine.

1
Introduction

Twenty-five percent of our planet's land surface is over 1,000 m above sea level. Here in fragile highland and mountain environments live 10 percent of the world's population, primarily in Asia, Africa, and South America (Staszewski 1957). One process that characterizes the developing mountainous nations of these continents is the alarming increase of population, often exceeding 3 percent each year (United Nations 1975). The impact of spiraling human numbers is upsetting delicate ecosystems, degrading or exhausting limited resources, and threatening the ways of life of peoples who, until recently, had successfully coped with their mountain habitats.

The small, mountainous, landlocked country of Nepal is a striking example of such acute social, economic, and environmental problems. An examination of this developing country brings into focus these problems in both time and space. Within a 160 km north-south cross section, altitude ranges from less than 100 m to over 8,000 m above sea level. Local relief between valley bottom and adjacent ridge or summit often is 5,000 m and occasionally is 6,000 m. A diverse succession of biogeographic belts of subtropical, temperate, subarctic, arctic, and even desert-steppe environments is found within this cross section.

Superimposed on and interacting with these diverse environmental belts are economies of equally diverse ethnic groups. Generally speaking, three major ethnic zones are found: in the high Himalayan regions of the

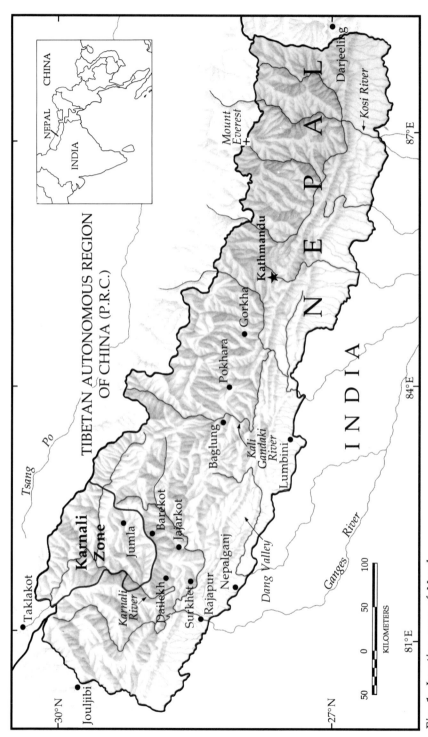

Fig. 1. Location map of Nepal

north between 2,500 and 4,600 m are found Tibetan-speaking Mongoloid people; in the middle valleys between 1,000 and 2,500 m are various Tibetan-Burman and Indo-Aryan speaking peoples; in the southern reaches of the country below 1,000 m live Indo-Aryan peoples (Bista 1972).

Nepal's growing population, now numbering more than twelve million persons, is exacerbating the country's environmental degradation. His Majesty's Government wrestles with this problem and a myriad of associated problems in order to maintain and, it hopes, to improve the economic and social well-being of the people.

BACKGROUND AND SCOPE

Alexander von Humboldt (1817), while working in the Andes, was the first to recognize the relationship of differences in vegetation to the vertical zonation of climate. In recent years several studies of horizontal and vertical zonation of climate and vegetation in mountainous regions have been made, particularly by Carl Troll (1959) and some of his students. One of these, Ulrich Schweinfurth, made a valuable contribution on Himalayan vegetation (1957). Yet such studies of vegetation have excluded humans as one of the communities within the habitat. Such an omission is unfortunate, for humans have significantly altered the natural or wild vegetation in most areas of the world (Thomas 1956). Such is certainly the case in the Himalaya, where the wild vegetation of the country is preserved only in scattered fragments and where, therefore, classifications of "natural vegetation" are misleading and limited or only of theoretical value. Moreover, the validity of this argument is further supported by the presence of ethnic zonation in various mountain regions. Within such zones human beings should be considered animals that interact in response to climatic and other environmental influences.

The Nepal Himalaya is a striking case in point. Since 1951 when Nepal opened her borders and ended 105 years of Rana isolation (Kumar 1967; Regmi 1958) considerable research by Nepalese and foreign scholars has been carried out. Until very recently the areas that have received most attention, outside the valley of Kathmandu, have been the Gandaki and Kosi drainages of central and eastern Nepal. The Karnali drainage of western Nepal has not been as well studied, primarily because of its more remote location, far from Kathmandu and the consequent problems of access.

Although extensive work of a descriptive or taxonomic nature has been undertaken by geologists, soil scientists, agronomists, zoologists, botanists, ethnologists, demographers, and to some extent geographers, with few exceptions interdisciplinary studies of a cultural-ecological nature have been neglected.

Instead unidisciplinary studies across the broad spectrum of physical and social sciences have been the rule. Moreover, these studies have focused on a scale of a single village, nation, or region.

Village studies have been the purview principally of anthropologists and ethnologists, who until recently have usually worked with a small group, band, or village, normally in a relatively isolated environment where traditional patterns of life predominate. For example, if information is gathered on agriculture, the influxes of the modern world are usually kept at bay. In these refuge environments the sample size is small and the temporal perspective is normally one year (e.g., Hitchcock 1966). But most of the world's populations do not exist and function in such an encapsulated manner. Instead their cultures, societies, and environments are parts of larger, multiethnic systems whose varied environments and large populations are undergoing change.

National overviews, such as those by Toni Hagen (1961), Pradyumna Karan (1960), and Wolf Donner (1972), are favored by geographers and economists, as well as development planners. Because of the gross scale of the data employed they tend to obscure important regional and subregional variations and nuances. Intermediate-scale regional studies, such as Harka Gurung's work on the Pokhara Valley (1966) or Christoph von Fürer-Haimendorf's ethnography of the Sherpas of Solu Khumbu (1964), obviate some of the problems mentioned above but still have not fully integrated or linked their findings within broader temporal and spatial contexts.

Indeed what are lacking are multiscale studies that link and integrate findings within a broader temporal and spatial framework. Specifically, attempts to understand the articulations between and among households within a village, villages within a valley or subregion, subregions within a regional montage, regions within a nation, and nations within an international scale are missing.

My own interest in the mountain ecosystems of Nepal was stimulated in the early 1960s when I took part in two expeditions to the Solu Khumbu region in northeast Nepal (Bishop 1962, 1963). During the time that I spent on these expeditions, as well as during later travels in the Kali Gandaki drainage of central Nepal, totaling fifteen months, I was struck by the seasonal and diurnal pulsations of human activities, the great mobility of people in pursuing these activities, and the interaction of various ethnic groups within, between, and among the environmental zones of Nepal. I became concerned with complex questions involving the dynamics of human occupance in mountain environments and human modification of these environments that could explain the nature of both the cultural and physical landscapes that I was observing.

These questions focused on the interrelationships of varied and limited natural resources in often harsh landscapes; the biogeographic processes going on in these environments; the cultures and livelihood pursuits of varied ethnic groups; the articulation of economies through the movement of people, animals, and goods; the response of the people to change-effecting forces; and the cultural and environmental constraints on these people that, in turn, affect their ability to cope with the increasing pressures on their limited energy and land resources and on their often precarious ways of life.

At the same time, I became convinced that to answer these questions and so understand Nepal and the Nepalese, a different research approach was called for, an interdisciplinary one that would provide a multidimensional perspective comprised of environmental, cultural, historical, and temporal components. Furthermore, such a perspective should crosscut and interrelate diverse scales of household, village, region, and nation.

This construct owes much to the ideas of Pierre Dansereau (1966) on ecological principles, Maximilien Sorre (1961) on the concept of *genre de vie*, Julian H. Steward (1963) on the theory of culture change, H. C. Brookfield's (1962) use of a general systems overview for comparative analysis, and particularly the application of specific ecologic viewpoints by Fredrik Barth (1956) in studying the distribution of ethnic groups and cultures in parts of Asia and by Harald Uhlig (1969) in identifying various Himalayan agricultural landscapes.

PROBLEMS AND OBJECTIVES

The study presented here is a systemic regional synthesis with an interdisciplinary cultural-ecological point of view. It focuses on Karnali in northwestern Nepal (figure 1), the largest of Nepal's fourteen administrative zones and a microcosm of the country's exacerbating environmental and ecological stresses (Cool 1967). The central theme of the research is the relationship of humans to the biota of their habitat and their modifications of that habitat. As such it examines the ways the people of Karnali Zone— Indo-Aryan speaking Paharis or hill Hindus and Mongoloid Bhotia of Tibetan origin—traditionally have coped with constraints on their ways of life and how their old methods are holding up today under new and more intense stresses.

For purposes of analysis, the point of view was adopted that Karnali Zone, an intermontane basin complex that constitutes the upper reaches of the Karnali River drainage basin, is an open, macroscale system containing a number of subregional or microscale systems, which themselves are composed of groups of villages made up of a number of households.

Study of existing literature and discussions with a variety of scholars as well as my own personal observations in central and eastern Nepal encouraged three tentative conclusions:

1. All the movements of people, animals, and goods have both a three-dimensional spatial component and a temporal component.
2. The Karnali Zone system, while open, existed in a relatively steady or homeostatic steady state for a century and a half prior to 1951.
3. Since 1951 external sociopolitical forces have been destroying the steady state or homeostatic condition that had prevailed for one and a half centuries and rapid changes have taken place, creating an unstable system.

These tentative conclusions constituted a general conceptual and working framework within which the specific objectives of the research could be placed. In subsequent study I identified, described, and analyzed the rapidly changing cultural-ecological systems of Karnali Zone. I did not, however, seek to deal with all of the cultural and environmental variables present in the system; instead I emphasized the movements of people, animals, and goods, and seasonality.

In order to eliminate the mass of peripheral information that often obscures key issues, a simplified model of Karnali Zone's subsistence economic system was constructed, based on field research. This explanatory model permitted identification of the essential physical, biotic, cultural, political, historical, and technological components and processes of the system and provided a useful heuristic device to realize the following specific research objectives:

1. To discover and treat those key factors that govern or constrain the movements of ethnic groups within and between their habitats;
2. To determine the manner and degree to which these groups by their movements are ecological agents that alter the natural landscape; and
3. To assess the significance of economic, political, and social forces that recently have changed and/or are changing these movement patterns.

To avoid problems common in the traditional village research, regional studies, and gross national overviews discussed above, the work was designed to provide both a historical perspective and a multiscale spatial perspective at four levels: (1) Karnali Zone, a region linked with other zones of Nepal, Nepal as a nation, and other states such as India and Tibet; (2) subregions within Karnali Zone, linked internally and externally with other regions; (3) villages within subregions; and (4) households within villages.

PROCEDURES

The field work for this study was carried out in Nepal over a period of twenty months from October 1968 through May 1970. Of this time fifteen months were spent in Karnali Zone and covered the Nepalese calendar year 2026 V.S. (from mid-April 1969 to mid-April 1970). The scope of the project, as well as the remote location of the study area, demanded considerable logistical organization and a large field force.

My wife, Lila, and our two young children, Tara and Brent, not only accompanied me to Nepal on this project but were an integral part of it. Based upon our experience, the advantages (to say nothing of the joys) of a family participant observation approach in foreign field research cannot be overemphasized. The presence of my entire family, combined with the long period we lived in Karnali Zone, in time allowed us to be accepted and trusted by the local population to a degree that would have been impossible had I worked alone. This acceptance was reflected by the high quality and credibility of information furnished, often voluntarily, by my informants. Without question our children were passports of information.

Moreover, both Lila and Tara contributed to the project research observations; Brent was only two to four years old at the time. Lila provided substantial assistance in collecting data, particularly from women. Tara was able to furnish valuable information on home life because she was permitted free movement in high-caste Hindu homes whose doors were closed to both Lila and me because of pollution beliefs and practices. In addition, because of the acculturation processes she underwent in the field and her total command of the local Nepalese vernacular, the nuances she gave to the interpretation of many conversations she heard were of value to the entire research team (Bishop and Bishop 1971).

In addition to my family, my field team consisted of three Nepalese assistants and a four-man camp and logistical support group. Through the cooperation of Tribhuvan University's Research Council, with whom I was affiliated as a research associate, Indra Narayan Manadhar, who had a master's degree in geography from that institution, was able to work with me. Ramchandra Lal Shresta, with a master's degree in political science from Tribhuvan University, was our principal translator. Ang Tsering Sherpa, who had six years of prior experience working on Swiss Agricultural projects, and whose mother tongue was Tibetan, assisted in the collection of a variety of data.

In order to minimize the amount of time my wife and I, along with our field assistants, had to devote to the normal and necessary activities of daily living and thus be free to direct our maximum energies to the research project, four Sherpas were employed to run our commissary and handle our trekking logistics. Of these, Danu and Kancha were old friends from previous expeditions.

Because of the scarcity of food in Karnali Zone and our desire not to burden the local economy with the needs of a group of this size, we elected to operate in a mostly self-sufficient manner. This required the purchase of over 4,000 man-days of food in Kathmandu and its transport by air to our base of operations at Jumla-Kalanga, the zonal headquarters of Karnali.

While in the field, we traveled over 2,500 km in order to carry out the research. Because of the size and composition of the field team, it was possible to divide into several teams when simultaneous data collection was required.

The integrative, multidisciplinary, multiscale objectives of this study called for equally integrative multiscale procedures in data collection if problems inherent in a program of this size were to be obviated.

Field data methods that included archival searches where possible, participant observation and oral histories, questionnaires, cartography, and photography were employed at several or all of the following scales: national, zonal, district, panchayat (see Appendix A), village, and household.

At the national level, information was obtained from appropriate departments of His Majesty's Government in Kathmandu, such as the Department of Hydrology and Meteorology, the Central Bureau of Statistics, the National Planning Commission, and the Home and Panchayat Ministry, as well as foreign research or development organizations, including the United Nations, United States Agency for International Development, and the German Research Scheme Nepal Himalaya.

In the Karnali study area itself (figure 2), which had never before been systematically worked by scholars, no reliable base data were available. Therefore, my team and I had to generate much background data that the researcher might otherwise expect to be readily available.

A survey to provide information for a cultural-ecological synthesis of the study area and to permit identification of the distinctive subregions or microsystems of Karnali was carried out at the panchayat/village level. Potentially quantifiable data involving a spectrum of key cultural and physical variables that operate in a multidimensional time-space matrix and that are significant to the cultural, ecological, economic, technological, and political dynamics of that matrix were collected with the use of a seventy-category questionnaire.

Testing of this instrument was carried out in five panchayats of Dolpo District of Dhaulagiri Zone on the eastern border of Karnali, thus tying in my area with that under study by Corneille Jest (1974) and James Fisher (1972). After slight modification, the questionnaire was employed to sample thirty-five (37 percent) of the Karnali Zone's ninety-four village panchayats.

In addition, the study area was tied to the southern part of the Karnali River drainage by sampling ten panchayats in Bheri and Rapti zones for comparative purposes.

During the time these field investigations were carried out, Humla District as well as the northern part of Mugu District were closed by His Majesty's Government to foreign visitors. Therefore, information on the panchayats of these areas had to be generated in a variety of indirect ways: some informants from these closed areas were interviewed when they visited the zonal headquarters at Jumla-Kalanga; Ramchandra journeyed to Humla and carried out a survey of four panchayats in that district; information on upper Humla was supplied by Dr. Melvin Goldstein, who worked in that area subsequent to my field period and after it had opened. This information was augmented in 1972, when I was able to visit upper Mugu briefly, as well as in 1974 and 1976, when my wife returned to Karnali Zone.

On the basis of information derived from this heavy panchayat-scale survey, which was conducted over an eight-month period, seventy-four households from nineteen representative villages in the central core area of Karnali Zone were selected for a more intensive questionnaire survey. The households of each village represented both an ethnic and economic cross section of that village. Moreover, the seventy-four-unit sample exhibited a close fit with the ethnic and economic composition of Karnali Zone as a whole. The use of the household unit seemed justified, for it is the most important economically coordinated unit in the study area. Collection of quantifiable data from this sample permitted systematic analysis of daily and seasonal labor budgets, extent of human and animal movements, specialization and exchange, ceremonial obligations, and so on. Moreover, this scheme permitted a determination of the range of responses to change-effecting forces introduced into the system and allowed the identification of those responses that are cultural and those that are individual.

Both of these systematic panchayat and household surveys were designed to provide data compatible for comparison with those derived by Charles McDougal and presented in his work on village and household economy south of Karnali Zone (1968).

While carrying out these surveys, information valuable for a historical perspective was obtained by collection of oral histories. Moreover, His Majesty's Government allowed me access to both the revenue office tax records in Jumla-Kalanga dating from 1830 as well as more recent land reform survey data; these too contributed to the historical perspective.

In addition, the flow of people, animals, and goods into and through Jumla-Kalanga was enumerated for the study year 2026 V.S. (1969-70). The quantities and value of goods being transferred as well as their origins and destinations were measured by Tamang enumerators fluent in Nepali,

Fig. 2. *Map of Karnali Zone*

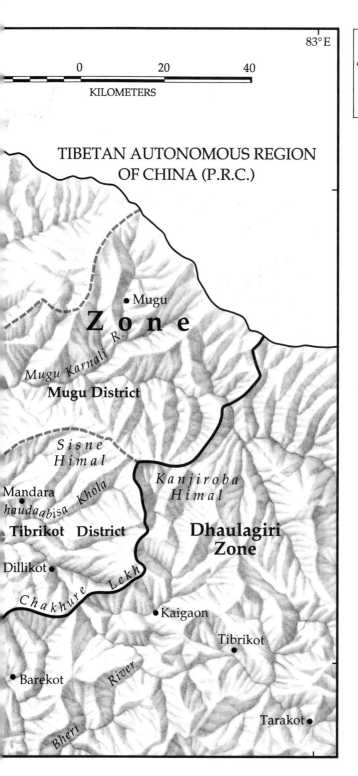

83°E

0   20   40

KILOMETERS

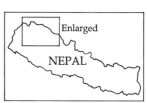

Enlarged

NEPAL

TIBETAN AUTONOMOUS REGION
OF CHINA (P.R.C.)

• Mugu

Z o n e

Mugu Karnali R.

Mugu District

*S i s n e
H i m a l*

Mandara
•

Khola

haudaabisa

*K a n j i r o b a
H i m a l*

Tibrikot   District

**Dhaulagiri
Zone**

Dillikot •

C h a k h u r e   L e k h

• Kaigaon

Tibrikot
•

• Barekot

River

Tarakot •

Bheri

Hindi, and Tibetan, who monitored the four trails leading into the zonal headquarters. The number of people and animals, their home villages and destinations, the routes followed, the times taken for the journeys, and the purposes of the trips were determined.

The households of four Jumla-Kalanga Bazaar shopkeepers were also surveyed to provide an insight into such families' economies; these data are not incorporated with that from the seventy-four rural households. Moreover, a record was maintained of the business operations of all twenty-nine shopkeepers in Jumla-Kalanga during 2026 V.S.

In cooperation with the Department of Hydrology and Meteorology I installed four simple, unmanned weather stations at appropriate locations (Jumla, Dillikot, Burma, and Gum) and obtained both continuous temperature records and monthly rainfall records for 2026. At these sites soil samples were also obtained. Finally, during our travels throughout the zone as well as to Dhaulagiri Zone and Bheri Zone in the east and south respectively, a botanical collection of 200 specimens was made to be identified later and tied into the work of J. D. A. Stainton (1972).

At all scales of inquiry emphasis was placed on the study of spatial structures and variables that determine their arrangement and interaction. The density, distribution, and dimension of these variables were located and measured. Moreover, the sequence of these structures over the calendar was determined.

In this monograph my findings are presented in three parts. A perspective of both the physical and cultural landscapes of Karnali Zone within a broad pan-Himalayan context is provided in chapters 2, 3, and 4. Here the historical perspective is emphasized. Without an appreciation of this historical dimension it is impossible to fully understand current processes, for what went on in the past is reflected in the present-day scene. In chapters 5, 6, and 7, the contemporary livelihood pursuits of the Karnali population are examined topically. Then, in the concluding chapter (8), these pursuits are integrated with the aid of a cultural-ecological subsistence system model. When pertinent, detailed quantitative data at household, panchayat (groups of villages), and regional scales are introduced throughout the monograph.

Nepalese terms are defined when they first appear in the work, and a glossary of these terms is provided in Appendix A. All weights and measures in use in Karnali Zone are converted to metric system; these and their metric equivalents appear in Appendix B.

2

Harsh Himalayan Habitat

Above the low alluvial plains of the Indus, Ganges, and Brahmaputra rivers towers the stupendous rampart of the Himalaya—the abode of snow.[1] The greatest mountain system in the world, it stretches in a broad arc for 2,400 km and separates the Indian peninsula from the Tibetan Plateau of Central Asia. The upper Indus River at Nanga Parbat (8,116 m) in Pakistan marks the northwestern end of the range, while the Tsang Po forms its southeastern boundary where it cuts through the mountains below Namcha Barwa (7,755 m) to become the Brahmaputra River in Assam. North of the Himalaya lie paralleling trans-Himalayan ranges such as the Zaskar, Ladakh, and giant Karakoram ranges of Kashmir and Ladakh and, to the east, the Tibetan border and Kailas ranges. All are part of the southern margin of the Tibetan Plateau, which itself averages 4,500 m above sea level (figure 3).

In breadth the Himalaya span 160 to 249 km, building in height successively through three major zones. The Sub-Himalaya or Siwalik Hills, the lowest and youngest wrinkle north of the plains, rise to over 1000 m. Behind this ridge are *Dun* valleys like Dehra *Dun* in the Kumaon Himalaya of India, the Surkhet and Dang valleys of western Nepal, and the Rapti Valley of central Nepal. Beyond rise the Lower Himalaya in a succession of ridges *en echelon*, sometimes to about 3,500 m. Within these middle ranges

---

1   Ancient Sanskrit compound: *himā*, "snow," and *alāya*, "abode" (Mason 1955:3).

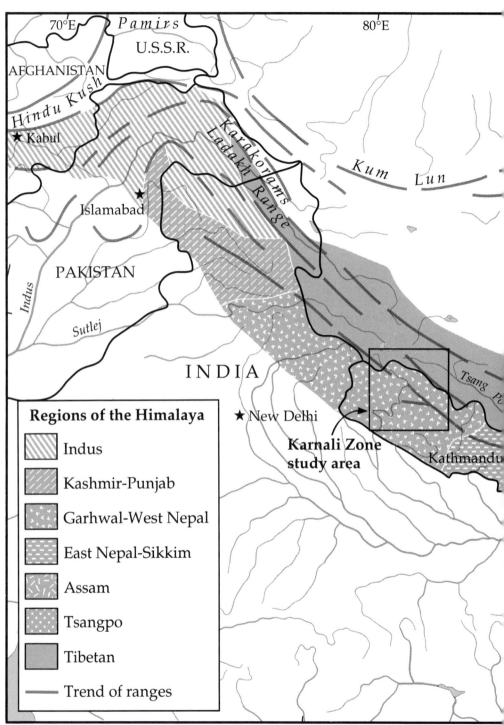

Fig. 3. The Himalayan system as regionalized by C. Troll (1967) according to

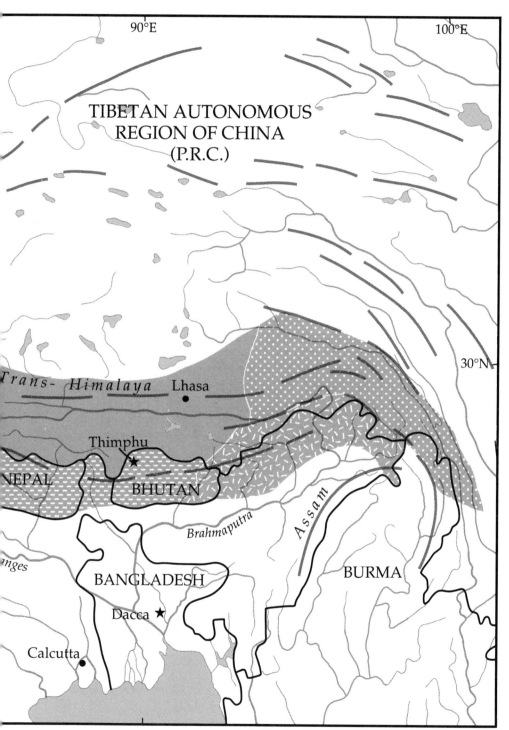

its horizontal climatic belts

are low temperate valleys such as the Pokhara Valley of central Nepal and the Kathmandu Valley. Finally, the glaciated Great Himalaya itself culminates in crests with an average elevation of 6,000 m. Indicative of the tremendous scale of this range are over 100 summits whose elevation exceeds 7,000 m; twelve of these summits (all in Nepal) are over 8,000 m.

Yet despite this barrier, the Indus, Tsang Po, and Brahmaputra rivers, as well as many major tributaries of the Ganges, actually rise on the Tibetan Plateau. After flowing for long distances parallel to the ranges they turn south, cutting deep gorges through the Himalaya. Even more puzzling, these gorges are always near the highest peaks.

For millennia the Great Himalaya barrier has had a profound and intimate effect on the peoples who live in its shadow, an effect that is reflected in their mythologies, religions, literatures, politics, and economies. It is understandable why even today nearly three-quarters of a billion people in India, Pakistan, Nepal, and Bhutan view the greatest of mountain ranges with wonder, veneration, and sometimes terror.

KARNALI TEXTURE, GRAIN, AND RELIEF

The nation-state of Nepal extends longitudinally for 800 km between the Mahakali River in the west and the Mechi River in the east (figure 1); thus it comprises the middle third of the long sweep of the Himalaya. The Karnali River watershed constitutes most of the western section of the Nepal Himalaya. It drains 42,690 km^2 north of Chisapani, where it cuts through the Siwalik Hills to the Gangetic Plain. Of this area 46 percent, or about 20,000 km^2, is drained by its two major tributaries, the Seti River in the West and the Bheri River in the east.

The political unit of Karnali Zone upon which this study focuses is delimited primarily by interfluves and occupies 13,000 km^2 or 30 percent of the watershed's upper reaches (figure 2). Another approximately 2,000 km^2, or 11 percent, is drained by the Humla Karnali River in Tibet and 3,000 km^2, or 17 percent, by the headwaters of the Langu Khola in Dolpo District of Dhaulagiri Zone.

Within the Karnali drainage the three major physical zones of the chain, mentioned earlier, span about 240 km from south to north between the Indian and Tibetan borders and present a topography somewhat more complex than that found in central and eastern Nepal (figures 4 and 5).

Moreover, the geology of western Nepal corresponds in general to the topography (Hagen 1969; Ohta and Akiba 1973). In turn, the major topographic expressions are delimited by major thrust faults associated with overfolded and transported nappe sheets as well as transverse faults that reflect associated block movements. In the lower southern part of the region the strike of structural folds trends WNW-ESE while in the northern half the strike is

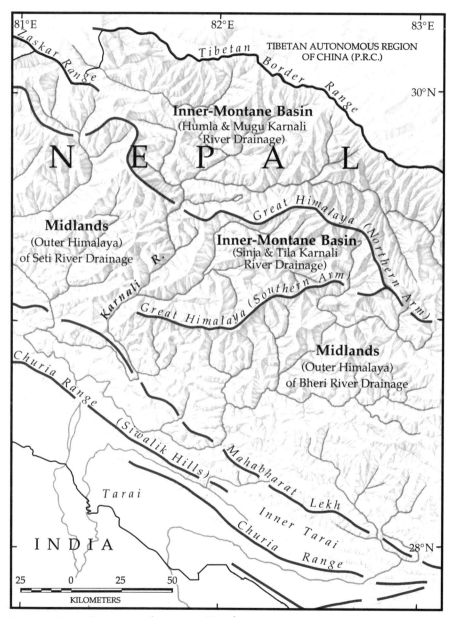

Fig. 4. Physical regions of western Nepal

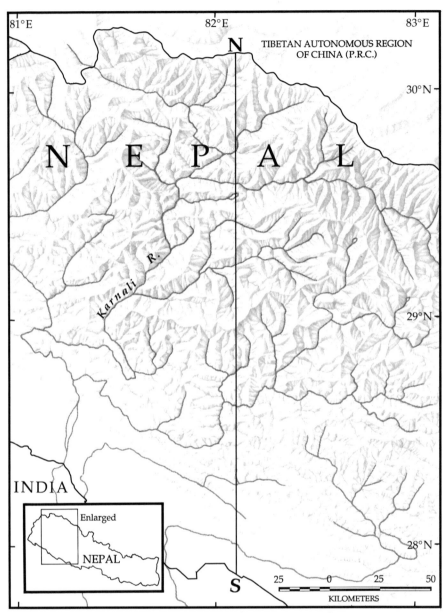

Fig. 5. North-south cross section through western Nepal

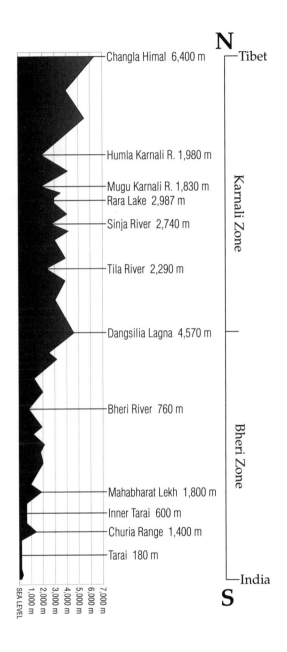

*Fig. 6. Aerial view of the Karnali inter-
montane basin, looking north*

NW-SE. Ohta and Akiba consider the southern half of the Karnali drainage south of the Chakhure-Mabu Lekh, or ridge, to be the westward extension of the Nepal Himalaya; the northern half is the eastern extension of the Kumaon Himalaya (1973:221).

In western Nepal the Siwalik Hills are a series of ridges *en echelon* and are also known as the Churia and Dundwa ranges. Reaching about 1,500 m, they are composed of poorly sorted Tertiary sandstones, shales, and loosely cemented conglomerates, the detritus worn from more elevated ridges to the north by late mountain building processes.

The Siwalik Hills separate the northern extension of the Ganges Plain (known as the Tarai in Nepal), which nowhere is above 200 m, from the inner Tarai *Dun* valleys such as Surkhet, Dang, and the western Rapti, which are about 600 m in height. Both the Tarai and the inner Tarai valleys of Nepal are fairly flat areas of late Pleistocene or Recent alluvial deposits. They constitute the agricultural breadbasket of the country, where one-third of the population farms two-thirds of its agricultural land.

North of the inner Tarai rises the Mahabharat Lekh, the southern-most ridge of the Lower Himalaya or Midlands. This zone reaches to about 2,500 m and is made up of Paleozoic metasediments such as phyllites, crystalline schists, and quartzite. It is in the Nepal Midlands as well as in some intermontane basins beyond the Great Himalaya that two-thirds of the country's population live on one-third of the country's arable land.

In the upper reaches of the drainage (Karnali Zone) the topography and underlying geology become more complex, for here the Great Himalaya are found in two arms. The southern one is the Chakhure-Mabu Lekh, composed of gneiss. It is thought to be the southern edge of a nappe sheet detached from its root zone in the Tibetan border ranges further north. With an average height of more than 4,000 m the Chakhure-Mabu Lekh is the western extension of the Dhaulagiri Himal[2] and terminates at the Karnali River. It is both the southern border of the Karnali Zone study area and the topographic boundary that separates the lower Himalaya or Midlands from the inner Himalaya.

The northern and higher arm of the Great Himalaya trends northwest from the Kanjiroba Himal through the Sisne Himal (6,400 m), the Saipal Himal (7,000 m), and Api (7,100 m); it continues in the Kumaon Himalaya of India and includes that country's highest summit, Nanda Devi (7,817 m). These high himals are composed of Tibetan Tethys sediments that were deposited in southern marginal basins of the Tethys Sea before the major mountain-building took place. The main Tibetan Tethys sedimentary basin lies further north beyond the Tibetan border ranges.

Between the Sisne and Saipal himals of the Great Himalaya, erosion by the upper Karnali River drainage has reduced the northern arm to a

---

2   In Nepal the word *himal* designates an individual mountain range or massif.

chain of lower *lekhs,* or ridges, 3,800 to 4,800 m in height. These are composed of Paleozoic and Mesozoic metasediments such as phyllites, quartzites, and in some places thick limestone layers.

The upper Karnali River catchment contains two low intermontane topographic basins. The southern one lies between the two arms of the Great Himalaya and is drained by the Tila and Sinja Karnali rivers (figure 6). To the west the main Karnali River cuts through both mountain arms and is only 1,500 m above sea level at the confluence of the Humla and Mugu Karnali rivers. These two tributaries occupy the second and northern intermontane basin between the Great Himalaya's northern arm and the Tibetan border range, 5,000 to 7,000 m in height. This trans-Himalayan range, composed primarily of gneisses and granites, separates the Karnali River drainage from that of the Tsang Po in Tibet.

Fluvial erosion in the Karnali River system has kept pace with mountain building processes. Late Pleistocene and Recent alluvial terraces and fans are important features. Over time geologic and hydrologic processes have combined to produce the texture, grain, and relief we see today.

The country opens to the southwest and is deeply incised by a superimposed dendritic drainage pattern that predates the orogeny that produced the Himalaya (figures 7 and 8). One striking feature of the drainage is Rara Lake, the nation's largest, with an area of 1,000 ha, which is perched at approximately 3,000 m above the deeply cut Mugu Karnali River (figure 9). It has survived the ongoing tectonic forces taking place in the Great Himalaya, although its drainage has changed from east to west, most probably during the late Pleistocene.

This combination of geologic and hydrologic processes has produced in the upper Karnali catchment area a topography unique to the Nepal Himalaya. Karnali Zone occupies a major breech in the mountains that is actually an intermontane basin complex. Indeed, the area does not generally exhibit the extremely jagged and confining relief found in the Great Himalaya of central and eastern Nepal. Instead the land forms are less rugged and the country is more open.

MONSOON CLIMATE REGIME

Like the Great Himalayan ramparts, the rains that fall during the Indian monsoon[3] climate regime have a profound effect on the lives of the quarter of the world's population, 80 percent of whom are farmers, who inhabit South Asia. The amount and intensity of the precipitation and where and when it falls dictate to a large measure the success or failure of their

---

[3]   The word "monsoon" is derived from the Arabic word *mausin,* which means "season."

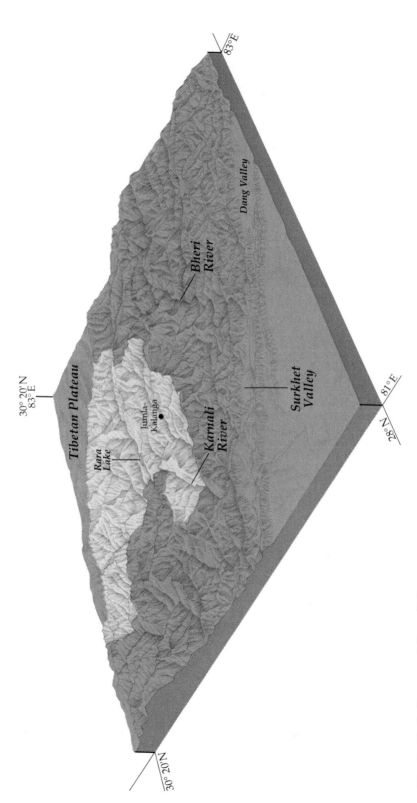

Fig. 7. Block diagram of Karnali Zone

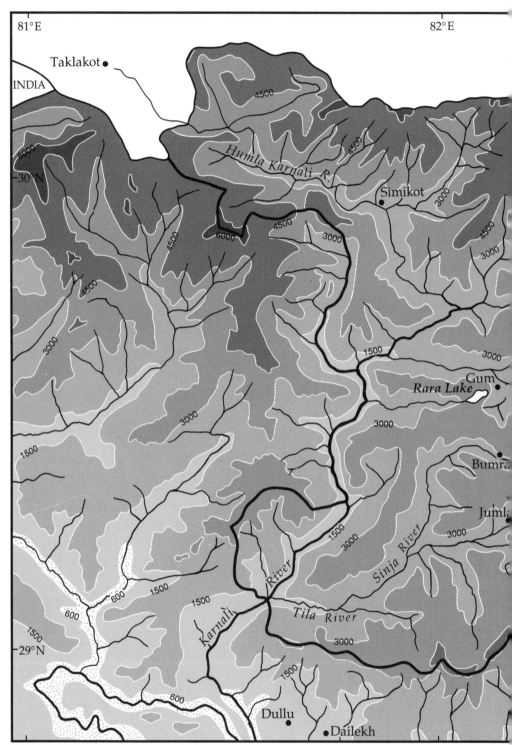

Fig. 8. *Topographic map of Karnali Zone*

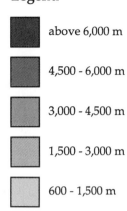

Legend

■	above 6,000 m
■	4,500 - 6,000 m
■	3,000 - 4,500 m
■	1,500 - 3,000 m
■	600 - 1,500 m
▨	below 600 m

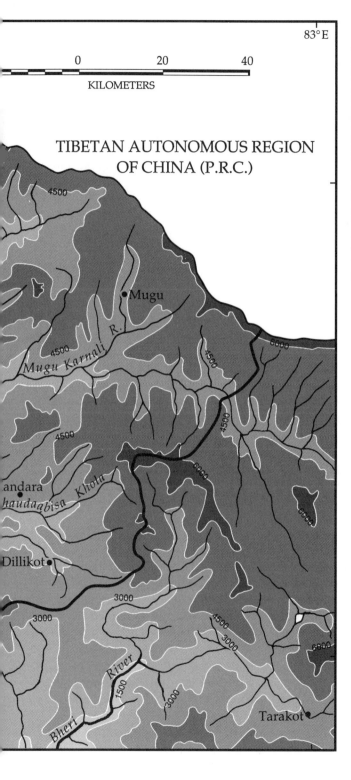

83°E

0   20   40

KILOMETERS

TIBETAN AUTONOMOUS REGION
OF CHINA (P.R.C.)

4500

•Mugu

Mugu Karnali R.

4500

4500

6000

4500

4500

6000

6000

andara
haudaabisa Khola

Dillikot•

3000

3000

4500

3000

1500

Bheri River

3000

Tarakot•

6000

crops, and so is inexorably linked to their well-being, and even to their survival.

The original explanation for the seasonal behavior of the monsoon by Edmond Halley (1686) was based on observations of surface winds over coastal regions of the Indian peninsula. These showed a marked reversal between cool, dry, land winds in winter and warm, rain-bearing winds in summer. Subsequent data from the growing network of synoptic surface meteorological stations throughout South Asia and adjacent areas, aerological information obtained above the surface since World War II, the findings of the International Indian Ocean Expedition in the early 1960s, and the more recent weather satellite observations have shown this theory of large-scale alternating and thermally driven land and sea breezes to be simplistic in the extreme.

In reality the Indian monsoon results from a complex of interacting phenomena. Both thermodynamic and hydrodynamic processes, often associated with the relief of the subcontinent's coastline, the western Ghats, the Himalaya as well as lesser flanking ranges to both east and west, and the extensive and lofty Tibetan Plateau, affect air-mass circulation, not only at the surface but in the mid and upper troposphere and the lower stratosphere as well. They also produce significant waves, pulsations and perturbations in the air masses. As Chang (1967) points out, "the [Indian] monsoon circulation like the atmosphere elsewhere is but a gigantic engine powered by rapidly transmuting various forms of energy—thermal, latent, potential, kinetic."

The several schools of theory that exist on the Indian monsoon indicate that full understanding of the phenomenon is still lacking. But if a complete explanation for the forces that dictate the monsoon regime of South Asia has yet to be achieved, the surface climate and weather that result from these forces are well known.[4]

The subcontinent has not one but several climates. All reflect the region's most significant characteristic—great variability of rainfall over space and time, both seasonally and from year to year. It is this variability that makes the lot of the farmer so precarious and helpful prediction by the meteorologist so difficult. Furthermore, most if not all of South Asia's weather characteristics, particularly its rainfall vicissitudes, can be explained by the orographic controls of great height and arcing east-west trend that the Himalaya impose at all seasons.

Before examining the weather of the western Nepal Himalaya in detail and Karnali Zone in particular, a brief discussion of the salient aspects of

---

[4] For a discussion in depth of the Indian monsoon, see Pedelaborde (1963) and Das (1972); an excellent review article is that by Hamilton (1976).

the seasonal variation in Indian monsoon climate regime, focused on the northern half of the subcontinent and emphasizing the crucial role of the pan-Himalaya, is indicated.

Fig. 9. Aerial view looking west of Rara Lake (2,981 m) above Mugu Karnali River (1,760 m)

The Winter Monsoon

Cool, clear, and generally dry conditions prevail in the northern half of South Asia during the winter months. The northeast monsoon, known also as the land trades, prevails in the lower troposphere over the lowlands. As in most trade wind areas, it is characterized by diverging and subsiding dry continental air. H. Flohn (1969) sees this condition as a "Föhn effect" caused by the cool, heavy air draining the southern flanks of the Himalaya, which are snow covered as low as 2,500-4,000 m, as well as escaping from the Tibetan Plateau through valley breeches in the mountains. In the upper troposphere westerly winds prevail which reach the ground in the Himalaya. At their core is the subtropical westerly jet stream that flows from North Africa to southern China. During the winter the westerly jet, a key factor in monsoon circulation, is channeled south of the Tibetan Plateau and Himalaya and is well established at about 27°N over the Ganges Plain.

Because of its height, size, and position, another effect of the Tibetan Plateau is to extend the cold of the winter Siberian anticyclone, centered over Turkistan, far to the south. But the higher Himalaya on its southern fringe prevents the high, cold polar air mass from reaching the South Asian lowlands. As a result, winter daytime maximum temperatures on the Ganges Plain reach 20° to 30°C while those in the Himalaya show a decrease of 5°C per thousand meters of elevation.

This clear and dry winter picture is broken about six times each month by western disturbances. Many appear to be continuations of Mediterranean depressions; others are locally generated. All are ushered over the subcontinent from the northwest by the subtropical jet stream, bringing precipitation to Kashmir and the western Himalaya, as well as to the adjacent lowlands of the Punjab, Uttar Pradesh, and the lower Ganges Valley as far as Patna (86°E).

The amount of winter precipitation that results from these disturbances varies considerably and increases markedly with elevation. At some locations in Kashmir and high in the Himalaya, snowfall even produces a winter secondary precipitation maximum and, in turn, spring and summer melt waters that are indispensable for irrigation. Although less falls in the lowlands, it is essential for the success of winter crops. Little evaporation takes place during this cool season, allowing the meager moisture to be highly effective for the growth of wheat and barley.

The Premonsoon

With the northward march of the sun through the spring equinox toward its summer solstice, the weather becomes increasingly hot while generally dry conditions continue. The atmosphere becomes more hazy, owing to dust in the lowlands and fires along the mountain flanks where farmers burn pastureland grasses to encourage new growth. During March snow cover in the Himalaya and on the Tibetan Plateau is slow to melt because of the high reflectance of solar radiation from its surface, and the albedo is about 85 percent (Bishop et al. 1966). As a result the highlands remain cool while the lowlands to the south warm rapidly with daytime temperatures reaching 40°C. Anticyclonic subsidence now combines with a stronger sun.

This continuing thermal contrast, however, begins to weaken in early April as the snow in high elevations recedes, albedo decreases, and the air above begins to warm. Once the Tibetan Plateau is free of snow, solar insolation heats the ground, which then heats the air above to a point where it is much warmer than the air at the same level over the lowlands. In turn the ascending air over the lowlands begins to draw in humid currents from the south. Now converging winds of the lower troposphere and diverging winds of the middle troposphere combine with the prevailing westerlies above to produce periodic and violent premonsoon storms.

In northwest India and Pakistan these storms produce little rain because of relatively dry air in the lower troposphere but are marked by towering cumulus clouds, thunder squalls, and violent dust storms known as *andis*. However, to the southeast over the lower Ganges, where moist, southerly maritime air has begun to replace the dry northeast monsoon, thunderstorms called "nor'westers" begin in late March and increase in frequency, intensity, and rainfall during April and May. These usually occur during the late afternoon and early evening following a buildup of cloud associated with unstable air during the day. Here total precipitation in May can reach 125-250 mm but increases in the Himalaya to the north with elevation, as well as to the east, over Bangladesh, Assam, and upper Burma. In addition, tropical storms, including hurricanes, in the Bay of Bengal region contribute to the severe weather that precedes the summer monsoon.

The Summer Monsoon

For most of the people living in the northern half of the Indian subcontinent the term "monsoon" is synonymous with the summer rainy season upon which their lives depend. Moisture-bearing tropical maritime air from the southwest advances up the Bay of Bengal bringing monsoon rains first to Burma in late April and May. In the ensuing weeks it spreads rapidly north and west over the subcontinent, always preceded by the turbulent weather discussed above. If this disturbed weather is particularly severe over the Ganges or in the Himalaya it is difficult to recognize when pre-monsoon thunderstorms end and the actual summer monsoon begins.

Important basic changes in air-mass circulation set the stage for the rapid spread or burst of the summer monsoon. During May and June a heat low (a thermal high with corresponding low barometric pressure) builds up in the northwest and gradually extends southeast over northern Pakistan and India, where it is known as the monsoon trough. At the same time the subtropical westerly jet stream in the upper troposphere begins alternately to disappear and reappear south of the Himalaya. With each disappearance the southwest monsoon surges and bursts forward. Finally, the westerly jet disappears altogether to relocate north of the Tibetan Plateau at 40°N as an extensive anticyclone dominates upper air circulation above the subcontinent and Tibet. The Himalaya now perform the crucial role of deflecting the summer monsoon's northward movement up the Indo-Gangetic plains.

The summer monsoon circulation pattern is, therefore, exactly opposite that of the winter. It is one of cyclonic or counterclockwise movement of low-level, warm, moist maritime air below clockwise anticyclonic movement of cooler, dry continental air.

The arrival of the summer monsoon can vary as much as a month (Hamilton 1976:179). Normally it reaches Calcutta at the head of the Bay of

Bengal in early June, New Delhi in the Indo-Gangetic lowlands by July 2 with a standard deviation of seven to eight days, and finally Kashmir in a feeble fashion by mid-July. With its arrival the increased frequency and amount of cloud and rain bring slightly cooler temperatures to the Ganges Plains and adjacent mountains, while the Tibetan Plateau, in the rain shadow of the Himalaya, becomes extremely hot for its latitude and altitude.

During the summer months the plains and lower Himalaya receive more than 70 percent of their yearly precipitation. However, this is not a time of continuous rainfall. Instead it is one of periodically disturbed weather with cloud and rain, about once every six days, interspersed with fair weather lulls. This pulsating rhythm of alternately degenerating and regenerating moist maritime air combines with rain-making processes. At any lowland location the convective rainfall brought about by low-level convergence and upper air divergence is less than that which is orographically induced at windward locations in the lower Himalaya to the north. Furthermore, the amount of summer rain decreases from southeast to northwest as the moist maritime wedge of air becomes steadily thinner and dryer.

When a succession of high-level westerly disturbances or depressions, which are not totally absent during the summer, pass over the Himalaya, the rainfall pattern of the northern subcontinent is interrupted by what are known as breaks. Although the westerlies do not reach the ground to produce surface depressions, they do seem to draw the monsoon trough to the southern edge of the Himalaya, and thus create a northward shift of monsoon circulation. The result is abnormally heavy rainfall in the Himalaya that often causes landslides, while heavy flooding may take place in the adjacent plains. To the south the subcontinent experiences a cessation of rain during these breaks, which usually last some three to ten days. When prolonged breaks in the monsoon occur, sever drought and famine can be disastrous to the farmer.

Therefore, the salient feature of the summer monsoon in the northern subcontinent is the great variability of the rainfall over time and space. Because of the phenomenon discussed above, the northeast flood plains and adjacent lower Himalaya receive high precipitation; the amount diminishes to the northeast, finally to arid conditions in Rajasthan as well as in the rain shadow behind the Great Himalaya. Moreover, the amount of rain that falls at any site varies considerably from year to year. In general this temporal variability is inversely proportional to the amount of rain that falls.

The Postmonsoon

Starting in September in northwest Pakistan and Kashmir, the southwest monsoon begins a slow withdrawal as the thermal monsoon trough weakens. This retreat takes about twice as long as the monsoon advance, but moist maritime air has completely disappeared from the Indo-Gangetic Plain and adjacent Himalaya by mid-October, and from all the subcontinent by early December.

Associated with this withdrawal during the fall months is the disappearance of the easterly summer jet stream over the peninsula and the reappearance of the subtropical westerly jet stream south of the Himalaya as the dynamic features of circulation aloft take up their cool-season positions. During the retreat frequent hurricanes again develop over the Bay of Bengal, often bringing devastating floods to the Ganges and Brahmaputra lowlands such as those of 1970.

By the end of October the Himalaya have returned to their winter regime of cool, clear, and generally dry weather.

KARNALI WEATHER

The following discussion of the salient weather features of western Nepal is based upon short-term observations in the field as well as the limited rainfall and temperature figures available from HMG's Department of Hydrology and Meteorology. Because of the paucity of weather stations in the area, the questionable reliability of measurements at some stations, and the short and inconsistent span of years that these stations have been operating, the data are of limited and varied precision and require great care in treatment. Nonetheless in conjunction with known climatic features they do furnish a valuable base for the analysis of Karnali's weather and climate.

Figures 10 through 12 and table 1 are presented here and additional information is provided in Appendix C. Of particular importance are the climatic water-balance diagrams in figure 12. Based upon C. W. Thornthwaite and J. R. Mather's methods (1957), these graphically illustrate the interrelationship of heat and moisture processes, topography, soils, and vegetation; they indicate, albeit in a gross fashion, the amount and seasonal distribution (i.e., deficit or surplus periods) of soil moisture so crucial to crop and vegetation growth.[5]

The Karnali River catchment of Nepal reflects the seasonal rhythm of the Indian monsoon regime outlined above. Here, as throughout the Himalaya, topography exerts a particularly dominant climatic control that contributes to great local variation in duration, intensity, and timing of both sunshine and rain, as well as barometric pressure and winds. Moreover, the particular arrangement of texture and grain—elevation, relief, and orientation of topographic features—in western Nepal produces a distinctive

---

[5] For detailed discussions of water balances see Thornthwaite and Mather (1955); and Yoshino (1971).

weather and climate that differs from the central and eastern regions of the country. Specifically, the low open intermontane basins of Karnali Zone that lie in the rain shadows north of the Api-Saipal Himal and the Chakhure-Mabu Lekh have a climate that is markedly dry and warm. Although much cooler and wetter than the Vale of Kashmir lying 850 km to the northwest, Karnali Zone shows significant similarities to this large intermontane basin of India.

In the lower reaches of western Nepal south of Karnali Zone's major orographic barriers, the climate is more typical of that found along the southern flanks of the Himalaya. Here local variations more obviously resolve themselves into broad climatic belts that are determined solely by elevation. Nepalganj, at an elevation of 181 m in the Tarai 30 km south of the first ripple of the Himalaya, has a subtropical, subhumid climate typical of that portion of the Ganges Plain. With about 1,300 mm of rain each year, of which 85 percent occurs during the summer monsoon months of June, July, August, and September, it shows a slight water surplus during the rainy season.

During the summer monsoon, the increasing elevations from the Siwalik Hills through the Midlands mechanically induce rainfall from moisture-laden southerly winds drawn into the hills by warm, rising air to the north, a phenomenon that is reflected in data from Chisapani and Dailekh. At the former site, 225 m above sea level at the break in slope between the Tarai and the Siwalik Hills, the annual precipitation is more than 2,100 mm, of which 92 percent occurs during the summer monsoon. This greater precipitation gives Chisapani a subtropical, humid, premontane climate with ample summer water surplus but significant winter water deficit. The coefficient of rainfall variability (the standard deviation expressed as a percentage) for a period of years is 7.3 compared to 28.7 at Gularia, a site near Nepalganj; this illustrates the rule that the variability of rainfall from year to year at a site is generally inversely proportional to the amount of rainfall that the site receives. At both Nepalganj and Chisapani the arrival of summer rains brings a swift, marked decrease in temperature and relief from the stifling heat and dust of the premonsoon.

In the midlands at Dailekh, 1,000 m higher than Chisapani, there is somewhat less precipitation, about 1,600 mm annually, since moisture is gradually extracted from the air during its northward movement. But the climate still remains subtropical and humid, although there is less of a winter water deficiency. Higher still, summer rainfall becomes increasingly less intense but more continuous. Mist and cloud, accompanied by a steady drizzle, limit insolation and control the upper limit at which cultivation of crops is possible. On the southern flanks of the Chakhure-Mabu Lekh in western Nepal this limit is about 3,000 m; in central Nepal it is 2,500 m, while in the eastern part of the country it is as low as 2,000 m.

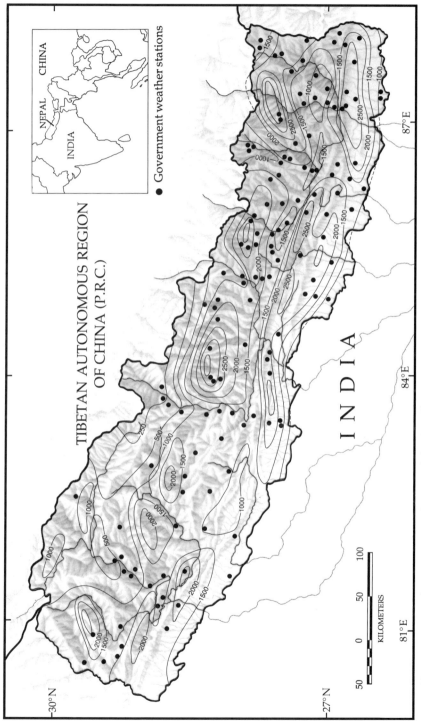

Fig. 10. Mean annual precipitation for Nepal (1964-68)

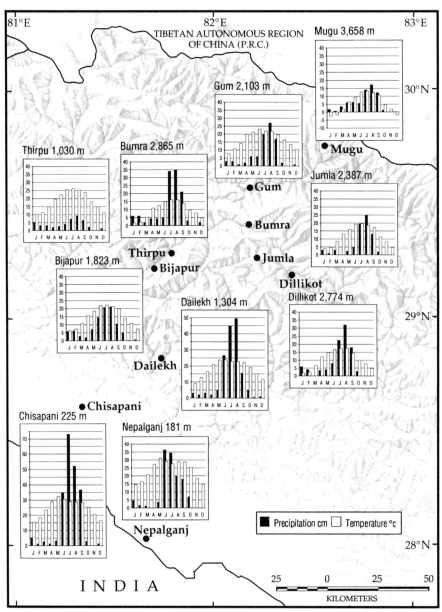

Fig. 11. *Temperature and precipitation for selected stations in western Nepal*

The importance of the Chakhure-Mabu Lekh as a climatic barrier is evident from a comparison of annual rainfall from stations south and north of this high ridge. Jumla, at 2,387 m, receives an annual precipitation of 665 mm, only 42 percent of that of Dailekh. The similar effect of the Api-Saipal Himal, which marks the western border of Karnali Zone, is equally striking. Chainpur at 1,304 m on the southwest flank of this barrier receives almost 1,500 mm each year, while Bijapur at 1,800 m in the main Karnali drainage gets only 1,000 mm.

However, the dry conditions of Karnali Zone's intermontane basins are only partially explained by these rainfall barriers. The orographically induced diurnal wind circulation in the valley bottoms and on adjacent lower slopes of the Karnali River and its Tila, Sinja, Mugu, and Humla tributaries plays an especially significant role by reducing rainfall and increasing insolation. Throughout the year, but particularly during the spring, summer, and fall months, strong southerly or up-valley winds blow from about 11 A.M. to sunset in response to the insolation of the highlands and, in turn, of the adjacent air. The author has often experienced winds of over 85 km per hour at Jumla. The combination of up-valley and up-slope air circulation produces a pronounced Föhn effect over the valleys as dry descending air warms above the valley bottoms to prevent cloud formation and curtail rain. Furthermore this Föhn condition reduces the expected nighttime reversal of winds to a degree where northerly down-valley winds are normally weak or absent. When flying above the solid cloud cover during the summer monsoon, one can easily locate these valleys by the absence of cloud cover above them.

A comparison of the annual rainfall of Jumla (665 mm) and Gum (880 mm), at 2,387 m in the Tila Karnali Valley and at 2,103 m in the Mugu Karnali Valley respectively, with that received at nearby higher locations clearly reveals the control on rain that the valley winds impose. Bumra at 2,865 m high in the Sinja Valley receives about 1,200 mm of precipitation each year; Dillikot at 2,774 m on the upper Tila River gets about 1,000 mm. While the climate of Jumla and Gum is a warm, temperate, subhumid one with a moderate water deficiency in winter and a water surplus in summer, that of Bumra and Dillikot is cooler and more moist with only a small deficiency of water during the winter and a much higher water surplus during the summer.

The most striking example of the effect of valley winds, however, is found at lower elevations along an 80 km stretch of the main Karnali River between the confluence of the Mugu and Humla rivers (1,500 m) and the entrance of the Tila River (1,000 m). In this deeply incised valley, which trends north-south, the strong valley winds have a desiccating effect. Along the river at 1,030 m, Thirpu receives 470 mm of rain annually, of which only 58 percent falls during the summer monsoon. At no time during the

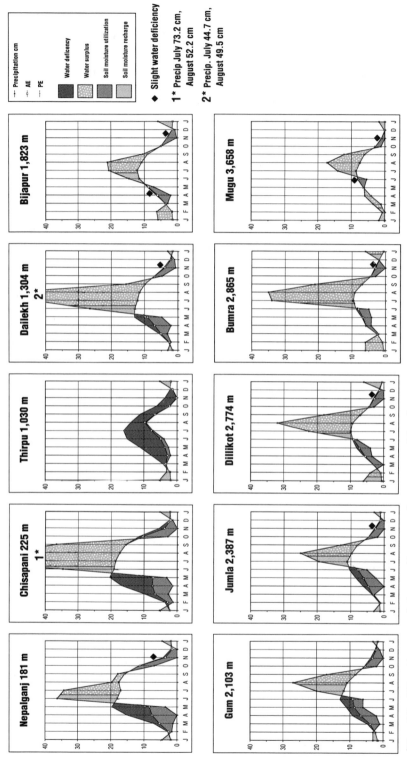

Fig. 12. Climatic water-balance diagrams for western Nepal

TABLE 1. Weather data for selected stations in the Karnali Basin in 2026 V.S. (1969-70).

	Latitude Longitude	Coldest month (°C) Driest month (mm)	Warmest month (°C) Wettest month (mm)	Temp. spread (°C)	Mean annual temp. Total annual precipitation	% of Precipitation Summer	Winter	Coefficient of rainfall variability
Nepalganj (181 m)	28 06'N 81 37'E	Dec. (14.5) Apr. Nov. Dec. (nil)	May (31.1) June (364)	16.6	23.6° 1,264 mm	85	15	28.7a
Chisapani (225 m)	28 39'N 81 16'E	Jan. (15.5) Nov. (6)	May (32.4) July (727)	16.9	24.8° 2,156 mm	92	8	7.3
Thirpu (1,030 m)	29 19'N 81 46'E	Jan. (10.4) Nov. (nil)	July (26.2) Aug. (94)	15.8	18.6° 470 mm	58	42	21.0
Dailekh (1,304 m)	28 51'N 81 43'E	Jan. (9.1) Nov. (7)	June (23.8) Aug. (495)	14.7	18.4° 1,580 mm	86	14	14.8
Bijapur (1,823 m)	29 14'N 81 38'E	Jan. (6.4) Nov. Dec. (nil)	July (22.2) June (262)	15.8	14.6° 983 mm	77	23	24.0
Gum (2,103 m)	29 33'N 82 10'E	Jan. (7.9) Nov. (nil)	June (23.2) Aug. (270)	15.3	16.7° 880 mm	80	20	
Jumla (2,387 m)	29 16'N 82 11'E	Jan. (3.9) Nov. (nil)	July (19.7) Aug. (152)	15.8	12.2° 665 mm	85	15	25.0
Dillikot (2,774 m)	29 12'N 82 22'E	Jan. (1.8) Nov. Dec. Mar. (nil)	Aug. (17.4) Aug. (320)	15.6	10.5° 1,010 mm	80	20	
Bumra (2,865 m)	29 24'N 82 08'E	Jan. (1.6) Nov. (nil)	July (16.1) Aug. (350)	14.5	9.6° 1,225 mm	78	22	
Mugu (3,658 m)	29 45'N 82 33'E	Jan. (-2.7) Nov. (nil)	July (13.1) Aug. (172)	15.8	5.6° 686 mm	71	29	49.0

a Gularia

year does a water surplus accrue; semiarid conditions prevail. Bijapur, on the other hand, is 800 m higher on the slopes above the river. With an average of 75 more rainy days each year, it gets over twice the amount of precipitation (983 m), of which 77 percent falls during the summer season. In contrast to the valley below, warm, temperate, subhumid conditions and a significant water surplus prevail.

Another important orographically induced feature of rainfall in Karnali Zone (as throughout the Himalaya) is the local thunderstorm that releases heavy, if short-lived, deluges. At Jumla, for example, on July 16, 1969, such a storm released over 10 percent of that site's annual precipitation in a twenty-four-hour period. The inopportune occurrence of such storms during critical agricultural periods often has disastrous results, and will be discussed later.

Strong insolation and radiation, as well as low humidity, combine with the open nature of the terrain to partially offset the area's northern latitude (4° further poleward than the eastern end of the country), and give Karnali Zone's intermontane basins relatively warm temperatures. Moreover, thermodynamic processes over the wide, high expanse of the Tibetan Plateau, referred to by Flohn (1969) as a thermal engine, also contribute to this condition. Here the level at which greater cloud cover with lower insolation and higher humidity affects vegetation, agriculture, and human activities is much higher than that in the Midlands; this critical level can be as high as 4,000 m, depending on the local topographic expression. Moreover, at these higher elevations greater winter precipitation occurs in the form of snow, owing to the capture of moisture from periodic western disturbances. Snowfall is not only heavier in Karnali Zone than it is further east, but it is also slower to melt in the spring because of the area's more northerly latitude.

This picture is particularly evident at Mugu (3,659 m) where 29 percent of the yearly precipitation occurs during the winter months. There conditions are also more continental because of latitude. Because of the seasonal distribution of precipitation (about 700 mm yearly), low winter temperatures, high evaporation, and swift spring melt and runoff of snow, moisture is ineffectual and subalpine, semiarid conditions prevail.

SOILS, FORESTS, AND FAUNA

In western Nepal, as throughout the Himalaya, the complex of soils, animals, and plants is arranged in a striking vertical (altitudinal) succession of differing biotic belts, each a sensitive expression of geologic, orographic, and climatic factors already discussed (figure 13). Furthermore, human exploitation, alteration, or destruction of components in the biotic complex are reflected in the composition of the belts. Although these actions have

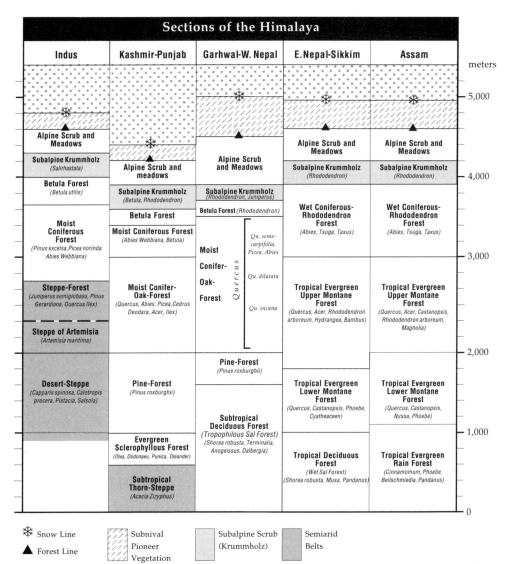

Fig. 13. Vertical zonation of vegetation in sections of the Himalayan system. After C. Troll (1967).

been selective and variable over both time and space, no belt remains free of their impact today.

U. Schweinfurth (1957), in constructing his valuable map of the vertical and horizontal distribution of vegetation in the Himalaya from all available sources, was forced to leave blank, indicating "biologically unexplored," much of western Nepal. Subsequent work of J. D. A. Stainton (1972) did much to fill in those gaps. Both authors followed the pioneering survey of H. G. Champion (1936) in delineating their forest types. The following discussion of vegetation is based on both their work and that of the author.

Little detailed information exists on the heterogeneous mountain soils of western Nepal, which remain unmapped. Not surprisingly, most of the pedologic research done so far has concentrated on the important agricultural lowlands of the country. However, data from Jumla, Dillikot, Bumra, and Gum, the sites of my four weather stations, do shed some light on the soils of the zone's intermontane basins. These data are more appropriately presented in chapter 5 (table 12).

The belt below 1,300 m in the lower reaches of western Nepal is one of subtropical deciduous forest, primarily sal (*Shorea robusta*). On the relatively flat fluvial deposits of the Tarai, the *bhabar*—or narrow and gently sloping belt of alluvial gravels immediately south of the Siwalik Hills—and the similar inner Tarai, Surkhet, Dang, and western Rapti valleys,[6] known in Nepal as *bhitri mardesh*, or "the flat ground on the inside" (Stainton 1972:18), soil composition and water availability are the dominant factors in determining forest type.

Although sal is the principal forest here, it will not grow in waterlogged flat areas of the Tarai, nor on recently deposited alluvium braided streams. There it is replaced by *Acacia catechu* and *Dalbergia sissoo* and in more moist river and gully environments by tropical evergreen forests.

Lowland soils are generally sandy or silty loams that reflect variable fluvial sorting and permeability. Under sal they can be fairly deep and moderately fertile; even waterlogged soils can be fairly productive when properly drained and cultivated after clearing. However, improper drainage results in enhanced salinity, high alkalinity, and low fertility, as is the case near Napalganj (Bhatt 1970:19).

On the highly porous alluvial gravels of the *bhabar*, streams are intermittent, flowing on the surface only during the summer monsoon. Because of this water scarcity few villages are located here and the sal forests have been less affected by humans. In the inner Tarai valleys where the alluvial soils of sands and clays mixed with gravels are generally poor, the

---

6   The Rapti Valley of western Nepal should not be confused with the Rapti Valley of central Nepal southwest of Kathmandu.

water shortage is not as critical. In the intervening Siwalik Hills, as well as in the low outer foothills of the Midlands north of the inner Tarai, brown, neutral to slightly acidic loams and clayey loams that are fairly rich in organic matter have developed under the forest cover from sandstone, shales, and metasediments. Here terrain aspect begins to play a role in determining forest type; semideciduous hill forests cover the southern slopes while sal still predominates on the northern slopes.

Historically these lower reaches of western Nepal contained the country's most extensive forests. Many environmental factors contributed to malarious conditions, which in turn deterred human occupance and exploitation. Only in the Dang Valley, the old habitat of Tharu tribal people whose sickle cell blood group traits contributed to their resistance to malaria (Srivastava 1958:221), did deforestation and cultivation take place centuries ago. However, since 1965 these forests have been disappearing at a rapid rate. A successful malaria eradication program initiated in 1954 by the United Nations and USAID has permitted widespread land reclamation programs to be carried out in an attempt to relieve the growing population pressures of the Midlands to the north.

In the deeply incised dendritic drainage of the Karnali catchment basin subtropical deciduous forests penetrate far to the north into the Midlands. For example, sal is found more than 80 km north of the plains near Jajarkot in the Bheri River valley.

Northward through the Midlands and the intermontane basins of Karnali Zone to the Tibetan border ranges, altitude and aspect replace soil formation and water availability as the most important determinants of forest types. In addition, the drier conditions of western Nepal, relative to the eastern regions of the country, contribute to a greater prevalence of western Himalayan species in the forest composition of the various belts.

The Midland forest belts between the Mahabharat Lekh and the Chakhure-Mabu Lekh are more like those of Kumaon (Osmaston 1927) to the west than those to the east in Nepal. Above the subtropical deciduous forest is a forest succession of *Pinus roxburghii* (1,000-2,000 m), temperate mixed oak and conifer (1,400-3,900 m), subalpine birch (3100-4100 m) and moist alpine scrub (3,700-4,300 m).

Pinus roxburghii, a conifer indigenous to the Himalaya, grows in a narrow but almost pure belt and shows a preference for dry, well-drained, open sites on both north- and south-facing slopes. *Quercus incana* dominates more moist gullies while *Euphorbia royleana* is common on steep, hot, and dry slopes. The character of this pine forest has been considerably altered, primarily by fire. In the summer animals are grazed on luxuriant grasses within the open stands; during the dry winter months these grasses and fallen pine needles are susceptible to fire. The fire resistant qualities that allow *Pinus roxburghii* to survive also make it a valuable wood for building purposes.

The wider and more varied temperate mixed oak and conifer forest that succeeds *Pinus roxburghii* is not only the most prominent type on the southern flanks of the western Himalaya, but because of both its extensive distribution and its biotic characteristics, it is the belt most affected by human actions. Furthermore, alteration or disruption of this forest cover in western Nepal has particularly serious consequences on lowland and plains agriculture, owing to increased runoff, erosion, siltation, and flooding.

Below 2,400 m, where winter snows rarely fall, *Quercus incana* and *Quercus lanuginosa* dominate southern exposures, while more luxurious *Quercus dilatata* forests are found in more moist gully and north-facing environments. Broad-leafed horse chestnut, walnut, and maple forest (*Aesculus indica, Juglans regia, Ulnus wallichiana*) is found along streams on all aspects. This is the temperate hill belt that has been most used for settlement and agriculture. Besides extensive clearing, fires from the *Pinus roxburghii* forest below and widespread lopping for fodder have further reduced the natural cover. In uncultivated locations some *Rhododendron arboreum* remain. The latter, which is less prevalent here than further east, survives because it is neither good fodder nor firewood.

Above 2,400 m greater humidity and reduced insolation contribute to cloud forests of *Quercus semecarpifolia* mixed with those of fir (*Abies pindrow*), hemlock (*Tsuga dumosa*), and occasionally *Pinus excelsa* as a secondary growth. Here, where climatic conditions are less favorable for agriculture and settlement, forests are more extensive. Yet in many locations they too have been altered or destroyed by shifting cultivation and grazing associated with temporary summer settlements. Moreover, the rate of conversion from temporary settlement and shifting cultivation to permanent settlement and cultivation has accelerated in the last three decades in response to escalating population pressures.

With increasing elevation these temperate oak and conifers give way to a subalpine belt dominated by birch (*Betula utilis*) but also containing stands of *Abies spectabilis* and *Quercus semecarpifolia*. These timberline forests are in turn replaced by moist alpine scrub, of which the principal species is *Juniperus recurva*, near the crest of the Chakhure-Mabu Lekh.

Soils of the western Nepal Midlands have developed from a variety of metasediment parent rocks under equally variable aspect, moisture, and vegetation conditions. Generally speaking, those dryer elevations below 2,400 m have a Brown Hill soil of the type already mentioned. In the cloud forest above the soils are predominantly Brown Submontane sandy loams or sandy clay loams. When these occur beneath undisturbed coniferous cover, they are true Brown Podzol soils with fairly well-developed profiles, a high accumulation of organic matter near the surface, an absence of free lime, and an acidic pH (Rajan and Rao 1971:67).

The biotic complex of Karnali Zone differs greatly from that of the Midlands to the south. The drier climate, more open northerly location, and, very important, the longer and more intensive history of human occupance (discussed in chapters 3 and 4) are reflected in a more varied and complex pattern of vegetation with an even greater prevalence of western Himalayan species. Much of the original vegetation of the intermontane basins, particularly that of the Tila, Sinja, and Mugu river valleys and their adjacent slopes to as high as 3,300 m on south and east exposures, was destroyed many centuries ago. Extensive forests can now be found only in higher and more moist secondary and tertiary drainages where cloud forest conditions have helped deter human destructive exploitation until very recently (figure 14).

Below 2,400 m *Quercus incana* and *Quercus lanuginosa* as well as *Pinus roxburghii* are now found mostly along the main Karnali River and in the lower Humla Karnali Valley below Simikot. In the hot, low, arid valley of the main Karnali between 1,000 and 1,500 m xerophytic species such as *Dalbergia sissoo* and *Acacia catechu* grow in a thin belt beside the river. Above this belt treeless, wind-parched slopes with "cactus forests" of *Euphorbia royleana* (figure 15) rise for as much as 1,000 m to a level where villages occur on the edge of the fast disappearing *Pinus roxburghii* and *Quercus incana–Quercus lanuginosa* forest. Elsewhere below 2,400 m the oaks generally have been replaced by terraced fields and heavily grazed grassy slopes.

In the lowest and hottest southwestern corner of the zone, banana, orange, fig, and mango grow as village trees. Scattered cedar (*Cedrus deodara*), a western Himalayan conifer, still grow on dry limestone in the lower Tila Valley. A few very old trees even survive upstream near Jumla, where they stand out in the often dry, barren landscape, mark the sites of shrines, and owe their existence to their religious significance.

Below 2,100-2,400 m and in the upper timberline, which varies between 3,700 and 4,000 m in Karnali Zone, is a wide belt of temperate forest, predominantly conifer, that bears strong resemblance to the western Himalayan conifer forests of Kashmir.

Below 3,300 m these forests are principally pine and spruce (*Pinus excelsa* and *Picea smithiana*). The pine is more prevalent, growing in extensive, pure stands on south-facing slopes where it is often a secondary growth. Because it regenerates faster than the spruce, it occupies locations originally covered by *Picea smithiana*. Pure stands of this spruce now are confined to more protected north- and west-facing slopes. The low-altitude fir, *Abies pindrow*, is rarely found, except in Humla where tall forests grow

Fig. 14. Cloud Forest

on similar slopes. Interspersed with these pine and spruce forests are broad-leafed forests of horse chestnut, walnut, and maple (*Aesculus indica, Juglans regia, Ulnus wallichiana*), which occupy more moist watercourses and gullies. Although fairly thin, they are widespread and give the landscape the look of a European woodland (Stainton 1972:94). Low-altitude meadows, important for grazing, are also common within the conifer. Here the pine is prevented from colonizing by yearly fires. Cypress (*Cupressus torulosa*) and poplar (*Populus ciliata*), the latter sometimes associated with buckthorn (*Hippophae salicifolia*), grow along watercourses and irrigation canals. Cypress is also found around villages, where apple and peach also thrive.

Fig. 15. Cactus forest of Euphorbia royleana.

Above 3,300 m, especially in the high country that separates the Tila, Sinja, and Mugu valleys, the composition of the forest belt changes considerably and consists of high-altitude fir, oak, and birch (*Abies spectabilis, Quercus semecarpifolia, Betula utilis*). Sometimes these are found together in a mixed forest. More commonly, altitude, aspect, winter snows, and cloud combine to produce a patchwork pattern of pure forest in which all three species reach timberline. Therefore, a clearly defined birch belt above the temperate conifer forest, like that south of the Chakhure-Mabu Lekh, is obscured or absent.

Although pure *Abies spectabilis* forests are less extensive than in the Midlands, they do dominate here, particularly on northern and western slopes that have a consistent winter snow cover. On the other hand, *Quercus semecarpifolia* forests grow only on southern slopes where snow melts early in the spring. It is in this high-altitude oak that shifting cultivation is now prevalent (figure 16). *Betula utilis* is generally confined to gullies and steeper slopes, again with north or west exposures, where deep snowdrifts collect in winter and remain until May or June. On avalanche scars and old scree slopes the birch often descends deep into the fir.

Meadows are another important component of this patchwork pattern. These occur both within the forests and on their upper fringes where people have cleared the trees by cutting and burning for grazing grounds, or *patans* (figure 17). *Juniperus wallichiana* sometimes colonizes in these meadows, while bamboo (*Arundiaria* spp.) often occurs as a secondary growth in the bordering fir and oak following fire.

Above 4,000 m alpine scrub and meadow extend toward the snow line, which occurs at about 5,000 m. The scrub, which consists primarily of *Juniperus wallichiana* and *Rhodedendron* species, is more common on northern exposures; the meadows, heavily grazed in July and August, prefer the southern slopes. Unlike the *patans* of the forest belt, these are not manmade; nor are they subjected to yearly fires (figure 18).

Within Karnali Zone the composition of the forest belts, like that of the belts above timberline, changes with latitude and reflects a pronounced northward increase in dryness. Moreover, tree line, along with other altitude limits such as frost line, snow line, and the maximum height of settlement and cultivation, rises northward in response to the increase in mass elevation (Uhlig 1976:554).

In the dry reaches of the Humla Karnali and Mugu Karnali valleys, flanked to the north by the Tibetan border range and to the south by the Great Himalaya, *Pinus excelsa, Betula utilis,* and *Juniperus wallichiana,* species well suited for high altitude and dry conditions, are the principal upper forest trees. *Quercus semecarpifolia* penetrates only the lower Humla Valley and is absent in the Mugu Valley, probably because of human intervention. In both valleys *Pinus excelsa* replaces *Abies spectabilis* as the predominant conifer. Here again fire in these semiarid environments contributes to the prevalence of the pine, besides reducing the total number of species present. Although the birch and juniper are normally the forest-line trees, with the former favoring northern exposures and the latter south-facing slopes, the pine sometimes grows to timberline. It has been reported

Fig. 16. Slash-and-burn cultivation of barley on a southeast exposure in Quercus semecarpifolia–Abies spectabili forest at 3,300 m. Betula utilis occupies the avalanche slope in the
background.

above 4,000 m in the Limi Valley of northwest Humla.[7] Dryness also ac-
counts for large stands of spruce (Picea smithiana) in the Humla Valley below Simikot (3,000 m) and even to below Mugu village (3,650 m).

---

7   Melvyn C. Goldstein, personal communication, October 1976.

On the mountain flanks above these dry inner valleys the change from forest to alpine scrub and meadow is not as well defined as it is further south. Juniper is common to both belts, and its transition from forest tree to dwarf shrub not only is gradual, but is predicated more by dryness than by altitude. Both the lower and upper limits of the alpine scrub and meadow belt, about 4,200 m and 5,200 m respectively, are higher than in the south, and snow line is as high as 5,800 m at some locations in the Tibetan border range.

Fig. 17. Burned-off grazing grounds (patans) on the Churchi Lekh (3,900 m), looking west between Rara Lake and the Sinja Karnali Valley

In the headwaters of the Humla Karnali to the west in Tibet and the Langu Khola to the east in Dolpo, true alpine steppe vegetation replaces scrub and meadow. In these arid regions *Caragana*, *Lonicera*, and *Artemesia* species grow to 5,200 m.

The array of soils in Karnali Zone is as varied as the vegetation. Below timberline they are predominantly residual Brown Podzol submontane soils that developed under forest vegetation, Regosols of recently deposited alluvium on the terraces and fans in the valley bottoms, and poorer Lithosols or mixtures of parent rock debris such as scree that have been deposited at the bases of slopes by gravity.

The fertility of these intermontane basin soils is related not only to their genesis but, in places, to the length of time they have been cultivated or grazed. Where under forest cover or where cultivated for only a short period of time, the soils are moderately fertile with a 2-7 percent organic content and a pH value of between five and seven. Where cultivation has gone on for centuries without sufficient fertilizer, the soils are always lime deficient with pH values as low as 4.8 and often bankrupt in phosphorous. In general, they exhibit high permeability, which in turn contributes to both high-surface and subsurface runoff in the watershed and a soil moisture deficit during six months of the year (March to June and October to November).

Above the timberline mountain meadow and skeletal soils predominate. Their composition is more dependent upon altitude, aspect, and denudation than it is upon the type of metasediment, gneiss, or granite parent rock present (Bunting 1965:123). Soil texture and structure also vary according to the proportion of gravel, rock fragments, and shaley material they contain. The meadow soils are acidic and of moderately shallow depth in which the buildup of organic material from grass roots is helped by the relatively low temperatures of those elevations. Moreover, the grasses are a binding material and prevent the loss of soils by wind action and snow melt as long as they are not seriously disturbed by grazing. Where steeper slopes allow better drainage these soils display a herbaceous cover; but because they are thinner, they become gravel fields when eroded. Because of their relatively thin formation, mountain meadow soils can also be viewed as skeletal soils (Rajan and Rao 1971:68).

High in the northern reaches of the zone where semiarid and arid conditions prevail, the soils are classically skeletal type. There physical weathering is intense, whereas chemical and bacterial action is minimal. Soils are acidic, thin, of a sandy loam or loam texture, and lacking both clay and humus as binding agents and are highly susceptible to erosion, especially by wind. They contain a meager supply of plant nutrients that sustain only hardy types of natural vegetation and are not suited for cultivation.

As is the case throughout the Himalaya, the environmental belts in Karnali Zone constitute distinctive wildlife habitats that support fauna assemblages quite different from those of the plains (Mani 1974). There, like the flora, Palaearctic animals from the north and west meet and mix with those from the Oriental realm to the south and east. However, because of this transitional situation, there is less diversity of species here than there is to the east and west. In the temperate forests Oriental species tend to be more prevalent; above the timberline and in the more arid northern part of the zone Palaearctic fauna predominate (Prater 1971:15-17; Fleming et al. 1976:14-15). Many of these species migrate seasonally through these ecological belts. Throughout the area, however, the indiscriminate killing of wildlife and modification of its habitats by humans have restricted the range and reduced the populations.

A variety of mammals inhabits the forest belts. Some species more commonly associated with the lowlands, such as barking deer (*Muntiacus muntjak*), penetrate the lower reaches of the intermontane basins. Indian porcupine (*Hystrix indica*) are below 2,400 m in both open land and forest. The Indian wild boar (*Sus scrofa*) seem to be ubiquitous. A few leopard (*Panthera pardus*) and smaller cats are reported, and marauding tiger (*Panthera tigris*) are seen each year. On an August night in 1970 a tiger raided our farmstead base camp, where it killed one of the landlord's dogs; before carrying off its prey, it also attacked and seriously injured a large Tibetan mastiff watchdog.

Fig. 18. High patans

Langur monkeys (*Presbytis entellus*) and hill foxes (*Vulpes montana*) are also found near cultivated areas. And on one occasion I watched a red or lesser panda (*Ailurus fulgens*) race across a meadow at 2,800 m on the edge of the forest, a jackal (*Canis aureus*) in hot pursuit.

Other animals shun heavily populated and deforested situations. Otters (*Lutra lutra*) live along streams in wooded areas while stone martens (*Martes foina*) range more widely in the forests. Another wide-ranging mammal is the Himalayan black bear (*Selenarctos thibetanus*), which prefers steep, forested slopes. Every summer several maulings or deaths from bear attacks occur in the zone. For example, in 1969 a woman was killed at dusk in the forest on a tributary of the Tila River 15 km from Jumla.

More isolated forests are the habitats of the goat-antelopes, serow (*Capricornis sumatraensis*), and grey goral (*Nemorhaedus goral*). On high, rocky slopes and cliffs within these forests the tahr (*Hemitragus jemlahicus*), a wild goat, is sometimes found. Musk deer (*Moschus moschiferus*), although heavily hunted, still survive in many birch forests above the conifers. Himalayan weasels (*Mustela sibirica*) roam some timberline environments.

In the open alpine belts above timberline a different faunal association with fewer species reflects harsher conditions. Himalayan mouse-hare (*Ochotona roylei*) and marmot (*Marmota himlayana*) are prevalent small mammals. Fairly large groups of blue sheep or bharal (*Pseudois nayaur*) are found high in the upper reaches of Humla and Mugu, despite intensive hunting. A few Greater Tibetan sheep (*Ovis ammon hodgsoni*) as well as wolves (*Canis lupus*) still live in the highest and most isolated reaches, although they face imminent extinction (R. Jackson 1979).

Finally, the fishes of Karnali Zone are also of some importance to humans. Such species as *Oreinus richardsonii* and *Nemacheilus rupecola*, along with *Barbus sps.* and the sucker *Pseudochencis suleatus*, are found in the rivers and streams as well as in Rara Lake (Bhatt 1970:147-50).

FROM THE ENVIRONMENTAL ARENA TO THE HUMAN ARRIVALS

The continuous mutual interaction of geologic, orographic, climatic, and biotic factors at work in Karnali Zone gives it a special character that distinguishes it from the rest of Nepal. For here northern, eastern, southern, and western physical and biological components blend in a transitional natural landscape in which western Himalayan influences tend to hold sway. The net result is a dry and warm inner Himalayan intermontane basin region surrounded by high mountains that is more like the intermontane basin of Kashmir than the nearby Pokhara or Kathmandu valleys of midland Nepal.

Within Karnali Zone the clear-cut arrangement of ecological components in a succession of differing altitudinal and latitudinal belts is modified by the area's texture, grain, and relief. Dendritic drainage produces great variation in topographic aspect within a small area; in turn, aspect imposes a profound control on weather, soils, and vegetation, and thus contributes to a pattern of diverse climatic and biotic associations (figure 19). In addition, the variable impact of the human population accentuates the mosaic quality of the pattern.

Finally, the environmental situation—a composite of all components discussed above—has impeded, and continues to impede, human access to Karnali zone and its resources. It not only limits movements to trail travel and affects the location, pattern, and density of the trail network (the spatial factor) but imposes seasonal restrictions on use of the trails (the temporal factor). Where, when, and with what ease people, along with animals, can move to, from, and within the Karnali Zone arena are shown in figure 20.

Access to and travel within and between the Sinja-Tila and Humla-Mugu intermontane basins are topographically controlled. Low routes enter this arena only from the southwest through the Karnali River breech and then spread northwestward up the drainages. High routes cross both the Chakhure-Mabu Lekh in the south and the Tibetan border range in the north, which bound Karnali Zone's two innermontane basins. The Api-Saipal Himal to the west and the Sisne-Kanjiroba Himal to the east are barriers through which no routes exist. Travel over these routes is restricted during the year by conditions that vary in type, severity, and duration with altitude.

Below 2,400 m rapid spring snow melt and runoff from higher elevations and subsequent summer rain swell the rivers. Floods periodically carry away bridges, particularly those in the main Karnali and Mugu Karnali valleys; important crossings are closed for periods of a few days to several weeks. Similarly the metasediment bedrock, chiefly gneiss, is very susceptible to erosion where stabilizing vegetation has been removed; landslides and washouts frequently block or cut the trails (figure 21). Travel at these low levels is therefore easier and conditions more dependable during the winter and spring. Temperatures at this time are moderate and snow is never a deterring factor.

At intermediate elevations between 2,400 and 3,600 m conditions allow generally uninterrupted movement throughout the year. On the one hand routes in these secondary and tertiary drainages are seldom closed by either summer flooding or winter snow; on the other hand, summer landslides and winter snow cover do combine with a higher frequency of steep grades and rocky surface to make travel more strenuous (figure 22).

Above 3,600 m the combination of greater altitude and generally more rugged terrain makes travel most difficult and practical only during the summer and fall. Snow and low temperatures in winter and spring are the chief constraining factors. Both the Chakhure-Mabu Lekh and the lower northern arm of the Great Himalaya between the Sinja-Tila and Humla-Mugu drainage basins are snow-covered for three to five months (between December and May). After severe storms, travel over these high routes is

---

Fig. 19, opposite. Landsat imagery mosaic of the Karnali River drainage showing about 80,000 km at a scale of approximately 1:1,500,000. Courtesy of Wolfram U. Drewes.

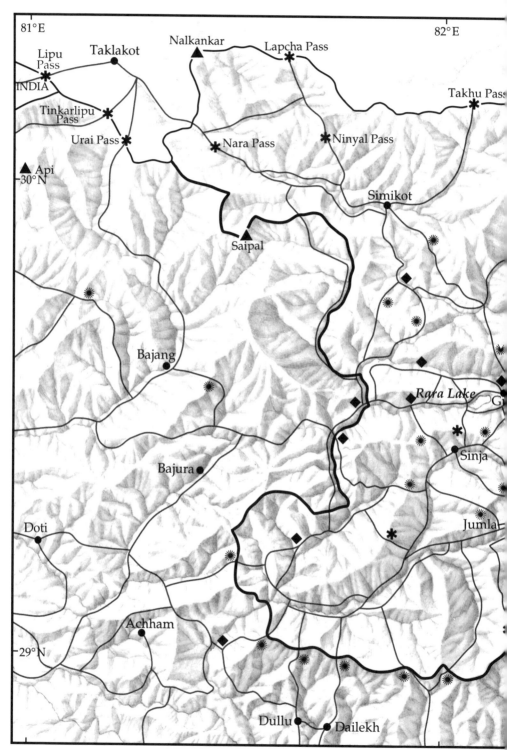

Fig. 20. Karnali Zone trails and seasonal travel restrictions

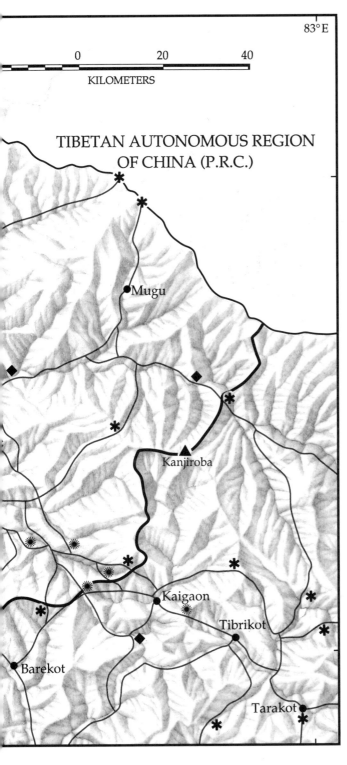

83°E

0   20   40

KILOMETERS

TIBETAN AUTONOMOUS REGION
OF CHINA (P.R.C.)

●Mugu

◆

◆

✳

✱

▲
Kanjiroba

❋
❋
❋
✱

✱

●Kaigaon
❋

✱

✱

◆

Tibrikot●

✱

●Barekot

Tarakot●
✱

▲ Peaks over 6,800 meters

✱ Trails blocked by snow
   for 3-6 months in winter-
   spring

❋ Trails periodically
   blocked by snow for 2-10
   days

◆ Trails subject to major
   spring-summer flooding,
   bridge washouts, and/or
   landslides

Fig. 21. Removal of the coniferous forest cover near Dillikot at 2,300 m on the north side of Mabu Lekh has contributed to severe erosion.

Fig. 22. *Snow-covered trail between Sinja and Rara*

impossible for periods of two to ten days in some places and for as long as a month or more in others. Abnormally early November or December storms on the Chakhure-Mabu Lekh (figure 23) are sometimes fatal for travelers caught in exposed positions. In the Tibetan border range, routes to the high passes are snow-covered for five to six months (mid-November to early June), and travel impossible for four months or more.

Although the important Humla Karnali River route to Tibet is snow-free at its border sector, it is closed during the winter; further downstream the rugged terrain forces the trail out of the valley into high adjacent mountainsides. In eastern Mugu, on the other hand, the trail along the Langu Khola into northern Dolpo is confined to its steep-walled gorge and rarely can be traveled. It has been negotiated only in winter when both water level and temperatures are at or near their lowest.

Fig. 23 Early snow on Chakhure Lekh

In sum, a variety of environmental factors orchestrates seasonal rhythms of movement, both interregional ones within the Karnali Zone arena and intraregional ones between the zone and adjacent areas in which spatial dimensions expand and contract like an accordion. High routes that are often more direct are passable only during the snow-free summer and fall; low and longer routes can best be followed during the dry, flood-free winter and spring. Moreover, north-south movements are generally more difficult than east-west movements. In the latter case they are possible only in the southern part of the zone where, again, seasonal restrictions are in force. Routes leading eastward to the middle reaches of the Bheri River in Dolpo are more easily traveled in summer and fall; those leading westward beyond the main Karnali River to the Seti River midlands are better followed during the fall and winter.

In a still broader spatial context that encompasses the Indian plains and the Tibetan Plateau, two major seasonally regulated barriers to human movement are of special historical significance: the malarial lowlands south of the temperate Midlands, and the lofty snow and ice-clad mountains within which the upper Karnali basins are temperate enclaves. The lowlands could be safely traversed only in the dry season (November to May); the mountains even now can be crossed only during the summer monsoon and early fall.

3
Cultural Kaleidoscope
Genesis and Growth

OVERVIEW

The present distribution of Himalayan peoples (figure 24) is the culmination of a long history of penetrations by Mongoloid tribes from the east and north and by Caucasoid groups from the west and south. The lofty mountains were effective deterrents to direct, large-scale mass migrations through the passes from the north. Malarial lowlands presented fewer obstacles as wave after wave of various ethnic groups sought new land or opportunity to loot and plunder, while fleeing drought,[1] population pressures, or political upheaval in their original homelands. Therefore, penetrations of the lower mountainous Himalaya were most often flanking movements, inexorably linked to and paralleling major migrations into and through the great river-plain corridors of South Asia.

In the eastern Himalaya of Assam, Bhutan, and Sikkim north of the Brahmaputra River, Mongoloid groups always held sway. In the west, Caucasoid Pahari (hill Hindus) now predominate on the mountain flanks above the Indus and Ganges plains from western Kashmir through the Kumaon Himalaya; Tibetans occupy adjacent higher inner-Himalaya and trans-Himalaya reaches to the north.

---

1   For a valuable perspective on changing climate in Asia see Tabuchi and Urushibara 1971.

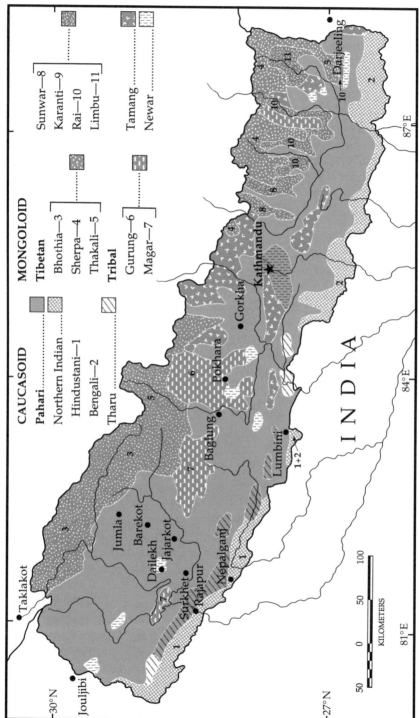

Fig. 24. Ethnographic map of the Nepal Himalaya. SOURCE: Atlas Narodov Mira (1964).

In the Nepal Himalaya, the central segment of the great mountain arc, Pahari, Bhotia of Tibetan origin, and Mongoloid groups (e.g., Limbu, Rai, Tamang, Gurung, Magar) all meet. A continuous Pahari wedge extends eastward through the entire width of the Midlands, or lower Himalaya. Indo-European-speaking plains Hindus identical to those of north India inhabit the Tarai and inner Tarai to the south as do tribal Tharu in western and central Nepal. To the north, a noncontiguous wedge of Tibeto-Burman speaking tribes extends westward through higher Midlands and some inner Himalayan reaches (2,000-3,500 m), thus often separating the Pahari from Bhotia who inhabit the inner Himalayan valleys and trans-Himalayan reaches. The distribution of these ethnic groups conforms to environmental belts. In turn, each belt constitutes a distinctive cultural area, the present product of past social, political, economic, and ecological processes. Although considerable cultural variation exists among regions within each belt, primarily owing to particular combinations of historical events and environmental factors, each displays considerable cultural continuity—an east-west or west-east continuum—at the country scale.

The following are a few key cultural characteristics of the Pahari, tribal, and Bhotia belts in the triple-tiered meeting ground of the Nepal Himalaya (Bista 1972), which furnish both a framework and a useful point of departure for focus on western Nepal and Karnali Zone.

A. Pahari cultural belt
   1. A genetic stock of Indo-Aryan Caucasoids, pre-Aryan Mongoloid indigenes, and their admixture
   2. Nepali, an Indo-Aryan Sanskrit-based language
   3. A predominance of Sanskritic Hindu religious beliefs and practices
   4. A caste system less rigid than that of northern India
   5. Strict avoidance of beef
   6. A sedentary agricultural economy

B. Tribal cultural belt
   1. A pre-Aryan and/or recent Mongoloid genetic stock
   2. Tibeto-Burman languages as the mother tongue, with Nepali generally spoken as a second language
   3. A combination of native animist, Lamaist, and Hindu religious beliefs and practices
   4. Originally casteless
   5. Consumption of liquor and meat varying with degree of Hinduization
   6. Agriculture, pastoralism, trade, and home industry the basis of economy, with agriculture now the most important

C. Bhotia cultural belt
   1. Mongoloid genetic stock

2. Tibetan dialects as the mother tongue, but moderately bilingual (Nepali)
3. Lamaist and/or Bonist religious beliefs and practices
4. A society in which caste is not a pervasive element
5. Consumption of liquor and meat, including beef
6. Agriculture, pastoralism, trade, and home industry the basis of economy, with agriculture now the most important

From the Karnali River watershed westward to the border, the distribution of Himalayan peoples and their attendant cultural ingredients is analogous to that of the area's flora and fauna discussed in chapter 2. There is much less ethnic diversity here than there is further east. Western Pahari elements predominate. Eastern tribal elements (Magar) thin and finally end south and west of the Chakhure-Mabu Lekh; Newar enclaves are recent phenomena, the result of migrations from the Kathmandu Valley in the past two hundred years.

Most important, the intermontane basins of Karnali Zone are populated primarily by Pahari. Over 92 percent of the population is hill Hindu, living in direct contact with a small Bhotia minority that is now confined to peripheral trans-Himalayan border reaches in northern Humla and Mugu, as well as enclaves on the western flanks of the Sisne Himal and Kanjiroba Himal.

Karnali Zone's cultural history has been one of successive major socioeconomic stages (cf. Bobek 1962:218-47):

1. Specialized hunting and fishing tribes, probably with some cultivation and incipient social stratification
2. Pastoral nomadic societies with some cultivation and more or less developed social stratification
3. Clan peasantry with solidifying social stratification; pastoral nomadism a subbranch
4. Rural feudalism under princely domination
5. Recent exposure to urban rent capitalism

Therefore, the present-day cultural landscape of Karnali Zone reflects a distinctive *genre de vie* that has evolved during at least two millennia of human occupance. Current culture traits such as ethnic composition, language, religious beliefs and practices, settlement patterns, land-tenure systems, livelihood strategies, social and economic institutions and hierarchies, and political power are products of the past. As such, all are the outgrowth of a series of migrations, conquests, and economic and political dominations with their attendant cultural borrowing, mixing, adjustment, and adaptation. Furthermore, these components together governed and continue to govern the ways in which the people of Karnali Zone manipulate their milieu.

In order to understand both the composite of cultural controls and the processes of human interaction with the environment, it is necessary to trace the sequence of events that has led to today's situation. Moreover, such a perspective places Karnali Zone in its proper pan-Himalayan context.

THE COMING OF THE KHASA

The early history of Karnali Zone is obscured by the absence of archeological evidence and written records prior to the eleventh century A.D. However, common cultural characteristics throughout the Pahari belt, particularly its linguistic composition (Grierson 1916), as well as historical evidence from northern India, other Himalayan areas, and Tibet, furnish the basis for a broad-brush and somewhat speculative picture.[2] They indicate a sequence of events in western Nepal and the backwater of Karnali Zone that began with the infiltration by Aryan Khasa from the northwest, an infiltration that paralleled but lagged behind those of the Indus and Ganges plains (table 2).

The first historical reference to the Khasa appears in the Mahabharata, an epic of early Indian literature, which suggests that they were a tribe of pastoral nomads who began pushing southeastward through the lower Himalaya about 1000-800 B.C., a thousand years after the initial Aryan incursions into the great river valleys. They "were a warlike tribe, and were well known to classical writers who noted as their special home the Indian Caucasus [the Hindu Kush] of Pliny" (Grierson 1916:7). Organized in clans of warriors with hereditary chiefs, priests, and pastoralist-farmers, they observed animist beliefs and practices that may have involved human sacrifice and cannibalism. Furthermore, "They were considered [by their Aryan predecessors on the plains] to have lost their claim to consideration as Aryans and to have become Mlechchhas, or barbarians, owing to their non-observance of the rules for eating and drinking observed by the Sanskritic peoples of India" (Grierson 1916:7).

The Khasa were not the first to occupy desirable sites in the lower Himalayan mountain tracts. Pollen analysis of lake bed deposits from both Haigam Lake in the Kashmir Valley and from the Naukutchiya Tal near Naini Tal in the Kumaon Himalaya indicates forest clearing, cultivation (probably of wheat or barley), and subsequent abandonment prior to the fifteenth century B.C. (Kishu-Mittre in Hutchinson, 1974:4-5). However, intensive farming accompanied by large-scale deforestation did not occur until between A.D. 700 and 1500. It should be remembered that on the plains to the

---

2 For in-depth historical sequences or analysis for India, see Basham (1963), Cohn (1971), and Majumdar (1971); for Tibet, see Snellgrove and Richardson (1968), and Stein (1972); for Nepal, see Regmi (1961, 1965, 1969); and for the Himalayan borderlands from Ladakh to Assam, see Rahul (1970).

TABLE 2. Historical development of Karnali and adjacent regions.

Year	Ganges Plains N. India	Kumaon/Indian Himalaya	Karnali (N.W. Nepal)	Kathmandu Valley	Tibet
1950	Indian Independence – 1947		Return of the Shah dynasty to power in Nepal		Tibetan autonomous region of China annexed by PRC in 1950
1900	British Raj				
1800	Annexed by British (1816)	Annexed by British (1816)	Shah dynasty controls Nepal until 1846	Rana family oligarchy (1846–1950)	
1700	Mughal administration (1526–1859)	Conquered by Gorkha (1790)	Annexed by House of Gorkha (Nepal) in 1788	Conquered by Gorkha (Shah dynasty) in 1768	Manchu protectorate (1720–92)
1600			Jumla princedom a Baisi state (15th–18th centuries)		Rule of the Dalai Lamas (1642–1950)
1500					
1400	Delhi sultanate	Rise of Chands (Rajputs)		Malla Period (ca. 13th–18th centuries)	
1300			Western Malla kingdom (12th–14th centuries)		
1200	Muslim invasions	Petty states			
1100					Religious kings (630–1642)
1000					
900	Region states (7th–13th centuries)	Katyuri princedoms	Tribal periphery of Katyuri domain	Licchavi Period (ca. 3d–13th centuries)	
800	Pala & Sena dynasties				
700					Tibetan military expansion (7th–9th centuries)
600					

			500
Katyuri Kingdom (under Gupta suzerainty)			
Classical Gupta Period (4th–9th centuries)			400
	Immigration of Khasa from northwest		300
		Kirati Period (ca. 7th century B.C.–3d century A.D.)	200
		Tibeto-Burman nomadic tribes	100
Political fragmentation 2d century B.C.–3d century A.D.	Immigration of Khasa from northwest		A.D.
			B.C.
Mauryan Empire (Asoka) Gautama Buddha 563–483*	Tibeto-Burmese tribal immigrations (from southeast)		
Aryan expansion and civilization			1000
Aryan invasions from northwest			

*Born in present-day Nepal

south farming was practiced much earlier. Radiocarbon dating indicates cultivation of a variety of food grains (in both the Ganges and Indus lowlands) prior to 2500 B.C. In the Indus, it was associated with the Harappa civilization before the arrival of any Aryans.

References to the Khasa in the Mārkandēya Purana, an early Nepali religious text, suggest that they had reached western Nepal by the third to fifth centuries A.D. (Grierson 1918:5). On the basis of the above evidence concerning predecessors of the Khasa, as well as general ecological considerations, we can assume that in Karnali Zone, as well as in the Midlands to the south and to the west in the Indian Himalaya of Kumaon and Garhwal, the Khasa sought out locations that offered: (1) good forest pasture for their horses, sheep, goats, and cattle, (2) floodplains and alluvial terraces for easy cultivation of barley and wheat, and (3) command of trading routes. The ecological situation would indicate that the Khasa first occupied the lower Tila and Sinja river valleys and later the upper Tila, Mugu, and Humla valleys (figure 3). There, as they became more and more sedentary and village-based, a noncontiguous settlement pattern of Khasa pockets separated by forests emerged, similar to that of earlier Aryan movement and settlement in the Ganges Valley.

In this process the Khasa may well have come in contact with numerically inferior indigenous hunters and gatherers, probably Mongoloid Kirati.[3] If so, the Khasa either displaced or absorbed them at the lowest servant and laborer level of their stratified tribal social organization, thus accounting for the absence today of any discrete non-Tibetan Mongoloid group in Karnali Zone. As Berreman (1972:16-19), among others, points out, this initial absorption laid the groundwork for the present-day mixed ethnic composition of Pahari culture.

In tracing the subsequent cultural history of Karnali Zone, certain facts constantly must be borne in mind: (1) developments in western Nepal were closely associated with those in Kumaon and Garhwal (rather than those of central and eastern Nepal) until at least the period of Gorkha conquest in the late eighteenth century; (2) invading armies were always a heterogeneous mix of conquered peoples led by a dominant group, tribe, or clan; (3) moreover, new settlers in Karnali Zone were incorporated into the extant society; (4) penetration of culture from the centers of power, which waxed and waned in northern India, was at first slow and often rendered superficial on the mountainous frontiers; (5) if the lower Himalaya of Garhwal, Kumaon, and western Nepal was a pioneer fringe, then Karnali Zone in turn was a frontier fringe of the Midlands.

---

[3] *Kirata* means "to roam on the edge" and can refer to all Mongoloid tribes of the Himalaya (Slusser 1982).

Long before Khasa settlement in western Nepal most Himalayan peoples from Kashmir to the Valley of Nepal (the Kathmandu Valley) were undergoing Indianization processes of varying type, magnitude, and intensity. Of special importance was the dissemination of Buddhism by the zealous Asoka (ca. 321-187 B.C.). From his capital at Pataliputra (present-day Patna) on the middle Ganges, this Mauryan king spread Buddhist religious philosophy northwestward to Kashmir and beyond; by the fifth century A.D. it had not only filtered through the Pamir to reach China by way of inner Asian trade routes, but had been well established in the lower Himalaya kingdoms.

At this time such hill kingdoms were becoming increasingly important through their control of trade between inner Asia and north India. The Licchavi dynasty was now in control of the Kathmandu Valley; in Garhwal and Kumaon (and perhaps in the western Nepal Midlands to some extent) the Katyuri kingdom was gaining strength. Both numbered among the kingdoms and chiefdoms along the frontier fringe that fell loosely within the sphere of influence of powerful kingdoms on the Ganges.

Between the fourth and seventh centuries A.D. the Gupta dynasty held paramount power over all of northern India, exacting tribute from these mountain states as well as from the tribal republics of Rajasthan. At the same time, the Gupta brought classical Indian civilization to its apex. This period was marked not only by urban prosperity and an attendant surge of science and the arts, but also by continued development and refinement of a stratified social order based on the exclusiveness of the ritually pure holders of power. As a result the economic order (agriculturally based networks of villages) functioned with increasing social fragmentation.

Gupta political administration, supported by land-based revenues, was more decentralized than in the past (e.g., the Mauryan period) and of necessity made a greater practice of paying provincial governors and district officials with income-generating land grants in lieu of direct cash payments from the royal coffers. Such a loose administrative system permitted governors of distant regions, far from direct control by the central authority, to function somewhat autonomously and to break away whenever that authority weakened.

Toward the end of the Gupta period (sixth to seventh centuries) successive waves of warring seminomadic tribes of Turkish and Mongol speech known collectively as Huns spread out from central Asia to attack the Roman Empire, Persia, and northern India. At first the Gupta withstood these invasions and absorbed the barbarian hoards into their society, at the price of both increased militarism and decreased social flexibility. But with the death of Harsha (A.D. 647), who led a classical revival from his capital at Kanauj near Delhi after the Huns overran the Gupta briefly at the end of the

fifth century, the empire finally crumbled. Gupta suzerainty over its minions could no longer be maintained and South Asia slipped into the Middle
Ages, a period that was to last a thousand years.

The seventh to twelfth centuries were marked by almost constant
warfare, both among the small petty kingdoms and chiefdoms that were the
splinters of the empire and with the invaders, first the barbarians, then
Muslim Turks as Islam emerged in the Middle East and spread. Hermann
Goetz aptly described these events as: "an avalanche . . . the most different
racial and cultural type[s], fleeing one before the other [were] pushed onward
in order not to be subjected, dragged on as vassals or voluntary associates of
the victor, constantly changing their leaders, federations swelling to count-
less numbers with victory, breaking up with defeat . . . reforming under new
leaders, part of them settled at last on the frontier as defenders against the
next impact of the same avalanche, or [were] deported to distant provinces
where they would be harmless amidst a foreign population" (1953:3).

Dynasty replaced dynasty as each conquering warrior clan in turn imposed itself on an already mixed population, lowering in position some
conquered classes in the stratified social order while maintaining with little
modification the extant economic and political structures by incorporating
the displaced princes into the secular administration. Brahman priests always retained their ritual superiority and associated positions of power. Various powers on the plains (the Pratihara clans of Gurjara tribal origin from
Rajasthan; the Pala dynasty from Bengal and Bihar; the Rashtrakitta dynasty
out of the Deccan Plateau) struggled for control of Kanauj and the Punjab.
Regional states rose and fell.

Throughout the Himalayan borderlands independent kingdoms,
from Kashmir to the Kathmandu Valley, emerged only to feel the impact of
Tibetan military expansion, which spilled over the Himalayas and temporarily blocked plains influence. Under the initial leadership of Grong-
btsan-sgam-po (d. A.D. 650), a powerful kingdom grew in southeastern Tibet.
During the seventh to ninth centuries it extended its domination westward
to include Hunza, Swat, and Kashmir and southward over the Himalaya
crests, even reaching the plains. But with the disintegration of Tibetan authority, which coincided with but was not related to the rise of the Gurjara
in Rajasthan and their control of Kanauj and the Punjab (ca. A.D. 840-910),
control of the petty hill kingdoms returned to the native princes.

In western Tibet three closely linked kingdoms now grew in power,
known as Purang, Guge, and Maryul, stretching from Mustang (Lo) to
Ladakh (Snellgrove and Richardson 1968:112). These kingdoms, which were
established by displaced descendants of the Lhasa kings who had migrated
westward after A.D. 866, were responsible for the development of Tibetan
Buddhism at a time (ninth to eleventh centuries) when it was neglected in
central and eastern Tibet. To the south of the Himalaya in the middle and

lower Ganges the Pala kingdom of Buddhist persuasion extended its influence northwestward into the Punjab and the peripheral Himalayan hills at the expense of the Hindu Gurjara-Pratihari. But in the process both were weakened by the stress of continued warfare.

During the eleventh century the Pala of Bihar and Bengal were succeeded by the Sena dynasty of strong Brahmanical persuasion. In the aftermath of conflict and change on the plains to the south, the Licchavi kingdom in the Kathmandu Valley began to crumble. Yet there Buddhism and Hinduism continued to coexist as they have for centuries, both maintaining less orthodox tantric elements that reflected older tribal animism with its leanings toward the mystical and magical and the propitiation of awe-inspiring and terrible forces of nature. This situation survives today.

Most important to the ensuing cultural history of Karnali Zone was the state of affairs at this time to the west in Kumaon. There Katyuri kings, probably of Khasa origin like most of their subjects, but claiming a linkage with nobility of the Ganges Plain, reigned supreme over the Himalaya from Garhwal to Doti in far western Nepal from the ninth through the eleventh centuries.[4] During this period Buddhism, which had been well established in earlier Katyuri times, was completely obliterated by zealous Brahmans who carried the current anti-Buddhist movement from the plains to the hills. Buddhist Khasa were either absorbed or dispersed. It seems safe to assume that many of the latter group moved eastward beyond the Katyuri periphery, thus continuing the Khasa migrations into the upper Karnali drainage and the Karnali study area. In Kumaon Hinduism came to permeate all aspects of life.

These processes of Brahmanization intensified as successive waves of Muslim invaders, beginning with the raids of Mahmud of Ghazni in the early eleventh century, brought new turmoil to the Ganges. Plains Hindus in increasing numbers sought sanctuary in the hills as their homelands were overrun. In turn these new immigrants eroded Katyuri power and contributed to their collapse. By the twelfth century, the Katyuri kingdom had dissolved into a number of petty principalities, some ruled by Katyuri nobility, others dominated by plains immigrants, and still others controlled by Khasa chiefs.

THE GURJARA LEGACY

All of the peoples in the early medieval scenario just outlined affected the course of history in western Nepal and Karnali Zone to some degree, either directly or indirectly. Of special importance were the Gurjara, whose influence on social, economic, and political developments was pronounced.

---

4   Doti's capital was at or near present-day Silgarhi-Doti on the Seti Karnali River.

Many key aspects of Pahari society past and present, such as prominent elements in its language, dominant upper strata in its social structure, and its associated pervasive feudal framework, along with the close similarity of these elements to those of Rajasthan, can best be explained by early Gurjara penetrations of both the Indian plains and the Himalayan borderlands and subsequent interaction between the two regions.

Although the origins of the Gurjara are obscure, scholars generally agree that they were, in fact, a collection of barbarian tribes of mixed ethnic stock who entered the northwest corridor on the heels of the Huns. Opinions differ, however, on the sequence of ensuing Gurjara movements and the routes they followed. Grierson's reconstruction (1916:8-16), based primarily on linguistic evidence, appears most plausible and is supported by written archeological evidence from the Indian Himalaya (e.g., Goetz 1955).

The Gurjaras . . . invaded India about the sixth century A.D. and occupied [more rapidly than their Khasa predecessors had] the . . . [mountain] tract, then known as Sapādalaksha . . . [Khasa and Gurjara alike] spoke an Aryan, but not necessarily Indo-Aryan language. Of these Gurjaras the bulk followed pastoral pursuits and became merged in and identified with the preceding Khasa population. Others were fighting men, and were identified by the Brahmans with Kshatriyas [the warrior rank]. In this guise they invaded the Eastern Rajputana from Sapādalaksha, and, possibly, Western Rajputana from Sindh, and founded, as Rajputs, the great Rajput states of Rajputana. (Grierson 1916:4)

Thus, linkages were established between Sapadalaksha and Rajasthan that were to persist to the present.

On the plains the Gurjara swiftly underwent varying degrees of ritual and secular processes of Indianization that reflected the uncertainty and stress of the times. The Indian society of which they were now a part rapidly rigidified in the face of accelerated inroads by Muslim (Turk and Afghan) invaders. Intricate and interrelated social, economic, and religious hierarchies, although displaying considerable local or regional variation, had long since evolved from the original Aryan class order. Now they became steadily more inflexible, permitting a numerically small minority to hold economic and political power by controlling and regulating all aspects of society.

On the basis of birth or genus all people were assigned to castes (*jati*), which were grouped within broad ranks (*varna*) or occupational divisions. The three economically and politically dominant Aryan social classes of priests and scholars (Brahman), rulers and warriors (Ksatriya), and merchants (Vaisaya), twice-born followers of common gods and ritual, were served by a fourth *varna* (Sudra) of many craftsmen, laborers, and agriculturalists (i.e., peasants), caste groups that were excluded from Brahmanical ritual. In addition to these four *varna*, ritually polluted occupationals, namely field laborers and scavengers, fell within a fifth rank of untouchable or Dom (or Dum) castes, who also served the twice-born as serfs and slaves.

Through this system Brahman lawmakers, in consort with the Ksatriya ruling classes from whom they were granted land, legitimized high-caste exploitation by religious justification of privilege and thus permitted the functionaries of a decentralized feudal[5] economic-political hierarchy of king, vassals, peasants, serfs, and slaves.

In the hills Indianization proceeded at a much slower pace. Although the hill Gurjara were as quick as their plains kin to disassociate themselves from a name that labeled them unclean barbarians,[6] their relative isolation on the Sapadalaksha fringe of the major plains powers deterred outside influence. Infiltration of orthodox aspects of Hindu civilization was at first slow and superficial but then accelerated as upper-class Brahmans and Ksatriya from Rajasthan reimmigrated, "seeking refuge from Musalman oppression in the hills from which they had originally issued" (Grierson 1916:15).

As Khasa/Gurjara peoples of the lower Himalaya underwent continuing Indianization processes over this protracted period, both ritual and secular facets of the plains situation were perforce modified or ameliorated. Regional variations on this common theme developed as historical events produced differing social and economic mixes. In turn, each mix adjusted to its own particular environment. Such a distinctive variation developed in the Karnali River watershed as an outgrowth of seventh through twelfth century conditions there and in surrounding regions.

THE RISE OF THE KHASA MALLA

Political Origins and Territorial Expansion

Conditions on the Sapadalaksha fringe to the east of Doti (i.e., the main Karnali River and its major tributaries) during this period remain murky owing to a dearth of reliable historical data. Yet subsequent events would indicate that here too Khasa chiefs probably of Gurjara origin controlled scattered populations predominantly Khasa but of a more mixed composition than further west. With the fragmentation, weakening, or collapse of the powerful states on their periphery, these less Indianized groups, which were swelling in size from both internal growth and increasing immigration, became stronger. From this new and expanding Karnali center of

---

5   From the Latin *feudum*, a piece of land that is granted in return for service. For a discussion of Indian feudal structure and its variance with that of medieval Europe see Thorner (1956:133-50).

6   The name Gurjara is common only in seventh and eighth century writings. Today it is retained (in varying forms) solely by scattered nomadic herders (Barth 1956; Nitzberg 1970; Brar 1971).

strength, a Khasa dynasty emerged, known as Malla,[7] which forged an extended regional kingdom during the twelfth to fourteenth centuries that was the foundation for the cultural unity of Nepal's dominant Pahari society today.

Beginning with the twelfth century the cultural history of Karnali Zone and western Nepal becomes increasingly clear. The contents of royal inscriptions, land grant plates or tablets of clay or copper, genealogies, or *vamsavali*, and Tibetan chronicles, along with the architectural style and the location and distribution of stone temples and sculpture, roadside monuments and markers, and public works (e.g., water reservoirs and conduits and fountains) tell the story of the rise and fall of the western Malla kingdom. In combination these data furnish a valuable if far from complete picture of its spread and extent and the concomitant development of its social, economic, and political institutions and hierarchies.[8]

On the basis of Tibetan chronicles Tucci contends that "about the 11th century, two aryan-speaking tribes broke into Western Tibet. The one took control of Purang and the other of Guge" (1956:108). Both went "so far as to Tibetanize their habits and names" (Tucci 1956:109). In the early twelfth century Nagaraja, the founder of the Khasa Malla dynasty and a descendant of the ruling family of Guge, moved his capital to Sija, present-day Sinja, 24 km northwest of Jumla-Kalanga. Sharma (1972:17), on the other hand, presents an equally plausible argument. Based on Yogi Naraharinath's belief that Nagaraja's home village (Khari) was located in the upper Mugu Karnali Valley before he established his kingdom at Sinja, Sharma maintains that the Malla dynasty originated in Karnali Zone. He further maintains that Nagaraja brought Guge and Purang within the sway of his Khasa kingdom by conquest, since reference to this line of kings begins with him in the Tibetan chronicles.

Whether the invasions of Tibet occurred in the eleventh century or in the early twelfth century, both scholars agree that the "invaders from the south Himalayan countries were . . . Khasa, who as a war-like aristocracy controlled a fluctuating mass of other tribes, those K'ri ta (Kirata) or Mon to which the old Tibetan chronicles make allusions" (Tucci 1956:109).

During the twelfth century Nagaraja's successors extended and solidified their kingdom. From the time of Kradhichalla the dynasty ruled from

---

[7]   This Khasa dynasty and kingdom of western Nepal is referred to as western Malla or Khasa Malla in order to prevent confusion with a twelfth to eighteenth century dynasty and kingdom in the Kathmandu Valley also known as Malla.

[8]   The discovery and initial analysis of evidence of the existence of this western Malla dynasty was made by the Tibetan scholar G. Tucci (1956, 1962); following Tucci's exploration, Yogi Naraharinath collected a plethora of written materials, which are published in valuable reference works (Itihas Prakash Mandal 1955-56; Naraharinath 1966). Prayag Raj Sharma subsequently studied the art and architecture of the Karnali River basin (1972).

two capitals on a seasonal basis: Sinja remained the summer capital while Dullu, 10 km west of Dailekh in the Midlands to the south of Karnali Zone, was the winter capital. By the reign of Kradhichalla's son Krachalla (A.D. 1207-23), who was responsible for the first datable inscriptions, the dynasty controlled extensive portions of Kumaon and Garhwal. Krachalla's heir Ashokachalla was "described as the great king of the Sapadalaksha mountains—the Khas country" (Sharma 1972:18).

Late in the thirteenth century these rulers began looking eastward as their military strength increased. On three occasions between 1287 and 1289 Khasa armies under Jitari (the elder son of Ashokachalla) sacked and burned the weak and fragmented principalities of the Kathmandu Valley. It also seems likely that Jitari's reign signaled continued eastward migration of Khasa people into the central Midlands and/or Khasa domination and absorption of indigenous groups they encountered.

Jitari was the first Khasa ruler to drop the suffix "-challa" from his name and add the suffix "-malla." As Sharma astutely points out (1972:42) he probably did so only after being exposed to the practice in the Kathmandu Valley. There a dynasty of Licchavi origin was emerging that already had assumed this honorific (meaning "protector"), thus emulating the more sophisticated dynasties of India.[9] It is, therefore, important to keep in mind that these two Malla dynasties were in no way related.

Most, but not all, Khasa Malla incursions of the Kathmandu Valley were military forays. Ripumalla apparently visited the valley in 1312 as a pilgrim to worship at both Hindu and Buddhist shrines; at the same time he also traveled to the birthplace of the Buddha at Lumbini in the central Tarai (figure 1).

The last Khasa Malla incursion occurred in 1327 during the reign of Adityamalla, at which time the valley was pillaged once more.

In 1328 Pratapamalla died without an heir and the Malla kingdom was passed to another line of Khas nobility. Punya Pal of Gela was married to a princess of the royal family; after the coronation in Sinja, he dropped the Pal designation and assumed the -malla suffix of his wife's lineage.[10]

---

[9]   The -malla honorific suffix was first assumed by the Palavas of south India in the seventh century; gradually its use as a status symbol spread first westward and then northward to be adopted in the Kathmandu Valley in A.D. 1200 (Slusser 1982, chap. 4).

It also should be pointed out that in the Tibetan chronicles the Tibetan family suffix "-IDe" was added to all Khasa rulers' names through Ashoka, but from Jitari onward the -malla suffix was used. This indicates an end of Khasa-Tibetanization (D. Regmi 1965: pt. 1, p. 712) or, more likely, the increased strength of the Khasa dynasty's control over its trans-Himalayan minions.

[10]   The location of Gela, like that of Khari, has not been definitely determined. Perhaps the present-day village of Gela on the lower Tila Karnali was Punya Pal's home. Tucci (1956:108) believes that it was located in Purang and that Punya Pal unified the domains of the Guge

All evidence indicates that the Malla kingdom reached its zenith during the time of Prithivimalla, Punyamalla's son, who ruled in the mid-fourteenth century (ca. 1334-58). His domain encompassed territory as extensive as that of the present-day area of Nepal (142,000 km$^{2)}$ and not only included the Tibetan provinces of Guge and Purang but also that of Lo, present-day Mustang in north central Nepal (Jackson 1976:46-48). In the Midlands to the south of the Himalayan crest, it stretched eastward to Kashikot overlooking the Pokhara Valley (figure 1) westward into Kumaon and Garhwal and southward through the inner Tarai valleys of Dang and Surkhet to the plains.

With the rise and expansion of the western Malla, the Karnali drainage ceased to be the eastern frontier fringe of the Kumaon kingdoms. Instead it became the center of a powerful Karnali Khas kingdom, with two nodes comprising its core: the Dailekh-Dullu region on the southern flanks of the Chakhure-Mabu Lekh, and the main Karnali Valley, as well as the lower Tila and Sinja Karnali valleys, north of the *lekh* in the Karnali Zone study area. Within its own extended frontiers now lay the former core of more Indianized Katyuri principalities to the west in Kumaon, as well as Kirati tribal territories on its periphery to the north, east, and south.

From Tribal to Feudal Society

The rugged terrain and the seasonal variability of the monsoon climate, as well as the distances involved, made Malla control of its territories difficult, and were important factors that contributed to the emergence of a feudal structure during the rise of the Karnali Khasa. Owen Lattimore's description of feudalism is most apt in the case of the Malla. He sees it as "a complex organization . . . [that] emerges in a period when, in the relationship between these aspects of society, military striking power has quite wide geographical range, but transportation is so cumbrous and expensive that the exchange of food and goods of daily consumption cannot be organized within a common market as wide as the periphery to which military operations can reach" (1962:543-44).

Indeed, as the western Malla kingdom grew and developed, Karnali Khasa society evolved from one of tribal structure (Bobek's [1962] stage of clan-peasantry with solidifying social stratification) to one of feudal structure (what Bobek classifies as rural feudalism under princely domination) in response to interacting social, economic, and political factors as well as to the historical events and environment constraints already mentioned. The pro-

---

and Purang through marriage. It should be noted that the practice of a sonless father bringing a son-in-law to stay in his house is known as *dolaji* and still prevails in Karnali Zone among the Matwali Chhetri Khas descendants (Sharma 1971:43-66).

cesses of change in the fabric of Karnali Khas society were those of Indianization, which first the Gurjara of the plains had undergone in Rajasthan and then the people of the lower Himalaya in Kumaon and Garhwal had experienced. Now during the Malla period it was the Karnali Khasa's turn to undergo intensifying processes of Indianization. At the roots of these changes, as elsewhere, were the control and allocation of resources. Most important, the control and allocation of land became the basis of Malla power.

In a most astute treatment of frontier feudalism, Owen Lattimore (1962:525-26) states that "historically, when we find frontier affairs recorded primarily in terms of negotiations with 'barbarian' chiefs, the society of the frontier people in question is still tribal; when the most important administrative events recorded are allocations of territory, the social system is passing from the tribal to the feudal." Such was the case for the Karnali Khas under the Malla during the twelfth through fourteenth centuries.

Although observations on early Malla times are conjectural and far from conclusive owing to the relatively small number of archeological remains, good indirect evidence from neighboring regions does permit some reasonable assumptions. Toward the end of the Malla era (late fourteenth century) useful inscriptions increase considerably in number, reliability, and informative content. But like earlier ones, they were written by and primarily concern the royalty and aristocracy in the style of the time and thus reflect the bias of the dominant segment of society. Yet, if treated with caution, it is possible to filter fact from folklore and, reading between the lines, to glean a valuable, if again somewhat speculative, picture of the common person's lot as well. Moreover, it is not always possible to separate the discussion into discrete social, economic, and political spheres, for all crosscut each other; their components interact not only among themselves but with those of the physical environment to produce the distinct cultural fabric of the kingdom.

As the tribes of the Karnali catchment basin entered the Malla era during the twelfth century they constituted a plural or polyethnic society that was stratified not only culturally but spatially.[11] The Khasa, with their social hierarchy of chiefs and warriors, priests, farmer-pastoralists, and no doubt slaves, were growing in number because of both natural biological increase and immigrations from Kumaon and were continuing to displace or

---

11   Charles Winich's definition of "tribe" is appropriate here: "A social group, usually with a definite area, dialect, cultural homogeneity and unifying social organization . . . which has a leader . . . [and] a common ancestor as well as a patron deity. The families or small communities making up the tribe are linked through economic, social, religious, family, or blood ties" (1956:546). Furnivall's definition of plural society is also appropriate here: "A poly-ethnic society integrated in the market place, under the control of a state system dominated by one of the groups, but leaving large areas of cultural diversity in the religious and domestic sectors of activity" (Barth 1969:16).

absorb indigenous Mongolian tribes such as Magar and Kirati. They were the dominant ethnic group, not only numerically but politically and economically, on the southern Himalayan slopes from Doti and Achham to Dullu and Dailekh, as well as north of the Chakhure-Mabu Lekh in the valleys of the main Karnali River and the lower Tila and Sinja Karnali rivers.

In what is now the Karnali Zone study area Khasa clans lived in loosely to tightly clustered villages depending upon terrain and occupied both the most agriculturally productive and the most easily worked alluvial terraces and fans between 1,000 and 2,500 m (figure 25). They also controlled the important trade routes between the Ganges Plain and Tibet that passed through their territory, routes also significant for Hindu pilgrim traffic to Lake Manosarowar and the abode of Siva, and Mount Kailas, on the plateau north of Taklakot (figure 2). Khasa farmland was allocated by village headmen or clan leaders on a family freehold basis while the mixed oak and conifer-covered hillsides above the break-in-slope were held in common and used for pasture, wood fuel, and numerous plant and animal resources.

On the periphery of the Khasa core territories Bhotia occupied other ecological niches in the headwaters of the Karnali drainage and in the north, where they continued to live as discrete though dominated tribes. Following a more mobile way of life than the Khasa, their livelihood was based on pastoralism and trade rather than on agriculture and was interdependent with that of their valley neighbors. Thus symbiotic relationships were already at work that had social and spatial dimensions and that operated within and across both ethnic and ecological boundaries.

Cultural Accomplishments and Contributions

The establishment and solidification of Malla power during the twelfth century and subsequent territorial expansion brought the Karnali Khasa not only increasing economic prosperity but a protracted period (thirteenth and fourteenth centuries) of continuity and stability, one sufficient for tremendous development and change to take place both in the cultural landscape of the region and in the Karnali Khasa society that the landscape reflected. Although their cultural accomplishments never rivaled those achieved by the people of either the Indian Himalaya or the Kathmandu Valley, under the Malla dynasty the Karnali Khasa, and particularly those few in positions of authority, did reach a level of well-being, culminating during the reign of Prithivimalla, the likes of which they neither had enjoyed before nor have since. All developments were at first slow but sustained (thirteenth century) and then accelerated (fourteenth century),

---

Fig. 25 (opposite). The Sinja Karnali Valley with paddy growing on the southern exposure at 2,600 m

and propelled Khasa tribal society, in which economy, religion, and political administration were not as yet specialized social institutions but egalitarian and based upon kinship or local clan ties,[12] to its feudal form in which occupational specialization reflected increased social, economic, and ritual stratification, and land-based political power was held by the elite strata who wielded it to their own exclusive benefit.

The Malla court, at Sinja during the summer and Dullu during the winter,[13] became a center for the arts and learning. Contemporary inscriptions lauded Sinja for its music, song, and dance (Itihas Prakash Mandal, 1955-56: vol. 2, pt. 1, pp. 54, 63). Buddhist monks, Brahman priests, scholars and tutors, artists, and craftsmen from abroad took residence and settled there, encouraged by the prevalent policy that exempted them from taxes and in some cases granted them land from which they could derive income.

A profusion of stone images, Hindu temples, Buddhist *chaityas* and *stupas*, palaces and audience halls, edict pillars and boundary markers, as well as rest houses, fountains, irrigation conduits, and reservoirs in which water could be retained for drought periods, are found today throughout the region, particularly in the Jumla, Achham, and Dailekh Khasa core areas (figures 26, 27, 28). Their remains attest to the extent of Malla building projects, which, it is safe to assume, could have been carried out only with considerable use of corvée or slave labor. Of particular note are the temples, smaller and more simplified versions of those built during the late Katyuri period (eleventh to fourteenth centuries) in Kumaon (Sharma 1972:20, 22).

The Karnali Khasa domain, like the Kathmandu Valley, was a refuge for Buddhism, which Brahmans had forced from Kumaon by the eleventh century and which Muslim invaders had completely obliterated from the Ganges Plain by the end of the thirteenth century. Inscriptions indicate that Malla rulers were Buddhist and that monasteries flourished at Sinja. But at the same time Brahmanism was making steady inroads and was coexisting with Buddhism. Deities of both were commonly worshiped. Finally, during the reign of Prithivimalla (1334-58) Brahmanism gained supremacy, at least among the royalty and aristocracy. However, one can presume that a large portion of Khasa society (the lower strata), along with Bhotia groups on the periphery, continued to retain their Buddhist persuasion and/or their ancient animistic beliefs and practices.

The ascendancy of Brahmanism was only one of many manifestations of increasing Hinduization that the Karnali Khasa underwent during

---

[12] Marshall Sahlins (1968:15) points out that "in tribes, production, polity, and piety are not as yet separately organized, and society not as yet a holy alliance of market, state, and church."

[13] The proverb *Siñjā Hāt, Dullū Birāt* ("Sinja market, Dullu capital") is popular among the people of Karnali even today.

Fig. 26. Guardian lions at the site of the Malla palace, Lāmāthāda above Sinja

the fourteenth century. These accelerated processes were all most likely linked to an event in the Rajasthan state of Udaipur in 1303. That August the capital of Chitor fell to the Mongols after a bloody defense by Rajput warriors that was preceded by "that horrible rite, the *Johar*, where females are immolated to preserve them from pollution or captivity" (Tod 1914, 1:215). In the wake of these Muslim hoards Rajput refugees, usually of princely families, sought safety and a new life with their country cousins in Himalayan sanctuaries. For the first time they began to penetrate western Nepal, usually via Kumaon.[14]

---

[14] Hamilton (1819:15) states that Rajputs arrived in Nepal no earlier than 1306. Although he gives no explanation for that specific date, one can deduce that he based it on the fall of Rajasthan to the Muslims.

Fig. 27. Stupas at Michagoan, 3 km west of Jumla-Kalanga

Two Karnali Khas developments emerged in the fourteenth century that were to have an enduring effect, for today they constitute important cornerstones of eastern Pahari or Nepalese culture and contribute to its distinctive regional character: the Nepali language and the special Nepalese version of the Hindu caste system.

The Nepali language of today has been called at various times Gorkhali, or "the language of the Gorkhas"; Parabatya, or "mountain language"; and Khas-kura, or "language of the Khas."[15] Belonging to the Indo-Aryan family, it is of Sanskrit derivation and one of the Pahari languages of the lower Himalaya. Ralph L. Turner's contention (1965:xiii) that "the close resemblance, noted by Grierson, of the Pahari languages with the Rajasthani is due rather to the preservation of common original features than to the introduction of common innovations" supports the theory of the Gurjara connection between the Khas of Kumaon and Karnali and the Rajasthani of

---

15 For a valuable summary of Nepali see Turner (1965:xii-xviii).

the plains discussed earlier. But as these ancient Pahari tongues evolved in different regions they developed independently and with considerable borrowing from the languages of other ethnic groups they came in contact with or absorbed. Thus, as Turner points out (1965:xiv), the evolution of Nepali was influenced by other Indo-Aryan languages found to the south and, even more, by the Tibeto-Burman tongues found to the north and east. The earliest known example of medieval Nepali is a bilingual royal decree inscribed on a copper plate during the reign of Adityamalla and dated 1321 A.D. (Sharma 1972:34). It is written first in Nepali using the Nagari script[16] and then in Tibetan.

Caste: Components and Regional Variations

The most integral aspect of Indianization that the polyethnic population of Karnali underwent during the final phase of Malla rule was the introduction of the Hindu caste system, modeled after the ancient and orthodox Brahmanical system of the plains. Although a vast and continually expanding literature exists on the Hindu caste system, no single acceptable definition can be put forth. However, there is wide agreement among South Asian scholars on the attributes of the system, and most are germane to the case of Karnali.[17]

Caste is the multifaceted status hierarchy composed of all members of society, each of whom is ranked within the broad, fourfold Hindu class (*varna*) divisions or within the fifth class of untouchables or outcastes. Each caste, or *jati*, is ideally an endogamous group in which membership is hereditary and permanent. At the core of the caste structure is a rank order of values bound up in concepts of ritual status, purity, and pollution. Furthermore, caste determines an individual's behavior, obligations, and expectations. All social, economic, religious, legal, and political activities of a caste society are prescribed by sanctions that both determine and limit access to land, positions of political power, and command of human labor. Therefore, within such a constrictive system, wealth, political power, high rank, and privilege converge. And hereditary occupational specialization is a common feature. Caste is functionally significant only when viewed in a regional or local context and at a particular time.

Himalayan scholars attribute distinctive regional variations in culture, notably manifested by caste structure differences along the hill-Hindu belt of the Himalayan frontier fringe, to a variety of factors. Berreman believes cultural differences among Pahari regions, as well as local homogene-

---

[16] The Devanagari alphabet in which Nepali is written today was a later development.

[17] For a representative selection of major works on caste see: Bailey (1957); de Reuck and Knight (1967); Dumont (1970); Fürer-Haimendorf (1966); Hutton (1963); Leach (1966); and Marriott (1960).

Fig. 28. Small temple over spring at Gothi Chaur, 20 km east of Jumla-Kalanga

ity, are the products of "cultural drift" caused by the degree, duration, and kind of isolation the populations involved have experienced (1960:788-89). Although remote location and environmental factors impose varying constraints on human mobility and contact, both diurnal movements and seasonal migrations involving communication and exchange are also important aspects of the rhythmical ways of life over time and space in all Himalayan regions.

Therefore, many scholars such as Barth (1969) and Nitzberg (1972) question the importance of the role of isolation as a chief cause for cultural differences. Barth believes that contact and interdependence of different ethnic groups, both within and among regions, foster cultural differences and permit them to persist (1969:9-10). Majumdar (1962:77) maintains that regional variations are due instead to the survival of aspects of pre-Hindu tribal matriarchal social organization. Brar (1971:23-24) contends that regional differences in social stratification are not completely tied to ethnic composition. He ascribes as the primary factor the variations in interaction between dominant and subordinate classes of a population and the degree of the latter's acceptance of the former's ideology. Similarly, Srinivas (1962:46) attributes the differences exhibited both within and among Pahari regions to "delayed Sanskritization," or the failure to adopt the orthodox Brahman sex code.

In fact both the exposure and relative isolation or insularity of the lower Himalayan areas have played roles of importance that have varied from region to region and from time to time. Interwoven with historical events and ecological factors, these circumstances were important contributors not only to distinctive regional variations in general and caste structures in particular but also to the fluidity and change of those structures over time.

In table 3 the major caste divisions of three Pahari regions—Garhwal, Kumaon, and the upper Karnali drainage of western Nepal—illustrate both distinctive differences among themselves and their common differences with the orthodox Sanskritic system of the plains.[18] Stratification based on concepts of purity and pollution reflects ritual status reinforcement of the political and economic status hierarchies of their tribal precursors. Missing from all Pahari caste systems are the Vaisaya and Sudra classes (Berreman 1972:202). The absence of large urban centers or permanent marketplaces precluded the former, while assignment of Khas farmers and laborers to Ksatriya status eliminated the latter.

From afar, plains Hindus had long viewed the Khasa stratified polyethnic tribal amalgam on their frontier fringe as having nebulous caste status. Moreover, the frequent occurrence of cross-class marriage, not only among the Khasa but between Khasa and other tribes, as well as other relaxed egalitarian and pragmatic tribal practices, were both foreign and objectionable to orthodox Hindus on the plains. Although the highest secular strata of rulers and warriors were judged to fall within the Ksatriya *varna*, their polluting use of meat, liquor, and the plow, their worship of household and village gods, and their practice of blood sacrifice were repugnant

---

[18] Several analyses of distinctive regional caste systems along the Pahari belt from Kashmir to Kumaon that are valuable in understanding or comparing the Karnali case include: Brar (1971); Nitzberg (1978); Berreman (1972); and Sanwal (1976). For a detailed discussion of caste in Karnali see Campbell (1978:83-190).

TABLE 3. Regional comparison of major caste divisions.

Orthodox Sanskritic Caste Hierarchy of the Plains	Central Indian Himalaya, Garhwal (2-fold)[1]	Kumaon (4-fold)[2]	Western Nepal, Karnali (3-fold)[3]
1. Brahman (priests and scholars)	1. Brahman clean	1. Imigrant Brahman	1. Brahman (immigrant and Khasa) Twice-born (wear sacred thread)
2. Ksatriya (rulers and warriors)	1. Rajputs clean (immigrant) / 1. Khasiya clean (indigenous)	2. Imigrant Rajputs / 3a. Khasi Brahman / 3b. Khasi Jimdar (small owners/cultivators)	1. Chhetri Twice-born (wear sacred thread) / 2. Matwali Chhetri (Khasa) (drink liquor) Tribals: Bhotia Magar
		— Line of the Twice-Born —	
3. Vaisaya (merchants and traders)	Absent in the Pahari Belt (no large	Absent in the Pahari Belt central places or urban market centers)	Absent in the Pahari Belt centers)
4. Sudra (farmers, artisans and laborers)	Absent in the Pahari Belt (no large	Absent in the Pahari Belt central places or urban market centers)	Absent in the Pahari Belt centers)
		— Line of Pollution —	
Untouchables (outside society)	2. Unclean Dom	4. Dom	3. Dum (unclean occupationals)

[1] After G. Berreman (1972)
[2] After R. D. Sanwal (1976)
[3] See J. Hitchcock (1978)

and earned the bulk of the Khasa—farmers, pastoralists, and laborers—the label of *mlĕchchhas*, or barbarians, who were at best no better than Sudra.

As the Brahmans established the system, their own orthodox views were tempered by practical secular considerations. Acculturation was therefore a two-way street, as it was in other Hinduized Himalayan regions from Kashmir to Kumaon, and in the Kathmandu Valley as well. The caste system that evolved in Karnali accommodated many pre-Hindu Khasa practices. These included cross-class marriage, secular marriages involving a bride price, elopement based on love, matrilocal residence with son-in-law adoption, widow remarriage including levirate,[19] and divorce.

Srivastava (in Fürer-Haimendorf 1966:163) points out that in Kumaon the interaction between Hindu and tribal "produced an 'accommodative' social adjustment which has shown a tendency to become relatively stable and mutually acceptable." Such was the case with Karnali, where the introduction and early development of its caste structure, like other processes of Hinduization, most clearly resembled that which their Kumaon antecedents had undergone several centuries earlier; although it was similar in general to Kumaon, at least initially, it also was markedly looser in construct and exhibited important differences in detail.

In contrast to the fourfold division of society in Kumaon, a broad threefold division emerged in Karnali. Of special significance was the difference in the ranking of Brahmans and Ksatriya. In Kumaon, immigrant Brahmans and Rajputs (Ksatriya) had wrested total power from the indigenous Khasa in all but the most remote and economically insignificant backwater areas. Under the Chands (see table 2) the reduction of the Khasa in status was manifested by a caste hierarchy that ranked not only immigrant Brahmans but also immigrant Ksatriya above the indigenous Khasa, Brahmans, and Ksatriya alike (Sanwal 1976:38). On the other hand, when the caste system was introduced to Karnali in the late fourteenth century, powerful Khasa Malla ruled a society into which the invited Brahmans and other immigrants were assimilated. Since the dispossession of the existing power structure was out of the question, the Brahmans worked within the existing power, not only ritual but political, which would allow them to accrue economic benefits in Khasadesa, the Malla-controlled Karnali kingdom that was their new home.

The caste system that developed reflected both Khasa strength and Brahman pragmatism, for it made no significant distinctions in status ranking between recent immigrants and indigenous Khasa.[20]

---

19 The marriage of a widow to her deceased husband's brother.

20 John T. Hitchcock (1978) also points out these basic differences between Kumaon and Nepalese caste structure and the key historical role played by the Karnali Khasa-Malla kingdom in the distinctive development of the latter.

Caste: Karnali's Distinctive Brand

Karnali's distinctive caste structure was, in effect, a Brahmanical formalization of pre-Hindu tribal social criteria such as ethnic origin, occupation, affluence, and political power, all of which were related to the control and use of resources. To these now were added religious standards of judging status ritually by the degree of purity or pollution inherent in occupational, dietary, commensal, and connubial practices (see tables 4 and 5).

Immigrant Brahmans accorded all Khasa "clean" status, which encompassed two of the three major social divisions: Tagadhari, who were twice-born wearers of the sacred thread (the *jamai*) and Matwali, who drank liquor (*mat*) and therefore were not twice-born. Of the Tagadhari, Brahmans (figure 29) ranked highest in purity and were subdivided into two *jati*, or castes: Upadhaya and Jaisi. Immigrant Brahmans from the plains or from Kumaon belonged to the ritually superior Upadhaya *jat* and adhered to the strictest Hindu *dharma* and *karma*,[21] such as marriage to virgin Brahman brides. Only Upadhaya were entitled to perform priestly duties for the other Tagadhari. In all likelihood the Jaisi *jat* was initially composed of Khasa priests to whom the Upadhaya gave Brahman status. Subsequently the Jaisi also included the product of marriage between Upadhaya men and Brahman widows (i.e., nonvirgins). Barred from performing religious rites by the Upadhaya, the less pure Jaisi were astrologers or *josi*, from which word their caste designation was derived.

Collectively, the Brahmans held and maintained a monopoly on education and the role of guru. This afforded them access to their real power: administrative posts in the late Khasa Malla feudal structure. In return for service as ministers, emissaries, scribes, tutors, doctors, and astrologers, those Brahmans received royal grants of land or even fiefs, known as *birta*, which they held in perpetuity and from which they derived tax-exempt income.[22] Often these posts were hereditary, such as that of Adhakari, the

---

[21] *Dharma* is the Hindu code of moral and religious duty, law, and custom; it was strongly influenced by Buddhist precepts; it implies dynamic qualities of movement and change, the chief characteristics of natural law, and constitutes a behavioral model for a society that varies according to caste, family, or stage in the life cycle. As such, *dharma* legitimizes all rights and privileges within the social hierarchy, which are in turn protected or enforced by penalties or sanctions (*danda*). Thus social, economic, political, and religious security for the Tagadhari classes is assured (see Stutley and Stutley 1977:76).

Karma is any act or its performance, either good or bad, by an individual that has a significant relationship to that person's caste *dharma*. All *karma* express kinetic processes of natural (or biological) laws that over one's lifetime accumulate or accrue as merit or sin and thus ultimately determine one's destiny or fate (Stutley and Stutley 1977:142-43).

[22] An inscription dated 1356 records such a land grant made by Prithivimalla to a Brahman (Itihas Prakash Mandal, 2013 V.S. [1956: pt. 1, pp. 49-52]). In it the grant is referred to as *vritti*, a Sanskrit term meaning "livelihood" from which the corrupted Khas-kura term *birta* was derived. The relationship between Brahman and crown is revealed in another passage of

chief judicial minister who formulated and enacted *dharmic* law. It was the Adhakari who assigned caste rank and, in the case of the Khasa, awarded or withheld the sacred thread.

Khasa royalty (the Malla) and aristocracy (vassal clan chiefs), as well as a few new princely Rajput settlers, were patrons of the Brahmans and automatically assumed Tagadhari status on the basis of their control of land and power. As such they constituted the upper crust of Ksatriya (known in Nepal by the Khas-kura derivative "Chhetri"). Only during the eighteenth century did they acquire (or assume) the special caste designation of Thakuri, derived from the Sanskrit *thakura*, meaning "chief" or "man of rank," which both signified their ritual and social supremacy and differentiated them from the inferior Chhetri composed primarily of Khasa commoners.[23]

The Thakuri adopted most ritual restrictions observed by the Brahmans. No doubt at this time in history they universally eschewed using the plow. They did, however, eat wild boar in addition to sheep and goats. They also retained some unique orthodox practices in keeping with their rules and chief warrior heritage. Although they would no longer eat buffalo, it was their exclusive role to decapitate these sacrificial animals with the *kukuri* (Nepalese short sword) at religious festivals. They also continued to practice matrilateral cross-cousin marriage, which was thought incestuous by other Tagadhari (Campbell 1978:95-96).

The bulk of the Khasa, however, were commoners, able to command little or no prestige or power (figure 30). Instead, they constituted an important, even vital, labor pool for the higher strata of the feudal hierarchy. Therefore, it was expedient for the Brahmans to award Chhetri *jat* status to a considerable number of commoners, principally to small owner-cultivators who lived in close proximity to the elite and who still retained proprietary rights to their fields as a result of original settlement and clan allocation of land. Their elevation to Tagadhari rank, justified by their long history of sexual liaison with aristocrats, assured the dominant minority, Brahman

---

the proclamation (p. 55): "The giver of land lives in Heaven for 60,000 years and the confiscator of land . . . lives in Hell for the same period of time . . . . He who takes away even one coin of anothers gold, one cow or a parcel of land measuring one finger lives in Hell until fourteen Indras reign in Heaven. He who usurps land given by himself or given by others lives in shit for 60,000 years as a worm. He who saves a cow from a marsh, a Brahman from slavery, a man from the termination of his livelihood, a Brahman from murder, is absolved of all sins committed from his birth to his death."

[23] Mary Slusser (1982, chap. 3, pp. 4-5) provides a full explanation of the often confusing term *thakuri*. It is important to note that the use of *thakura* as an honorific by the Malla kings of the Kathmandu Valley beginning in the fourteenth century may be the basis for the present-day caste designation. However, there is no evidence that the honorific was ever used by Khasa Malla or subsequent Baisi and Chaubisi rulers in western and central Nepal.

TABLE 4. Evolution of social stratification in Karnali.

Early Malla (ca. 12th–14th Centuries)	Late Malla (ca. 1350–present)	Orthodox Varna
Khasa Priests →	**Brahman** **Tagadhari** Upadhaya (immigrants) Jaisi (Khasa)–Sanyasis (holy men returned to the real world)	Brahman
Khasa (including assimilated Gurjara?) Rulers → Aristocracy → Warriors →	**Thakuri** (Rajput immigrants and "pseudo-Rajput" Khasa) **Tagadhari** **Chhetri** — — — — Line of Twice-Born	Ksatriya (twice born)
Khasa Commoners → Small cultivators Pastoralists **Kirati** (on periphery) Pastoralists and traders →	**Matwali Chhetri** **Newar** (from Kathmandu ca. 1900) **Matwali** **Gharti** (slaves, freed in 1925) **Bhotia**–Mugali, Humlese — — — — Line of Pollution	Vaisaya **Line of Twice-Born** Sudra (clean) **Line of Pollution**
Laborers, serfs, and slaves → (of unknown origin)	**Dum** (occupationals) **Unclean** Kami, Sarki, Damai, Badi (transients)	Untouchables

TABLE 5. Diet and work sanctions by caste in 2026 V.S. (1969-70).

	Brahman	Thakuri	Chhetri	Matwali	Bhotia	Dum
Meat Consumption (in descending order of purity)						
Sheep and Goat	yes	yes	yes	yes	yes	yes
Wild boar[a]		yes	yes	yes	yes	yes
Chicken				yes	yes	yes
Buffalo					yes	yes
Pig					yes	yes
Cow						yes
Task Performance (in descending order of purity)						
Hunting[b] or fishing		yes	yes	yes	yes	yes
Plowing		avoided	yes	yes	yes	yes
Castrating animals			avoided	yes	yes	yes
Artisan occupations (metal and leather working, tailoring)						yes

[a] Other wild game, fish, and *Cannibis* have no purity connotations and thus can be consumed by all castes.
[b] Sacrificial killing of buffalo is the status right of Thakuri.

and Thakuri alike, a source of ritually suitable soldiers and domestic servants. In addition, it greatly increased the number of Tagadhari "clients" that Upadhaya priests could "service."

The balance of the Karnali Khasa commoners fell within the Matwali class stratum. Less affected by processes of Brahmanization, they continued their impure practices of consuming alcohol and chicken and remained, in the eyes of the Brahmans, unfit to wear the *jamai* of the twice-born. Yet on the basis of the universal Khas claim that their progenitors were warriors, these Matwali Khas cultivators and pastoralists were recognized by the Brahmans as fallen Ksatriya. They were, therefore, Chhetri, and clean, albeit less pure, and as such belonged to the Matwali Chhetri *jat*.

Over the ensuing centuries the Matwali Chhetri of Karnali have continued to remain relatively impervious to Brahmanical pressures. Today they retain in their distinctive social and religious beliefs and practices the most vivid pre-Hindu tribal Khasa vestiges of any Pahari group or caste in Nepal. Although the subject of considerable recent study, the Matwali Chhetri are still incompletely understood.[24]

---

[24] See Bista (1972:3-4); Campbell (1978); Fürer-Haimendorf (1971:7-24); Sharma (1971:43-60); Shresta (1971).

Fig. 29. Brahman with grandson

Close cooperation and interdependence between the Khasa and the tribes in pursuit of both livelihood and conquest constituted the cornerstone upon which the Karnali Malla kingdom had grown and prospered. Therefore, when the caste system was introduced it was appropriate and practical for the Brahmans also to accommodate those endogamous Mongoloid tribes of cultivators, herders, and traders on the periphery of the dominant Caucasoid Khasa and encompass them within the clean Matwali stratum, although at a lower ritual rank than the Matwali Chhetri. Thus, political stability within the polyethnic Malla domain was facilitated and economic intercourse continued without being seriously hampered by Brahmanical sanctions involving ritual purity and pollution.

These were principally Bhotia tribes who lived on the northern and eastern fringe of the Karnali drainage (figure 31). Of Bon or Buddhist persuasion, they spoke Tibeto-Burman dialects, particularly those of western Tibet, and generally exhibited Tibetan clan-kinship patterns, livelihood technologies, clothing, and diet (e.g., the consumption of alcohol and meat, even beef [yak]). Included too were Magars, a tribe of generally sedentary cultivators, already noted for their fighting prowess, who also spoke Tibeto-Burman dialects. Although only speculation, it seems likely that Magar ancestors had composed one of the indigenous Kirati tribes in the upper Karnali that the invading Khasa had absorbed or displaced. By the late fourteenth century Magars survived in the lower Himalaya hills south of the Chakhure-Mabu Lekh and in greater numbers in the Bheri River catchment basin to the east (Hitchcock 1966).

In time these Mongoloid tribes would undergo varying degrees of Hinduization or acculturation depending on the type and intensity of their association with Khasa/Pahari. Most of the Magar adopted Hindu social and religious beliefs and practices akin to those of the Matwali Chhetri. The majority of Bhotia tribes, such as Humli and Mugali, the Bhotia of the upper Humla Karnali and Mugu Karnali rivers, maintained most of their discrete Tibetan way of life, but some, like the Byansi living in high valleys close to the juncture of present-day India, Tibet, and Nepal, have acquired through Sanskritization[25] a status again similar to the Matwali Chhetri (Srivastava, in Fürer-Haimdendorf, ed. 1966:161-211; Manzardo, et al. 1976:84-118).

The lowest of the three major divisions in the Karnali caste structure was that of the ritually impure and therefore untouchable Dum (figure 32). To this, the closed stratum that was separated from the clean castes by a hard line of pollution precepts, the Brahmans consigned all landless laborers, ar-

---

[25] Sanskritization is "the process by which a 'low' caste or tribe or other group takes over the customs, ritual, beliefs, ideology and style of life of a high . . . caste," in order to improve its position in the local caste hierarchy and thus improve its economic and political position (Srinivas 1967:67-68).

Fig. 30. *Chhetri woman.* © *National Geographic Society.*

tisans, and slaves of mixed and questionable ethnic origin. These were the descendants of either slaves who had accompanied the Khasa to Karnali or indigenous tribal groups whom the Khasa conquered but did not absorb biologically into their own ranks.

Originally this class had performed a spectrum of tasks for their Khasa masters but by late Malla times the Dum, like all segments of society, had developed varying occupational specialties in addition to their common, menial labor roles. Thus, by the end of the fourteenth century, the Dum stratum was subdivided into several endogamous occupational castes, which the Dum themselves ranked by status.

Kami, or metalworkers, comprised the highest Dum caste and were further divided into subcastes according to specialty: Sunar (goldsmiths), Lohar (ironworkers), Tomatti (coppersmiths), and Tirva (potters). Generally conceded to be of lower status were Sarki, or leatherworkers, although this *jat* and the Kami accepted each other's boiled rice (*bhat*), one of the most functional indicators of status ranking within all Himalayan Hindu caste structures. Below the Sarki were the Damai, or tailors, who in addition to their primary specialty also served as musicians at various clean-caste ceremonies. Some Damai also performed religious services for the other Dum, who were not permitted to avail themselves of the Brahman priests.

Lowest in status among the Dum *jat* were the Badi, itinerant singers, dancers, and prostitutes who periodically wandered through Karnali but did not live there permanently. By virtue of their occupational specialties the Badi were considered untouchable even by the Kami, Sarki, and Damai.

All Dum were free from most clean-caste restrictions. Not only did they drink liquor and eat chicken and buffalo, but they also ate cattle that had died of natural causes. Nor were they bound by Brahmanical requirement to wash more than their hands before eating. The few pollution restrictions they did follow, those related to aspects of the life cycle such as birth, menstruation, and death, were observed in a casual or token manner. However, the Dum did take great care not to pollute clean-caste members with whom they had close daily association; except in the case of children, they avoided touching clean persons; nor were they permitted to give Tagadhari or Matwali water.

The landless Dum were the essential labor force, and in essence a form of property, of the landed Tagadhari, whose own purity precepts prohibited them from using the plow or engaging in other polluting occupational pursuits. Therefore, the *dharma* or *karma* of the Dum was to serve their high-caste masters. In return for their specialized, earthbound services and their common labor at planting and harvesting times, as well as carpentry and house construction, the Dum received food, shelter, and other material needs. Both this Dum/landlord relationship and the Brahman

Fig. 31. Bhotia elder

priest/clean client (i.e., the same landlords) relationship, again involving an exchange of service for food and gifts, was the heart of the social-religious-economic structure in the more Brahmanized core areas of Karnali. This structure was a regional variant of the *jajmani* system of northern India.[26]

Kinship Ties

Berremen (1972:199-200) points out that caste is the ultimate extension of the kin group and can best be defined in terms of the social and geographical limits of marriage networks. Among the Tagadhari and Matwali Chhetri of Karnali the functional kinship unit is the *thar*, which can best be viewed as a Brahmanical refinement or ordering of the tribal clan. Within each clean *jat* of Khasa clan or immigrant origin are a number of subcaste

---

[26] See Kolenda (1963:11-31) for a basic review of the Hindu *jajmani* system's ingredients, scope, and function.

Fig. 32. Dum smoking a brass and clay pipe, or sipa

thar, whose members trace their descent patrilineally from a common ancestor. Falling outside of Brahmanical society, and unable to trace their lineages, the Dum were not divided into *thar*.

But while the *thar* is the basic functioning exogamous kin unit in Karnali, and throughout the Pahari regions of Nepal, and marriage ideally is between members of two different *thar* of the same *jat*, another broad and ancient Sanskritic kin grouping, the *gotra*, is also recognized. *Gotra* lineage is of greater purity than the *thar*, and thus more closely adheres to the orthodox *dharmic* patrilineal ideal, for it is traced to one of seven mythologically patriarchal progenitors. The *gotra* kin units reflect Brahman efforts in very early times (fourth century B.C.) both to clarify marriage and inheritance laws and to maintain dominant status among the four *varna* (Stutley and Stutley 1977:102). *Gotra* lineage sometimes crosscuts *thar* lines and if prospective marriage partners are discovered to have the same *gotra*, the precedence of *gotra* exogamy is occasionally invoked and the union prevented.

Thar designations, which are like western surnames, were often derived from village or occupation names. Karnali *thar* names mentioned in late Malla inscriptions, and still common, include Adhikārī, Bhandārī, Joṡī, Kārki, Kadkā, Rāul, Thāpā. A list of *thar* found today in the study area is included in the caste outline of Appendix D. It should be noted that in the case of Chhetri it is seldom possible to ascertain from a *thar* name whether a person is twice-born Tagadhari or a Matwali. In addition some *thar* are the product of cross-caste marriage. The position of these mixed-caste *thar* in the hierarchy was less a function of the relative ritual status of the families involved than of their economic status.[27]

Within each *thar* are a number of branches, known as *bāsā* in Karnali, each of which denotes a particular *thar* subgroup's village or region of origin and adds a geographical dimension to the *thar* lineage for a shorter and more recent genealogical time span. Thus, for example, Kalikot (*bāsā*) Bista (*thar*) living today in the Kathmandu Valley know that they are descendants of Bista who migrated eastward from the Kalikot region of the lower Tila Valley after the caste structure was established in Karnali.

Mesh of People, Places, and Pursuits

From the preceding exposition on the introduction and early development of Karnali's hierarchical caste structure during the latter half of the

---

[27] For example, the Himal *thar* within the Thakuri *jat* was composed of the progeny of Brahman men and Chhetri women. Although of somewhat lower rank, Himals could still intermarry with pure Thakuri *thar*. Another example was the Khatri *thar* within the Chhetri caste, the product of marriage between Chhetri men and Thakuri women. For a full discussion of cross-caste marriage among the Nepalese Pahari, see Fürer-Haimendorf, ed. (1966:11-67).

fourteenth century, it is apparent that the degree of Hindu orthodoxy a family, clan, or group observed was then, and is today, significantly affected by its social and spatial proximity to the centers of Brahmanical and secular power. It is equally apparent that this Hindu caste system not only increased both intergroup and intragroup social stratification but also more sharply defined the spatial stratification of those groups that had occupied distinctive altitudinal belts or niches for some time.

In the Khasa Malla heartland north of the Chakhure-Mabu Lekh the twice-born Brahmans and Chhetri controlled prime, though limited, agricultural land bordering braided floodplains in the major valleys between 1,000 and 2,500 m, as well as adjacent forest and pasture slopes that rose 500-1,500 m above the river bottoms. The great majority of the Dum also lived in these major river valleys in close proximity to their Tagadhari masters. Matwali Chhetri lived between 1,500 and 3,000 m in less productive side or tertiary valleys and higher, more mountainous reaches. Bhotia continued to occupy even higher and more removed Karnali headwaters to the north and east, generally above 3,000 m.

A landmark agricultural innovation in Karnali's mixed economy, another facet of Hinduization during the Malla period, was the successful introduction of paddy cultivation in the major river valleys. There the terrain most readily lent itself to sophisticated and controlled irrigation techniques like those long employed for paddy culture in ecologically similar Kashmir.[28] With this imported knowledge the powerful Tagadhari marshalled forced labor, or *bisti*, for the construction of extensive canal networks that channeled water to rich alluvial terraces that late Malla inscriptions referred to as *alika*, meaning "lush" or "fertile" (Shresta 1971:56). Thus, wet rice could now be grown despite the region's low and variable rainfall.

The development of irrigation brought the Tagadhari elite increased economic prosperity and further widened the gap between them and the

---

[28] Rice is known to have been grown in northern India as early as 2,500 B.C. (Hutchinson 1974:59) and N. J. Vavilov contends that the southwestern Himalaya (i.e., Kashmir) was a gene center of its cultivation (Grist 1965:4). Harald Uhlig, the leading authority on rice cultivation in the Himalaya, points out that the cultural landscape of Kashmir under the Buddhist Ashoka (third to second centuries B.C.) was very probably based on rice, and that later (seventh to ninth centuries A.D.) noted engineers under Hindu kings planned and supervised the construction of vast irrigation works that permitted Kashmir's paddy culture to become firmly established (1973:80).

Although rice cultivation was implemented wherever possible by the Khasa as they migrated eastward, its practice in Karnali probably did not occur until the twelfth to fourteenth centuries, when the Mallas could harness the human energy needed to carry out vast irrigation works. Although this contention cannot as yet be verified by extant information, its logic is supported by legends in the oral histories I collected in the field.

Matwali living at higher elevations. On their irrigated fields, the *khet*,[29] a crop sequence of winter barley or wheat and summer rice was cultivated, while on unirrigated bottomlands below 1,800 m cotton was raised. In contrast, the Matwali Chhetri grew a dry-crop sequence of winter barley and summer millets, or perhaps grain amaranth, in sloping unirrigated fields, or *pakho*,[30] which produced lower and more variable yields. Land reclamation in this altitudinal belt was more difficult than in the major river valleys and generally involved slash-and-burn techniques on steep, forested slopes followed by arduous terracing. One can speculate that in still higher, more removed, and climatically more severe Bhotia areas agriculture was limited at that time to a meager crop of buckwheat or other hardy, old-world food grains during the short summer. Instead their Tibetan-type economy was based almost entirely on animal husbandry and trade, the two other prominent livelihood components in Karnali.

The livestock raised and the husbandry practiced reflected an adjustment to the ecological belt or niche that a caste or group occupied and further emphasized the position of that group in the social hierarchy. For the Tagadhari and Matwali Chhetri cultivators cattle raising was most important for traction in the fields and for fertilizer, as well as for milk. Then, as today, water buffalo also may have been raised for milk and ghee, or purified butter, by Tagadhari living in the lower southwest stretches of the major valleys below 1,800 m. Chhetri warriors also raised and trained horses in great numbers for cavalry operations, which were important in Malla military maneuvers. Contemporary inscriptions mention that ducks were domesticated and both donkeys and pigs raised.[31]

At intermediate and high elevations Matwali Chhetri and Bhotia maintained flocks of sheep for wool and for the transport of trade goods. Even more important to the Bhotia were their herds of yak, used for high altitude transport and trade, meat, and milk products.

Grazing patterns within and between ecological belts varied spatially and temporally according to altitude and latitude, and therefore also varied according to the animal involved. In the Tagadhari belt the pattern was a simple transhumance similar to that followed in the Alps, while in the higher belts more extensive movement of animals was necessary. The Matwali Chhetri used high mountain pastures in summer, then drove their flocks south to low valley locations for the winter. Wide-ranging cyclical

---

[29] *Khet* is the term used today for irrigated land in the hill regions of Nepal on which paddy can be grown.

[30] *Pakho* is the term for unirrigated agricultural land in the hills and highlands of Nepal on which only dry crops can be grown.

[31] Because of Hindu pollution precepts, one would suspect that by late Malla times domesticated pigs were kept only by the Dum.

pastoralism was practiced by the Bhotia, who grazed their herds in the Trans-Himalayan mountains and steppes in summer, then moved them north to the Tibetan Plateau pastures for the winter.

Trading was closely integrated with agriculture and animal husbandry, similarly following seasonal rhythms and reflecting the environmentally imposed travel constraints outlined in chapter 2. Both human and animal carrying power was employed, depending on the terrain encountered. Under the Malla, Karnali's trail networks were extended and improved. Of special note were the wide and gentle trails built in the Sinja and Tila valleys over much of the route linking the summer capital and market center at Had Sinja and at the winter capital, Dullu. Malla inscriptions indicate that horse-drawn chariots could be used on this route. Portions still exist today and are referred to by the local inhabitants as the "royal road."

Trade, both among the ecological belts and niches within the upper Karnali catchment basins and between the Karnali core area and other regions of the kingdom (western Tibet, the lower Himalayan hills to the south and west, and the inner Tarai lowlands), articulated the economy of the Malla domain, for it permitted regional production and consumption to be balanced over the course of the year. The seasonal circulation of food grains, animals and animal byproducts, handicrafts, items from the wild biota, and perhaps copper from mines in the Langu and Chaudhabisa headwaters, was oriented northward with Tibet in summer and southward with the Gangetic Plains in winter.

From early Malla times, and quite likely even earlier, such items as wood, yak tails, and musk were important trade items. Although not mentioned in contemporary inscriptions, salt from playa flats on the Tibetan Plateau also had to have been a key item.

In spite of the fact that the Malla heartland yielded little of value in luxury goods, it did lie astride important trade routes through the Himalaya and thus controlled the traffic of such items between China and India; but trade in luxury goods, or cesses on their passage, had little effect on the body of Malla society. Instead the wealth derived from these activities, like the spoils of war, accrued primarily to the benefit of the elite.

Malla rulers held ultimate control over all lands within the kingdom, which they parceled out at their pleasure. They not only awarded tax-exempt *birta* grants, already mentioned, but endowed temples and other religious or philanthropic enterprises with tax-exempt land grants known as *guthi*. In an effort to preserve and enhance solidarity in the Karnali core area, the Malla permitted many Chhetri warriors to enjoy similar freehold landed gentry status on the basis of original settlement.

The Malla also granted taxable land revenue, in lieu of salaries, to officers, officials, and selected chiefs or clan leaders. In later centuries these grants were known as *jagir*. These vassals held sway over village or valley fiefdoms in the Khasa sectors of Karnali and in important conquered agricultural areas outside the heartland. With a portion of their revenues they were responsible for levying troops in time of war against external enemies and for paying tribute to their Malla overlord, whose court they were obliged to attend on certain occasions. An inscription tells of the presentation of bull elephants by vassals to Prithivimalla in recognition of his suzerainty (Itihas Prakash Mandal, 2013 V.S. [1956], vol. 2, pt. 1, p. 54). Sometimes suzerain-vassal alliances were cemented further by marriage.

In the case of the Bhotia highlands the Malla out of necessity followed a policy of laissez-faire. Their farmland was meager and of little or no revenue-generating value. Wealth remained primarily in the form of mobile herds, which were difficult, if not impossible, to cess. Therefore, it behooved the Karnali kings to maintain tribal loyalty if the remote northern and eastern frontier fringes of the kingdom were to remain tranquil, the trails to Tibet and beyond kept open, and important Bhotia trading services sustained. Consequently the Malla imposed only the mildest sanctions or controls on the Bhotia.

Although all land-grant recipients of royal benevolence theoretically held only revenue rights to the land, many grants were hereditary, which meant that the holders did, in fact, possess tenure. In some cases, such as that of the Chhetri gentry, the holders apparently even had the right to mortgage or sell their land.

The elite Tagadhari grantees siphoned off the wealth of land and village, taking as revenue 50 percent or more of the yields and reducing the actual cultivators to a state of subsistence agriculture and tenancy. Thus, the bulk of Malla society was now a peasantry whose production, with simple implements and family labor, had to both satisfy their own basic food requirements and fulfill their obligations to the holders of political and economic power.[32] The burden of taxation was therefore borne primarily by the peasant cultivators.

References to "thirty-six" taxes indicate that the Malla system of taxation was a version of that imposed in Kumaon and other feudal kingdoms during the middle ages, where thirty-six property taxes, primarily on land, and another thirty-two miscellaneous taxes on goods and services known as "writer's fees" were collected (Sanwal 1976:43; 118-19). Although few Malla levies were identified, it is known that there were cesses on wool, raw cotton, and cotton cloth. The use of two types of coins, the silver *tanka* and the copper *daam*, in the kingdom suggests that the economy was at least par-

---

[32] For analyses and description of the complexities of peasantry and the spectrum of peasant societies in South Asia and elsewhere, see Redford (1956); Nash (1966); Wolf (1966); Shanin (1971).

tially monetized and that some taxes were paid in coin rather than in kind. It is unclear, however, whether the Malla kings minted their own coinage.

With the establishment of the feudal hierarchy, the Malla administration became increasingly decentralized and fragmented. Territorial expansion and a type of patrilineal inheritance, by which the lands of a household head were divided equally among all sons, were important contributing factors. As vassal feudatories multiplied, the gap or social space between king and commoner widened. And more and more intermediaries diverted income from both the peasant cultivators and the crown.

The rulers' revenue problems were compounded by the markedly high density of tax-exempt *birta, guthi,* and Chhetri landed gentry holdings at the center of the kingdom in the Tagadhari lowlands. There also lived the largest Dum population, whom Prithivimalla freed from taxation. Because of the continued lack of sufficient funds in the crown coffers, the Malla were obliged to levy special taxes for public works, temples, palaces, and royal functions that caused a further depression of the peasantry. Operating from such narrow and tenuous bases of economic and political power, the ruling, religious, and aristocratic elite gradually intensified their strategies for the mutual protection of privilege.

By the end of the fourteenth century the overlapping and interrelated social, economic, and political hierarchies of the Malla kingdom were well meshed with the tiered, mountainous environment and the varied, though limited, resources it furnished. In the Khasa heartland specifically, ethnic composition, language, religion, caste, livelihood pursuits, and administrative structure had all combined with terrain and location to create a distinctive cultural landscape. Although it subsequently underwent periodic modification, much from the Malla period survives today to make the upper Karnali catchment unique among hill regions of Nepal.

4

Cultural Kaleidoscope
Stagnation and Recent Change

The Baisi and Chaubisi Princedoms

After the reign of Prithivimalla (ca. the late fourteenth century) the Khasa Malla kingdom rapidly fell apart. The allegiance of the various vassal chiefs within its domain, always tenuous at best, could no longer be sustained, and fiefdom after fiefdom asserted its independence. In the Karnali, Seti, and Bheri drainages more than a score of petty hill principalities known as the Baisi (in Nepali, "twenty-two") kingdoms rose in its stead. At the same time a similar number of small states known as the Chaubisi ("twenty-four") kingdoms emerged in the Gandaki drainage to the east (figure 33). Of the latter group only a few, such as Parbat (Malibam), Galikot, and Piuthan, had been formally under Khasa Malla sway. Viewed in a pan-Himalayan context the Baisi and Chaubisi states were only segments of a vast array of princedoms or mini-kingdoms stretching in diminishing density from Kashmir to Sikkim that struggled for viability in the fifteenth century. This state of affairs lasted for the next 350 to 400 years. For most of these petty principalities

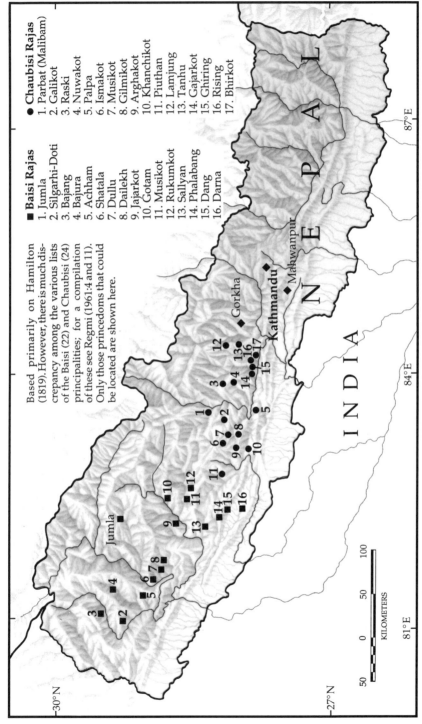

Baisi Rajas
1. Jumla
2. Silgarhi-Doti
3. Bajang
4. Bajura
5. Achham
6. Shatala
7. Dullu
8. Dailekh
9. Jajarkot
10. Gotam
11. Musikot
12. Rukumkot
13. Sallyan
14. Phalabang
15. Dang
16. Darna

Chaubisi Rajas
1. Parbat (Malibam)
2. Galikot
3. Raski
4. Nuwakot
5. Palpa
6. Ismakot
7. Musikot
8. Gilmikot
9. Arghakot
10. Khanchikot
11. Piuthan
12. Lamjung
13. Tanhu
14. Gajarkot
15. Ghiring
16. Rising
17. Bhirkot

Based primarily on Hamilton (1819). However, there is much discrepancy among the various lists of the Baisi (22) and Chaubisi (24) principalities; for a compilation of these see Regmi (1961:4 and 11). Only those princedoms that could be located are shown here.

Fig. 33. The Baisi and Chaubisi princedoms

the protracted period of chaos came to an end with Gorkha unification and its aftermath in the late eighteenth and early nineteenth centuries.[1]

Continental Considerations

Developments not only in the Himalaya but on the Indian peninsula to the south and in Tibet and inner Asia to the north directly or indirectly affected the lives of the Karnali peoples between the fifteenth and eighteenth centuries and subsequently during the nineteenth and twentieth centuries. Overextension of the Mughul Empire, particularly into the Deccan Plateau and South India, led to administrative inefficiencies and decay and economic bankruptcy. This trend culminated during the reign of the Muslim zealot Aurangzeb (1659-1707), whose bigoted dislike of Hinduism and unorthodox Islamic practices and whose oppressive revenue demands on the peasants combined to destroy any semblance of solidarity. Hindu reaction gained strength and internal revolts followed. By the mid-eighteenth century a mosaic of both Hindu and Muslim regional powers emerged, including the Marathas in the west, the Sikhs in the northwest, Oudh and Bengal in the middle and lower Ganges Valley, and the Nizam of Hyderabad in the south.[2]

This period was also marked by the European Renaissance, the great age of navigation, and western intrusions into the subcontinent via the sea. Lured by Marco Polo's vivid account of Indian riches, the Portuguese, Dutch, Danes, English, and French all established commercial bases along the coastal periphery of the Mughul Empire and penetrated its interior seeking trading concessions in spices, silks, saltpeter, indigo, and cotton goods. By the mid-eighteenth century French and English merchant companies had become the chief contestants for economic control. This struggle, similar to that taking place in North America, became one front in the Seven Years' War (1756-63) waged by the two European powers and their indigenous allies on several continents. Clive's overwhelming victory at the Battle of Plassey (June 22, 1757) virtually destroyed French claims in India, and later English victory globally not only assured the East India Company

---

[1] A pan-Himalayan historical resume of this period is found in Rahul (1970). More precise and detailed information on the petty states of the Indian Himalaya, including Garhwal and Kumaon, is contained in Atkinson (1882-86); Traill (1828) recorded important observations in Kumaon.

For valuable insights and information on life in the princedoms of the Nepal Himalaya during this period, particularly in the Baisi and Chaubisi kingdoms, but also in those farther west beyond the Mahakali River, see Hamilton (1819, reprinted 1971). For recent works of high scholarship, the reader is referred to Ludwig F. Stiller's analysis of the Baisi-Chaubisi princedoms (1975:33-76) and Mary Slusser's cultural history of the Kathmandu Valley (1982).

[2] For a detailed temporal and spatial picture of this changing political mosaic on the Indian subcontinent, see Schwartzberg (1978).

supremacy among the European concerns in India but led to subsequent territorial expansion and, ultimately, British imperial domination of the subcontinent.

Changes were also occurring north of the Himalaya, where since the early thirteenth century, Mongols had held varying degrees of control over Tibet. There an inner Asian brand of feudalism had developed that, with its intertwined relationship between Mongol overlord protector and Tibetan religious king–Buddhist prelate, was not unlike the secular and sacred patron-priest system of Hindu South Asia. At the same time Kublai Khan had finished the horde's conquest of Cathay, founded the Yuan dynasty (1260), and furthered the cultural connection between Tibet and China. When a century of "Chinese" suzerainty ended with the expulsion of the last foreign Yuan emperor and the establishment of the native Ming dynasty (1363-1644), Lamaist Buddhism in one form or another had not only penetrated all strata of Tibetan society but also had spread far to the east with its Mongol purveyors.

The end of foreign overlordship in Tibet was followed by a period of distinctive indigenous political and religious development. Over the next two hundred years the strength and influence of various eastern Tibetan kingdoms, centered in the lower Tsang-Po drainage, rose and fell. All had these things in common: they strove to revive the traditions and glories of the early religious kings (ca. the sixth to ninth centuries); they enjoyed the support of the powerful Kar-ma-pa or Red Hats Buddhist sect; they maintained religious and commercial contacts with both Mongolia and China. By 1565 the kings of Tsang had risen to consolidate militarily their hold over most of the plateau principalities.

During this same period a reformed Buddhist school, the Gelupa or Yellow Hat sect, was founded by Tsong-kha-pa (1357-1417), Tibet's most famous scholar, with the support of nobility and commoner alike, in the Lhasa area. Based on austerity, meditation, monastic discipline and, at least initially, the principle of having secular matters totally in the hands of lay princes, it grew and spread. In 1577 So-nam Gyatso, Tsong-kha-pa's third chief abbot successor and an avid missionary, visited Mongolia, where he converted Altan Khan and his tribe and received from that powerful Mongol chief the title of Dalai Lama ("lama of all within the seas").[3] Thus at a time when the Gelupa sect was engendering increasing jealousy and resistance among the other sects and their patrons were competing for power, Mongol-Gelupa ties were established that soon led to the traditional protector-prelate relationship and foreign intervention.

---

[3]   As the second reincarnation of Gedun Truppa, Tsong-kha-pa's nephew and immediate successor, So-nam Gyatso was considered the third Dalai Lama. For a valuable recent work on Tibetan history, see Snellgrove and Richardson (1968).

In the wake of early seventeenth-century internal squabbles and military encroachment by the king of Ladakh into western and central Tibet in 1640, which further weakened Tsang control, Gu-shri Khan of the Dzungar Mongols invaded eastern Tibet, with the encouragement of Gelupa followers whose cause he championed. By 1642 he had captured Lhasa, killed the last Tsang king, displaced the Kar-ma-pa lamas, installed himself as a protector "King of Tibet," and invested the fifth Dalai Lama as the chief religious prelate under whom a Tibetan regent tended to the secular administration of the kingdom.

Under the great fifth Dalai Lama Tibet reached the zenith of its cultural revival. He built the famous palace-monastery on the Potala hill at Lhasa. And, as an astute diplomat, he visited Peking shortly after the Manchus had conquered China and founded another foreign dynasty, the Ching (1644-1912). Within a short time his domain stretched from Mount Kailas to the upper Yangtze River. However, after the Dalai Lama's death in 1682, rapidly deteriorating affairs in Lhasa, coupled with renewed Mongol strength and militancy on the Ching frontiers, eventually led to Chinese intervention.

In 1720 the Manchus defeated the Mongol protectors in Tibet, established imperial garrisons at key locations, and enthroned the popular seventh Dalai Lama. In an attempt to create an effective counterbalance to the Dalai Lama, they also conferred the Panchen Lama, chief abbot of the large Gelupa monastery of Tashilhumpo near Shigatse, with considerable feudal powers.

The eruption of new violence at Lhasa in 1750, this time involving the imperial representatives there, provoked another Chinese military response, which further strengthened Manchu suzerainty. The Tibet government was reorganized once more: the kingship was abolished, replaced by a council of ministers under the supervision of Chinese residents known as Ambans, and the Dalai Lama was given supreme temporal power over the country's religious hierarchy similar to that which the fifth Dalai Lama had enjoyed.[4]

It is also important to note that the seventeenth and early eighteenth centuries were a time of European merchant and missionary penetration into and through the Himalaya, including the Nepalese sector, and contact with Tibet (Sandberg 1904). For example, in 1624 Antonio d'Andrade, a Jesuit father from Goa, established a mission at Tsaparong, the capital of Guge in western Tibet; its brief existence ended in 1640 when the troubles with Ladakh began. Eventually, in 1707, a Capuchin mission gained a transi-

---

[4]   A detailed examination of the Tibetan feudal order, which existed in this form until 1951, is provided by Carrasco (1951).

tory foothold in Lhasa; Tibetan religious resistance to Christian proselytizing and a dearth of funds from Rome forced its withdrawal in 1745. A more successful Capuchin mission was founded (1795) in Patan in the Kathmandu Valley, which had long been an important entrepôt between Tibet and India.

Karnali Chaos

Although the various extant historical records give no explanation for the demise of the western Malla, it is evident that both external and internal forces were at work. The growing strength of powers on its periphery and splintered leadership within its core regions in the upper Karnali drainage combined to erode Khasa Malla strength and cohesion.

The Tibetan chronicles indicate that by the reign of Abhayamalla, Prithivamalla's son and apparently the last of that dynasty, the Tibetan provinces of Guge and Purang had broken away (Tucci 1956:130). To the east in the Valley of Nepal (the Kathmandu Valley) the growing cohesiveness of non–Khasa Malla kingdoms, coupled with the strength of Makwankpur (south of the valley) and Palpa (controlling the central lowland), now barred further Khasa Malla expansion in that quadrant. Similarly to the west in Kumaon the rising power of the Chands began to emerge at the end of the fourteenth century.[5]

At the same time continuing waves of Islamic Mongol conquerors out of Afghanistan brought intensified strife to the plains of northern India. For example, the devastating raid of Tamerlain in 1398-99, during which he massacred 100,000 prisoners near Delhi and sacked that city before withdrawing via Hardwar, Dehra Dun, and the Siwalik Hills, heralded the breakup of the Muslim-Turk sultanate (Smith 1923:252). Such incursions, as well as the subsequent establishment and spread of Mughul authority[6]—particularly Akbar's bloody conquest of Chitor in 1568, a repeat performance of the bloodbath of 1303—and Aurangzeb's religious persecution of Hindu Rajputs in 1679-80, escalated the ripple effect that earlier Muslim invasions of northern India had initiated on the lower Himalaya. Now Hindu Rajputs in increasing numbers sought refuge in the hills, not only in what are now the Indian districts of Himachal Pradesh, Garhwal, and Kumaon, but in the Nepal foothills as well.

The accelerated infiltration of such immigrants, usually via Kumaon, into the Karnali Khasa kingdom played an important role in the replacement of the ruling Malla by other families claiming Rajput descent. The tur-

---

5   Of Rajput origin, members of the Chand clan apparently fled from the plains several centuries earlier and settled in Kumaon on the west bank of the Mahakali River. For a detailed history of the Chands, see Atkinson (1882-86), vol. 2, pp. 443-697.

6   Established by Babar in 1526 and ending with the mutiny of 1857.

moil that ensued in turn was a catalyst for increased Khasa (Thakuri aristocracy and Chhetri warriors) movement eastward into the Gandaki drainage, where along with Rajput arrivals they helped shape the course of events in the Chaubisi kingdoms.

A number of factors combine to confound our understanding both of these early shifts in power in the western Malla domain and of many subsequent events and processes there and throughout the Baisi-Chaubisi territory. Many valuable records from Baisi times have been lost, stolen, or destroyed by fire.[7] Genealogies (*vamsavali*) and official orders (*tamrapatra*) inscribed on gold or copper plates have been reused by unknowing families; the former melted down and converted to bullion and the latter used to repair copper pots (*taulos*) in which rice is boiled. Some of the *vamsavali* that still exist show signs of alteration or genealogical tampering at one time or another by families who sought to improve by documentation their lineage purity or their claims of Rajput origin. This confusion is compounded by similar, and even more frequent, discrepancies in the oral histories of the Karnali *thar*.[8]

Most of these machinations may never be unraveled and understood fully. One in particular is the claim today by all Karnali Thakuri, as well as most of the *jati* throughout Nepal, that they are the descendants of Rajput princes who entered the Nepal Himalaya during the Baisi-Chaubisi period. This claim quite obviously cannot be universally accepted, for historical evidence shows that the Thakuri are in fact a mix of many Khasa (including Gurjara?) and some Rajput; in the case of central Nepal they also include a few Magar. The question of which Karnali Thakuri *thar* claims are spurious and which are authentic is not only unresolvable but irrelevant to this study. What is important is that Rajput settlement in Karnali Khasa territory, both before and during the Baisi times, made an impact that was strikingly disproportionate to their few numbers.

Other difficulties also hinder interpretation of the written and oral records. They include the evolutionary changes in the Khas-kura language and the associated changes in proper names, particularly in place names

---

[7] For example, in February 1924, hundreds of important gold, copper, and paper documents were consumed by fire in the fort (*kot*) at Chhinasim (Jumla-Kalanga) while all the population were bathing in the Tila River on the occasion of a lunar eclipse (Itihas Prakash Mandal 1956, vol. 2, pt. 1, p. 119).

[8] Most of the oral histories I collected in Karnali go back no further than the beginning of the Baisi period (ca. 1400). Usually they are involuted blends of fable and fact that augment and generally conform to written records; or they replace lost documents and thus constitute an almost exclusively oral tradition. As one would expect, both their time span and their credibility vary considerably, usually, but not always, according to the education and therefore the caste ranking of the informant. All require judicious interpretation; while many are of little value in any work, others furnish valuable information, particularly with regard to the temporal and spatial dimensions of settlement patterns and marriage networks.

*Fig. 34. Aerial view of Jumla-Kalanga, look-
ing southwest over the extensive irrigation
system on the Tila Karnali River floodplain
and alluvial terraces (2,330 m)*

such as villages; these discrepancies sometimes make it difficult, occasionally impossible, to fit past with present-day locations.

Yet, despite the inconsistencies and breaks in continuity in these
records, it is still possible to extract from them much valuable information
on both events and processes in Karnali during the muddled and disordered
Baisi-Chaubisi period. The quality and reliability of this information steadily
improve as the course of history is traced from the fifteenth century to the
eighteenth century.

Kalyal Consolidation of Jumla

Contemporary inscriptions indicate that soon after Abhayamalla's
reign (ca. 1400) the core of the Malla kingdom had splintered into three separate regions, each controlled by a different ruler. Dailekh, south of the
Chakhure-Mabu Lekh, had broken away by 1396 under the Khasa ruler
Samsaravara. At Sinja another Khasa king, Medinavarna, ruled between
1393 and 1404, after which he moved his capital to Chhinasim (present-day

Jumla-Kalanga, figure 34) on the Tila Karnali while a Rajput interloper, Baliraja, controlled territory around Sunargaon, 24 km downstream from Chhinasim and commanding an important trade route between Sinja and Jajarkot (south of the Chakhure-Mabu Lekh; see figures 20 and 77). Although a joint land grant issued by Baliraja and Medinavarna in 1404 (Itihas Prakash Mandal 1956, vol. 2, pt. 1, pp. 109-12) indicates the existence of two Jumlas, apparently Baliraja or his immediate scion incorporated Medinavarna's domain soon after that date into a single Jumla and subsequently consolidated their control over what had been the Khasa core of the Malla kingdom.

For fifteen generations (from 1404 to 1788) Baliraja and his line of successors, known as the Kalyal kings (of the Sahi *thar*), ruled Jumla, the largest, most populated, and most powerful of any Baisi or Chaubisi principality. However, Kalyal power was a far cry from that of Prithivimalla. Jumla encompassed only about one-ninth of the territory held by the last great Malla (16,000 km^2 versus 142,000 km^2). Valuable agricultural lands to the south, particularly in the inner Tarai valleys of Dang and Surkhet, and key trade routes to the west were no longer sources of wealth.

After the Khasa vassal in Doti broke away from his Jumla overlord in the early fifteenth century, he briefly controlled not only the upper Seti River drainage but large areas of Kumaon beyond the Mahakali River. Thus, he deprived the Kalyals of important westernmost trade routes that funneled through Taklakot to Guge and Purang. However, under Raja Bhanti Chand (1437-59) Kumaon soon threw off the yoke of Doti and gained command of those routes.

Unlike most of the other petty hill states, Jumla still controlled enough agricultural land, forest, and mineral resources and trade routes to remain economically and politically viable, albeit on a greatly reduced scale. Because of this, Kalyal strength was sufficient to command from not only Baisi but Chaubisi rajas or chiefs at least a degree of the allegiance enjoyed by the Malla. Most acknowledged Jumla's superiority with little more than lip service. Hamilton observed that the power of a Kalyal king consisted of three privileges: "Each chief sent him an annual embassy, with presents; he bestowed the mark of royalty (tika) on each heir, when he succeeded; and he had a right to interfere in keeping the stronger from overrunning the weaker, and to exhort all chiefs to preserve the balance of power. Except persuasion, however, no means seem to have existed to enforce cooperation" (1819:283).

Given the disparate political and economic viability of the petty hill states, a balance of power was difficult to achieve or maintain. Efforts to overcome these disparities, such as subsidiary alliances among various Chaubisi princedoms, often cemented by marriage or by family (lineage) ties, were transitory and of limited success. More often the Baisi-Chaubisi period was one of chronic feuding, fluctuating boundaries, and erratically rising and falling dynasties as noble houses vied for limited resources.

Although the institutional framework of society in all of the mini-kingdoms of the lower Himalaya was generally similar during this last stage of medieval history, the Mahakali River still divided distinctive regional cultures of the Pahari belt. In the Baisi and Chaubisi states to the east, the social and religious structures remained relatively less rigid then those in the west. On the other hand, the feudal political-military organization of the Baisi and Chaubisi states was patterned after the ancient Hindu system, in contrast to those west of the Mahakali, which were based on Islamic organization (Hamilton 1819:101-2). This latter case reflects greater and longer contact with, and incursions by, Muslims from the plains.

During these troubled times the way of life in the Karnali core kingdom of Jumla, like that in all Baisi and Chaubisi principalities, underwent many modifications and changes. While a few, such as power shifts among the elite, were abrupt and often violent, most were more gradual or subtle responses to exacerbated religious, social, economic, and political pressures or intensified Hinduization processes that were already at work in the late Malla period. All contributed to an increasingly structured and decentralized feudal order.

Economic and political fragmentation proceeded as the Kalyal kings of Jumla continually alienated themselves from their primary source of power by parceling out land not only to Brahman and Chhetri faithful in the form of *birta* and *jagir* grants, but to members of the royal family itself.

The kings' relatives, particularly their brothers, were either awarded large fiefdoms or left the Sahi court at Chhinasim to carve out princedoms on their own. It can be assumed that brothers were particularly troublesome or rebellious because of the rule of primogeniture, by which the throne was inherited exclusively by the eldest son. Therefore, it is not surprising that most lands held by members of the immediate family were usually far removed from the capital. A *vamsavali* translated by Tucci (1956:122) indicates that five brothers of Visésaraj (ca. 1500) went north to lands in the Humla drainage that presumably had been Bhotia domain; the brother of Bahādur Bāh (ca. 1650) went to lands around Rara Lake, including the villages of Chhapru and Rara. Over the centuries brothers of numerous kings went eastward to fiefdoms centered on the Byas River, and Juphal, Dunahi, or Ralli villages in the Tibrikot region (figure 35) of the upper Bheri River valley. The brother of Suratha Śāh (ca. 1724) went to Tiprikot Tara (today the village of Tarakot) in a Magar enclave known as Tichurong that marked the eastern extension of the Jumla kingdom.[9]

Since the days of Baliraj another Thakuri house, that of the Raskoti rajas, had controlled a small princedom on the western fringe of Jumla beyond the Karnali River (see figure 3). Apparently both subsequent military aid for and marriage ties with the Kalyal house permitted the Raskoti to extend their authority over not only the neighboring trans-Karnali princedom of Sanni but the entire southwestern lowlands of Jumla (the lower Tila River valley and the middle section of the Karnali River north of its confluence with the Tila). A joint accord, dated April 1620, between Vikram Sahi of the Kalyal house and Saimalsahi of the Raskoti house, allegedly first cousins, delimited Raskoti territory, spelled out responsibilities for mutual assistance, indicated Raskoti recognition of Kalyal suzerainty and, significantly, stated that the Raskoti *thar* abandoned its Astri *gotra* in favor of the Sahi's (Kalyal) Rabi *gotra* (Itihas Prakash Mandal 1956, vol. 2, pt. 1, pp. 132-33).[10]

---

[9] For a more detailed discussion of Tichurong history see Fisher (1972:23-32).

[10] All the vassals of the major fiefdoms within Jumla as well as many chiefs of other Baisi princedoms that broke away traced their lineage to either the Kalyal or the Raskoti house.

Fig. 35. *Tibrikot commanding the Bheri River in western Dolpo. South-facing Brahman and Chhetri homes of the Pahari elite lie above terraced* khet *fields, while below and to the right a cluster of Dum dwellings is confined to a steeper, west-facing slope. On the crest of the promontory is a fifteenth-century fortress shrine.*

Thus, as Jumla was subdivided and subdivided again, the old elite was destroyed, displaced, or particularly in the case of Khasa Chhetri, lowered in political and economic status by a new elite that sought to maintain control over a more stratified and complex feudal hierarchy. In order to legitimize their privileged status and strengthen their exploitive command of all resources, both environmental and human, this new Brahman-Thakuri consortium intensified and entrenched all facets of Hinduism.

The Baisi era in Jumla witnessed the continued construction of temples and shrines dedicated to the pantheon of Hindu deities (the major gods Ganeh, Vishnu, and Siva and their incarnations), although the Kalyals were unable to sustain the distinctive architectural scale of the Malla. Within two centuries the Malla style disappeared (Sharma 1972:33). Ruins also indicate that during that same period the practice of Buddhism in any state-supported overt form by the Karnali Khasa also disappeared.

Increasing emphasis was placed on the adherence to Brahman *dharmic* dictates, which were embodied in the caste system and manifested by religious, connubial, commensal, and occupational practices already mentioned. These manifestations of rank in the Karnali social hierarchy, particularly those of Tagadhari exclusiveness, were underscored further by a variety of caste symbols. For example, special forms of dress and jewelry, as well as the right to whitewash house exteriors, were reserved for the Brahmans and Thakuri. Moreover, the use of caste-specific honorifics was called for when a person of lower caste addressed a higher caste member.

Of special significance was the power of the Kalyals at the apex of the hierarchy. The king's right to rule and enforce the laws of *dharma* was supported by the inherent principle of *danda*, meaning staff, rod, and scepter, symbolizing power and sovereignty and embodying the ancient Hindu concepts of universal law and order (Stutley and Stutley 1977:68-69). Therefore, it was not only the king's right but his religious duty to punish offenders.

Under medieval Hindu law, which addressed a spectrum of land-tenure matters, caste behavior, and criminal infractions, both crimes and punishments were fraught with inequities, all reflecting relative power and prestige: Brahmans could not be sentenced to death, no matter what the offence; all persons were guilty until proven innocent; trial by ordeal was commonly employed; punishments ranged from outcasting, branding, banishment and enslavement to imprisonment, mutilation, and a variety of death sentences.

Grassroots Religious Reaction

The subservient bulk of the Khasa (Chhetri and Matwali Chhetri alike) who bore the brunt of the Kalyals' onerous brand of power, were loath to accept either the *dharmic* dictates or the Brahmanical deities in which those dictates were embodied. In an effort to counter or ameliorate the pressures imposed by the new elite, the Khasa commoners not only marshalled but modified their egalitarian and pragmatic tribal ways, as well as many of the old animistic and Buddhistic beliefs and practices to which they still clung. This movement was manifested by the emergence during the Baisi era of a family of incarnating gods (twelve Masta brothers and assorted sisters, maternal uncles, nephews, daughters, et al.) who were imbued with non-*dharmic* values and who spoke to the Khasa through the medium of oracles or shamans known as *dhami*.[11]

---

[11]   The first known reference to any of these gods is found in a land grant inscription dated 1625 (Itihas Prakash Mandal 1956, vol. 2, pt. 1, p. 137).

Since Tucci (1956) and Snellgrove (1961) first called attention to the brothers Masta, these incarnating gods have received the attention of several scholars, including Marc Gaborieau (1969:19-50) and P. R. Sharma (in Shresta, ed. 1971:91-104). For a detailed analysis and dis-

The life histories *(pareli)* of the gods, which are actually autobiographies recited by the *dhami* when they are possessed by the gods, reveal that the events, trials, and tribulations of their lives paralleled those of the Khasa whose cause they championed. They were closely associated not only with the Tibetan or Bhotia tradition of pre-Malla and Malla times, but with recently introduced Hindu tradition as well. The *pareli* of the best-known gods, the brothers Masta, indicate that they assumed human form in the Baisi princedom of Bajang (in upper Seti drainage, west of Jumla) on the order from their father, the Hindu deity Indra. From Bajang they wandered eastward into the Karnali and Bheri drainages and the Baisi territories of Achham, Dailekh, Jajarkot, and, in particular, Jumla.

During the course of their wanderings the Masta gods were continually engaged in contending with needs, upholding rights, and overcoming plights that replicated those of the mortal Khasa. With divine power they performed great deeds and achieved stunning victories. Uninhabited areas were explored and made useable, often only after supernatural forces had been foiled or vanquished. Trails and bridges were built, fields were cleared, and lakes were drained; irrigation canals, storage tanks, and fountains were constructed. Exploitation by misguided, greedy, corrupt, or evil earthly Kalyal rulers was avenged or curbed. Injustices, commonly involving inheritance, land, or water rights, were redressed.

Early in their odysseys the Masta exhibited mostly Bhotia cultural traits, but later as their contact with the Hinduized populace increased, they too became acculturated (Campbell 1978:295-96). Finally, each settled in and presided over a different geographical domain.

The fact that most of the Masta brothers derived their names from the villages in which their principle shrines were located suggests that these gods were, in fact, a Baisi era development of an older collection of village gods (figure 36).

Campbell (1978:323) states that "the hidden gods of Jumla Brahmanism are thus identified with patrilineal hierarchy and respect while the family of incarnating gods identify themselves with matrilineal affection and equality." Together these two groups of deities founded a kinship system that reduplicated the two value systems bound up in human kinship in Karnali.[12]

---

cussion of not only Jumla's non-*dharmic* values and oracular religion but also its *dharmic* values and Brahmanical religion, see the exhaustive comparative work of Gabriel Campbell (1978).

[12] Campbell refers to the orthodox Hindu deities as "hidden gods" in order to distinguish them from the family of incarnating gods who speak through *dhamis*.

Fig. 36. Masta shrine at Garjiaŋkot, 12 km east of Jumla-Kalanga

The successful integration of the Masta family of incarnating gods into the Hindu framework indicates that it was prudent and practical for the Brahman-Thakuri consortium to remain fairly flexible and to accommodate the Chhetri–Matwali Chhetri grassroots movement. Thus the social construct that ordered and orchestrated all facets of life in the Kalyal kingdom continued to be a mix of two seemingly contradictory, but balancing, sets of values, one *dharmic* and one non-*dharmic*.

During both the Baisi era and the ensuing centuries as this Karnali Khasa brand of Hinduism spread eastward it underwent continued change and refinement in response to more stringent, orthodox Brahmanical inputs or political pressures. But in Jumla, historical events and environmental factors permitted the *dharmic*/non-*dharmic* blend to persist to a much greater degree. Today its components constitute the woof and the warp of the area's social fabric and give Karnali's culture an elasticity unique among the Pahari regions of Nepal.

Adjustment and Entrenchment of Lifestyle

The period of Kalyal rule witnessed the continued adjustment of Jumla's agriculturally based but diversified economy to feudal forces, environmental and resource constraints, and population pressures. All of these governing factors varied in degree or intensity from fiefdom to fiefdom. Only by increasing royal regulation of all facets of life, particularly society's exploitation and exchange of available resources, could a sufficient level of livelihood—surplus for the elite minority and subsistence for the commoner majority—be maintained.

Land grants and permits from this era not only demarcated fields but indicated just where the individuals in question could graze cows and sheep, cut wood, gather leaves and twigs, dispose of waste, and settle people. Some of these documents spelled out the right to raise sheep, sell milch cows and colts, and derive income from trade concessions; others constituted free transit permits between Tibet (Bhot) and India (Medesh). An increasing number were concerned with Kalyal expropriation of holdings and the transfer of land from one individual in disfavor to another currently in favor; these manifested the *dharmic* principle of "what the lord gives he can also take away." Occasionally even a Dum was awarded a land grant for services rendered.

Most documents now mentioned not only the standard "thirty-six and thirty-two" taxes but also a number of additional ones, such as four road taxes (i.e., transit duties) and another four tolls on the use of bridges, ferries, and fords (*ghats*). This increasing tax burden led to a corresponding peasant indebtedness to wealthy Tagadhari who charged 25 to 50 percent annual interest on loans. As a result, more and more households could free themselves from their stultifying financial obligations only by committing family members to indentured servitude with the moneylenders.

One particularly illuminating *tamrapatra* states that Sudarson Sahi dunned the entire population with a special roof tax in order to finance the construction of a new palace at Chhinasim between 1745 and 1751 (Itihas Prakash Mandal 1956, vol. 2, pt. 1, pp. 149-51). It not only indicates the king's ability to marshall a large labor force, including over 1,500 slaves, *jajmani*, and hired laborers and 200 Brahman supervisors, but also provides a detailed picture of mid-eighteenth century building techniques, procedures, and costs.[13]

Karnali's economy continued to depend on the seasonal exchange of indigenous products grown, collected, or extracted not only in its own subregions but in neighboring hill regions to the south (principally the Baisi princedom of Jajarkot) and trans-Himalayan areas on the Tibetan Plateau to

---

[13] An English translation of a portion of this *tamrapatra* is found in D. R. Regmi (1961:7-8).

the north (see chapter 3). But political, social, and ecological constraints, common to all the Baisi and Chaubisi states, also prevented the generation of any specialized trade such as that long enjoyed in the Kathmandu Valley. Thus limited to the exchange of only subsistence requirements, Jumla was unable, or had no reason, to develop any well-articulated internal market system. In turn, the absence of market centers forestalled the growth of either a merchant class or a broad spectrum of Dum occupational specialists such as were found on the Indian plains.

Therefore, if Jumla was to be assured a continued source of luxury goods for its Tagadhari elite and critical revenue for its royal treasury, it had to maintain friendly relations with Tibetan principalities and retain control over at least a portion of the transit trade between plateau and plains. Like their Malla predecessors, the Kalyal kings strove for these objectives throughout the Baisi era. Deprived at first of important routes to both western and central Tibet (via the Mahakali and Seti drainages on their western periphery and the Kali Gandaki drainage on their eastern periphery) and confronted later with constant and powerful foreign warfare on the former front,[14] they concentrated their attention on the more vulnerable eastern avenue through the strategic trans-Himalayan principalities of Lo (Mustang) and Thak Khola.

Efforts to reestablish the suzerainty the last Malla had enjoyed over these lucrative entrepôts brought Jumla into continuous armed conflict not only with Lo and its Thak Khola vassals but with other states (Ldakh, the central Tibetan principality of Gung-Thang, and the hill-Hindu princedoms of Parbat and Doti) that were either Lo's allies or were themselves contestants for this important trade (Jackson 1978:195-227). Kalyal fortunes waxed and waned but eventually prevailed. By the mid-eighteenth century Lo was forced to recognize Jumla's unquestioned suzerainty by payment of annual tribute.

At the same time, the Kalyals courted commercial concessions from the rising power of eastern Tibet. In 1679 the Jumla king himself visited the fifth Dalai Lama and in 1729 a trade mission was sent to Lhasa. Thus Jumla ultimately was able not only to derive financial benefit from all transit trade flowing through the upper Kali Gandaki but to divert a portion of that traffic westward into its own domain via the corridor of the upper Bheri and Tila Karnali rivers, where it helped meet the demands of a growing population.

---

[14] The seventeenth and early eighteenth centuries were especially chaotic times as Lakakh, Garhwal, and Kumaon struggled to wrest control of Himalayan passes and plateau territory from Tibetan princedoms. For example, with that aim Bir Bahadur Chand invaded the Purang area in 1670, defeated the Tibetans there, and destroyed the fort at the trade center of Taklakot (Rahu 1970:92-93, 102).

During the protracted Baisi era Jumla's population swelled significantly, if erratically. Despite losses caused by recurrent warfare, disease, drought, and emigration, there was apparently a net increase in indigenous ranks. Moreover, these were periodically augmented by immigration as not only Rajputs and their followers from the plains but some Tibetans from the plateau fled homeland troubles and took refuge in Karnali.

This upsurge exacerbated the pressures on, and competition for, fields, forests, and grazing grounds that were first evident in late Malla times. By the reign of Baliraja the most choice irrigable bottomland in the Khasa core valleys already had been put to plow and evidently supported a considerable population. The ensuing period of Kalyal rule was, in turn, the time of the most rapid, extensive colonization of higher and less agriculturally productive secondary and tertiary drainages and upland interstices separating the major valleys.

A number of different stimuli, all either direct or indirect manifestations of population pressure, prompted this spread of settlement. For example, many families, especially Chhetri, who were dispossessed of their valley lands during the Kalyal regime were indisposed to remain on in a tenant capacity. Members of other households sought relief from inhibiting field fragmentation caused by Hindu inheritance practices, whereby each generation divided holdings into smaller and more scattered parcels.

Whether the spread of settlement was on a family scale or on a larger, more controlled, institutional scale, such as the areal extension of an old fiefdom or the founding of a new one, it involved one of two processes. One was the outright colonization of virgin lands and the establishment of new villages. The other was the gradual conversion of semipermanent (i.e., seasonally occupied) clusters of fieldhouses (*kateros*) and animal shelters (*goths*) in upland pastures to permanent residences. Although often far removed from the valleys, these new communities generally maintained close social and economic ties with their parent villages. This evolution from season-satellite to permanent, independent village was common historically throughout the Pahari belt of the Himalaya and probably constituted the chief means of uphill migration.[15]

By the end of the Kalyal regime Jumla boasted nearly 600 villages varying in size between several score and a few hundred people. Although extant records give no hint of Jumla's total population at this time, the mention of 22,000 "roofs" in a Nepalese chronicle (Regmi 1961:4) does provide us with a clue. Assuming that the average family size in Karnali was the same as today (5.9) and allowing that a number of these roofs may well

---

[15] Joel Andress (1966) provides a detailed examination of this process near Mussoorie in the lower hills of Garhwal.

have been *kateros,* it seems safe to speculate that Jumla's population had reached somewhere between 100,000 and 130,000.

With population growth and the surge of settlement into the higher reaches of Karnali came a corresponding increase in environmental alteration and deterioration. The extensive forest clearing (with ax and fire) for wood fuel, lumber, and pasture or plot, the extended grazing of livestock, and the intensified terracing of steep slopes had the cumulative effect of modifying both the heat budget and water balance (and therefore the macroclimate) in the settled areas. This impact was obviously most severe on the lower slopes adjacent to the major valleys, which had been settled first and which continued to support the densest concentrations of people. All available evidence, albeit indirect, suggests that by the mid-eighteenth century these slopes had been stripped of most forest cover, particularly the most useful *Pinus roxburghii, Quercus incana, Quercus lanuginosa,* and *Cedrus deodara* between 2,100 and 2,400 m (see chapter 2).

Thus, as the era of petty Baisi and Chaubisi princedoms neared its end, the patterns and processes of life in Karnali, initiated by the last Malla and developed by the Kalyals, were firmly and deeply entrenched. The secular and sacred institutions composing Jumla's feudal order not only maintained but widened the social/spatial gap between king and commoner. Although it had not yet reached a critical level, the large population now taxed the resources at its disposal. The overall effects were the continued stagnation of society and the downward spiral of its quality of life.

GORKHA UNIFICATION

Expansion and Containment

The rise to power of a line of Rajput immigrants east of the Kali Gandaki drainage during the late medieval times portended the eventual unification of all feudal princedoms and tribal territories between the Mahakali and Mechi rivers into the nation-state of Nepal. In 1559 Dravya Shah, whose older brother ruled the Chaubisi princedom of Lamjung in the hills east of the Pokhara Valley, conquered a small (approximately 400 km²) and resource-poor state centered on the ridge town of Gorkha (see figure 33) and founded the Shah dynasty—the House of Gorkha—from which the present ruler of Nepal, King Birendra Bir Bikram Shah, is descended in an unbroken line.[16]

---

[16] Valuable political and economic analysis of Nepal during and immediately after Gorkha unification is provided by Regmi (1971) and Stiller (1975, 1976).

It should be noted here that the term "Shah" was an honorific title that the Rajput line had assumed, or had allegedly received from the Mughul emperor of Delhi, and adopted as its *thar* surname.

The reigns of Dravya and succeeding Shahs were marked by continual feuding with neighboring principalities, particularly Lamjung, as Gorkha struggled to enlarge its territory and thus control the trade and resources upon which its survival depended. It was not until the reign of the gifted Ram Shah (1606-33) however, that Gorkha achieved any significant economic viability and emerged as an acknowledged political power. Contained by the stronger petty Hindu princedoms of Lamjung, Kaski, and Tanahu to the west, Ram Shah extended his domain in the other three quadrants, which were mainly populated by Magar, Gurung, Tamang, and Bhotia clans. Soon Gorkha's frontiers encompassed 2,600 km^2 and stretched north to Tibetan passes, east to the Trisuli River, and south to the Tarai.

Ram Shah's accomplishments were not limited to military conquests. He maintained friendly relations with states as far afield as that of the Mughul emperor in Delhi and Udaipur, the ancestral home of the Shahs in Rajputana; he encouraged and regulated trade with the Newars of the Valley of Nepal; he established a system of weights and measures; he developed or modified administrative, land tenure, taxation, and interest and loan policies in vogue at that time; and, most significant, he codified the eastern Pahari brand of Hindu law currently invoked in various forms throughout the Baisi and Chaubisi princedoms (Regmi 1961:17-22).

The territorial frontiers attained by Ram Shah remained essentially the same for more than a hundred years after his death. Not until the reign of Prithvi Narayan (1742-75) the strong, energetic, and charismatic Shah who is considered the father of the Kingdom of Nepal, was there further Gorkha growth.

Upon ascending the throne at the age of twenty, Prithvi Narayan Shah continued the efforts of his forefathers to expand eastward. His primary objectives were the strategic Valley of Nepal and the lucrative industry and commerce of its Newar kingdoms (Kathmandu, Patan, and Bhaktapur); the sparsely populated tribal (Rai and Limbu) hills beyond, through which ran other important trade routes between Tibet and India; and the agriculturally productive lowlands to the south. In addition, many of these areas were a much needed source of land with which he could pay or reward his supporters and army, not only the high-caste officers but the lower-caste troops as well.[17] Whenever possible Prithvi Narayan Shah used diplomacy or coercion in his campaigns of annexation. When opposed, he employed his initially small but tenacious army of Thakuri, Khasa, Magar, and Gurung. Those who cooperated he rewarded; those who resisted he ruthlessly punished.

---

[17] This policy of awarding *jagir* grants to the levies or sepoys was an innovative policy introduced by Prithvi Narayan to satisfy their lust for land and thus to assure their loyalty and support (Stiller 1973).

The key to further expansion and increased power, the Valley of Nepal, proved difficult to obtain. Despite Narayan's capture of Nuwakot on the Trisuli River in 1744, which cut off some Newar traffic with Tibet, and his subsequent encirclement and blockade of the valley, which completely severed its connection with Tibet and with southern allies and India, the valley continued to hold out. Not until 1769 and the capture of Bhaktapur (present-day Bhadgaon) was Prithvi Narayan Shah finally able to achieve complete control of this rich prize. At last, with the valley secured and his capital moved from Gorkha to Kathmandu, he was able to expand more rapidly his kingdom's frontiers, safe from the jealous and restive Chaubisi rajas at his rear. At the time of his death (January 11, 1775) Prithvi Narayan Shah had realized his objectives of controlling all territory east of the Marsyandi River between Tibet and India as far as the borders of Sikkim.

During the following three decades the Kingdom of Nepal continued to expand under a succession of regents, notably Bahadur Shah (1785-94), who was a younger son of Prithvi Narayan, and prime minister Bhim Sen Thapa (1806-37), a member of one of the *bharadari* ("noble") families who surrounded the Shahs. Now annexation efforts were primarily directed westward, not only to secure additional trade routes and land but to stabilize those more densely populated Pahari principalities that had spawned the House of Gorkha and its Tagadhari followers. By 1789 all Chaubisi and Baisi princedoms, including Jumla, had been annexed. The following year the Chand states of Kumaon were conquered and in 1803 Dehra *Dun* fell and Garhwal was obtained. By 1808, with their sights on Kashmir, Gurkha[18] forces had pushed on through the Indian Himalaya and captured the fort at Kangra. The Kingdom of Nepal had reached its greatest size (approximately 200,000 km^2) and stretched over 2,000 km between the Sutlej and the Tista rivers.

Nepal's rapid territorial burgeoning not only increasingly taxed its available resources (land and treasury), but inevitably propelled it into conflicts with plateau and plains powers. Disputes (with Lhasa) over trade and coinage arrangements that the Newars had long enjoyed and that the Shahs now controlled percipitated Nepalese invasions of Tibet in 1788, and again in 1791 when Shigatze and Tashilhumpo monastery were sacked and great

---

[18] In order to alleviate present-day confusion attention must be drawn to the distinction between the terms Gorkha and Gurkha. The former is the town and kingdom that rose to prominence under the Shahs (i.e., the House of Gorkha); the latter is an English corruption of Gorkha originally applied to the soldiers of Gorkha (i.e., the Gorkhali). In the nineteenth and twentieth centuries the Gurkhas of Nepal became famous as mercenary troops in British and Indian service. Unfortunately, the term Gurkha is often used incorrectly today to imply that these people are a single ethnic group, tribe, clan, or caste. In reality Gurkha units, since the days of Prithvi Narayan Shah, have been drawn from a number of Nepalese tribes, principally Magar, Gurung, and Limbu.

quantities of loot were carried back to Kathmandu. However, these successes were short-lived, for China responded once more to her Tibetan vassal's troubles. In 1792 a large Manchu army crossed the Himalaya, advanced down the Trisuli River to within 40 km of Kathmandu, and exacted a peace settlement. Although trade soon resumed, Nepal not only lost both coinage concessions and booty but agreed to send delegations to Peking every five years bearing token gifts.

Conflicts with the British along the kingdom's new southern borders had more profound and lasting effects. In 1765 the East India Company had been ceded Bengal and Bihar and by 1801, with the surrender to the company of much territory by the Nazir of Oudh, it not only controlled all of the Ganges Plains but had a common frontier with Nepal along almost all of the Tarai. Gorkha possession of these malaria-infested, fertile, and often forested lowland fringes was increasingly crucial for the maintenance of their growing armies. The British on the other hand sought a more limiting and defensible boundary along the crest of the Churia range (Stiller 1976:1-24).

Continued disputes over the lowlands, as well as Nepal's alarming westward advance in the adjacent hills, finally led to the Nepal–East India Company war of 1814-16. Early Gorkhali victories, in the course of which the poorly led company forces were given hard lessons in mountain warfare, did not elicit hoped-for help from the Marathas and Sikhs. The British, with their superior resources and firepower, notably artillery, soon prevailed and confined Nepal within frontiers that have remained relatively unchanged ever since, and thus ended forever Gorkhali expansion.

With the Treaty of Sagauli and its immediate aftermath Nepal was required to relinquish much recently annexed territory (figure 37). Holdings east of the Singalila Ridge and the Mechi River were returned to the Sikkim Raja. Pahari principalities west of the Mahakali River were lost, with Kumaon and part of Garhwal ceded by the British. Tarai possessions reverted to the Nazim of Oudh and to the company. However, in a move to stabilize his Bengal and Bihar borders by obviating the problem of possible future encroachment, the British restored to Nepal its eastern Tarai territory in December 1816. In addition, Nepal agreed to accept a British Resident in Kathmandu.

In less than a century the House of Gorkha had unified militarily or politically a panoply of medieval principalities and tribal territories whose societies reflected the spectrum of Himalayan traditions—Hindu, Buddhist, Khasa, Magar, Gurung, Newar, Kirati, and even Islamic. However, integration into a modern nation-state of these diverse cultural regions that remained within Nepal's boundaries after 1816 did not follow. Instead, as will be seen in the case of Jumla, a combination of environmental, economic, social, and political factors from international to local level, permitted new or continued exploitation of the bulk of the peoples by a few privileged and

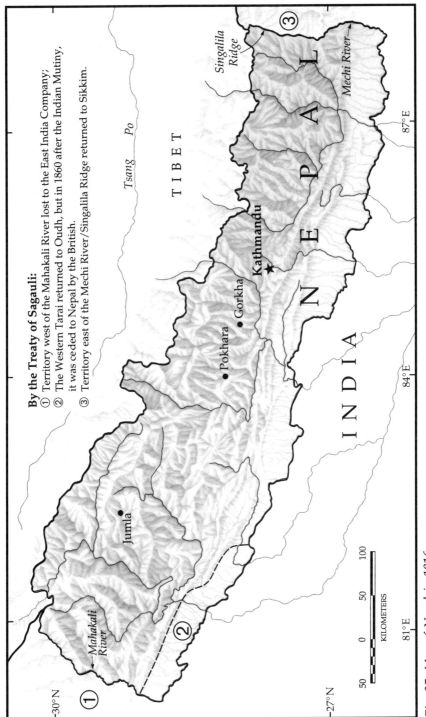

By the Treaty of Sagauli:
① Territory west of the Mahakali River lost to the East India Company;
② The Western Tarai returned to Oudh, but in 1860 after the Indian Mutiny, it was ceded to Nepal by the British.
③ Territory east of the Mechi River/Singalila Ridge returned to Sikkim.

Fig. 37. Map of Nepal in 1816

elite Pahari. All government policies pursued throughout the provinces were designed to preserve the status quo under a feudal umbrella. At this same time, suspicion of foreigners and their alien influences in general, and fear of further British intervention in Nepalese affairs in particular, led the kingdom on a course of isolationism and mercantilism.

Thus stultified in all sectors and denied any fruitful avenues for growth and development, every echelon of Nepalese society and its concomitant way of life stagnated. This homeostatic state of affairs continued until 1951.

Annexation of Jumla

As the largest and strongest of the Baisi and Chaubisi principalities Jumla proved to be a particularly thorny obstacle to the Gorkhali's westward expansion. Unlike some neighboring rajas, such as those of Mustang (Lo), Jajarkot, and Bajura, the last of the Kalyals, Sobhan Sahi, chose to ignore overtures for peaceful annexation that would have permitted him to retain his princedom in a quasi-independent vassal capacity. Instead, he united the elite and peasantry of Jumla's far-flung fiefdoms in the common cause of resistance and assembled an army of 22,000 (Hamilton 1819:287).

In 1787 Bahadur Shah mounted a two-pronged attack from the east via the Bheri River corridor and the upper Langu Khola in Dolpo. Although the Gorkhali eventually captured forty-five villages in the Tibrikot region and blocked Jumla's chief avenue of trade with Tibet, they could not reach the Kalyal's core area in the Tila drainage. Only after a second army attacked from the south were Jumla's mountain defenses breached and its numerically superior troops overcome. Advancing from Jajarkot in the late summer of 1789, this fresh Gorkhali force quickly captured Dailekh and Dullu, crossed the Mabu Lekh, and descended into the lower Tila Valley.

Although the easy capture of the capital at Chhinasim that September (Stiller 1975:185) toppled the Kalyal dynasty and sent Sobhan Sahi and many of his family and noble supporters fleeing to either Tibet or Oudh, it brought the Gorkhas control of only the southern portion of Jumla. It took another year of hard fighting to wipe out organized resistance in the northern reaches of Mugu and Humla.

Even then Jumla's tumultuous populace, encouraged by the confusion the Nepal-Tibet war produced, continued to rise in widespread, if sporadic and short-lived, insurrections against their oppressive conquerors. Only when the last such mutiny was quelled in 1793 was this new province of Nepal permanently pacified.

The governmental measures instituted in Jumla after annexation by the Kingdom of Nepal were essentially the same as those it introduced throughout the Baisi-Chaubisi hill regions in the west. While preserving and working through Jumla's existing feudal framework for its own ends, the centralized authority in Kathmandu introduced administrative, labor, land tenure, taxation, trade, and judicial policies that were, in fact, mere intensifications and modifications of, or additions to, those in force under the Kalyals.

However, the new order was markedly more repressive than the old and soon brought about several significant and lasting changes within the indigenous society of Jumla. The economic status of its upper echelon Thakuri and Brahmans was altered or rearranged; the living standards of the majority of its clean-caste families were depressed or lowered; the plight of its growing peasantry (cultivator-tenants and landless laborers) was further exacerbated. In the face of these repressions Karnali Khasa in great numbers migrated from their homelands in an effort to escape Kathmandu's harsh local rule and to find new lands. Coupled with the high war losses Jumla had suffered, this exodus substantially reduced the region's population.

Jumla, like most major western principalities attached by conquest and in which military units were garrisoned, fell under the jurisdiction of a district governor, or *subba*, who was an army officer sent from Kathmandu to replace the raja at the apex of the regional power hierarchy. Geographically far removed from the central government, the *subba* of Jumla exercised extensive civil and military authority in implementing and enforcing Kathmandu's dictates in an area whose importance was as much strategic as economic (see Appendix E). His chief responsibilities were to keep the peace and to exact from the district and its populace resources and revenues that, at least until 1816, were needed to help meet the mounting demands of Nepal's war efforts.

Marshalling of the Labor Force

The government's seemingly endless labor requirements placed a heavy burden on the population, particularly the peasantry. A compulsory labor system, known as *jhara*, was introduced that forced all adult males to render unpaid service according to their community location, caste status, or occupational specialty. Only nobility and government officials were exempt. Even Brahmans were required to perform *jhara* duty for several decades; the Upadhaya until 1813 and the Jaisi until 1839 (Regmi 1971:104).

Obligations included not only work in quarries and copper mines, construction and maintenance of trails, bridges, buildings, and fortifications, but service as mail runners and porters to carry military supplies, sick persons, tax revenues, luxury goods for the court, and the loads of traveling royalty. These services were essential to a smooth-running transportation and communication network within Jumla and between this insular district and Kathmandu to the east and the war fronts to the west.

After 1804 a relay system known as *hulak* was employed to permit mail and material to move rapidly around the clock. The porters, or *hulaki*, carried for only a short distance and passed their loads to porters from the next village or relay station. The linear distance measurement of the *kos*, or "postman's mile," equal to 3.658 km (2.27 miles), was introduced at this time. Traditionally, Karnali travelers had logged distance by *sipa* (a clay tobacco pipe) "smokes"—how far they walked in the forty-five minutes or so one pipeful lasted. Today this more practical "*sipa*-time" method prevails for all but government travel.

Kathmandu had to contend with both environmental and human obstacles to efficient and fast travel. On high and remote trail segments, where people often perished in snow storms, *dharmashalas* (rest houses) and shelters were built. Ferrymen on the Karnali River, which could not at that time be bridged because of its great width, were instructed to "carry on your work at the *ghat* [ferry crossing]. . . . If you obstruct the army's use of the ferry you will be deprived of all your property" (Itihas Prakash Mandal 1956, vol. 2, pt. 2, p. 9).

Because the porter relays required the continual service of *hulaki* in great numbers and left them little or no time for their normal livelihood pursuits, resentment was widespread. In order to stem rising discontentment and thus assure dependable human carrying power, the government first exempted the porters from some taxes and later paid them a minimal cash wage (Regmi 1971:115).

Such privileges, however, did not extend beyond the *hulaki*. Moreover, exploitation of the entire *jhara* system was rampant, despite occasional government efforts to stop abuses. Villagers were forced not only to carry the personal loads of soldiers and officials without compensation, but also to furnish them free food. Some villagers were even pressed into unpaid service by high-caste pilgrims traveling to Lake Manosarowar and Mount Kailas. An examination of the contemporary official documents dealing with complaints published in *Itihas Prakash* indicates that the farther a village was from the *subba*'s headquarters at Chhinasim, the more subject to abuse were its people.

Refashioned Land Tenure and Taxation

Immediately after annexing Jumla, Kathmandu confiscated all tax-exempt *birta* and *guthi* holdings that had not been awarded by former Kalyal rajas or could not be substantiated by documentation. This move was designed to increase *raikar* (crown) holdings and revenues in an area where so much land was in freehold tenure. The Jumlawalas most affected by this policy were the thread-wearing Brahmans, Thakuri, and Chhetri with only small freeholdings, and thus with little political power or economic leverage. They were lowered in the economic hierarchy to varying levels of tax-paying landholder, cultivator, or tenant. Pollution precepts made this turn of events additionally disruptive and abhorrent to the Brahmans so affected. Those unable or unwilling either to reestablish themselves in other livelihood pursuits or to revert to farming joined the growing ranks of emigrants who fled the area.

On the other hand, influential Brahmans and Thakuri who did retain large *birta* holdings or who ingratiated themselves with the new government were able to maintain their position and prestige through patronage, although sometimes at a lower economic standard. They too were now subject to financial obligations to Kathmandu. Some had to pay a special fee or *salami* in recognition of their *birta* confirmation. A large number were required to pay an annual property levy known as *sirto*, which stemmed from the vassal tribute made to the Kalyal kings during the previous regime. However, the economic benefits that most of these Tagadhari elite continued to accrue usually outweighed their financial and labor obligations to the state. Some with readily available cash were even able to expand their landholdings at the expense of others by assuming and paying off the obligations or back taxes of those in arrears. Thus, as wealth begot wealth, the range of economic well-being within both Brahman and Thakuri castes widened.

For the first few years Kathmandu paid salaries to its troops stationed in Jumla from land revenues collected in the district. This departure from the more prevalent practice of assigning them *jagir* grants was possible because, since late Malla times, rents and taxes usually had been paid in cash. However, the costs of maintaining eighteen companies (see Appendix E) comprising between 2,500 and 4,000 officers and men were great.[19] As financial demands escalated with continued war efforts and as growing numbers of Jumlawala migrated in the face of economic hardships, leaving their farmlands abandoned and unproductive, Jumla soon was unable to generate revenue sufficient for its own needs. In some years cash collected in Kumaon and other districts had to be diverted to Jumla so that its military payroll could be met (Regmi 1971:93).

Beginning in 1805 Kathmandu introduced a number of measures to alleviate this situation and to increase revenues generally in Jumla. In an effort to both reduce and simplify its financial obligations to its military per-

---

[19] A company during the Gorkha unification period consisted of between 140 and 200 officers and sepoys. The annual cost in pay and maintenance of the "occupation" forces in Jumla was therefore somewhere between ten and twenty lakhs of rupees (i.e., one and two million rupees). At present-day conversion rates, that would amount to approximately $100,000 to $200,000 (see Stiller 1975:283-84).

sonnel, the government terminated the salary system and began awarding specific *jagir* land grants as it did in most other regions of the country. This change, in turn, gave rise to increasing abuses of the peasantry, despite periodic government attempts to prevent them, for *jagir* holders (*jagirdars*) exercised a considerable amount of de facto autonomous power over their tenant-cultivators. They not only extracted excessive rents, in food grains as well as in cash, but often summarily evicted tenants whose production dropped or whose payments fell in arrears.

To counter the loss of land revenues and the reduction of the labor pool that emigration produced, Kathmandu imposed strict controls on human movement. In addition, it encouraged the immigration of Tibetans and Indians. A homestead policy was enacted that gave settlers who reclaimed land a four-year exemption from taxes.

Farmlands were "scrutinized," or surveyed, in 1805 and again in 1830-37 in order that all holdings be enumerated, registered, and included in new tax schedules. An additional and important motive for the 1805 survey was to determine which *birta* holdings remained to be confiscated. Tax assessors and surveyors may have actually measured or chained the more valuable *khet* lands to determine their area.[20] Two systems of land measurement were used in *khet* areas: the *mato muri* (0.0127 ha) and the *ropani* (0.0509 ha), 100 *mato muri* or twenty-five *ropani* were equivalent to one *khet muri*.[21]

However, in the more extensive and widespread upland *pakho* areas, which were more difficult to measure, the scrutinizers usually made just a count of farmsteads. When they did try to determine the extent of holdings, they could perforce make only estimates. These were based on the *hule*, or plow unit, the amount of land a bullock team can plow in a day, and were imprecise in the extreme because of the variability of such factors as slope, quality and condition of both team and soil, and skill of plower.

The outstanding and consistent feature of the new government's land-tax policy, like those of earlier regimes, was its very lack of consistency and uniformity. To this Kathmandu added a stringent and regressive brand of rigidity. The ancient Adhiya system of produce sharing between freehold or state landlord and cultivator or tenant was applied to new homesteads from which rents were collected in kind. In all other holdings cash assess-

---

[20] The contention of informants in the Revenue Office (*Mal Adda*) in Chhinasim that these early surveys did chain *khet* holdings (with a device known as a *tanga*) is supported by contemporary references. However, it would appear that the consistency and accuracy of these measurements are open to question.

[21] For a more detailed breakdown of these systems the reader is referred to the glossary of weights and measures in Appendix B. It should be noted that use of both *muri* and *ropani* systems probably predates the Gorkha period.

ments remained in effect. Under the Kalyals these were also based on, or had evolved from, the Adhiya sharing criteria and involved various remission mechanisms that made some allowance for years of poor harvest.

Although the new cash assessments known as *thek tiro* that Kathmandu promulgated in 1805 did not call for any appreciable rise in rents, they were now fixed and inflexible, for no remissions whatsoever were permitted. Thus by design the peasantry was required to absorb the entire loss in productivity that droughts, hailstorms, floods, and landslides frequently inflicted. Only when another survey, such as that of 1830-37, was carried out to add newly claimed lands to the revenue register could a cultivator or tenant whose lands had been depleted hope for any redress or relief.

The *thek tiro* tax was paid on all *khet* lands on the basis of size and irrespective of varying quality. A similar but lower cash assessment called *serma* was paid on those *pakho* lands whose size had been estimated. In these cases the land tax took the form of a special homestead levy called *saune fagu*.

Besides its land taxes the state also imposed a number of miscellaneous household taxes of the genre collected since late Malla times. These individual home obligations varied greatly according to a family's location, caste, and economic status. Important house taxes included those on the use of grazing grounds, the collection of medicinal herbs, the production of milk products, the sale of sal and wool, and the operation of water mills (*ghattas*). Other fixed taxes were levied at the village scale and included duties on the sale of falcons, horses, honey, printed cotton cloth, and musk. These village taxes were divided among the households that each village contained.

For administrative purposes Kathmandu subdivided Jumla District into eighteen *daras*, which were reflections of the vassal domains and fiefdom groupings in the Pahari core region and peripheral tribal territories of the Kalyal period. The map of Jumla (figure 38) suggests the striking and significant inverse relationship that generally existed between the size of a *dara* and its duration of sedentary (i.e., agricultural) human occupance, its extent of prime (*khet*) lands, its density of population, and its economic importance. Humla and Tibrikot *daras*, however, were exceptions to this pattern, owing to protracted Pahari penetration, settlement, and agricultural activity in the deeply incised lower Humla River valley and the similar western section of the Bheri River corridor.

Within each *dara* the village, or sometimes a group of villages, was made the basic revenue unit, or *mauja*. For each *mauja* a contract was awarded to an influential man or village leader who collected all taxes from the households under his jurisdiction. These collections were made in several installments between mid-July and mid-April and were geared to local harvest times of the principal summer and winter food grains. In return for

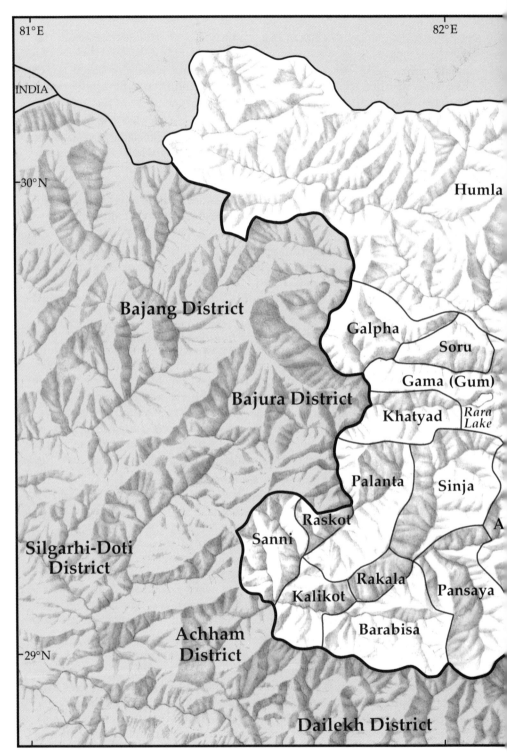

81°E   82°E

INDIA

30°N

Humla

Bajang District

Galpha

Soru

Gama (Gum)

Bajura District

Khatyad   *Rara Lake*

Palanta   Sinja

Raskot

Silgarhi-Doti District

Sanni

A

Rakala

Pansaya

Kalikot

Achham District

Barabisa

29°N

Dailekh District

Fig. 38. Map of Jumla District and its daras

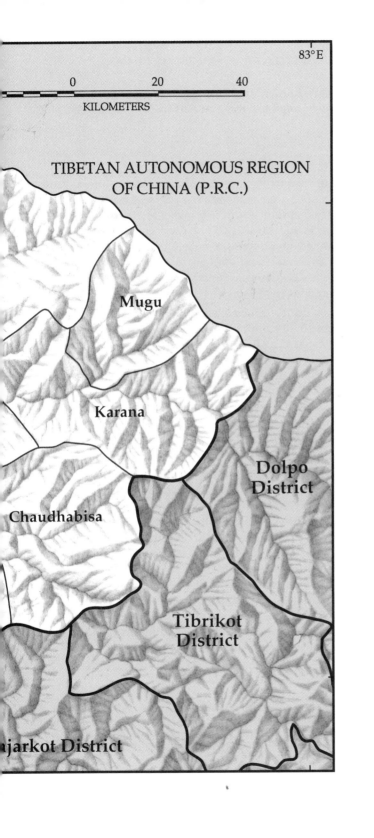

83°E

0　　　　20　　　　40

KILOMETERS

TIBETAN AUTONOMOUS REGION
OF CHINA (P.R.C.)

Mugu

Karana

Chaudhabisa

Dolpo
District

Tibrikot
District

ajarkot District

his services the tax collector, known as a *jimmawal* in predominantly *khet* areas and a *mukhiya* in *pakho* regions, was entitled to keep as much as 10 percent of his take.

Contracts, Regulations, and Entrenched Stagnation

By instituting the contractual system of tax collection in Jumla, Kathmandu not only made use of and perpetuated existing regional feudal hierarchies but placed the onerous task of extracting revenues from the populace on the indigenous *jimmawals* and *Mukhiyas*. For their part these collectors were vested with, or assumed themselves, a degree of prestige and power formerly held by the Kalyals' vassals and administrators, which many in fact had been. As such, they wielded power transcending that required to meet their contracted fiscal obligations to the state.

The tax collectors' authority touched all facets of village life and included the right and responsibility not only to arbitrate most local disputes but to try judicial cases concerning all but fifth-generation Tagadhari. Only very serious judicial matters were referred to the district governor at Jumla-Kalanga (headquarters) in Chhinasim. Both district and local officials were instructed to award "punishment or fines or both" for a spectrum of caste-*dharma* violations that included "cow-slaughter,[22] abortion, and sexual relations between kith and kin" (Itihas Prakash Mandal 1956, vol. 2, pt. 2, p. 29). It would appear that judicial fines were another important source of revenue for the government of Nepal.

Both the content and number of official state orders or *Lal Mohars* (literally "red seals") and correspondence that dealt with religious matters— not only dharmic dictates but *guthi* land grants and priestly duties—indicate that state efforts to foster and enforce Hindu orthodoxy exceeded those of the Kalyals. Of special note was the zealous support Kathmandu's administrative cadre and military personnel gave the Siva-associated temples of Candan Nath and Bhairan Nath in Jumla-Kalanga (figure 39). This support was in the form of extensive local *guthi* land grants and a variety of special cesses on the district's populace. In the face of these circumstances the Sanskritization process accelerated among Matwali Chhetri *thar* and *bāsā* as these Khasa groups sought to ease economic-cum-religious pressures by joining the ranks of the thread-wearing Chhetri.

---

[22] Immediately after unification a ban on cow slaughter was vigorously pursued in Jumla as it was throughout Nepal. Those who deliberately ignored the ban were beheaded; those who killed a cow in ignorance were heavily fined. In 1805 a proclamation was issued stating that such criminals would henceforth be either executed or enslaved (M. C. Regmi 1969). Apparently the Dum were the primary target of this measure, for the ban did not apply to Bhotia slaughter of yaks.

Fig. 39. *Candan Nath and Bhairan Nath temples at Jumla-Kalanga*

As we have seen, economic activities collateral to farming (animal husbandry, home industry, forest product collection, trade) were the basis of most miscellaneous household and village revenues. These pursuits were closely tied to the movements of people, and their animals and goods, in interregional and intraregional temporal and spatial patterns that were well established and regulated by Kalyal times. Moreover, they generally constituted household, village, or fiefdom resource and trade monopolies, important cornerstones of all feudal systems.

The new government preserved the patterns of movement with rigidly enforced regulations and maintained the monopolies with a variety of contracts and concessions. It issued a myriad of instructions spelling out just where, when, and often with whom, families, villages, or *dara*s could graze animals, hunt, exploit the wild biota, or trade. For example, the people of Tibrikot Dara were told to confine their winter trading and grazing (sheep and goats) to Piuthan, while those in Jumla, i.e., Asi Dara, were instructed to go only to Dang and Sallyan: "Those who transgress the traditional rule shall be heavily fined or punished (Itihas Prakash Mandal 1956, vol. 2, pt. 2, p. 41). Similar dictates concerned the patterns of summer trading with Tibet. Kathmandu awarded monopolistic hunting, trading, timbering and mining contracts on an annual basis to individuals, again on preferential basis, which brought in both additional revenues and needed commodities.

All of the revenue policies and procedures imposed on Jumla by the House of Gorkha during the early nineteenth century favored a reshuffled and loyal local elite as they tightened the exploitative vise on a burgeoning and overburdened peasantry. The peace that followed the Treaty of Sagauli in no way altered this state of affairs, although Kathmandu was now free from the sapping costs of waging war. Rather than turn to programs of internal growth and development, it continued to follow the retrogressive course of feeding feudal appetites by rigorously milking its provinces of whatever wealth they would yield.

In Jumla fixed taxation, restrictive contracts and monopolies, and repressive regulations continued to rob cultivators and tenants of what little freedom of choice and action they had enjoyed. The cumulative and combined effect was to strangle the bulk of the agriculturalists in the vicious downward spiral of subtenancy, insecurity, indebtedness,[23] indentured servitude, and even slavery. One result of these processes was the marked increase in the number of farming families who could achieve no more than a bare subsistence level of living. Another was the general decline in agricultural productivity.

Additional and interrelated factors contributing to this reduced productivity were the abandonment of holdings and the declines in the labor force due to out-migration. The presence today of "fossil" terraces in many upland *pakho* areas that predate annexation attests to this subsequent condition. Although available information permits only conjecture, it would appear that between annexation (1788) and the mid-nineteenth century (ca. 1860) Jumla's population may have dropped as much as 40 percent (from approximately 130,000 to about 75,000 or 80,000).[24]

The reduction in their numbers actually brought the people who remained in Jumla mixed blessings. Although it contributed to some severe socioeconomic hardships, it also temporarily removed or reduced many of

---

[23] Tagadhari moneylenders extracted exorbitant annual interest rates of 50 percent or more on loans; one document (Itihas Prakash Mandal 1956, vol. 2, pt. 2, p. 33) indicates a rate of 71 percent.

[24] The former figure was discussed above; the latter estimate is based on extant Jumla tax records.

the stresses that a previously growing population had been exerting on the natural environment. In upland areas the competition for field and forest resources diminished. Throughout the district the rate of deforestation due to wood fuel and construction demands slowed. Moreover these demands, particularly in the densely populated and denuded *khet* lowland, were closely regulated (Itihas Prakash Mandal 1956, vol. 2, pt. 2, pp. 135-43),

In sum, Jumla was relegated to the role of backwater peripheral province after its incorporation into the Kingdom of Nepal. Far removed from Kathmandu, this once important Karnali Khasa heartland became a frontier buffer district which, relative to other districts, was of little or limited economic (revenue) value. Under the heavy Gorkha yoke Jumla's peoples soon were mired in a constricting and exploitative feudal order more stifling that that which they had endured under the Kalyals. For all but the highest strata in this firmly entrenched and stagnant society, the standard of living was marginal, stressful, and precarious. Finally, the peasantry's deep suspicion and resentment of both the "foreigners" from Kathmandu and the policies they perpetuated were embodied in a popular Jumla proverb: *Rājālāgyo kāl lāgyo:* "If the king is after you, it is like death."

THE RANA OLIGARCHY (1846-1950)

The depressed way of life that the House of Gorkha imposed or entrenched in Jumla continued relatively unchanged until the mid-twentieth century. However, after 1846 this static condition, which was common to the entire country, was maintained by "new management" in Kathmandu. That year both kingdom and crown fell under the control of a Khasa clan—the Ranas—who ran the realm exclusively for their own benefit. A brief account of the Ranas' rise and their regime is germane to our understanding of the final phase of feudalism in the upper Karnali drainage.[25]

The Ranas' Rise

The early decades of the nineteenth century were a time of rampant internecine conflicts within the House of Gorkha and between and among the principal noble clans (i.e., the Basnyat, Bhandari, Pande, and Thapa) surrounding the Shahs. For thirty-one years (1806-37) the Thapa, who were staunch supporters of Shahs, managed to hold sway thanks to the strong bond of Bhim Sen Thapa. However, with the prime minister's eventual demise, internal political instability increased as the various factions vied for power. Nine years later, on September 14, 1846, the struggles culminated

---

[25] A plethora of information exists on the history, politics, and polity of the Rana regime; valuable works include Kumar (1967), Levi (1905-8), London (1928), Rose (1971:128-74), and Wright (1877).

in a night of Machiavellian violence known as the Kot Massacre during which many chief political contenders from the prominent noble (Thakuri) families were slain. From this carnage emerged Jung Bahadur Kunwar, a clever and formidable potentate who inaugurated a single-family despotism in Nepal that was to last 104 years.

Born in 1817, Jung Bahadur was a grandnephew of Bhim Sen Thapa and the product of a Chhetri family, albeit of less political influence, who had rendered distinguished military service for the Shahs since the reign of Prithvi Narayan. In 1805 his father, Bal Narsingh Kunwar, had been awarded the hereditary civil rank of *kaji* (a king's minister) for capturing and strangling to death King Ran Bahadur Shah's assassin. One of eight sons, Jung Bahadur was himself married to a Thapa at age eleven, entered military service at sixteen, and served as a lieutenant in Jumla for two years (1835-37) when his father was posted there as a *subba* (Rana 1909:1-17). After the downfall of their relative and patron Bhim Sen, the Kunwars were stripped of rank and property. But this reversal in family fortunes proved to be only temporary, for Jung Bahadur possessed a special aptitude for connivance and survival amid the congenital court intrigue. He gradually maneuvered himself into posts of increasing importance in Kathmandu and ultimately played the key role, with both duplicity and force, in the Kot Massacre. The following day he was appointed prime minister and commander-in-chief of the army by the crown.

Thereupon, Jung Bahadur moved swiftly to consolidate and protect his position. He installed his brothers and other close relatives in all top military and administrative posts. He exiled those influential nobles who had not been killed or who had not already fled the capital. He also effected the banishment of several troublesome members of the royal family.

In an effort to solicit support from the Brahman class and to appeal to the religious feelings of all segments of society, the new premier restored the *birta* and *guthi* lands (predominantly *khet*) that had been confiscated in 1806 (Regmi 1963:88-91; 158-59). It is important to point out that since most of those lands had been reawarded as *jagir* and since Jung Bahadur could ill afford alienating the army, the dispossessed Brahmans were entitled to claim only unoccupied wastelands (in Jumla, usually uplands unsuitable for irrigation) of an area that would yield income no greater than that which they had lost. However, funds were to be furnished them to pay for their wasteland reclamation. In Jumla this order of 1846 had two important effects: it checked or decreased emigration from the district and it substantially increased the portion of Brahman *birta* that was *pakho*.

Subsequent events in 1847 gave Jung Bahadur the chance to further cement his control of the kingdom by replacing the current king, Rjendra Bikram Shah, with the seventeen-year-old heir apparent Surendra Bikram, who was easily coercible. For example, in order to enhance his social status and prestige Jung Bahadur extracted from the new king a royal decree in 1849 recognizing his claim that the Kunwars stemmed from an ancient Rajput family (Kumar 1967:158-59).[26] Furthermore, it conferred on Jung Bahadur and his family the honorific "Rana," which they took as their new *thar*, or clan name. With this pedigree that Ranas were elevated to high Thakuri status that permitted marriage with the Shahs.

With his position in the kingdom secure, at least for the moment, Jung Bahadur turned his attentions to northern India, where events did not portend well for his or his country's future. There British military might had completely shattered the once powerful Sikh kingdom in two wars (1845-46 and 1848-49) and the entire Punjab had been annexed. The Rana premier was quick to realize that if he continued Nepal's anti-British policies of the past few years the kingdom might well precipitate a similar armed confrontation and suffer a similar fate. Ever the pragmatist, he set about reversing the popular but dangerous antagonistic policies by courting British friendship. To that end, as well as to see and appraise personally the sources of British strength and to garner for himself foreign recognition and support (Levi 1905, vol. 2, p. 336), Jung Bahadur embarked on a visit to England in early 1850. He thus became the first South Asian potentate to ignore Hindu religious sanctions against crossing the "black waters." The trip proved singularly successful on all counts (Rana 1909:113-52).

Upon his return to Kathmandu a year later, the Rana prime minister resumed his quest of absolute power with newly acquired inspiration and ideas for more efficient military, civil, judicial, and administrative machinery. Since early Gorkha times Nepal's military-cum-civil governmental structure had been a blend of Hindu and Muslim (Mughul) organizational elements. Jung Bahadur now infused these with a few European principles and procedures. The army was reorganized along British lines and its training improved (Kumar 1967:91). The number and size of civil departments were expanded in order to increase the capacity and efficiency of the central government in land tenure management in tax and other revenue collection. In effect, a centralized yet feudalistic agrarian bureaucracy was developed to strengthen the political and economic authority of the Rana monolith. By usurping the monarch's right of patronage and his practice of *pajani*,[27] an annual review of the elites' performance and behavior, Jung Bahadur maintained control over all civil and military appointees.

---

[26] The Lal Mohar states that of four ancestral brothers, one had ruled Chitor while three had sought their fortunes in the Nepal Himalaya; of the latter, one became Rija of Taklakhar (i.e., Taklakot area now in Tibet), one resided in Jumla, and offspring of the third settled in Kaski.

[27] *Pajani* was an instrument of control that was first introduced by Prithvi Narayan Shah. It was "an institution by which the king renewed all civil and military appointments of the state every year, resulting in the continuation or confirmation of the previous appointments,

In order to make the law a firm and efficient instrument of administration, the prime minister enacted a new legal code (Muluki Ain) in 1854 that was to be applied uniformly throughout the realm. This was a formulation, based on the Hindu civil and criminal judicial principles already outlined, that encompassed crime and punishment involving the state, persons and property, caste, and political offences (Kumar 1967:114-31). It also included a few notable reforms such as the elimination of trial by ordeal and provisions that restrained the practice of *sati* (self-immolation by widows).

At this stage internal and international conditions seemed favorable for Jung Bahadur to improve the position of Nepalese traders in Tibet and to redress the ignominious defeat his country had sustained in 1791.[28] He also may have hoped that a successful Tibetan campaign would bring him enough popular support to depose Surendra Shah and take the throne for himself (Rose 1971:109). Elaborate military mobilization and logistical preparations were made in 1854; in western Nepal these centered in Jumla. After Tibet rejected Nepal's demands for exorbitant tribute and trans-Himalayan territory, including the Taklakot area, Jung Bahadur launched an offensive along the entire frontier the following spring. Although Nepal was victorious in this second Tibetan war (1855-56), its gains fell short of expectations and it settled for an annual Tibetan tribute of 10,000 rupees and extraterritorial rights for Nepalese traders in Lhasa. Moreover, this war effort, like previous ones, had imposed tremendous and unpopular labor demands on the people and seriously depleted the treasury: it required the services of an estimated 400,000 porters (*jhara*, compulsory labor) and cost almost 2.7 million rupees (Rose 1971:113-15).

Although Surendra's throne eluded Jung Bahadur, complete control of the country and its resources did not. In a surprise move at the war's conclusion he resigned as prime minister in favor of his brother Bam Bahadur Rana. And immediately he secured from the monarch the Chaubisi principalities of Kaski and Lamjung as a private estate over which he exercised total sovereignty with the title of maharaja and from which he personally derived 100,000 rupees in revenues annually (Kumar 1967:187). At the same time the prime ministership became an exclusive and hereditary Rana post. Furthermore, in order to obviate the problems that primogeniture inheritance continually produced (e.g., weak regents acting for minors) a system of agnatic inheritance was formulated. A Rana *Roll of Succession* was drawn up by Jung Bahadur which called for the prime ministership passing succes-

---

or modification in the nature and tenure of existing appointments, or dismissals and new appointments" (Kumar 1967:167).

[28] In Tibet a weak regent presided for a Dalai Lama in his minority; in China the Manchus had their hands full with the widespread T'ai P'ing rebellion (1850-64) and organized banditry (1833-68); the British were involved in the Crimean War (1854-56) with Russia.

sively to his brothers before going to his eldest son. Finally, when his brother Bam suddenly died in May 1857, Jung resumed the prime minister-ship, fused the post with that of maharaja of Kaski and Lamjung, and ex-tracted yet another Lal Mohar (official state order) by which King Surendra relinquished to him absolute powers of life and death. With this act the monarch was reduced to a titular figurehead whose role was merely ceremo-nial. Stripped of his de jure powers, the king was now only a spiritual head of state whom the people revered from afar as the reincarnation of Vishnu.

Thus, in a brief span of eleven years (1846-57) Jung Bahadur attained absolute de facto command of the kingdom and founded a family oligarchy in which the prime minister was above the law and accountable to neither the king nor the people. With supreme power over political, governmental, social, and religious affairs, he headed a medieval mode of rule in which family and state interest were one and the same. Despite a systemic struggle, often marked by violence within the Rana ranks themselves, this outmoded regime continued to survive until 1950 under eight succeeding prime min-isters. In large part its preservation was due to these Ranas' concerted efforts to submerge rival factions and families, suppress education, and prohibit foreign travel and commerce within the country. Free from British interfer-ence in the internal affairs of Nepal, the Ranas introduced few social re-forms. Those that were promulgated, such as the abolition of slavery in 1924, were token and in no way alleviated the plight of the vast majority of the rural population. Concessions to modernity were almost always con-fined to the three cities of the Kathmandu Valley, the only true central place in the country, where they benefited only the urban elite. These included the establishment of one high school and one hospital in 1890, the introduc-tion of electricity in 1903, and subsequently the sparse use of telephones, ra-dios, and automobiles (carried into the valley over the trails from India). In this way crown, nobility, and commoner alike were effectively isolated from the mainstream of life in South Asia which was moving toward modernity.

Developments in Jumla

The Rana regime brought Jumla's peasantry a 104-year continuation of exploitive and nefarious management by preserving the labor, land, taxa-tion, and legal systems employed by the Shahs. What few modifications or reforms the Ranas did introduce were designed to secure more revenue or to increase administrative efficiency rather than to improve local living conditions. Yet abuse, bribery, and corruption continued to be systemic. Kathmandu's dictates were often circumvented or manipulated by the local elite, as well as by the civil and military personnel, in order to permit per-sonal gain. As long as this consortium in remote Karnali met the Ranas' revenue demands and maintained tranquility (that is, squelched bothersome complaints before they reached the capital), its members had ample opportunity to fleece the populace without censure.

Under Rana impetus the civil components of district government grew both in size and relative importance. The military garrison based in Jumla-Kalanga was reduced to one or two companies after the Second Tibetan War and functioned chiefly as armed police. Their role was to enforce law and order, to accompany the governor (known as the Bada Hakim in late Rana times) on his travels and inspection tours through the district, and to guard the Revenue Office (*Mal Adda*) and jail at Chhinasim headquarters. In 1887 a district court was added to the administrative machinery. It was one of four lower courts in western Nepal that dispensed district-wide justice (that is, those cases that could not be handled at the village level) and fell within the jurisdiction of a lower court of appeals located in Doti (Kumar 1967:128-31). With these developments the number of villagers who were required to travel to Jumla, the district's capital, on so-called government business increased.

At the same time (ca. 1890) several Newars from Kathmandu who had previously worked in the area as government servants opened shop in Jumla-Kalanga, thus forming the nucleus for a permanent bazaar in the only truly central place the district could boast. Their clientele was limited to the civil servants and military personnel stationed there, for the visiting subsistence farmers could not afford the imported luxury items. Seeing the success of the Newars, a dozen or so local landed Brahmans, Thakuri, and Chhetri also opened shops. This resulted in a division of the limited market and soon forced the Newars, who previously did not farm, to buy land in order to make ends meet.

Two district-wide field scrutinizations and tax settlements were carried out under the Ranas to add newly reclaimed farmland to the revenue records and to increase the tax base. During the first (1868) the area-estimate of *pakho* lands was extended in order to apply the *serma* assessment to a greater number of upland holdings. During the second (1889) all *khet* holdings were assessed according to their productive quality. Four grades—*abal, doyam, sim,* and *chahar*—were determined on the basis of soil properties and irrigation facilities (Regmi 1963:56-59). *Abal* was premier-grade land most suitable for both a summer paddy crop and a winter wheat or barley crop. However, these moves brought Rana coffers only a meager increase in revenues from Jumla for they compounded the inherent chaos that characterized all facets of land tenure and taxation and exacerbated popular dissatisfaction. They bolstered a fertile field for bribery and collusion as landholders sought to avoid scrutinization and reduce assessments.

Developments in the lowlands to the south during the last half of the nineteenth century were also felt in Jumla. At the time of the Indian Mutiny (1857-58) Jung Bahadur Rana pursued his friendship policy with

England by personally leading an army of 8,000 Gorkhas against the rebels in Oudh and assisting the British in the relief of Lucknow. Nepal gained much more than booty and esteem from this timely action. In 1860 the British returned approximately 8,000 km^2 of territory in the western Tarai that Nepal had been forced to cede in 1816 (see figure 37). The Ranas and their cohorts were quick to claim for themselves in *birta* tenure the rich forests and valuable cultivatable tracts of the area. For their own ends they encouraged settlement (principally by Indians), land reclamation, and the growth of Nepalganj, a permanent market town on the border close to road and rail heads of the transportation network the British were building in northern India. Nepalganj soon replaced in importance the bazaars and seasonal trade fairs of the Dang Valley in the inner Tarai. Around 1890 the Ranas also established the large seasonal border market of Rajapur west of the major Karnali River debouchment.[29] Thus by Rana design these two new trade marts captured much of the annual winter traffic from the hinterland to the north.

It must be noted here that these developments took place at a time when Nepal's command of the Himalaya was on the decline. As a result of renewed British efforts to secure and control trans-Himalayan commerce, Darjeeling and Kalimpong eclipsed Kathmandu as important entrepôts by 1900. However, it should be remembered that such traffic via the Karnali drainage had always been insignificant compared to that through Kathmandu because of environmental constraints. Rana efforts in western Nepal were therefore chiefly concerned with monopolizing internal and Nepalese-Indian trade. The present-day activities of the Jumlawala in this field will be discussed in detail in chapter 6.

Population and Settlement Trends

The continued stale state of affairs in Jumla during the Rana regime was manifested by a markedly slow and sporadic regrowth of its depleted population (figure 40). Not until about 1940 did it even approach the size it probably had attained before annexation by Gorkha in 1788. Although available information precludes a full understanding of the demographic processes at work during this period and the subsequent two decades (1950-70), it is clear that a number of factors were involved. In spite of the fact that Rana polity checked emigration and attempted to encourage immigration, it also reduced the peasant family's level of nutrition (dietary intake) and made it more vulnerable during periods of drought by robbing it of an adequate food supply. In turn, persistent and widespread undernourishment and periodic famine combined with poor health, diseases, and epidemics

---

[29] Because of its susceptibility to periodic flooding, Rajapur has had three locations since its founding.

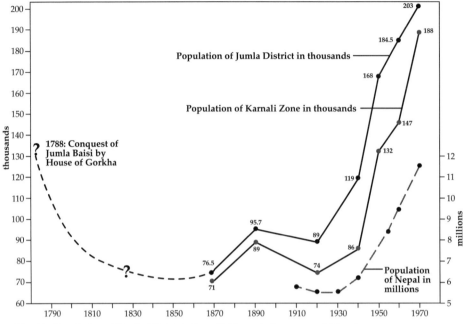

Fig. 40. Population of Jumla District, Karnali Zone study area, and Nepal

(burns, worms, dysentery, goiter, tuberculosis, malaria, measles, smallpox, etc.) to offset a high birthrate with a high death rate (a high incidence of infant and child mortality and limited life expectancy). One striking example was the influenza pandemic of 1918, which claimed between sixteen and twenty million lives in India (Davis 1951:41). The virus spread rapidly up the Karnali trade routes into Jumla, taking a heavy toll in many villages, particularly in the Tila Valley. There entire households were wiped out because no one in these families was physically capable of caring for the sick.

The antithesis of Jumla's slow population recovery during the nineteenth and early twentieth centuries was found in Kumaon and Garhwal. Between 1790 and 1815 these areas had suffered similar ravages of war, exploitation, and depopulation at the hands of Nepal. However, the arrival of British administration in 1816 brought security of life and property, revenue and land tenure reforms, economic development, famine relief, and other conditions that stimulated rapid population growth and settlement expansion (Andress 1966:107-20). By 1941 these regions of the Indian Himalaya contained twice the number of people they had before the Gorkha invasion.

In Jumla the last decade of the Ranas (1940-50) finally witnessed the beginning of the end of homeostatic conditions. The first signal was a Malthusian escalation in population growth that paralleled that of Nepal, South Asia, and the developing world as a whole (Davis 1951; Borgström 1973). In those ten years Jumla's population jumped from 119,000 to 168,000, an increase of 41 percent, as the death rate began to decline. Contributing factors were an improvement, however small, of the people's nutrition levels, which probably resulted from a lower frequency of drought years, increased use of maize as a food grain, and the initial inroads of modern medicines.

A singularly significant phenomenon in Jumla during Rana times was the fact that settlement did not expand beyond either the density or the areal extent it had reached by 1788 under the Kalyals. Because of the degree of depopulation in the early nineteenth century and the slow rate of regrowth over the following century, the district remained underpopulated in relation to its meager agricultural resources until the very end of the era. Some Rana dictates to the contrary, there was little need, opportunity, or desire to extend settlement such as occurred in the sparsely inhabited hills of eastern Nepal and the newly regained lowlands of the western Tarai or in economically stimulated regions of the Indian (British) Himalaya.

Therefore in Jumla, as in other Pahari regions of western Nepal (i.e., old Baisi and Chaubisi princedoms), the Rana years were ones of sluggish settlement recovery and entrenchment within previously occupied and exploited areas.

Abandoned farmlands, pastures, and forests were reclaimed. Wherever and whenever possible fields in the lower valleys were converted by heavy labor input from *pakho* to *khet* in an effort to obtain both higher yields and higher taxes. Revenue records show that there were approximately 1,300 ha of *khet* registered in 1830. In 1868 there were 1,345 ha, but by 1889 the amount had risen to 1,700 ha, an increase of 26 percent during the previous two decades. In 1950 Jumla contained 598 villages with an average of 380 persons and 48 households.

NEPAL IN THE MODERN AGE (1951 ONWARD)

Overthrow of the Ranas

Early twentieth-century political, social, and economic forces at work throughout the world, but particularly in India, portended the inevitable downfall of the Ranas and their outmoded, isolationist, and feudalistic regime in Nepal. Between World War I and World War II the growing strength of Mahatma Gandhi's nationalist movement, the emergence of political parties (especially the Indian National Congress party), and the Quit India campaign turbulently propelled the subcontinent toward independence from the British Raj. During this period the advent of a number of secret Nepalese political groups in India was closely linked to these developments. Composed primarily of exiles, but including dissident colleagues in Kathmandu, they sought to remove the Ranas from power and to introduce democratic rule in Nepal. Furthermore, when the British finally departed from South Asia in 1947, the Ranas lost the crucial support of an Indian government upon which they had long relied for noninterference in their own despotic domestic affairs.

The new and independent Government of India, which was dominated by the Congress party, not only pressured the Ranas to institute democratic reforms but provided the Nepalese Congress party support and a safe base of operations on the plains. At the same time the puppet Shah ruler, King Tribhuvan, quietly lent his support to the movement. All the while the Ranas clung myopically to their course of self-interest. What few belated reforms they did undertake, such as the formulation of a Nepalese constitution in 1948, were inadequate, halfhearted, and seldom implemented.

The popular movements gathered momentum and in a rapid series of events in 1951 the Rana regime was toppled and King Tribhuvan was restored to power as the leader of the democratic movement. Thereupon Nepal opened its doors to the modern world and began the difficult task of developing a politically, socially, and economically viable third-world nation.

This task was made especially precarious by Nepal's vulnerable position between two giant neighbors—India and the People's Republic of China, which had "liberated" Tibet in 1950.

During the following decade Nepal joined the United Nations, established diplomatic relations with an increasing number of nations from whom it sought financial aid and expertise in road building, agricultural and industrial development, health, and education. Those who became most involved and visible were India, the United States, the People's Republic of China, the Soviet Union, and the United Nations (Mihaly 1965).

The initial steps from a depressed past into a progressive present were shaky and beset with obstacles, for Nepal possessed few natural resources other than farmlands and forests (and hydroelectric potential). These were generally as undeveloped as its human resources. Ninety-four percent of the country's stratified, polyethnic, and predominantly agrarian population of eight million (in 1951) were scattered throughout the hinterland in 29,000 villages of 500 or fewer. The vast majority were both handicapped by ignorance and deeply conditioned to mistrust the motives of any foreigners, whether from the capital or abroad. Fewer than 10 percent of the male population, and fewer than one percent of the female population, were literate; most of the literate were concentrated in the capital (His Majesty's Government of Nepal 1958). Those few with any modern foreign (i.e., non-Brahmanical) education belonged exclusively to the same influential and privileged families who had held all important government positions during the Rana years. While this closed cadre now was frequently reshuffled within the antiquated and inefficient administrative structures, it was perforce not opened and augmented. These conditions seriously hampered not only the design but, even more, the implementation of appropriate development programs.

Thus, in a country so ill-prepared for modernization, particularly along the lines of developed western nations, the decade of the 1950s was one of little social or economic progress. It was, instead, a time of chronic political instability and confusion. During the first few post-Rana years, King Tribhuvan appointed a series of ineffectual governments. Upon this revolutionary and popular monarch's death in 1955, his son, Mahendra, assumed not only the crown but the prime ministership and began to quicken the pace of political and administrative reorganization. By 1959 he was able to promulgate a new constitution. General elections were held and a parliamentary democracy was established in which the Nepalese Congress party held control. At the same time the bureaucracy was restructured with a central secretariat commanding twelve ministries. The central secretariat replaced as the hub of government the palace secretariat that the king had previously relied upon. However, most of these innovations were short-lived.

On December 15, 1960, King Mahendra resumed absolute control of the country with a swift and bloodless coup. This move no doubt was motivated by his belief that Nepal lacked sufficient political sophistication to remain a unified, nonaligned, and independent nation-state in the face of continuing, ominous external developments, such as an unsuccessful Tibetan revolt against the Chinese in 1959-60 during which the Dalai Lama fled to India. Subsequently, the Sino-Indian war of October-November 1962 not only gave his beliefs further credence but had the effect of quelling political dissatisfaction and bringing country-wide support of his autocratic actions.

With his coup Mahendra immediately dissolved the parliament, placed key political leaders under arrest, and outlawed political parties. While he retained the central secretariat and its ministries, he reinstated the palace secretariat as the chief and supragovernmental body of the kingdom (Rose and Fisher 1970:72-74). In addition he quickly replaced the parliamentary democracy with a multitiered pyramidal and partyless panchayat system of government,[30] formalized by yet another constitution in 1962, with the monarch at the apex. This Panchayat Raj was designed to better reflect the traditional organization of Nepalese society and to develop more efficiently its human and natural resources and serve its needs. It was hoped that by decentralizing its administrative machinery the total population could become involved in the nation's struggles. This form of government remains in effect today in Nepal, the world's only surviving Hindu monarchy.[31]

---

[30] The term "panchayat" stems from the traditional village council of five elders.

[31] The reader is referred to Rose (1971:177-291), Rose and Fisher (1970), and Joshi and Rose (1966) for detailed discussions of domestic and foreign affairs developments in post-Rana Nepal.

Change-Effecting Forces in Karnali Zone

During the first two decades of post-Rana modern times (from 1951 to the period of my fieldwork in 1969-70) external events and developments, both of international and national origin, were felt in varying degree or intensity in the insular upper Karnali basins. All brought or forecast changes, usually positive but sometimes negative, in the lives of all segments of society. Their collective effect was to contribute to the escalating population explosion, destroy the steady or homeostatic state of life that had persisted for over a century, and propel the populace into a period of political, social, economic, and psychological readjustment. The following are but a few of the changes that affected Karnali.

One important administrative step taken by the Panchayat Raj was the 1962 reorganization of Nepal's internal divisions in order to achieve uniformity of area and population. The thirty-six districts of the Rana regime were replaced by fourteen first-order zones made up of seventy-five second-order development districts, fourteen third-order town panchayats (such as Nepalganj) with populations over 10,000, and some 3,800 fourth-order village panchayats, each a single village or cluster of villages with a population of approximately 2,000. This scheme was a systematic attempt to delimit zones and districts along major interfluves or rivers in a manner that would promote internal communication and transportation and economic self-sufficiency.

Most of the Rana's Jumla District became Karnali Zone (figure 41). With 13,200 km^2 it was the country's largest. The old eighteen *daras* were abolished in favor of four districts: Jumla, containing forty-nine village panchayats; Humla and Mugu, each with twenty panchayats, and Tibrikot with five panchayats. Approximately 2,800 km^2 of old Tibrikot Dara (with seventy villages and about 16,000 persons) in the Bheri River drainage were assigned to Dolpo District of Dhaulagiri Zone in three adjustments between 1962 and 1966. These moves created considerable confusion and dissatisfaction among many Bheri River villagers, for they forced them to reorient many of their movements to the zonal headquarters of Dhaulagiri at Baglung (see figure 1) instead of continuing their traditional, easier, and shorter travel to Jumla-Kalanga, now the headquarters of Karnali Zone.[32]

Following this reorganization a zonal commissioner replaced the Bada Hakim as the central government's chief representative and supreme authority in the zone. Under him were four assistant zonal commissioners (chief district officers) who were stationed in each district headquarters:

---

[32] It should be noted that in 1975 yet another adjustment of administrative divisions was instituted in Nepal (see Appendix I). This was based upon a number of lessons the government had learned over the previous decade. In the northwest all of Dolpo was made a fifth district of Karnali Zone, thus rectifying the Bheri River corridor problem.

Jumla-Kalanga in Jumla; Simikot in Humla; Gum in Mugu; Depalgaon in Tibrikot.

The recent advent of some egalitarian ideals in Kathmandu and, at the same time, a critical need for revenues, brought a number of post-Rana changes or modifications in the labor, land, and tax systems. One of the first was the well-received abolition of compulsory unpaid labor obligations for government purposes. With new land tenure and taxation legislation, culminating in the Lands Act of 1964, the government attempted to bring uniformity and reforms to the existing disarray of disparate systems and also to protect tenant cultivators from both exorbitant rents and arbitrary evictions. From a fiscal standpoint the legislation was intended to increase revenues from landholdings while making such taxation more equitable.

Although tax-exempt *guthi* tenure was retained, the *jagir* system was abolished (1952) and the pervasive *birta* system terminated (1959). The Lands Act of 1964 not only limited the rent a landlord could charge his tenants to 50 percent of the yields but also limited the amount of farmland a hill family could own to approximately four hectares.[33] Procedures for the redistribution of land in excess of this ceiling favored the owners of adjoining land or other owners rather than landless tenants.[34] Families with large holdings quickly devised many strategies to circumvent this new regulation. Indeed the program was so susceptible to corruption and engendered so much opposition among the Tagadhari strata of Karnali Zone that the government was impelled to hold the implementation of this reform in abeyance. As a result the Land Reform Survey carried out as part of the program was shelved and its valuable economic data never processed or analyzed.[35] Another unsuccessful facet of the Lands Act was the Compulsory Savings Program. Designed to divert agricultural capital derived from the surplus of the chief food-grain crop away from moneylenders, who were now prohibited from charging more than 10 percent interest on loans, and into other sectors of the Nepalese economy, it was initiated in 1964 but abandoned in 1969 because of alleged widespread embezzlement (Regmi 1976:206-7).

Regarding taxation, all miscellaneous fixed village assessments were terminated in 1951. Only the taxes involving land were retained. In 1966 the

---

[33] The family unit was defined as parents, minor children, and unmarried daughters under thirty-five years of age (Nepal 1964, sect. 7).

[34] It must be pointed out that in Nepal's western midlands and mountains (including Karnali Zone) only 19.28 percent of *khet* and 6.59 percent of *pakho* were tenant cultivated (Regmi 1976:193); the heaviest concentration of landless peasants was found in the Tarai and inner Tarai regions.

[35] Thanks to the cooperation of both His Majesty's Government of Nepal and the people of Karnali Zone, access to the Land Reform Survey data provided me an especially important source of information on the region's socioeconomic structure, which will be discussed in chapter 5.

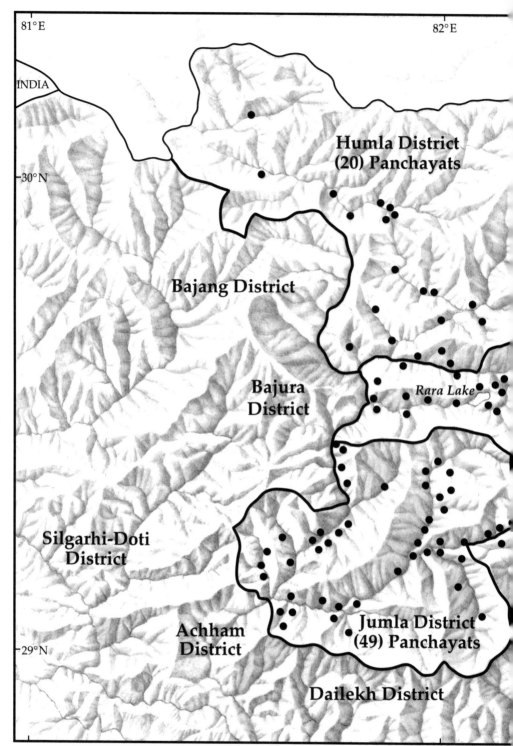

Fig. 41. Panchayats of Karnali Zone in 1970

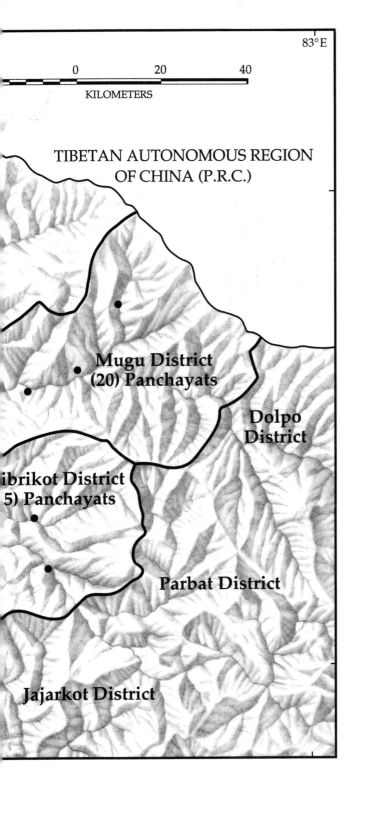

83°E

0   20   40

KILOMETERS

TIBETAN AUTONOMOUS REGION
OF CHINA (P.R.C.)

**Mugu District
(20) Panchayats**

**Dolpo
District**

**ibrikot District
5) Panchayats**

Parbat District

Jajarkot District

criteria for these assessments were modified somewhat to better reflect land quality. At the same time the rates were raised a moderate amount. All revenues now were to be collected in cash. The Rana's collection machinery remained in operation, but the *jimmawal*s and *mukhiya*s were permitted to keep only 2.5 percent of the revenue they garnered.

Without doubt these measures did improve in slight degree the economic status, and in some instances the earnings, of the small cultivators, tenants, and occupational caste Dum at the expense of larger landowners. They were, however, only compromise solutions to land reform and as such were as ineffectual in Nepal as were the programs in most other developing third-world nations (see Myrdal 1968; Warriner 1969). In no way did they appreciably alter the well-entrenched caste-based economic hierarchy of Karnali Zone; neither did other egalitarian reforms.

In 1963 the Legal Code (Muluki Ain) of Nepal was modified with the view to abolish discrimination on the basis of caste or community and legalize intercaste marriage. However, as was almost universally the case throughout the country, Karnali Zone's populace continued to follow their traditional social customs and practices. In some cases, at both individual and village scales, intercaste relationships became even less flexible and accommodative than before. Many Tagadhari attempted to counter the real or imagined deterioration of their political and economic status (relative to that of the Matwali Chhetri, Bhotia, and Dum castes) by intensifying or more stringently following ritual purity practices in order to protect themselves from inroads from below. Fearing that post-Rana developments would deprive them of the political and economic leverage they had long enjoyed, the Tagadhari reverted to their remaining source of power, religious sanctions, to maintain the status quo. As a result, many ritual-brother relationships (known as *mit*s) between members of high and low castes (e.g., Chhetri and Bhotia), which had bonded both social and economic pursuits for generations, began to break down. In other instances high-caste Pahari villages threatened to terminate long-standing economic symbiotic relationships (such as seasonal grain exchanges) with nearby Bhotia communities if the latter did not adhere to Hindu birth and menstruation pollution observances. It is important to note that a similar hardening of caste arteries took place in Kumaon as a result of liberalized British administration after 1815 (Sanawal 1976:126-34).

A number of facilities were introduced that manifested Nepal's efforts to promote social and economic growth. Most were supported by foreign aid, which by 1966-67 comprised 60 percent of the nation's development expenditures. Primary and middle schools were established throughout the zone and a high school was built in Jumla-Kalanga. The zonal headquarters began to grow as a regional service center with the opening of a branch of the Rastrja Banijya (a state-owned bank), a fifteen-bed hospital, an agricultural experiment station, and a cottage industry training program. A telecommunications station was also installed, with satellite substations in the district headquarters, which was part of a national network. And on a nearby alluvial terrace at 2,340 m a STOL airfield 500 m long was completed and operational in June 1968 (figure 42).

Fig. 42. Aerial view of the STOL airfield at Jumla-Kalanga. Occupying 4 ha of prime khet *farmland on an alluvial terrace at 2,340 m, it is 500 m in length.*

A particularly significant development was the advent of the transistor radio. Both privately owned radios and those distributed to the village panchayats permitted the people to broaden not only their awareness of the outside world in general but their understanding of their own nation's programs and goals in particular. While all of these developments engendered hope for the future and rising expectations, only a few produced immediate or visible improvements.

On the other hand, events in Tibet had serious and economically deleterious effects throughout the zone. After the 1959 abortive revolt of Tibet, the Chinese placed a number of restrictions on interregional trade and pasturing movements between inhabitants on both sides of the border. Travel of Tibetans into Nepal was curtailed. Just what items the Nepalese could trade in Tibet, and where, when, and at what rates of exchange that trade could be conducted along the border were strictly prescribed and en-forced. These regulations not only altered the customary movement pat-terns but reduced the volume of such traffic. With the exception of the Bhotia in Limi panchayat (in northwest Humla), herds from Nepal no longer could be pastured in Tibet during the winter.[36] In Karnali the most seriously affected were the Bhotia of northeast Mugu, whose livelihood was based primarily on this trade and pasturing and who lacked sufficiently pro-ductive farmland to fall back on. These developments triggered negative economic ripples throughout Karnali, which will be discussed in chapters 5 and 6.

Finally, it must be noted that the northern border regions of Nepal, including Karnali Zone, were the first affected negatively by such external forces and the last helped by the central government. Only after the mid-1960s did His Majesty's Government begin to pay particular attention to their often special problems. Even then the need to fashion programs that were appropriate for regionally distinctive conditions continued to be gen-erally overlooked or ignored for another five to ten years.

---

[36] Limi was able to maintain its traditional movement patterns by special arrangements with the Chinese (Goldstein 1975).

5
Settlements, Land, and Labor

OVERVIEW AND ORGANIZATION

The economy of Karnali Zone's multiethnic but predominantly Pahari and peasant population is fitted to the resources available in its heterogeneous environment and is based on intensive agriculture. However, rapid population increase, a number of environmental limitations, and a variety of cultural, social, and political constraints combine to prevent agriculture by itself from furnishing even a subsistence level of existence. Only by some combination of six livelihood pursuits—agriculture, animal husbandry, home industry, exploitation of the wild biota, trade, and seasonal out-migrations for work—can most of the population achieve subsistence. The presence and importance of these components vary among households in a single village, among villages in a valley, as well as from valley to valley and from area to area within the zone. In other words, there is a series of subsets, each consisting of these six components. The relative importance of each varies from subset to subset in both time and space.

The temporal diversity within this economic system allows all of its components to be articulated or tied together by the spatial movements of people, animals, and goods. Conversely, these movements, which are considerable, show varying periodicity and extent, or scale, for they reflect the peasant's adjustment to climatic variations and seasonality. These movements, furthermore, constitute labor responses to various needs or requirements of the peasant household, for it is only by generally frequent movements that the peasants can supply the needs of their families and bring their standard of living to a subsistence level.

As a whole, this economic system is based on symbiotic exchange and trade between and among the Pahari and Bhotia who occupy varied ecological niches or altitudinal belts within the upper Karnali catchment region, and by these groups with Tibet, the lower regions of Nepal, and India. With minor variations this intra- and interregional economy is an example of the multitiered large valley-and-basin system of high local relief, with the bottom tier based on an old paddy culture that Uhlig (1976) has discussed.

More specifically, Karnali Zone itself contains four distinctive socioeconomic regions, each of which displays a distinguishing mix of altitudinal range and terrain conditions, ecological energetics, quality and quantity of cropland, meadow composition, and population size. Within each region are one or more *daras*, which in this context are viewed not as obsolete administrative units but as contemporary economic units. As such, they constitute ten subregions that reflect both differences and similarities within and among the four major regions.

As a comparison of figures 41 and 43 indicates, the four political districts of Karnali Zone do not fit well with the four economic regions. Therefore, throughout the following systematic discussion of Karnali's economic components, zonal-scale information is always presented on the basis of economic region and subregion, while panchayat, village, or household information is always keyed to these regions. However, on occasion data are ordered both by economic regions and subregions and by political districts in order either to illustrate how such political ordering can obscure reality within Karnali Zone or to permit comparison of the data with those of other regions of Nepal (always ordered by administrative divisions). Furthermore, the inclusion of considerable detailed information in tabular form, which might appear extraneous or excessive to some, is intended to provide other Himalayan scholars or Nepalese development planners with a published source of potentially useful data that is not available elsewhere.

Finally, this organizational framework is designed both to facilitate integrated analysis of livelihood processes and their function, delimitation, and articulation in relation to scale, place, and time and to obviate the problems presented by Karnali Zone's multidimensional economic character, which exhibits such complexity of process in relation to scale, place, and time. As such, this framework at once describes and reflects the livelihood processes.[1]

---

[1] Implicit in this framework are organization principles and theoretical assumptions contained in the corpus of ecological, cultural-ecological, and peasant economics literature. Recent works include those of Margalef (1968, 1969), Bennett (1976), and Halperin and Dow

POPULATION AND SETTLEMENT PATTERNS

Contemporary Karnali's population of 186,000 (ca. 1968) is superimposed on the inner-montane basin complex of the zone according to physical conditions and availability of livelihood resources, principally farmland (table 6). Thus its density is in direct relationship to the scale of the dendritic drainage—primary, secondary, tertiary (figure 44). The ethnic composition and distribution of the population, while similar to the mountainous regions of Seti and Mahakali zones to the west, differ markedly from the highland regions further east in Nepal. The events and processes that led to Karnali's present-day pattern have already been discussed in detail in chapters 3 and 4. Older indigenous groups, such as Magar and Gurung, usually found at middle elevations in a hill-mountain belt between Pahari and Bhotia, are absent in Karnali Zone; long ago they were either absorbed or displaced by Pahari progenitors. Instead these dominant hill Hindus live in direct contact with Buddhist Bhotia.

With associated Dum or occupationals, Pahari of Brahman Thakuri and Chhetri castes comprise 93 percent of the population and occupy all but the highest parts of the zone. The minority Bhotia (4 percent) have their permanent habitations in the upper reaches of Mugu and Humla, as well as in a few isolated niches farther south in the high tertiary valley of Chaudhabisa and upper Tila. The remaining 3 percent of the zone's population, which I categorize in this monograph as "miscellaneous," is composed of a few non-Bhotia tribal families, a greater number of recent Hindu immigrants from the lowlands of Nepal or India who have settled in the exclusively Pahari areas of economic regions A and B, and some more Hinduized Bhotia at the Pahari-Bhotia interface who have assumed higher caste/status designation such as Tamang.

This polyethnic, multicaste population lives in some 654 villages that vary in size from fewer than 20 to more than 100 households. The average village has 48 households with a population of about 280. Village sites range in elevation from 800 m near the confluence of the Karnali and Tila Karnali rivers (economic subregions 1 and 2) to more than 3,800 m in the upper Humla and Mugu river drainages (economic subregions 8 and 9). Most, however, are located between 1,600 and 2,600 m above sea level (figure 41).

Village sites are determined not only by the location of farmland but also by the proximity to water, fuel wood, forests, and grazing grounds and by the aspect of the local terrain (i.e., the orientation and angle of slope). Solar insolation is of particular importance and all villages are situated to maximize the duration of sunlight they receive. Wherever possible, southern

---

(1977). Geographers have long been concerned with the location, distribution, and pattern density of human activities in relation to the scale of space and time. For a discussion of such scale and social interactions by a Himalayan anthropologist, see Berreman (1978).

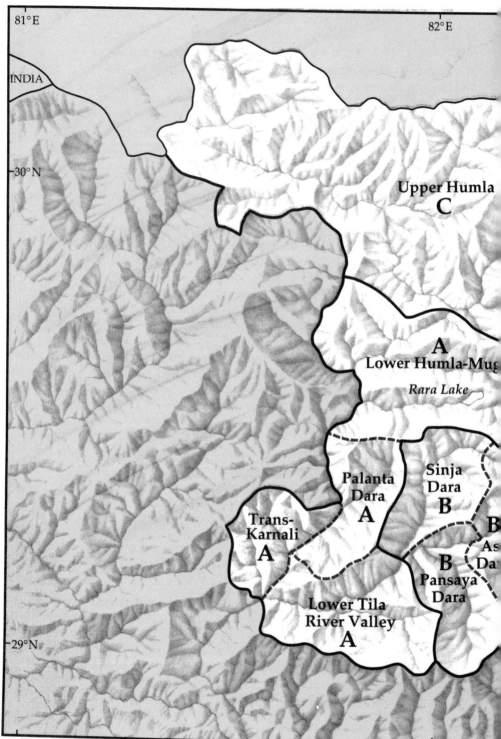

Fig. 43. *Map of economic regions and subregions of Karnali Zone*

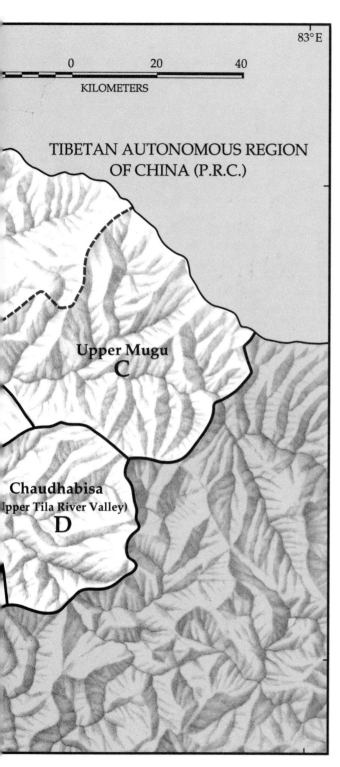

83°E

0   20   40

KILOMETERS

TIBETAN AUTONOMOUS REGION
OF CHINA (P.R.C.)

Upper Mugu
C

Chaudhabisa
(Upper Tila River Valley)
D

Regions

Region A
51 Panchayats (P)
333 Villages (V)
Trans-Karnali (9P &78V)
Sanni Dara
Raskot Dara

**Lower Tila River Valley
(11P &67V)**
Kalikot Dara
Barabisa Dara
Rakala Dara

Palanta Dara (7P & 36V)

**Lower Humla-Mugu
(24P & 152V)**
Khatyad Dara
Gama (Gum) Dara
Galpha Dara
Soru Dara

Region B
24 Panchayats
165 Villages
**Sinja Dara
(10P& 73V)**

**Pansaya Dara
(9P & 61V)**

**Asi Dara-Kalanga
(5P & 31V)**

Region C
16 Panchayats
129 Villages
Upper Humla (13P & 113V)
Humla Dara

Upper Mugu (3P & 16V)
Mugu Dara
Karana Dara

Region D
3 Panchayats
27 Villages
**Chaudhabisa
(Upper Tila River Valley)**
Chaudhabisa Dara

Key
P - Panchayat(s)
V - Village (s)

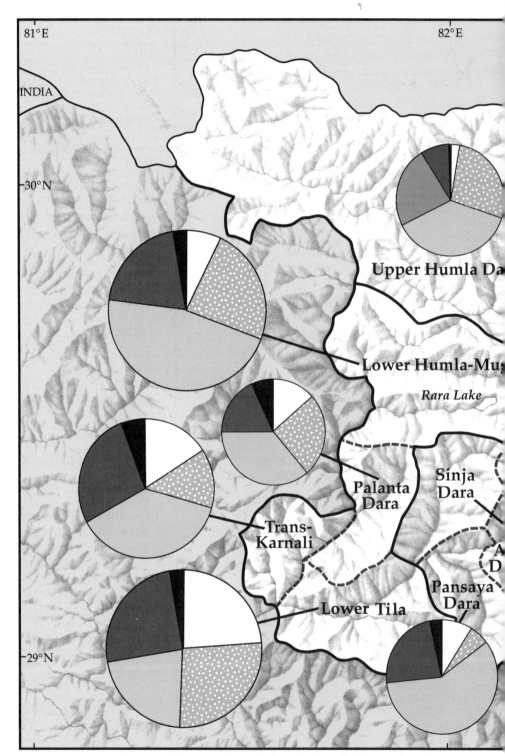

81°E

82°E

INDIA

30°N

Upper Humla Da

Lower Humla-Mu;

Rara Lake

Palanta
Dara

Sinja
Dara

A
D

Trans-
Karnali

Pansaya
Dara

Lower Tila

29°N

Fig. 44. Map of size and castes of population in Karnali Zone subregions

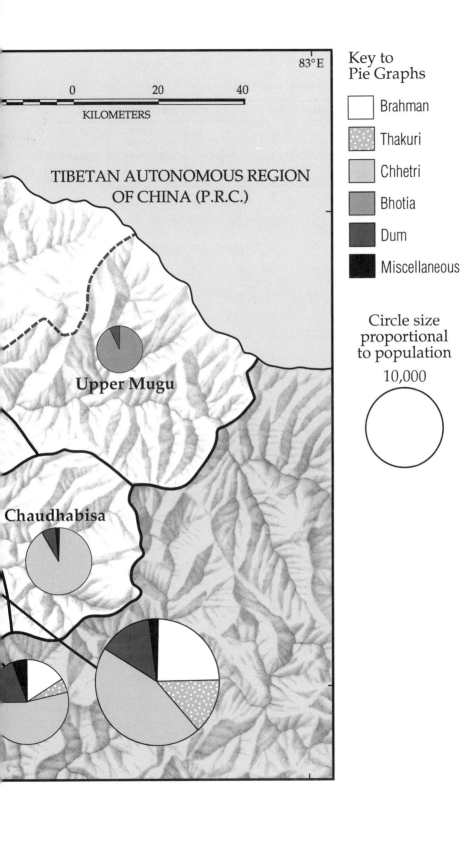

83°E

Key to
Pie Graphs

Brahman

Thakuri

Chhetri

Bhotia

Dum

Miscellaneous

Circle size
proportional
to population

10,000

0   20   40
KILOMETERS

TIBETAN AUTONOMOUS REGION
OF CHINA (P.R.C.)

Upper Mugu

Chaudhabisa

TABLE 6. Land cover in 2026 V.S. (1969-70).

Region	Area in km^2 (% of zone)	Above 4,500 m Alpine		Below 4,500 m Forest		Meadow, wasteland, and water		Farmland	
		km^2	%	km^2	%	km^2	%	km^2	%
Karnali Zone	13,200 (100.0)	2,747	21	5,478	42	4,825	37	149.6	1.1
Jumla District	2,817 (21.3)	nil	nil	1,838	65	925	33	54.0	1.9
Mugu District	2,992 (22.7)	1,209	40	843	28	907	30	33.0	1.1
Humla District	6,004 (45.5)	1,251	21	2,231	37	2,667	41	55.5	0.9
Tibrikot District	1,387 (10.5)	287	21	567	41	526	38	7.2	0.5
Region A	3,823 (29.0)	173	5	2,583	68	992	26	75.5	2.0
Trans-Karnali	390 (3.0)	—	—	302	77	75	19	12.7	3.3
Southwest Jumla	860 (6.5)	—	—	603	70	244	28	12.9	1.5
Palanta Dara	386 (2.9)	—	—	309	80	71	18	5.7	1.5
Lower Humla-Mugu	2,188 (16.6)	173	8	1,369	63	602	28	44.2	2.0
Region B	1,462 (11.1)	12	3	771	53	655	45	24.4	1.7
Sinja Dara	498 (3.8)	—	—	297	58	194	39	7.3	1.5
Pansaya Dara	545 (4.1)	nil	nil	276	51	258	47	11.5	2.1
Asi Dara–Kalanga	418 (3.2)	12	3	198	47	203	49	5.6	1.3
Region C	6,808 (51.6)	2,287	34	1,705	25	2,772	41	44.2	0.6
Upper Humla	4,726 (35.8)	1,093	23	1,578	33	2,014	43	40.4	0.9
Upper Mugu	2,082 (15.8)	1,194	58	127	6	758	36	3.8	0.2
Region D Chaudhabisa/ Upper Tila	1,107 (8.4)	276	25	420	38	406	37	5.5	0.5

SOURCES: Survey of India maps (1:50,000 scale); Army Map Service maps (1:250,000 scale); Government of Nepal revenue and land reform survey records.

exposures are sought, but the entrenched dendritic drainage of the zone precludes this orientation as a consistent pattern. In some secondary and tertiary valleys north-facing slopes receive as much exposure to the sun as south-facing slopes because of the lie of the land and the height and trend of nearby ridges. Moreover, east-facing slopes are preferable to west-facing ones as village sites; the morning sun is more reliable, owing to the orographically induced afternoon accumulation of cloud. In addition, villages are almost universally located where they do not occupy land that can be used for growing major food grains.[2] Whenever possible they are also located above prime agricultural land in order to facilitate the transport of manure from farmstead to field.

Fig. 45. The hillside village of Srinagar in Gama Dara (lower Humla-Mugu, economic region A). Popularly referred to as Gum, this large, flat-roofed Pahari community is the headquarters for Mugu District.

Hence, according to local environmental factors, Karnali's villages are loosely to tightly clustered settlements located either in the lower valleys along the break in slope where alluvial terraces or fans abut adjacent hillsides (frontispiece) or on upland slopes (figure 45) and promontories. Those

---

2   During the Rana regime some villages were even relocated, by order from Kathmandu, to bring more farmland into production.

at lower levels on flat or gently sloping ground are usually older and more compact. They generally exhibit a circular or elliptic form and a uniform density of houses to the village periphery where fields begin abruptly. Except for some compact Bhotia villages, those at higher elevations are more scattered or dispersed. They commonly are arranged in a linear pattern, either horizontally along the contour of a slope or vertically on a ridge spur, or in depressions or draws. Some no doubt reflect their fieldhouse origin and subsequent satellite village development.

Both the morphology of the villages and the design of the homes they comprise are expressions not only of the local physical environment but of cultural habitat, historical events and political controls, status and wealth, social, religious, and economic functions, and caste composition. Pahari villages predominate and are composed of one or more clean castes. Some, but not all, also contain a few Dum households. Other villages consist entirely of Dum. Within any multicaste village, a family's status dictates its house site, which is sanctioned, even selected, by a Brahman priest. Ideally the higher the caste the higher and more choice the home location. Dum houses are generally the lowest and most removed in a village (figure 35). However, the degree of spatial separation of caste house groupings in a village varies, not only according to degree of orthodoxy of its dominant families but also according to its physical conditions and limitations at the site. For example, in the Matwali Chhetri and Dum village of Talphi in the Chaudhabisa Valley (economic subregion 10) the Dum houses were originally on the village periphery. However, as the Matwali Chhetri expanded, their houses came to surround the Dum, who now occupy the village center. In all villages the individual houses or house complexes are separated to permit space for kitchen gardens, to avoid pollution from sweepings, to prevent a chain collapse of dwellings, and to reduce the possibility of fire spreading, always a concern. In January 1970 an unattended hearth fire in Mangri, a tightly-packed Bhotia community in upper Mugu, spread rapidly and destroyed over one-third of the village (figure 46).

The styles of houses in Karnali display not only striking regional differences but considerable variation in design and quality and technique of construction. In the exclusively Pahari lower southwestern reaches of the zone (trans-Karnali and lower Tila), the homes in most villages are similar to those in Kumaon (figure 47). They are detached or separated rectangular dwellings with plastered stone and mortar walls and steeply pitched roofs of straw, wooden shingles, or occasionally, in the case of wealthy families, slate. Most have two levels, the lower one a *goth*, or stable, used for winter quartering of livestock and the upper one used for living and storage. The space between the eaves is also used for storage. More affluent families may have three-storied houses with two living levels. They occupy the lower one (above the stable) during the winter to take advantage of the heat gener-

Fig. 46. A fire-damaged portion of Mangri, a Bhotia village in upper Mugu (economic region C). Construction of the homes is exposed by the various stages of repair. Note the Buddhist chortens and ghompa (temple) on the hillside beyond.

ated by their animals; the upper one they use during the summer. Dum houses are generally of one story, partitioned for both human and animal use. In front of all homes is a flat courtyard of flagstone or earth on which agricultural products are processed. Windows are usually small and few to conserve heat, and house interiors are not only dark but smokey, since chimneys are not used. House size and solidity, furnishings, and the presence and quality of a veranda or carved wooden casements and beams are indicators of family status.[3]

However, the majority of Pahari villages in Karnali Zone—those at higher elevations in the north and east as well as those in the Bheri River corridor of Dolpo—display a house style that reflects strong Tibetan (Bhotia) influence and thus differs greatly from that just described. Its most distinctive feature is its flat roof, or *thāro,* of beam and boards,[4] supporting hard-packed earth that must be tamped periodically. Ideally suited to the semiarid conditions that prevail throughout most of this inner-mountain area, this roof design is unique among the hill-Hindu regions of the Himalaya.

Fig. 47. A pitched-roofed Pahari village in the lower Tila (economic region A)

The flat-roofed upland Pahari houses are also usually two- or three-storied, with each level used in a manner identical to those in homes of southwest Karnali. On steep terrain they are built in tiers against the slope (figure 45). At these sites additional storage levels of less sturdy construc-

---

[3]   For a detailed discussion of Pahari houses in the Indian Himalaya, of which this type is a variant, see Andress (1966:46-72).

[4]   *Salo (Pinus excelsa)* is the most commonly used wood for house construction in the zone, although *chir (Pinus roxburghii)* or cedar *(Cedrus deodara)* are preferred for their fire and deterioration resistant qualities. However, today these species are usually either absent or scarce because of many centuries of human exploitation. Special permits from district officials are now required before any live timber may be felled for any purpose, including home building.

Fig. 48. A multifamily, semidetached rowhouse complex with common roofs in Chhapru, a Chhetri village on the northern shore of Lake Rara (Gama Dara). © National Geographic Society.

tion are often added, extending the house further up the hillside (figure 48). The flat roof of the bottom story *goth* normally functions as a porch or veranda for the living level; the *thāro* of the living level constitutes the principal food-processing area. Access between stories is afforded by external log ladders.

While some prosperous and/or high caste families have homes that are detached and separated from their neighbors, it is more typical for a number of families of a single caste, and usually of the same extended lineage, to live in a semidetached rowhouse complex and thus share common roofs. Each family thus occupies a vertical section or unit of the large rectangular structure that is considerably more dark and prone to smoke than the single-family dwellings already discussed. Dum also often live in such structures. Such multifamily complexes are another striking and unique feature of Karnali's cultural landscape that contrasts with all other Pahari regions.

The cost of building a house in Karnali varies between 50 and 500 $U.S. and is a major, if infrequent (every twenty-five to fifty years), family expense. A carpenter-mason from the occupational castes is contracted to provide expertise and direction, while the bulk of the common labor is generally furnished by men and women from other families in the village on a reciprocal or exchange basis. These neighbors are provided their meals for the days they participate in the cooperative building project. The completion of the house, which requires from one to five months to erect, is celebrated with a feast, and the new dwelling is sanctified with a special *puja*, or religious rite.

LANDHOLDINGS AND THE CASTE HIERARCHY

Karnali Zone, with a population of 14.1 per km^2 of total area, is the least densely populated zone of Nepal. This statistic, however, obscures ecological, and therefore economic, reality, for rugged terrain and harsh climate result in a dearth of land suitable for farming. Only 1.13 percent of the area is presently used for agriculture, the principal livelihood pursuit of the great majority of the populace. It is, then, much more pertinent to view population density in relation to arable area. The statistics presented in table 7 both bring this reality into focus and indicate interregional and intraregional differences in conditions. Data on Nepal and its major altitudinal/latitudinal belts are also included in order to permit a national perspective against which Karnali Zone can be compared.

More than 60 percent of Nepal's population live in the hills and mountains, which contain only about one-third of the country's farmland; less than 40 percent of the population live in the Tarai and inner Tarai lowland, where two-thirds of the arable land is located. Lowland population densities average 320 per km^2. In Karnali Zone, which makes up 19 percent of the total area in the western highlands but contains only 4.4 percent of their arable land, the population density is a staggering 1,243 per km^2, compared with an average figure for all of Nepal of 584.6 per km^2. Within the zone itself these densities vary considerably, from 413 in upper Humla (41 percent higher than that in the Tarai to the south) to 3,091 in Sinja Dara (over 950 percent greater than that in the western Tarai).

Of the 150 km^2 of arable land in Karnali, less than 21 km^2 (13.8 percent) is seasonally or perennially irrigated *khet* land on which paddy can be grown and double cropping of major cereal grains in a summer-winter (*kharif-rabi*) sequence is generally possible. Almost all of the Karnali *khet* (96.9 percent) is unevenly distributed in economic regions A and B. In these regions live 85 percent of the zone's populace, an indication of the close correlation that exists between population density and farmland quality (as measured by superior *khet* versus inferior, unirrigated *pakho* on which paddy cannot be grown).

It is important to note that estimates of the total irrigated arable land in all of Nepal (ca. 1969-70) range from 9.9 to about 12 percent (Chapagain 1976; Amatya 1975). There is, however, general agreement that almost three-quarters of the country's irrigated area lies in Tarai and inner Tarai districts where it seldom constitutes over 20 percent of the total cultivated land. Because of flat or gentle gradients and higher summer rainfall in these lowlands, paddy production is not limited to irrigated fields as it is in the highlands and is grown on more than 70 percent of the total arable land (Nepal 1972:26-42).[5]

These statistics indicate both the importance and the paucity of *khet* in the highlands. Thanks to a combination of environmental conditions, along with protracted human occupance and associated construction of both terraces and irrigation channels, Karnali Zone contains a relatively high proportion of *khet*. Yet, here too, the availability of land that can be irrigated is limited, as the data in table 8 illustrate. Over the past century (1868-1968) *khet* has been increased 54.9 percent (see figure 40), thus raising the average population density per hectare of *khet* from fifty-four to ninety (i.e., 9,000/km^2). This condition makes an increasing demand on the growing population to expand their arable land in upland areas that are suitable only as agriculturally marginal *pakho*.

Differential access to any of Karnali Zone's meager resources, but particularly to its scarce arable land and possession of the small proportion that is superior *khet*, has long determined and, conversely, has long been determined by, caste status. The information presented in table 9, a census of landholdings by caste, is derived from raw data recently collected by land reform survey teams. They clearly show the relationships between location, quantity, and quality of farmland, and caste/ethnic group distribution and density; the importance of cropland to economic rank as measured by caste

---

5   David Grigg points out that in the monsoon countries of South Asia irrigation is necessary where rainfall is less than 1,000-1,150 mm and desirable where it is less than 1,250-1,400 mm; it is also necessary for double cropping where rainfall is less than 1,500-1,650 mm (1970:260).

TABLE 7. Population vis-à-vis total and cultivated area in 2026 V.S. (1969-70).

	Population and total area			Population and cultivated area								
Region	Pop. (% zone or Nepal)	km² (% zone or Nepal)	Pop./km²	Total cult. area (km²)	% of Region (% of zone or Nepal)	Pop/km² total cult.	Km² irrigated[a]	% of Region (% of total cult.)	Pop./km² irrigated	Km² not irrigated[b]	% of Region (% of total cult.)	Pop./km² not irrigated
Karnali Zone	185,994 (100)	13,200 (100)	14.1	149.6	100.0 (1.13)	1,243	20.59	13.8 (13.8)	9,040	129.01	86.2 (86.2)	1,440
Jumla District	123,485 (66.4)	2,817 (21.3)	43.8	54.0	36.1 (0.41)	2,287	16.14	29.9 (10.8)	7,650	37.87	70.1 (25.3)	3,260
Mugu District	24,761 (13.3)	2,992 (22.7)	8.3	33.0	22.1 (0.25)	750	1.67	5.1 (1.2)	14,870	31.29	94.9 (20.9)	790
Humla District	27,847 (15.0)	6,004 (45.8)	4.6	55.5	37.0 (0.42)	502	1.63	2.9 (1.0)	17,080	53.82	97.1 (36.0)	520
Tibrikot District	9,903 (5.3)	1,387 (10.5)	7.1	7.2	4.8 (0.05)	1,375	1.15	16.0 (0.8)	8,610	6.62	84.0 (4.0)	1,640
Region A	107,246 (57.7)	3,823 (29.0)	28.1	75.5	50.5 (0.57)	1,420	11.68	15.5 (7.8)	9,180	63.94	84.5 (42.7)	1,680
Trans-Karnali	25,647 (13.8)	390 (3.0)	65.8	12.7	8.5 (0.10)	2,019	3.91	30.7 (2.6)	6,560	8.81	69.3 (5.9)	2,910
Lower Tila	33,413 (18.0)	860 (6.5)	38.9	12.9	8.6 (0.10)	2,590	3.54	27.5 (2.4)	9,440	9.31	72.5 (6.2)	3,590

SETTLEMENTS, LAND, AND LABOR 173

Palanta Dara	16,074 (8.6)	386 (2.9)	41.7	5.7	3.8 (0.04)	2,820	1.37	24.0 (0.9)	11,700	4.44	76.0 (3.0)	3,620
Lower Humla-Mugu	32,112 (17.3)	2,188 (16.6)	14.7	44.2	29.5 (0.33)	727	2.86	6.5 (1.9)	11,240	41.37	93.5 (27.7)	780
Region B	51,253 (27.6)	1,462 (11.1)	35.1	24.4	16.3 (0.18)	2,101	8.21	33.7 (5.5)	6,240	16.20	66.3 (10.8)	3,160
Sinja Dara	22,561 (12.1)	498 (3.8)	45.3	7.3	4.9 (0.05)	3,091	3.13	42.8 (2.1)	7,210	4.19	57.2 (2.8)	5,390
Pansaya Dara	17,911 (9.6)	545 (4.1)	32.9	11.5	7.7 (0.09)	1,557	2.30	19.9 (1.5)	7,780	9.23	80.1 (6.2)	1,940
Asi Dara	10,781 (5.8)	418 (3.2)	25.8	5.6	3.7 (0.04)	1,925	2.78	50.1 (1.9)	3,880	2.78	49.9 (1.9)	3,890
Region C	20,495 (11.0)	6,808 (51.6)	3.0	44.2	29.5 (0.33)	464	0.44	1.0 (0.3)	46,740	43.74	99.0 (29.2)	470
Upper Humla	16,676 (4.0)	4,726 (35.8)	3.5	40.4	27.0 (0.31)	413	0.44	1.1 (0.3)	28,030	39.93	98.9 (26.7)	420
Upper Mugu	3,819 (2.0)	2,082 (15.8)	1.8	3.8	2.5 (0.02)	1,005	—	—	—	3.81	100.0 (2.5)	1,010
Region D Chaudhabisa/ Upper Tila	1,000 (3.8)	1,108 (8.4)	6.3	5.5	3.7 (0.04)	1,273	0.25	4.6 (0.2)	27,520	5.23	95.4 (3.5)	1,340

(TABLE 7 continued)

Region	Population and total area			Population and cultivated area								
	Pop. (% zone or Nepal)	km² (% zone or Nepal)	Pop./km²	Total cult. area (km²)	% of Region (% of zone or Nepal)	Pop./km² total cult.	Km² irri-gated[a]	% of Region (% of total cult.)	Pop./km² irrigated	Km² not irri-gated[b]	% of Region (% of total cult.)	Pop./km² not irrigated
Nepal[c]	11,289* (100.0)	142,080 (100.0)	79.5	19,309	100 (13.6)	584.6	1,902	9.9 (9.9)	5,935	17,407	90.0 (90.1)	649
Western Hills and Mountains	3,610* (32.0)	68,900 (48.5)	52.4	3,094	16.0 (2.2)	1,166.8	196	6.3 (1.0)	18,418	2,898	93.7 (15.0)	1,246
E. Hills and mts. (incl. Kathmandu Valley)	3,390* (30.0)	40,510 (28.5)	83.7	3,241	16.8 (2.3)	1,046.0	28.4	8.8 (1.5)	11,936	2,957	91.2 (15.3)	1,146
Western Tarai	1,223* (10.8)	15,540 (10.9)	78.7	4,177	21.6 (2.9)	292.8	381	9.1 (2.0)	3,209	3,796	90.9 (19.6)	322
Eastern Tarai	3,066* (27.2)	17,130 (12.1)	179.0	8,797	45.6 (6.2)	348.5	1,041	11.8 (5.4)	2,945	7,756	88.2 (40.2)	395

a *Khet* in Karnali Zone
b *Pakho* in Karnali Zone
c Information for Nepal derived from D. P. Chapagain (1976)
* In thousands

TABLE 8. Increase in population and *khet* farmland, 1868-1968.ᵃ

Region	*Khet* (in hectares)			Population			Population/hectare			M² of *khet*/capita	
	1868	1968	Increase	1868	1968	Increase	1868	1968	Increase	1868	1968
Karnali Zone	1,328.9	2,058.6	54.9%	71,900	186,000	159.0%	54.1	90.4	67.1%	185	111
Jumla District	1,015.9	1,614.0	58.9	44,000	123,500	181.0	43.3	76.5	76.7	231	131
Mugu District	138.3	166.5	20.4	11,500	24,800	116.0	83.2	148.9	79.0	120	67
Humla District	113.2	163.1	44.1	12,600	27,800	117.0	113.1	170.4	51.5	88	59
Tibrikot District	61.5	115.0	87.0	3,600	9,900	175.0	58.5	86.1	47.2	171	116
Region A	693.5	1,168.2	68.4	38,900	107,200	175.6	56.1	91.8	63.6	178	109
Trans-Karnali	156.9	391.0	149.2	7,700	25,600	232.5	49.1	65.5	33.4	204	153
Lower Tila	241.4	354.1	46.7	11,200	33,400	198.2	46.4	94.3	103.2	216	106
Palanta Dara	95.7	137.3	43.5	5,900	16,100	172.9	61.7	117.3	90.1	162	85
Lower Humla-Mugu	198.8	285.8	43.8	14,100	32,100	127.7	70.9	112.3	58.4	141	89
Region B	574.2	821.1	43.0	20,400	51,300	151.5	35.5	62.5	76.1	281	160
Sinja Dara	233.6	312.9	33.9	9,700	22,600	133.0	41.5	72.2	74.0	241	138
Pansaya Dara	158.6	230.1	45.1	6,300	17,900	184.1	39.7	77.8	96.0	252	129
Asi Dara–Kalanga	182.0	278.1	52.8	4,400	10,800	145.5	24.2	38.8	60.3	414	258
Region C	52.0	43.9	-16.0	10,200	20,500	101.0	196.2	467.0	138.0	51	21
Upper Humla	52.0	43.9	-16.0	8,300	16,700	101.2	159.6	380.4	138.3	63	26
Upper Mugu	—	—	—	1,900	3,800	100.0	—	—	—	—	—
Region D Chaudhabisa/ Upper Tila	9.9	25.4	156.6	2,400	7,000	191.7	242.4	275.6	13.7	41	36

ᵃ Derived from Revenue Office records.

TABLE 9. Census of landholdings by caste, 2026 V.S. (1969-70).

Region	Number of homes	Population		Landholdings (ha)					
		Number	%	Khet	%	Pakho	%	Total	%
Karnali Zone									
Brahman	4,625	25,957	14.0	586	28.5	968	7.5	1,554	10.4
Thakuri	5,672	33,499	18.0	471	22.9	2,687	20.8	3,158	21.1
Chhetri	12,643	76,392	41.1	752	36.5	6,383	49.5	7,135	47.7
Bhotia	1,392	7,607	4.1	nil	—	1,415	11.0	1,415	9.5
Dum	5,711	36,325	19.5	171	8.3	1,188	9.2	1,359	9.1
Misc.	1,036	6,216	3.3	79	3.8	261	2.0	340	2.3
Total	31,079	185,996	100.0	2,059	100.0	12,901	100.0	14,959	100.0
Jumla District									
Brahman	3,957	22,381	18.1	489	30.3	650	17.2	1,139	21.1
Thakuri	3,427	21,031	17.0	340	21.0	695	18.4	1,035	19.2
Chhetri	7,542	48,004	39.0	571	35.4	1,812	47.9	2,383	44.1
Bhotia	—	—	—	—	—	—	—	—	—
Dum	4,132	27,082	21.9	148	9.2	519	13.7	667	12.3
Misc.	783	4,987	4.0	67	4.1	110	2.9	177	3.3
Total	19,841	123,485	100.0	1,614	100.0	3,787	100.0	5,401	100.0
Mugu District									
Brahman	208	1,074	4.3	28	17.0	106	3.4	134	4.0
Thakuri	842	5,159	20.8	66	39.6	599	19.1	665	20.2
Chhetri	1,888	9,823	39.7	60	36.1	1,597	51.0	1,657	50.3
Bhotia	721	3,631	14.7	nil	—	378	12.1	378	11.5
Dum	809	4,673	18.9	8	5.0	408	13.0	416	12.6
Misc.	81	401	1.6	4	2.3	42	1.4	46	1.4
Total	4,549	24,761	100.0	166	100.0	3,130	100.0	3,296	100.0
Humla District									
Brahman	312	1,734	6.2	33	20.0	190	3.5	223	4.0
Thakuri	1,347	6,993	25.1	58	35.8	1,384	25.7	1,442	26.0
Chhetri	2,190	11,118	39.9	62	38.0	2,443	45.4	2,505	45.2
Bhotia	665	3,940	14.2	nil	—	1,036	19.2	1,036	18.7
Dum	610	3,499	12.6	7	4.2	235	4.4	242	4.3
Misc.	130	563	2.0	3	2.0	95	18	98	1.8
Total	5,254	27,847	100.0	163	100.0	5,382	100.0	5,546	100.0
Tibrikot District									
Brahman	148	768	7.7	36	31.3	22	3.6	58	8.1
Thakuri	56	315	3.2	7	6.2	9	1.4	16	2.2
Chhetri	1,023	7,447	75.2	59	51.3	531	88.2	589	82.2
Bhotia	6	36	0.4	—	—	1	0.2	7	0.1
Dum	160	1,071	10.8	8	6.9	27	4.4	35	4.8
Misc.	42	265	2.7	5	4.3	14	2.2	19	2.6
Total	1,435	9,902	100.0	115	100.0	604	100.0	724	100.0

...ulation/hectare			Rank by land-holding			Number of plots			Plots/hectare			Average plot size (m²)		
	Pakho	Total	K	R	T	*Khet*	*Pakho*	Total	*Khet*	*Pakho*	Total	*Khet*	*Pakho*	Total
.3	26.8	16.7	1	5	4	45,808	25,592	71,400	78	26	46	128	379	217
.1	12.5	10.6	2	3	2	38,417	40,923	79,340	82	15	25	123	658	398
.6	12.0	10.7	4	2	3	75,915	162,327	243,242	101	26	34	99	382	293
—	5.4	5.4	—	1	1	9	16,063	16,072	450	11	11	22	877	877
.7	30.6	26.7	5	6	6	13,998	26,248	40,246	82	22	30	122	453	338
.8	23.8	18.3	3	4	5	5,515	5,699	11,214	70	22	33	143	459	303
.3	14.4	12.4	—	—	—	179,662	281,852	461,514	87	22	31	115	455	333
.8	34.4	19.6	1	3	1	38,329	20,581	58,910	78	32	52	128	317	193
.9	30.3	20.3	2	2	3	26,630	19,500	46,130	78	28	45	128	356	224
.1	26.5	20.1	4	1	2	56,300	74,196	130,496	99	41	55	101	245	183
—	—	—	—	—	—	—	—	—	—	—	—	—	—	—
.1	52.2	40.6	5	5	5	11,452	16,562	28,014	77	32	42	129	314	238
.7	45.2	28.2	3	4	4	4,510	3,351	7,861	68	30	44	148	329	225
.5	32.6	22.9	—	—	—	137,221	134,190	271,441	85	35	50	118	286	200
.8	10.2	8.0	1	5	3	2,241	1,015	3,256	79	10	24	127	1,042	412
.3	8.6	7.8	2	2	2	6,133	5,303	11,436	93	9	17	108	1,224	581
.3	6.2	5.9	4	1	1	6,492	18,701	25,193	108	12	15	93	855	658
	9.6	9.6	—	4	5	4	3,273	3,277	400	9	9	25	1,149	1,149
.7	11.5	11.2	5	6	6	970	4,003	4,973	117	10	12	85	1,020	833
.0	9.5	8.7	3	3	4	359	511	870	94	12	19	106	826	529
.7	7.9	7.5	—	—	—	16,199	32,806	49,005	97	11	15	103	1,000	667
.2	9.1	15.5	1	5	6	3,450	3,836	6,286	106	15	28	945	667	353
.6	5.1	4.8	2	3	3	5,051	15,760	20,811	86	11	14	116	877	694
.2	4.6	4.4	4	2	2	8,124	34,926	43,050	131	14	17	76	699	581
	3.8	3.8	—	1	1	5	12,723	12,728	500	12	12	20	813	813
.8	14.9	14.5	5	6	5	568	3,547	4,115	86	15	17	117	662	585
.1	5.9	5.7	3	4	4	297	1,190	1,487	89	13	15	112	800	662
.8	5.2	5.0	—	—	—	17,495	70,982	88,477	107	13	16	94	769	625
.3	35.1	13.3	1	3	2	1,788	1,160	2,948	50	53	51	202	189	197
.0	36.3	19.9	2	4	4	603	360	963	84	41	61	119	243	165
.5	14.0	12.6	4	1	1	4,999	39,504	44,503	85	74	76	118	134	133
	39.1	39.1	—	5	6	—	67	67	—	73	73	—	137	137
.2	40.3	31.0	5	6	5	1,008	2,136	3,144	126	80	91	79	125	110
.0	19.6	14.3	3	2	3	349	647	996	70	48	54	143	209	186
.1	16.4	13.8	—	—	—	8,747	43,874	52,621	76	73	73	132	137	137

(TABLE 9 *continued*)

Region	Number of homes	Population		Landholdings (ha)					
		Number	%	Khet	%	Pakho	%	Total	%
Region A									
Brahman	2,683	16,603	15.5	290	24.8	785	12.3	1,075	14
Thakuri	3,867	24,179	22.5	374	32.0	1,539	24.1	1,913	25
Chhetri	6,042	37,311	34.8	357	30.5	2,990	46.8	3,348	44
Bhotia	16	85	0.1	—	—	15	0.2	15	0
Dum	3,581	24,817	23.1	107	9.2	874	13.7	981	13
Misc.	678	4,257	4.0	40	3.4	180	2.8	220	2
Total	16,869	107,252	100.0	1,169	100.0	6,383	100.0	7,552	100
Trans-Karnali									
Brahman	567	4,087	15.9	113	20.0	150	17.0	263	20
Thakuri	483	3,553	13.9	85	21.9	159	18.0	244	19
Chhetri	1,121	9,572	37.3	118	30.3	394	44.7	513	40
Bhotia	—	—	—	—	—	—	—	—	—
Dum	877	6,996	27.3	56	14.1	139	15.8	194	15
Misc.	197	1,439	5.6	18	4.7	39	4.5	58	4
Total	3,245	25,647	100.0	391	100.0	881	100.0	1,272	100
Lower Tila									
Brahman	1,290	7,953	23.8	102	28.9	311	33.4	413	32
Thakuri	1,400	9,004	26.9	134	37.7	277	29.8	411	32
Chhetri	1,174	7,194	21.5	83	23.5	154	16.5	237	18
Bhotia	—	—	—	—	—	—	—	—	—
Dum	1,095	8,366	25.0	30	8.5	164	17.6	194	15
Misc.	116	902	2.8	5	1.4	25	2.7	30	2
Total	5,077	33,413	100.0	354	100.0	931	100.0	1,285	100
Palanta Dara									
Brahman	393	2,214	13.8	20	14.5	90	20.7	110	19
Thakuri	689	4,048	25.2	50	36.6	125	28.9	175	30
Chhetri	894	5,796	36.1	51	37.1	142	32.7	193	33
Bhotia	—	—	—	—	—	—	—	—	—
Dum	482	2,935	18.2	7	4.8	58	13.3	65	11
Misc.	180	1,081	6.7	10	7.0	19	4.4	29	5
Total	2,638	16,074	100.0	138	100.0	434	100.0	572	100
Lower Humla-Mugu									
Brahman	433	2,349	7.3	55	19.1	234	5.7	289	6
Thakuri	1,295	7,574	23.6	105	36.7	978	23.6	1,083	24
Chhetri	2,853	14,749	45.9	105	36.8	2,300	55.5	2,405	54
Bhotia	16	85	nil	nil	—	15	0.4	15	0
Dum	1,127	6,520	20.3	14	4.9	513	124	527	11
Misc.	185	835	2.6	7	2.4	97	2.4	104	2
Total	5,909	32,112	100.0	286	100.0	4,137	100.0	4,423	100

pulation/hectare			Rank by land-holding			Number of plots			Plots/hectare			Average plot size (m²)		
et	Pakho	Total	K	R	T	Khet	Pakho	Total	Khet	Pakho	Total	Khet	Pakho	Total
7.3	21.1	15.4	1	4	4	18,508	12,546	31,054	64	16	29	156	625	345
4.6	15.7	12.6	2	3	3	26,660	22,201	48,861	71	14	26	141	714	385
4.5	12.5	11.1	3	2	2	30,713	47,455	78,168	86	16	23	116	625	435
—	5.7	5.7	—	1	1	4	59	63	—	4	4	—	2,500	2,500
1.9	28.4	25.3	5	6	6	5,580	13,254	18,834	52	15	19	192	667	526
6.4	23.7	19.4	4	5	5	2,229	3,203	5,432	56	18	25	179	556	400
1.8	16.8	14.2	—	—	—	83,694	98,717	182,411	72	15	24	139	667	417
6.1	27.3	15.4	1	3	3	4,480	3,340	7,820	40	22	30	252	448	337
1.6	22.3	14.3	2	1	1	2,230	2,668	4,898	26	17	20	383	595	500
0.9	24.3	18.7	4	2	2	4,009	7,582	11,591	34	19	23	295	521	443
—	—	—	—	—	—	—	—	—	—	—	—	—	—	—
5.6	50.4	36.0	5	5	5	2,130	3,185	5,315	38	23	27	262	435	366
9.1	36.4	24.9	3	4	4	680	925	1,605	37	23	28	267	427	360
5.6	29.1	20.2	—	—	—	13,529	17,700	31,229	35	20	25	286	500	400
7.8	25.6	19.3	2	1	1	8,357	5,803	14,160	82	19	34	122	535	292
7.4	32.5	21.9	1	2	2	12,887	6,020	18,907	97	22	46	104	461	217
8.4	46.7	30.3	3	3	3	11,586	10,137	21,723	139	66	92	72	152	109
6.8	50.9	43.0	5	5	5	1,526	3,567	5,093	51	22	26	198	461	382
4.5	36.0	30.2	4	4	4	99	308	407	21	12	14	485	813	735
4.4	35.9	26.0	—	—	—	34,455	25,834	60,289	97	28	47	103	357	213
1.3	24.7	20.2	2	1	1	1,557	725	2,282	78	8	21	128	1,235	481
0.5	32.4	23.1	1	2	2	2,813	3,537	6,350	56	28	36	179	353	276
3.8	40.8	30.0	4	3	3	4,720	2,322	7,042	93	16	37	108	614	274
—	—	—	—	—	—	—	—	—	—	—	—	—	—	—
0.7	50.7	45.4	5	4	5	543	979	1,522	81	17	24	123	592	424
3.0	56.2	37.5	3	5	4	821	785	1,606	86	41	56	117	245	180
7.0	37.1	28.1	—	—	—	10,454	8,348	18,802	76	19	33	132	526	303
3.0	10.0	8.1	1	5	5	4,114	2,678	6,792	75	11	24	133	877	426
2.1	7.7	7.0	2	3	3	8,730	9,976	18,706	83	10	17	120	980	578
0.2	6.4	6.1	4	2	2	10,398	27,414	37,812	99	12	16	10	840	637
0.0	5.8	5.8	6	1	1	4	59	63	400	4	4	25	250	2,326
5.0	12.7	12.4	5	6	6	1,381	5,523	6,904	99	11	13	102	926	763
1.2	8.6	8.0	3	4	4	629	1,185	1,814	91	12	17	110	820	575
2.4	7.8	7.3	—	—	—	25,256	46,835	72,091	88	11	16	114	909	625

(TABLE 9 *continued*)

Region	Number of homes	Population		Landholdings (ha)					
		Number	%	Khet	%	Pakho	%	Total	%
Region B									
Brahman	1,855	8,895	17.4	289	35.2	123	7.6	412	16
Thakuri	911	4,743	9.3	77	9.4	143	8.8	221	9
Chhetri	4,553	26,503	51.7	352	42.9	1,156	71.4	1,508	61
Bhotia	—	—	—	—	—	—	—	—	
Dum	1,780	9,400	18.4	63	7.7	168	10.4	231	9
Misc.	318	1,712	3.3	39	4.8	31	1.9	70	2
Total	9,417	51,253	100.0	821	100.0	1,620	100.0	2,441	100
Sinja Dara									
Brahman	1,124	5,469	24.2	143	45.6	54	12.9	197	26
Thakuri	635	3,193	14.2	45	14.6	116	27.8	162	22
Chhetri	1,761	10,229	45.3	100	32.0	215	51.4	315	43
Bhotia	—	—	—	—	—	—	—	—	
Dum	564	3,161	14.0	16	5.2	31	7.4	47	6
Misc.	101	509	2.3	8	2.6	2	0.5	10	1
Total	4,185	22,561	100.0	312	100.0	418	100.0	731	100
Pansaya Dara									
Brahman	354	1,673	9.3	61	26.6	25	2.7	86	7
Thakuri	182	987	5.5	18	7.6	13	1.4	31	2
Chhetri	1,865	10,484	58.5	115	50.1	789	85.4	904	78
Bhotia	—	—	—	—	—	—	—	—	
Dum	855	4,168	23.3	28	12.0	86	9.4	114	9
Misc.	117	599	3.4	9	3.7	11	1.2	20	1
Total	3,373	17,911	100.0	232	100.0	924	100.0	1,155	100
Asi Dara–Kalanga									
Brahman	377	1,753	16.3	85	30.7	44	15.7	129	23
Thakuri	94	563	5.2	14	5.1	13	4.8	27	4
Chhetri	927	5,790	53.7	137	49.4	152	54.6	289	52
Bhotia	—	—	—	—	—	—	—	—	
Dum	361	2,071	19.2	19	6.9	51	18.3	70	12
Misc.	100	604	5.6	22	7.9	18	6.6	40	7
Total	1,857	10,781	100.0	277	100.0	278	100.0	555	100
Region C									
Brahman	87	459	2.2	6	14.0	61	1.4	67	1.
Thakuri	894	4,578	22.3	19	44.2	1,005	23.0	1,024	23.
Chhetri	1,225	6,192	30.2	17	39.5	1,740	39.8	1,757	39.
Bhotia	1,370	7,486	36.5	—	—	1,399	32.0	1,399	31.
Dum	292	1,651	8.2	1	2.3	127	2.9	128	2.
Misc.	26	129	0.6	—	—	40	0.9	40	0.
Total	3,894	20,495	100.0	43	100.0	4,374	100.0	4,417	100.

Population/hectare			Rank by landholding			Number of plots			Plots/hectare			Average plot size (m²)		
Khet	Pakho	Total	K	R	T	Khet	Pakho	Total	Khet	Pakho	Total	Khet	Pakho	Total
0.8	72.3	21.6	1	5	3	25,723	11,873	37,596	89	97	91	112	103	110
1.6	33.2	21.5	3	2	2	9,303	7,635	16,938	121	53	77	83	189	130
5.3	22.9	17.6	4	1	1	37,833	55,804	93,637	107	48	62	93	208	161
—	—	—	–	–	–	—	—	—	—	—	—	—	—	—
9.2	56.0	40.7	5	4	5	8,130	9,532	17,662	129	57	76	78	175	132
3.9	55.2	24.5	2	3	4	3,227	1,526	4,753	83	49	68	120	204	147
2.4	31.6	21.0	–	–	–	84,216	86,370	170,586	103	53	70	97	189	143
8.3	101.3	27.8	1	3	2	16,282	7,084	23,366	114	131	119	88	76	84
9.8	27.5	19.7	3	1	1	6,941	5,491	12,432	152	47	77	66	211	130
2.2	47.5	32.4	4	2	3	16,587	22,139	38,726	166	103	123	60	97	81
—	—	—	–	–	–	—	—	—	—	—	—	—	—	—
5.5	101.4	66.8	5	4	5	3,156	2,944	6,100	195	95	129	51	106	78
2.0	249.5	49.7	2	5	4	1,332	334	1,666	162	164	163	62	61	62
2.1	53.9	30.8	–	–	–	44,298	37,992	82,290	142	91	113	70	110	89
7.3	68.1	19.5	1	4	2	4,584	1,950	6,534	75	79	76	134	126	131
6.3	72.2	32.4	2	5	4	1,468	1,507	2,975	84	116	98	120	86	103
0.9	13.3	11.6	4	1	1	14,320	20,201	34,521	124	26	38	81	391	262
—	—	—	–	–	–	—	—	—	—	—	—	—	—	—
1.4	48.2	36.6	5	2	5	3,352	4,061	7,413	122	47	65	82	213	154
0.3	56.0	31.2	3	3	3	1,182	457	1,639	139	43	85	72	234	117
7.8	19.4	15.5	–	–	–	24,906	28,176	53,082	108	31	46	93	323	217
0.5	40.2	13.6	2	3	1	4,857	2,839	7,696	57	65	60	176	154	168
9.7	42.3	20.5	3	5	4	894	637	1,531	63	48	56	159	209	180
2.1	38.2	20.0	4	2	3	6,926	13,464	20,390	50	89	71	198	113	142
—	—	—	–	–	–	—	—	—	—	—	—	—	—	—
7.5	40.8	29.6	5	4	5	1,622	2,527	4,149	84	50	59	119	201	169
7.4	32.9	15.0	1	1	2	713	735	1,448	32	40	36	309	249	279
3.9	38.9	19.4	–	–	–	15,012	20,202	35,214	54	73	63	185	137	159
76.5	7.5	6.9	1	5	5	1,577	1,173	2,750	263	19	41	38	526	244
40.9	4.6	4.5	2	3	3	2,454	11,087	13,541	129	11	13	78	909	769
64.2	3.6	3.5	3	2	2	4,218	26,213	30,431	248	15	17	40	667	588
—	5.4	5.4	–	4	4	5	15,937	15,942	—	11	11	—	909	909
51.0	13.0	12.9	4	6	6	157	2,027	2,184	157	16	17	64	625	588
—	3.2	3.2	–	1	1	27	516	543	—	13	13	—	769	769
76.6	4.7	4.6	–	–	–	8,438	56,953	65,391	196	13	15	51	769	667

(TABLE 9 *continued*)

Region	Number of homes	Population		Landholdings (ha)					
		Number	%	*Khet*	%	*Pakho*	%	Total	%
Upper Humla									
Brahman	87	459	2.8	6	14.4	61	1.5	68	1.7
Thakuri	894	4,578	27.5	19	44.2	1,005	25.2	1,025	25.4
Chhetri	1,225	6,192	37.1	17	38.8	1,740	43.6	1,757	43.5
Bhotia	665	3,940	23.6	nil	0.0	1,036	25.9	1,036	25.7
Dum	245	1,379	8.3	1	2.0	112	2.8	112	2.8
Misc.	25	128	0.8	nil	0.6	40	1.0	40	1.0
Total	3,141	16,676	100.0	43	100.0	3,994	100.0	4,038	100.0
Upper Mugu									
Brahman	—	—	—	—	—	—	—	—	—
Thakuri	—	—	—	—	—	—	—	—	—
Chhetri	—	—	—	—	—	—	—	—	—
Bhotia	705	3,546	92.9	—	—	363	95.4	363	95.4
Dum	47	272	7.1	—	—	17	4.6	17	4.6
Misc.	1	1		—	—	nil	—	nil	—
Total	753	3,819	100.0	—	—	380	100.0	380	100.0
Region D Chaudhabisa– Upper Tila									
Brahman	—	—	—	—	—	—	—	—	—
Thakuri	—	—	—	—	—	—	—	—	—
Chhetri	823	6,389	91.0	25	96.9	497	95.0	521	95.1
Bhotia	6	36	0.5	—	—	1	0.2	1	0.2
Dum	58	457	6.6	nil	1.5	16	3.1	17	3.0
Misc.	14	118	1.9	nil	1.6	9	1.7	9	1.7
Total	901	7,000	100.0	25	100.0	523	100.0	548	100.0

opulation/hectare			Rank by land-holding			Number of plots			Plots/hectare			Average plot size (m²)		
het	Pakho	Total	K	R	T	Khet	Pakho	Total	Khet	Pakho	Total	Khet	Pakho	Total
72.9	7.5	6.8	1	5	5	1,577	1,173	2,750	250	19	41	90	524	246
236.2	4.6	4.5	2	4	4	2,454	11,087	13,541	127	11	13	97	909	758
363.6	3.6	3.5	3	2	2	4,218	26,213	30,431	248	15	17	40	662	578
—	3.8	3.8	6	3	3	5	12,723	12,728	500	12	12	20	813	813
585.0	12.4	12.3	5	6	6	157	1,878	2,035	181	17	18	55	595	553
492.3	3.1	3.2	4	1	1	27	515	542	104	13	14	96	769	735
380.3	4.2	4.1	–	–	–	8,438	53,589	62,027	192	13	15	52	769	667
—	—	—	–	–	–	—	—	—	—	—	—	—	—	—
—	—	—	–	–	–	—	—	—	—	—	—	—	—	—
—	—	—	–	–	–	—	—	—	—	—	—	—	—	—
—	9.8	9.8	–	1	1	—	3,214	3,214	—	9	9	—	1,124	1,124
—	15.7	15.7	–	2	2	—	149	149	—	9	9	—	1,163	1,163
—	16.7	16.7	–	3	3	—	1	1	—	17	17	—	599	599
—	10.0	10.0	–	–	–	—	3,364	3,364	—	9	9	—	1,111	1,111
—	—	—	–	–	–	—	—	—	—	—	—	—	—	—
—	—	—	–	–	–	—	—	—	—	—	—	—	—	—
258.8	12.8	12.2	1	1	1	3,151	37,855	41,006	128	76	79	78	131	127
—	39.1	39.1	–	4	4	—	67	67	—	73	73	—	137	137
,203.0	28.2	27.6	3	3	3	131	1,435	1,566	34	89	95	29	113	106
29.5	13.1	12.6	2	2	2	32	454	486	80	50	52	125	198	193
2,748	13.4	12.8	–	–	–	3,314	39,811	43,125	130	76	79	77	131	128

population per hectare of *khet, pakho,* or total arable land (the lower the caste density, the higher the caste economic rank); the hierarchical arrangement of castes on the basis of quality or quantity of landholdings, and the close fit of this economic hierarchy with the interrelated and interdependent ritual and social hierarchies of the zone. The information also shows important regional variations and anomalies in economic status, which usually reflect historical events or ecological conditions.

The Brahman and Thakuri elite, while a numerical minority (14 and 18 percent of the zone's population respectively), hold 31.5 percent of the arable land and 51.4 percent of all *khet.* At zonal and district scales they always rank first and second in *khet* holdings if not in *pakho* or total holdings. At the economic regional and subregional scales their control of *khet* generally holds, although the order of rank is reversed in lower Tila and Palanta Dara. Moreover, the few families of the miscellaneous category rank second in Sinja Dara and the Chaudhabisa/upper Tila, and first in Asi Dara, where 50 percent of all arable land is *khet,* thus indicating the ability of these fairly recent immigrants to secure superior land.

The Brahmans' traditional dominance of high-quality holdings, as well as their continuing predilection for paddy, is further evidenced by the fact that their rank in terms of total arable land varies directly with the amount of *khet* present. In economic subregions where *khet* exceeds 20 percent of the total farmland, the Brahmans rank first in total holdings (the only exception is in the trans-Karnali region, where they rank third after Thakuri and Chhetri). In upper Humla and lower Humla-Mugu (with 1 percent and 6.5 percent *khet* respectively) they rank fifth. Where *khet* is inappreciable or absent (upper Mugu and the Chaudhabisa/upper Tila), the Brahmans do not live. These relationships, while not as pronounced, also are evident in the case of the Thakuri.

Chhetri comprise the largest portion of the population in Karnali Zone (41.1 percent) and are numerically dominant in all but two regions (lower Tila, where they are outnumbered by both Brahmans and Thakuri; and upper Mugu, where, like Brahmans and Thakuri, they do not reside). They command 47.7 percent of all arable land in the zone but only 36.5 percent of its *khet.* As a result the Chhetri always rank regionally beneath their Brahman and Thakuri neighbors (and usually beneath the miscellaneous caste category) on the basis of *khet* holdings. However, on the basis of *pakho* holdings they rank either first or second, except in lower Tila, where they rank third. This condition generally indicates the upland or peripheral location of most Chhetri holdings within each region. Only in the Chaudhabisa/upper Tila (economic region D), where they make up 91 percent of the population and are principally Matwali, are the Chhetri at the top of the landholding hierarchy.

The Dum occupationals, who make up 19.5 percent of Karnali's population, are an important labor force that is an integral part of the Pahari economic structure. Therefore, their regional distribution and density are directly proportional to the presence of *khet*, and 94.2 percent are found in economic areas A and B. In region C they are concentrated in the southern portion of upper Humla. It should be noted that those few Dum families in upper Mugu are, in fact, occupational Bhotia whose livelihood is in no way tied to the Pahari. Only in recent times (generally since 1951 and subsequent land reform) have most Dum been able to secure ownership rights to cropland. They now hold a mere 9.1 percent of the zone's total arable land and 8.3 percent of its *khet*. Everywhere they rank at the bottom of the landholding hierarchy, with over twice the population density on total arable land— and four to ten times the density on *khet*—of the highest ranking caste.

Of the Bhotia, who comprise only one twenty-fifth of the populace, 51.8 percent are concentrated in the most northern reaches of upper Humla, while 46.6 percent live in upper Mugu, where they constitute the sole caste group (the few Dum excepted). Thus confined to these harsh highlands, they hold no *khet* and only the poorest 11 percent of the zone's *pakho*. As a result they must make up in quantity what they lack in quality. This condition is reflected by the fact that they rank first at the zonal scale in both *pakho* and total holdings. Upper Humla not only is better suited than upper Mugu for agriculture but has more extensive arable land. There the Bhotia rank third in *pakho* holdings with a density of 3.8 per hectare. That they do not rank first is due to the most northern Pahari penetration in all of the Himalaya. On the other hand, in the exclusively Bhotia domain of upper Mugu—the zone's most arid and least agriculturally productive area—the population density per hectare of *pakho* is 10.

Throughout Karnali the degree of disparity (i.e., the range) in landholdings between and among castes is primarily a function of land quality. The greater the proportion of *khet* in a region, the wider the range between high- and low-ranking castes. Furthermore, the range is significantly greater when measured on the basis of *khet* than on the basis of either *pakho* or total (combined) holdings. Conversely, the more marginal a region is agriculturally (and therefore locationally), the more equitable the distribution of arable land among the castes present.

It follows, then, that a salient aspect of family holdings is their generally minuscule size, which varies considerably with caste. The average amount of cropland held by Karnali Zone's 31,000 families is less than half a hectare, and the average per capita holding only 0.08 (800 m²). Brahman families hold an average of 0.34 ha, but theirs is primarily *khet*. Thakuri and Chhetri households have an average of 0.56 ha, indicating a greater importance of *pakho*. Bhotia families' holdings average 1.02 ha, a reflection of their total reliance on *pakho*. And Dum families command an average of only 0.24 ha. Within each caste group holdings also vary greatly in size. Some elite Pahari households have as much as ten or more hectares. However, it is important to point out that it is not unusual for some enterprising and relatively affluent Dum families to hold more, if not better, land than poor Pahari households.

Fragmentation into a great number of small and discontinuous plots is a common feature of all landholdings. At the zonal scale there are eighty-seven plots per hectare of *khet* and twenty-two plots per hectare of *pakho*. Here again, as the data in table 9 indicate, interregional and intercaste variation is considerable. The principal cause of land fragmentation is the type of patrilineal inheritance, practiced by Pahari and Bhotia alike, by which all male heirs receive an equal share of each field. With every succeeding generation the number of plots per unit area increases. Other contributing, and interrelated, factors that govern the extent to which arable land is fragmented include land quality, slope gradients, the suitability for irrigation, and the degree of terracing needed—on both *khet* and *pakho* fields.

Pakho predominates in the higher, more remote, or more recently claimed sites and is divided into few plots. Thus in economic region C the average number of plots per hectare of *pakho* is 13; and there the Bhotia's land contains an average of only 11 parcels per hectare and 19.1 per family holding, perhaps owing in part to their frequent practice of polyandrous marriage. On the other hand, in regions A and B polygamous Pahari peasant families' smaller holdings are frequently made up of fifty to a hundred or more plots (table 9). These are widely dispersed, from kitchen gardens adjacent to their homes to fields a distance of several hours, or even days, of travel. Generally a family's principal fields lie within one hour's walk from its village.

ORGANIZATION AND ALLOCATION OF LABOR

The household is the basic economic unit within all Karnali communities. The ability of any family to generate its livelihood requirements, and the level of economic well-being it can attain, depend upon not only the quantity and quality of land and other natural resources it has at its disposal but also the manner and degree to which it can efficiently exploit those resources with the human labor—itself a resource—at its command.

For all but a very few resource-rich households who can rely totally on the labor of others, family labor is most critical. Household composition (the number, age, and sex of its members), structure (whether nuclear, or joint, or extended), and caste play important roles in determining how effectively a family's labor force can be marshalled and allocated over the yearly round. At the root of the matter is the total number of persons who must be fed, clothed, and housed, and the number who are available to help satisfy those needs (i.e., labor demands). Healthy adults constitute potentially fully productive family members; children above the age of eight or ten are partially productive members whose inputs are often important; the elderly or infirm, as well as young children, are generally unproductive. Therefore, the intensity of family labor that most households must generate in order to reach at least a subsistence level varies with the proportion of workers (fully and partially productive family members) to consumers (all family members).[6]

The information contained in table 10 indicates the division of tasks by sex within the family unit and the times when those tasks are carried out during the year. It is presented as an aggregate of the household labor organization and allocation that prevail in the thirty-five panchayats sampled in Karnali (Appendix G, figure 100) and illustrates a number of salient features and patterns common throughout the zone. However, it must be borne in mind that within the parameters of this composite variations do exist in the assignment of tasks by sex, the times during which those tasks are performed, and the number of tasks in which a family must, or is able to, engage. These variations at once reflect and result from a family's caste and associated ritual restrictions and obligations (table 5), its economic status, its location and the attendant environmental conditions it faces, and the particular mix of livelihood pursuits it follows.

Both men and women work long and hard to cope with the harsh conditions of their habitat. Shared tasks include firewood chopping, clothing repair, and the watering, feeding, and herding of animals when they are kept at or in the vicinity of the homestead. The greatest concentration of shared tasks occurs at planting and harvest times, when the intensive labor of men, women, and children is required; but the great majority of tasks are generally sex-specific and, as such, differ markedly in type, timespan, location, and therefore in mobility, regularity, and monotony.

Men build and maintain the home and outbuildings and repair agricultural implements, as well as card and spin wool and/or cotton, and knit woolen garments. Whereas Pahari men also weave (cotton cloth), this task is performed only by women in Bhotia families, who work exclusively with wool. Most of the men's time is spent in tasks that lie outside home maintenance and industry. They plow, harrow, and irrigate the fields, and when necessary build and maintain terraces (often aided by the common labor of the women as in home construction). Beyond the homestead and extended arable land, men manage livestock in the grazing grounds, collect herbs in the highlands, fish, engage in intraregional and long-range trade, and work

6   This rule was expounded by A. V. Chayanov (1966) in his theory of peasant economy, which he based on studies of late nineteenth- and early twentieth-century rural Russia. It has subsequently been applied in economic analyses of other agrarian societies.

TABLE 10. Division of labor by sex: principal tasks and times.

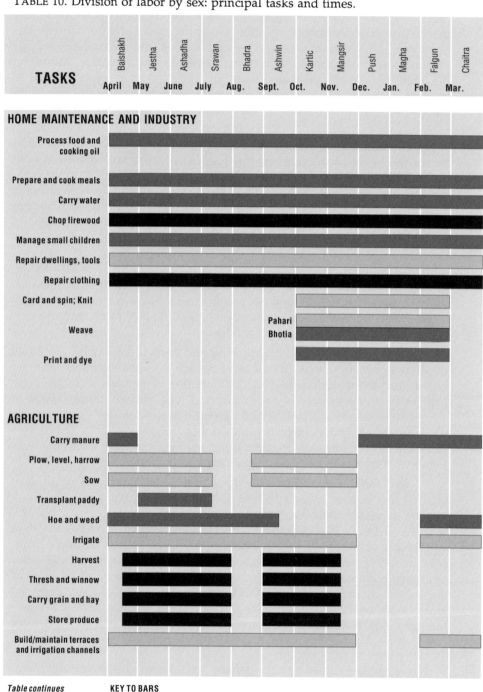

KEY TO BARS

Women only   Men only   Both Sexes

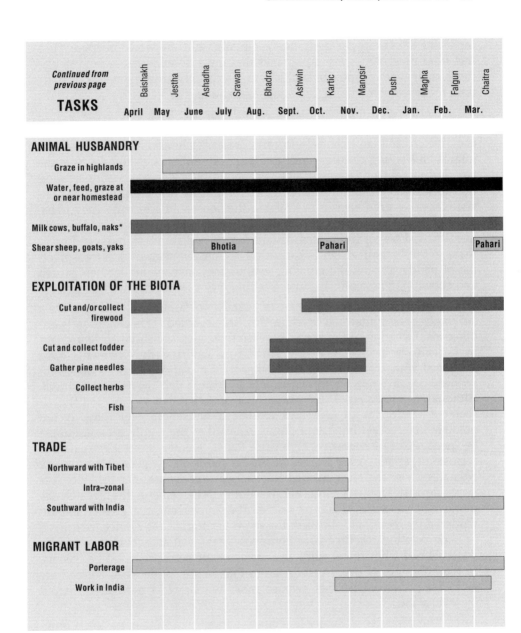

* A nak is a female yak.

as porters and migrant laborers abroad. Through all their endeavors, men represent the family vis-à-vis the community and the world beyond. Thus free from most time-consuming tasks that must be undertaken each day of the year by women, men generally have a strikingly greater amount of spare time for relaxation, talking, smoking, and sitting.

Women, on the other hand, are seldom idle from before dawn until after dark throughout the year. Each day they must process food, prepare and cook meals, milk and churn, and carry water. They also must tend to their infants and young children until the latter are old enough to take over the baby-sitting role with younger siblings and aid their elders generally. In addition to these tiresome diurnal homekeeping tasks women also are responsible for other arduous jobs essential to the household economy. They transport manure from home *goth* to the fields, collect firewood, fodder, pine needles, and leaves from often distant forests and meadowlands, and carry them to the homestead. In Pahari (*khet*) regions, women do the transplanting of paddy. During the growing seasons they manage the kitchen garden and spend long hours hoeing and weeding major field crops.

The economic contribution of women to family well-being is thus strikingly greater than the prestige they are accorded. This condition is another manifestation of the zone's pervasive caste-bound social structure. Yet in Karnali, as elsewhere in the Himalaya, historical developments have combined with economic reality to ameliorate in varying degrees their subservient position relative to that in which women find themselves in India. Although a discussion of the roles of women in Karnali society, and the associated intricacies of kith and kin-based household hierarchy, is not possible here, a few important points relevant to the family economy must be made.[7] Out of necessity, high-caste Pahari women are not relegated to seclusion (*purdah*) as are women of similar status on the plains. The lower a woman's caste, the more relaxed the *dharma* that dictates her behavior, the more flexible and extensive her freedom of movement, the greater the number of tasks she shares with men (or, conversely, the greater the aid rendered by men), and, in turn, the more egalitarian the family unit. Even in high-caste but resource-poor households that lack an adequate or ideally proportioned labor force, work arrangements, of necessity, must be flexible. In those families of every caste stratum that lack men, or when all men are away for prolonged periods, women must assume tasks normally reserved by and for men.

The diversity of family livelihood pursuits, as well as the great number of activities these pursuits demand and the diurnal and seasonal human

7   For detailed description and analyses of the role and status of women in South Asian society see Bennett (1977, 1978); Chaudhary (1961); Cormack (1953); Cadgil (1964); Wiser and Wiser (1963).

movements they entail, require intricate scheduling of the family labor force. It also calls for close coordination and cooperation with neighboring households and the village as a whole. For both household and village economies to function successfully, each family must contribute some of its labor or other resources for the common good of the community.

Some cooperative responsibilities occur only occasionally, such as contributing labor to home building, feeding portions of wedding parties, or extending credit or unencumbered aid to hard-pressed families in times of crop failure. Others occur yearly and are often rotated among families. In many Pahari villages families furnish, in turn, a male member who regulates and distributes the prescribed volume of channeled irrigation water to individual family holdings. Similarly they supply a herdsman who tends the animals of the village in nearby *patans*. At harvest times each participating household contributes a small amount of cereal grain to the current labor-contributing families.[8] An important example of more informal cooperation on a rotating basis is found where hydrological conditions permit *ghatta*, or flour mills. These are often built on privately owned land but operated with labor supplied by the owner's family and several other households. The mills are run during the eight-month period (mid-July to mid-March) when stream or channel does not have to be diverted for irrigation. For their services participating families generally retain one-twelfth of the grain that they mill for their neighbors.

The periodic demand for family labor, land, or money extends beyond village maintenance to cooperative development projects within and among panchayats. These efforts involve improvement of drinking water sources and trails, construction of new bridges, extension of major irrigation channels, and erection of government buildings, schools, and latrines. Some are local self-help endeavors; others are initiated and underwritten solely by the central government; most are joint ventures undertaken with matching funds from both the concerned communities and Kathmandu. While those families who supply labor or land sometimes donate these resources, they generally receive reimbursement at low or token rates. A common wage for labor on many projects is two rupees Nepalese Currency (about twenty cents U.S.) per day. The families on whose *khet* land the Jumla airfield was built received in compensation 350 rupees N.C. per *mato muri* (approximately $2,750/ha), a rate they claim is about one-third the current real value.

The greatest need for coordination and cooperation among Karnali households occurs during the acute and crucial periods of planting and harvesting when time and labor shortages are most severe. In order to alleviate these binds, most families must augment their own work force with outside

---

8   I found the exact amount to vary greatly according to a number of factors; Campbell (1978:79) reports that it often amounts to 48 lbs., or about 23 kg, per family in Jumla District.

labor. One strategy followed by many households, particularly those with *khet*, is to combine forces in a system of reciprocal or exchange labor known among the Pahari as *parma*. Most exchange labor is performed by women in the transplanting of paddy and calls for careful scheduling to achieve an equitable labor supply when and where it is needed. If exchange labor falls short of supplying the number of women needed by a family, additional women must be hired.

Hired field hands, tenant cultivators, and *jajmani* workers (Dum occupationals) furnish the bulk of the supplementary labor required by families with relatively large holdings. These three contractual systems draw from, organize, and mobilize the time and energy of land-poor households. In some cases they totally replace family labor in agricultural activities.

Under the hired labor or *majuri* system, members of any caste may be contracted for fieldwork on a daily basis. As a rule these hired hands, of necessity, work for the same families every year, although neither employer nor employee is under any obligation to maintain the relationship. Payment generally consists of four *mana* (2.27 l) of cereal grains plus two large bread (*roti*) meals of wheat, barley, millet, or maize. This daily wage is equivalent to seven or eight *mana* (4-4.5 l) of unhusked food grain and has a cash value of approximately four rupees N.C. In some parts of Karnali various combinations of grain, meals, and cash are now used in payment. Sometimes outside laborers also are retained on a permanent arrangement as household servants. In these instances they normally receive only their board and room, plus periodic presents of cash and clothing.

The perennial employment of tenant cultivators, who also may be drawn from the land-poor of any caste, is another strategy by which some high-caste owners of extensive and usually widely dispersed holdings solve their time and labor binds. If the arable land contracted to tenant families is located near the landlord's homestead, thereby permitting close supervision of the cultivator, the owner is able to collect 50 percent of the principal crop in rent each year. On the other hand, if the farmland assigned to tenants lies far from the owner's home where the cultivator's activities cannot be readily monitored, the absentee landlord usually demands a lower but fixed rent. The rate of this fixed rent varies between one-fourth and three-eights of the primary crop that is produced in a good year.

The case of a Brahman landlord living in Asi Dara illustrates these owner/tenant, time/distance, and land/labor interrelationships. Of the 14 ha of arable land this Brahman owns, 15 percent (2.1 ha) is high-grade *khet* located close to his home. This land he farms with family, exchange, and *jajmani* labor. Another 7 percent (0.99 ha) is lower-grade *khet* that lies within a half day's walk; this he leases to tenant farmers, from whom he receives one-half of the main crop (paddy). Nearly 78 percent (10.75 ha) is *pakho* land three to five days away in Dolpo District and, perforce, is farmed by tenant families. These distant holdings normally bring him a fixed rent equivalent to 25 percent of the average major crop yield. However, for the past two years (1967-69) he has been unable to collect any rent from his Dolpo tenants because of severe drought, crop failure, and near-famine conditions in the upper Bheri drainage.

The traditional and feudalistic Hindu *jajmani* system of caste-specific task specialization remains a prominent feature of labor organization in the Pahari core regions of Karnali. There unclean Dum, referred to in this context as *lagitya,* are the principal work force for Brahman, Thakuri, and thread-wearing Chhetri landowners (their clients, or *lagi*), to whom they are bound by deeply rooted and long-term (often hereditary) contractual relationships.

Some, but not all, Dum continue to practice the polluting occupational specialties that give them their caste identity.[9] However, the chief service that the Kami (metalworkers) and Sarki (cobblers) provide their landowner clients is skilled agricultural labor, particularly during the planting seasons. Of special importance is their service as plowmen (*hali*) for the Tagadhari, especially the Brahmans, who eschew earthly agricultural work in general and plowing in particular.[10] On the other hand, the lower-status Damai (tailors/drummers) must pursue almost exclusively their caste-specific occupations. But while they are not engaged by their *lagi* for skilled agricultural labor service per se, they do perform the ritually important, if ancillary, task of drumming when paddy is transplanted (see figure 49).

Mutual obligations based on caste *dharma* constitute the cornerstone of high-caste/low-caste labor relationships within the *jajmani* structure. A Kami or Sarki may have up to a dozen clients. Some Damai have as many as three dozen *lagi*. In return for his agricultural or caste-specific services the *lagitya* receives from each of his *lagi* a fixed quantity of the chief grain crops at harvest times, plus one (and in some cases two) *roti* meals on those days he performs the contracted fieldwork. He and his family may also receive gifts, such as extra paddy, a sacrificial goat, cash, or clothing, during religious festivals.

The amount of grain a client provides varies greatly, depending upon the size of his holdings and his affluence, and the type and amount of work the *lagitya* is expected to perform. The grain payment, known as *khulo,* can be as little as 12-16 *mana* (6-9 l); usually it is 48-64 *mana* (27-36 l). Plowmen generally receive a larger amount of grain, often as much as 100-120 *mana*

---

[9] Charles McDougal notes that in the far western hills of Nepal to the south of Karnali Zone only about half of the Dum families practice their caste occupation (1968:11). All evidence indicates that this condition also exists in my study area.

[10] For a description of these *jajmani* relationships in Dailekh District, see Caplan (1972:31-35).

(57-68 l) from a single *lagi*. In addition many *lagitya hali* are given small parcels of land (.5-1.5 *mato muri*; 64-191 m^2), which they are permitted to farm exclusively for themselves.

As a rule, a Dum family is able to generate only two to six months of its food-grain needs by *jajmani* labor. The balance must come from additional outside agricultural work (hired labor), the produce of its own fields, migrant labor, and in some instances piecemeal jobs that involve its occupational specialty. If these combined strategies fail to secure the family's minimum yearly requirements, the *lagi* will supply the balance.

Fig. 49. The paddy transplanting operation. Singing women place shoots 8-10 cm apart to the beat of a Damai drummer. Another occupational carries a hand leveling tool along an earthen bund in the middle field. Bullock teams pull a heavier harrow or leveling tool, while in the far field a plowman is at work.

Thus, we find that Karnali's labor force is organized in and articulated through four complex, interrelated, and often cross-cutting systems: family, exchange, hired, and *jajmani*. For the vast majority of families—those whose livelihood comes primarily from agriculture—a combination of these systems is vital.

Appendix G illustrates the use of and participation in these systems by seventy-four families living within three days' walk, without a load, of Jumla-Kalanga (see also figure 100).[11] These data clearly show the manner in which the proportions (the mix) of the labor systems employed differ among families according to the size of their landholdings and their caste. In the case of three wealthy Thakuri households, all fieldwork is performed by *lagitya* laborers. Furthermore, it can be seen that there is no correlation of caste, holdings size, or location with labor intensity. Instead the data exemplify the strikingly variable nature of agricultural labor inputs that result from an array of other human and environmental factors, some of which are included in Appendix G. This array places labor demands on every family that extend beyond sedentary agriculture to supplementary livelihood pursuits.

In sum, then, the labor force of Karnali Zone is mobilized and allocated in the following ways during the yearly cycle: from March through October the people are primarily required in their home villages for work in the fields. But during this time many also must be involved in movements of varying duration and extent. This is the time that food grains are exchanged for Tibetan salt and wool at border markets either in Tibet itself or in upper Humla and Mugu. It is the time for animals to be taken to the high pastures on the *lekh*s and shepherded. In some locations medicinal herbs are gathered. During this agriculture period, however, there are times when considerable buying and selling of food grains must be undertaken among the various valleys, or between high and low elevations, in order to meet immediate subsistence-level food requirements.

All of these activities have to be coordinated with the agricultural labor demands, particularly during those labor-intensive periods of planting, transplanting, and harvest. In these short periods not only is the total family labor force required in the fields, but often also exchange, hired, and *jajmani* labor as well. All of these demands on the family labor force impose a serious time bind on most households, one in which they are continually having to "rob Ram to pay Rana." This bind is even more serious in those areas where a winter-summer crop sequence is followed in *khet* fields.

During the nonagricultural season from December until late February a great out-migration to the south takes place. It is the time for the annual

---

11 Note that family holdings farmed by tenants are not included.

trading trip to the Tarai and to India. Many families living at very high elevations (2,700 to 3,700 m) take their animals to lower areas not only within the zone, but further south to the hills and valleys of Bheri or Seti zones. Moreover, many young people, particularly those of poor households, seek work to the west in the hills of Kumaon in India, in order to make enough money to buy their families' yearly needs in consumer goods. Although most return to their homes in the spring in time for planting, some remain for a year or more.

AGRICULTURE

In their agricultural pursuits, the Karnali farmers must contend with a diversity of spatial and seasonal ecological conditions—temperature and precipitation, soil quality, topographic expression and elevation—that have already been discussed in detail in chapter 2. Although the low and relatively warm incised major valleys in economic region A have 250 to 365 frost-free days, most of the zone has a short growing season of only 150 to 180 frost-free days and experiences severe winter frosts as well as late and variable spring frosts. And at great heights (3,500-4,000 m) on the northern fringe of economic region C only about 120 days are free from frost. Other important factors affecting plant growth are the depth and duration of winter snow cover in the highlands, the hot and dry premonsoon season (April through June), and the brief, humid summer period (July and August); these combine to create distinctive and limiting evapotranspiration and soil moisture regimes. In addition, the geologic structure, the type of parent rock, and the slope and orientation contribute to poorly developed soils, which range from thin, upland, sandy silty-loams to thicker, bottomland, silty clay-loams, and futher affect the moisure-retention characteristics of the arable land.

Crop Mixes and Vertical Zonation

Given this diversity of agroecological conditions, the farmers grow a wide array of crops. Major food grains are the most important. These include paddy or *dhan* (*Oryza sativa*), maize or *makai* (*Zea mays*), finger millet or *kodo* (*Eleusine coracana*), common millet or *chinu* (*Panicum miliaceum*), Italian millet or *kaguno* (*Setaria italica*), great millet or *junelo* (*Sorghum vulgare*), wheat or *gahun* (*Triticum vulgare*), and barley or *jau* (*Hordeum vulgare*). In high and agriculturally marginal areas buckwheat (*phaphar*) is also important. Two varieties are grown: sweet buckwheat or *mithe phaphar* (*Tagopyrum esculentum*) and sour buckwheat or *tite phaphar* (*T. tataricum*). In extreme northern Bhotia areas a Himalayan variety of wheat known as *naphal* is also a key crop. But the beardless or "naked" Tibetan variety of barley (*Hordeum himalayense*) known as *uwa*, which is important in high-altitude regions further east in Nepal, is relatively unimportant in Karnali. Where it is grown, it sometimes is not consumed, but reserved for trade purposes. In addition to these major summer and winter grains, a number of pulses (black gram, green gram, horse gram, and lentil), common or kidney beans, soybeans, and field peas are crops of importance, particularly for the Pahari, for they are ground into *dhal* to be eaten with boiled rice. Potato (*alu*) and amaranth (*marcia*), while important in some upland areas, are generally minor crops. In contrast, in the mountainous areas of central and eastern Nepal the potato is a crop of significance.

Mustard (*tori*) and Indian hemp (*Cannabis sativa*) are important field crops in some sub-humid temperate locations. Both are pressed and their oils extracted for cooking purposes. In the case of *Cannabis*, the plant is put to a variety of uses. The oil is often rubbed into the skin to ease sore muscles. Its fiber is twisted into serviceable twine and discarded stems are sometimes burned for fuel. As a narcotic it is occasionally smoked in the home or by pilgrims in the Siva temples at Jumla-Kalanga in two forms: as "grass," the dried inflorescence and small young leaves known as *ganja*; or as hashish, the resin that is laboriously hand-rubbed from fresh leaves and flowers by old women. However, hashish, known as *attar* in Karnali but generally as *charas* throughout Nepal, is primarily a trade item.[12] Tobacco is a more widely consumed narcotic. It is grown almost everywhere in the zone in small amounts, generally for home use.

Another fiber—cotton, or *ruwa* (*Gossypium arboreum*)—is important up to 1,800 m in the warm, semiarid Mugu and main Karnali valleys. Its highest concentration is in Galpha Dara of lower Humla-Mugu. Formerly a significant trade item, it is now raised in amounts sufficient only for local consumption. The variant grown here may be *Bengalense silow*, an annual short-lint cotton frequently cultivated in northern India.[13] Requiring a minimum of about 200 frost-free days, cotton is a distinguishing crop in economic region A. Commercial cottons are reported to grow at 1,500 m in Africa, but only 1,000 m in India (Purseglove 1968). To my knowledge, no cotton is grown at such heights elsewhere in the Himalaya.

Well over a dozen miscellaneous vegetables, condiments, and spices are grown in Karnali, principally as kitchen garden (*basi*) crops. These include cauliflower and cabbage, radish and turnip (especially important in the high Bhotia region of upper Humla and upper Mugu), tomato, eggplant, spinach, arum (*colocaria*), cucumber, pumpkin, bittergourd, sponge gourd, snake gourd, onion, garlic, chili, and coriander.

---

[12] For a general discussion of *Cannabis* and culture in Nepal, see Fisher (1975).

[13] Richard I. Forde, Ethnobotanical Laboratory, University of Michigan (personal communication, 1971).

TABLE 11. Crop calendars for selected Karnali villages.

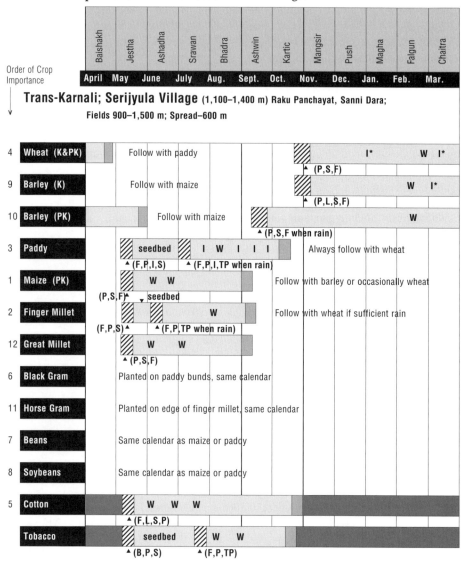

Order of Crop Importance	Crop	Baishakh April	Jestha May	Ashadha June	Srawan July	Bhadra Aug.	Ashwin Sept.	Kartic Oct.	Mangsir Nov.	Push Dec.	Magha Jan.	Falgun Feb.	Chaitra Mar.

Trans-Karnali; Serijyula Village (1,100–1,400 m) Raku Panchayat, Sanni Dara; Fields 900–1,500 m; Spread–600 m

4	Wheat (K&PK)	Follow with paddy ... I* ... W I* (P,S,F)
9	Barley (K)	Follow with maize ... W I* (P,L,S,F)
10	Barley (PK)	Follow with maize ... W (P,S,F when rain)
3	Paddy	seedbed I W I I I ... Always follow with wheat (F,P,I,S) (F,P,I,TP when rain)
1	Maize (PK)	W W ... Follow with barley or occasionally wheat (P,S,F) seedbed
2	Finger Millet	W ... Follow with wheat if sufficient rain (F,P,S) (F,P,TP when rain)
12	Great Millet	W W (P,S,F)
6	Black Gram	Planted on paddy bunds, same calendar
11	Horse Gram	Planted on edge of finger millet, same calendar
7	Beans	Same calendar as maize or paddy
8	Soybeans	Same calendar as maize or paddy
5	Cotton	W W W (F,L,S,P)
	Tobacco	seedbed W W (B,P,S) (F,P,TP)

KEY TO BARS

| Plant | Grow | Harvest | Fallow |

KEY TO LETTER CODES

(V)=village; (P)=panchayat; (B)=burn; (C&B)=cut & bend maize plants; (D)=dig; (F)=fertilize; (FG)=force germinate paddy; (H)=harvest; (I)=irrigate; (K)=*khet* fields; (L)=level (smooth or harrow); (P)=plow; (PK)=*pakho* fields; (S)=sew; (SB)=sew bed; (TP)=transplant; (W)=weed; (*)=when necessary

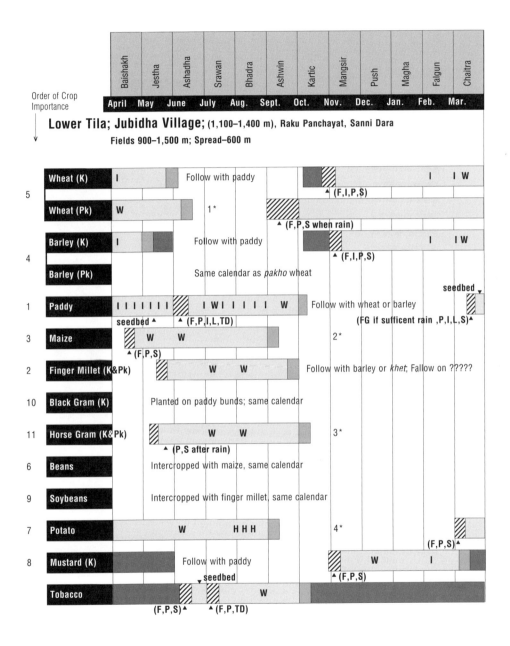

Lower Tila; Jubidha Village; (1,100–1,400 m), Raku Panchayat, Sanni Dara

Fields 900–1,500 m; Spread–600 m

1* Fallow the next year.

2* Follow with wheat or barley, if rain. Fallow if no rain.

3* If *khet* follow with wheat (K).

  If *pakho*, fallow and then maize, millet or repeat horse gram next year.

4* Follow with barley if sufficent rain; fallow if not.

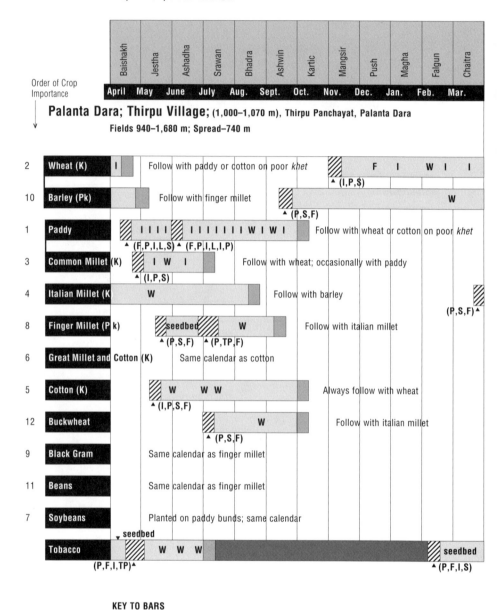

Palanta Dara; Thirpu Village; (1,000–1,070 m), Thirpu Panchayat, Palanta Dara
Fields 940–1,680 m; Spread–740 m

KEY TO BARS

| Plant | Grow | Harvest | Fallow |

KEY TO LETTER CODES

(V)=village; (P)=panchayat; (B)=burn; (C&B)=cut & bend maize plants; (D)=dig; (F)=fertilize; (FG)=force germinate paddy; (H)=harvest; (I)=irrigate; (K)=*khet* fields; (L)=level (smooth or harrow); (P)=plow; (PK)=*pakho* fields; (S)=sew; (SB)=sew bed; (TP)=transplant; (W)=weed; (*)=when necessary

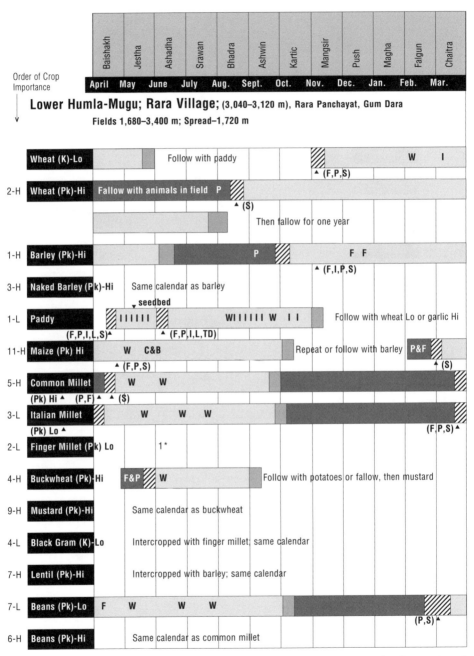

Order of Crop Importance

Lower Humla-Mugu; Rara Village; (3,040–3,120 m), Rara Panchayat, Gum Dara

Fields 1,680–3,400 m; Spread–1,720 m

(continues next page)

1* Same calendar as common millet; strip planted in same field as common
   millet and rotated yearly.

(continued from previous page)

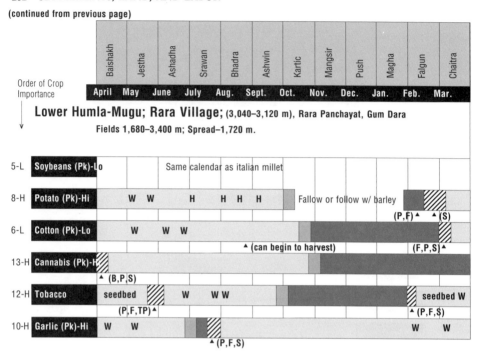

Baishakh	Jestha	Ashadha	Srawan	Bhadra	Ashwin	Kartic	Mangsir	Push	Magha	Falgun	Chaitra
April	May	June	July	Aug.	Sept.	Oct.	Nov.	Dec.	Jan.	Feb.	Mar.

Order of Crop Importance

↓

Lower Humla-Mugu; Rara Village; (3,040–3,120 m), Rara Panchayat, Gum Dara
Fields 1,680–3,400 m; Spread–1,720 m.

5-L Soybeans (Pk)-Lo   Same calendar as italian millet

8-H Potato (Pk)-Hi   W   W   H   H   H   H   Fallow or follow w/ barley
                                                      (P,F)▲   ▲(S)

6-L Cotton (Pk)-Lo   W   W   W
                                   ▲ (can begin to harvest)   (F,P,S)▲

13-H Cannabis (Pk)-H
     ▲ (B,P,S)

12-H Tobacco   seedbed   W   W W   seedbed W
               (P,F,TP)▲   ▲ (P,F,S)

10-H Garlic (Pk)-Hi   W   W   W   W
               ▲ (P,F,S)

KEY TO BARS

Plant	Grow	Harvest	Fallow

KEY TO LETTER CODES

(V)=village; (P)=panchayat; (B)=burn; (C&B)=cut & bend maize plants; (D)=dig; (F)=fertilize; (FG)=force germinate paddy; (H)=harvest; (I)=irrigate; (K)=*khet* fields; (L)=level (smooth or harrow); (P)=plow; (PK)=*pakho* fields; (S)=sew; (SB)=sew bed; (TP)=transplant; (W)=weed; (*)=when necessary

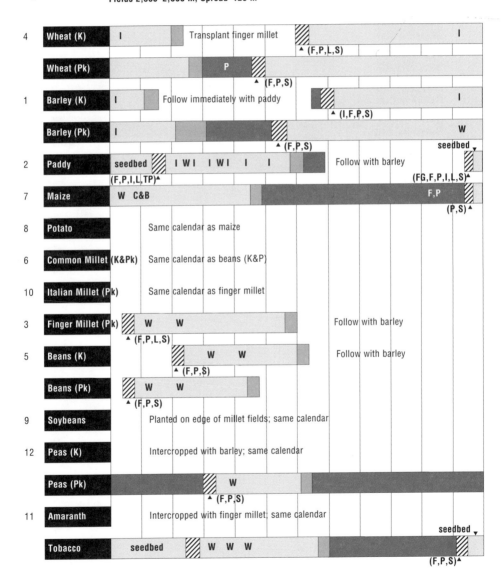

Order of Crop Importance

Sinja Dara; Ludka Village; (2,440–2,530 m), Ludka Panchayat, Sinja Dara
Fields 2,380–2,500 m; Spread–120 m

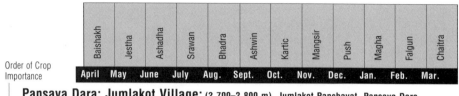

Order of Crop
Importance

	Baishakh	Jestha	Ashadha	Srawan	Bhadra	Ashwin	Kartic	Mangsir	Push	Magha	Falgun	Chaitra
	April	May	June	July	Aug.	Sept.	Oct.	Nov.	Dec.	Jan.	Feb.	Mar.

Pansaya Dara; Jumlakot Village; (2,700–2,800 m), Jumlakot Panchayat, Pansaya Dara
Fields 2,400–3,300 m; Spread–900 m

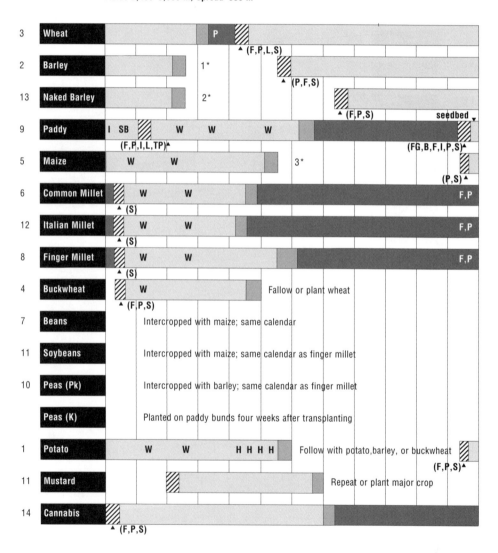

1*Follow w/ barley or buckwheat

2*Follow w/ barley, wheat or naked barley

3*If low in barley, plant barley immediately, if sufficient barley, fallow and repeat or potato

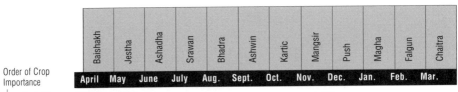

Order of Crop
Importance

Asi Dara; Chhina Village; (2,320–2,380 m), Chhina Panchayat, Asi Dara

Fields 2,270–2,500 m; Spread–230 m

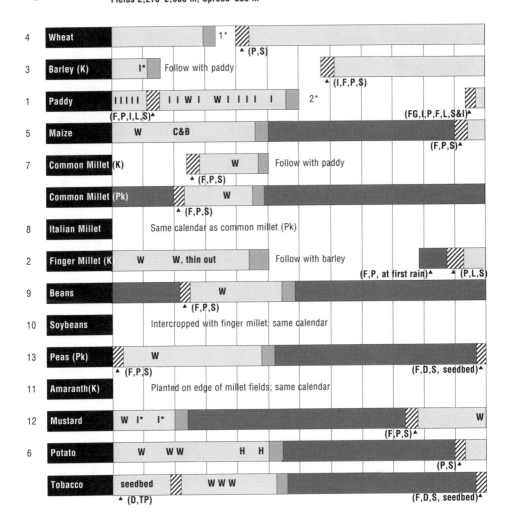

1* Follow with wheat, potato, or buckwheat

2* Follow with finger millet, or fallow

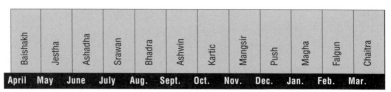

Asi Dara; Chhina Village; (2,320–2,380 m), Chhina Panchayat, Asi Dara
Miscellaneous Fields 2,270–2,500 m; Spread–230 m

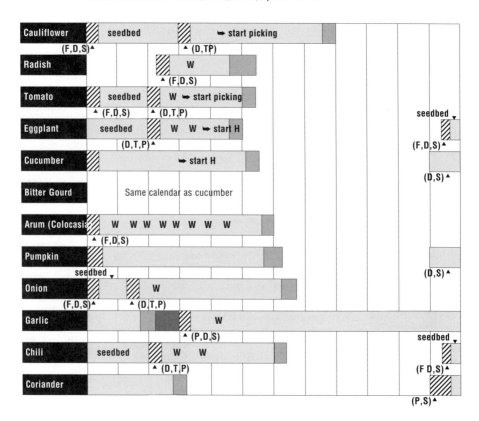

KEY TO BARS

Plant	Grow	Harvest	Fallow

KEY TO LETTER CODES

(V)=village; (P)=panchayat; (B)=burn; (C&B)=cut & bend maize plants; (D)=dig; (F)=fertilize; (FG)=force germinate paddy; (H)=harvest; (I)=irrigate; (K)=*khet* fields; (L)=level (smooth or harrow); (P)=plow; (PK)=*pakho* fields; (S)=sew; (SB)=sew bed; (TP)=transplant; (W)=weed; (*)=when necessary

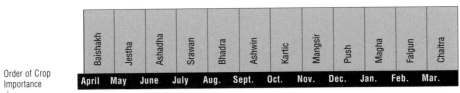

Order of Crop
Importance

Upper Humla; Simikot Village; (2,750–2,850 m.), Simikot Panchayat, Humla Dara
Fields 2,500–3,500 m.; Spread–1,000 m.

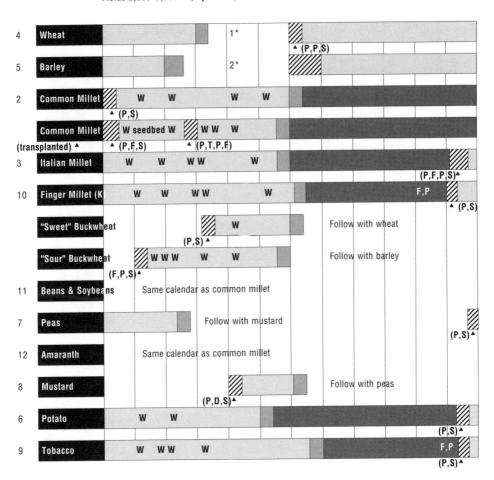

1* Follow with sweet buckwheat

2* Follow with common millet (transplanted)

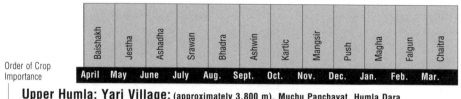

	Baishakh	Jestha	Ashadha	Srawan	Bhadra	Ashwin	Kartic	Mangsir	Push	Magha	Falgun	Chaitra
Order of Crop Importance	April	May	June	July	Aug.	Sept.	Oct.	Nov.	Dec.	Jan.	Feb.	Mar.

Upper Humla; Yari Village; (approximately 3,800 m), Muchu Panchayat, Humla Dara
Fields aprox. 3,600–4,000 m; Spread–400 m

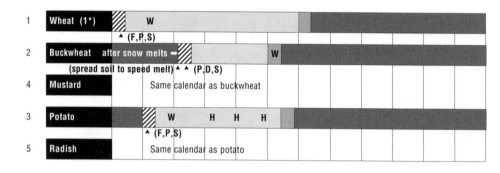

1 — Wheat (1*) — W — ▲ (F,P,S)

2 — Buckwheat — after snow melts → — W — (spread soil to speed melt) ▲ ▲ (P,D,S)

4 — Mustard — Same calendar as buckwheat

3 — Potato — W H H H — ▲ (F,P,S)

5 — Radish — Same calendar as potato

1*Himalayan Wheat (*NAPHAL*)

KEY TO BARS

Plant	Grow	Harvest	Fallow

KEY TO LETTER CODES

(**V**)=village; (**P**)=panchayat; (**B**)=burn; (**C&B**)=cut & bend maize plants; (**D**)=dig; (**F**)=fertilize; (**FG**)=force germinate paddy; (**H**)=harvest; (**I**)=irrigate; (**K**)=*khet* fields; (**L**)=level (smooth or harrow); (**P**)=plow; (**PK**)=*pakho* fields; (**S**)=sew; (**SB**)=sew bed; (**TP**)=transplant; (**W**)=weed; (*)=when necessary

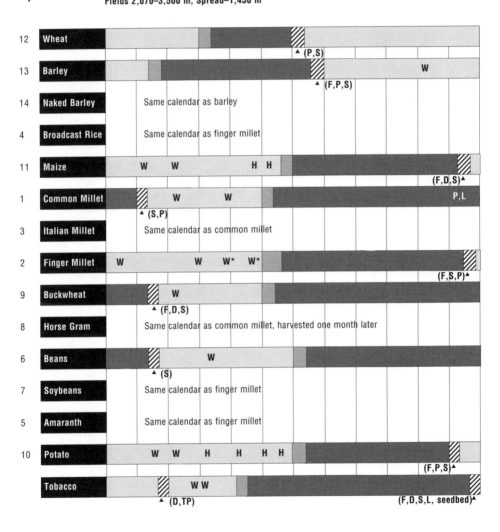

Order of Crop
Importance

	Baishakh	Jestha	Ashadha	Srawan	Bhadra	Ashwin	Kartic	Mangsir	Push	Magha	Falgun	Chaitra
	April	May	June	July	Aug.	Sept.	Oct.	Nov.	Dec.	Jan.	Feb.	Mar.

Upper Mugu; Mangri Village; (2,230–2,310 m), Dhunge Panchayat, Karana Dara
Fields 2,070–3,500 m; Spread–1,430 m

12 Wheat ▲ (P,S)

13 Barley   W ▲ (F,P,S)

14 Naked Barley   Same calendar as barley

4 Broadcast Rice   Same calendar as finger millet

11 Maize   W W   H H   (F,D,S)▲

1 Common Millet   W W   P,L   ▲ (S,P)

3 Italian Millet   Same calendar as common millet

2 Finger Millet   W   W W* W*   (F,S,P)▲

9 Buckwheat   W   ▲ (F,D,S)

8 Horse Gram   Same calendar as common millet, harvested one month later

6 Beans   W   ▲ (S)

7 Soybeans   Same calendar as finger millet

5 Amaranth   Same calendar as finger millet

10 Potato   W W   H   H   H H   (F,P,S)▲

Tobacco   W W   ▲ (D,TP)   (F,D,S,L, seedbed)▲

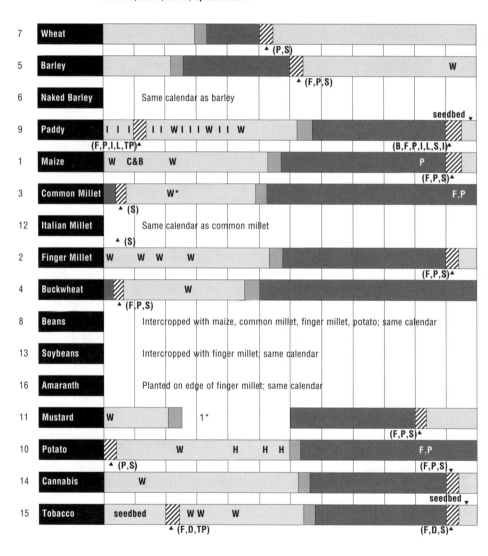

Chaudhabisa-Upper Tila; Luma Village; (2,590–2,650 m), Lum Panchayat, Chaudhabisa Dara
Fields 2,560–3,230 m; Spread–670 m

1*Can follow with transplanted finger millet

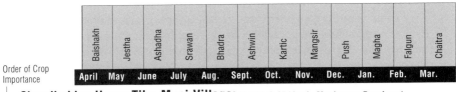

Order of Crop
Importance

Chaudhabisa-Upper Tila; Muni Village; (2,590–2,6510 m), Manisangu Panchayat,
Chaudhabisa Dara, Fields 2,590–3,110 m; Spread–520 m

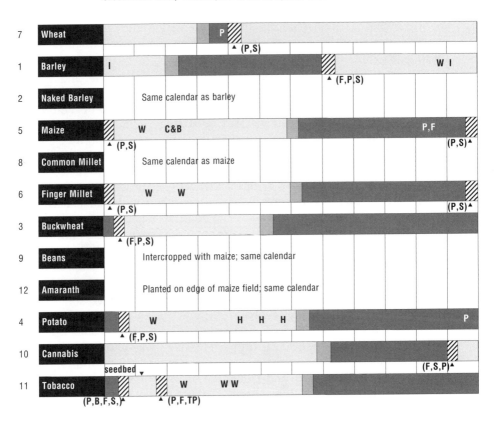

The cropping patterns and procedures for the major crops grown in twelve representative locations are presented in table 11. These regimes indicate the degree of agricultural varition that exists among the regions of Karnali Zone. The case of lakeside Rara village in lower Humla-Mugu (Gum Dara), which has a lower satellite village along the Mugu Karnali River, illustrates in detail the difference in local crop regimes that result from elevation and topography.[14] For Chhinagaon in Asi Dara the cropping patterns for miscellaneous minor crops (vegetables, condiments, and spices) are also included. Similar information on the major crops that are raised in five locations south of Karnali Zone (i.e., from the lower Himalaya to the Tarai) is provided in Appendix F for comparison.

Particularly notable in table 11 is the variety of elaborate, and in some instances unique, cropping practices that the astute peasant cultivators have perfected over the centuries in order to make maximum use of their sparse arable land or to increase their yields. One strategy followed wherever possible is double cropping, by which a summer-winter sequence of two crops is grown in a single field each year. Another involves intricate intercropping, the growing of two to four crops in a field simultaneously: Italian millet with common millet; mustard with buckwheat; potato with maize; lentil or field pea with barley; beans, pumpkins, or cucumbers with maize. Secondary crops commonly are planted around the edge of major cereals: pulses and beans on paddy bunds; amaranth, beans, and soybeans on the periphery of finger millet or maize fields. Even though the intercropping seems endless, each is fitted with care to the specific local conditions and the family's needs.

Crop rotation (the alternation of crops in a given field from year to year) is widely practiced, primarily in an effort to preserve soil fertility. Although rotations generally involve a two-year cycle of such crops as finger millet and barley, barley and wheat, or maize and potato, they can be more protracted. In Simikot panchayat (upper Humla) a five-year program is followed in some fields: wheat the first year; sweet buckwheat and fallow the second; field peas, mustard, and fallow the third; common millet and fallow the fourth; Italian millet, fallow, and the start of wheat again in the fifth.

The Karnali calendars also indicate the consistency with which crops are matched with elevation belts (the independent variable) and growing conditions according to their physiological characteristics. For example, although wheat is preferred to barley, it requires about one month longer to reach maturity. It therefore is the more important winter cereal only below 1,800 m in economic regions A and B, where it can be successfully fitted into

---

[14] It should be noted that Rara Lake ameliorates the severity of climate that is found elsewhere in the zone at 3,100 m.

a double-crop sequence; elsewhere barley generally is the major *rabi* crop (figure 50).

The millets are hardy, drought-resistant *kharif* crops that can be planted on poor upland *pakho*. Finger millet is preferred and is widely planted. Requiring five to six months to mature, it often is transplanted to allow for local growing conditions. In some instances it is densely broadcast in *khet* fields after barley harvest; about four weeks later the seedlings are transplanted in *pakho* fields, thus permitting paddy to be transplanted in the vacated *khet*. This technique is reported to increase finger millet yields twofold. Common and Italian millets, which require three to four months to mature, are considered poor man's crops and are usually grown in higher or less productive plots. They also are "emergency" cereals that can be planted on better land when abnormal conditions such as drought disrupt the usual scheduling and prevent the planting of preferred crops. The buckwheats are even more hardy and tolerant of poor growing conditions than the millets and replace them in extreme highland or *lekh* locations.

Of all the dry-farmed cereals, maize is the most sensitive to agroclimatic conditions and requires considerable moisture, particularly during its early stages of growth. It is also the most demanding of soil nutrients and thus rapidly exhausts the fields of their fertility. Because of these factors, maize is strikingly less important in Karnali Zone than it is on the lower Himalayan slopes to the south. At the regional scale it ranks first in importance only in the broad Chaudhabisa Valley of economic region D, where informants report that it was introduced thirty to forty years ago. There, and in adjacent areas (economic region B and lower Humla-Mugu in region A), a unique procedure is employed in its cultivation that evidently permits the maize plant to capture more soil moisture. During the second weeding several roots are severed and the plant bent in a manner that permits it to continue to grow upright as the remaining roots penetrate to a greater depth. The cultivators believe that this practice improves yields and reduces the chances of drought-induced crop failure.

The cultivation of wet rice in Karnali Zone reaches the highest elevation in the world (Uhlig 1978). Paddy is the major crop on irrigated land and is grown up to 2,680 m in the Sinja Valley and the upper Tila Valley (economic region B). Its extreme limit is reported to be about 2,740 m in the vicinity of Rimi village, Darma panchayat, in Humla Dara.[15] For paddy culture to be successful above about 1800 m, the seeds must be force-germinated inside the home. Traditionally this is begun on the twelfth of Chaitra (i.e., in the last week of March).[16] Procedures differ somewhat from valley to valley,

---

[15] Harka B. Gurung, personal communications, Dec. 1968.

[16] As has already been expounded, rice is of singular importance in determining not only economic but socioreligious status in the caste-based Pahari hierarchy of Karnali. All aspects of

depending on temperature. In the Jumla-Kalanga area of Asi Dara the un-husked kernels are dried in the sun for four days, then spread on birch-bark mats on the earthern floor, covered with pine needles, and sprinkled with stream water. This soaking is continued unabated for four days by the women of the home, who also constantly tend the fire in the hearth to maintain hothouse conditions. Thus prepared, the seeds are broadcast into a nearby seedbed. For the next few weeks this small plot is continually irri-gated (according to the height of the plants) and the seedlings fertilized three or four times with a special mixture of chicken droppings, paddy husks, and kitchen sweepings that has been rendered to a powder by burning. Early in Jestha (mid-May), when the seedlings have reached a height of 10-15 cm, transplanting begins (figures 50 and 51).

Thus we see that there are two distinct cropping systems in Karnali Zone, one based on irrigated *khet* and paddy culture, the other based on rain-fed *pakho* and the other major summer cereals. Both systems are found below 2,700 m, where the outstanding and identifying feature of each is double cropping. On the lower and better *khet* a sequence of summer paddy and winter barley or wheat predominates. On the higher or poorer *pakho*, millets or maize and barley or wheat are double cropped wherever condi-tions permit. As a rule the winter grains make up from 30 to 40 percent of the food grown. Above 2,700 m, when *pakho* alone is found, only a single dry-farmed crop can be grown in a given field each year, with the winter crops contributing a decreasing proportion of the annual production. Above about 3,500 m only summer crops are possible. However, it should be noted that at the highest and most arid limits of successful summer agriculture, in the Bhotia panchayat of Limi in northwest Humla, the fields must be care-fully terraced and irrigated in a manner similar to that employed on the *khet* lands of the Pahari.[17]

Therefore, in each of the four major economic regions of the zone a third dimension—elevation—creates significant variation in crop mixes and, in turn, food production. The villages of regions A and B engage inten-sively in one or both cropping systems according to the distribution of their fields. Those in regions C and D pursue generally less productive *pakho* farming almost exclusively. As table 12 graphically demonstrates, the dura-tion of time the farmer is forced to leave his meager fields fallow solely be-cause of agroclimatic conditions increases with altitude and latitude.

---

its cultivation and consumption are tied to and prescribed by Hindu ritual dictates. Moreover, paddy culture is deeply rooted in and perpetuated by ancient lore and legend. According to the people of economic region B, paddy was introduced by a wandering yogi or holy man named Candannath, who gave their ancestors seeds from Kashmir along with detailed instructions on just when and how to cultivate them.

[17] Melvyn G. Goldstein, personal communication, Nov. 10, 1975.

Manure, Terraces, and Tools

Fertilizer is especially important to Karnali crop production. All other determining factors remaining constant, it increases yields 50 to 100 percent whenever it is used. The farmers' perennial concern with obtaining what they perceive to be an adequate amount is underscored by the oft repeated proverb: "Without people there can be no king; without fertilizer there can be no crops." Lacking supplementary chemical fertilizers that have contributed to the green revolution in India, they continue to rely almost totally on manure. Their success in securing a sufficient dung supply and appropriately applying it to their plots depends primarily on the number of animals they are able to maintain given the fodder resources at their disposal. Also critical is the amount of time the household can devote to both the collection of pine needles and leafy organic matter from the forests to augment the dung and the subsequent distribution of the crudely produced compost from farmstead to field. Although some families do generate an adequate quantity of fertilizer, most do not. The majority of farmers interviewed state that their livestock furnish only about 50 percent of their minimum requirements.

Two basic and interrelated manuring systems are followed, which must be coordinated in both time and space. During those months (between October and May) when livestock are kept at or near the homestead, their manure is collected and mixed with needles and leaves at a ratio between 1:1 and 1:3, depending on the quantity of dung available. For example, each stabled cow, bullock, buffalo, or horse produces between 100 and 150 kg of fertilizer per month if this excrement is mixed with litter at a 1:2 ratio. Some families who lack livestock may board a few animals belonging to neighbors with limited feeding capability in order to secure dung. Others exchange fodder or grain for pure dung or buy loads of composted or prepared manure at a cost of about one rupee (ten cents) for 30-50 kg, depending on the mix ratio. Dum households often fill farmyard pits with kitchen waste, needles, and leaves to produce a nondung compost that supplements or takes the place of manure their *lagi* clients might occasionally give them. But only in the Bhotia villages of upper Humla and Mugu, where homes are built with indoor latrines, is human excrement collected and used as fertilizer along with manure.[18]

---

[18] Recent efforts by the Panchayat Raj to encourage all rural households in the country to build and use latrines have, so far, been largely unsuccessful among the Pahari of Karnali. So too have been government programs to reduce nutrient loss in the fertilizer that results from its inefficient or wasteful preparation, storage, and application.

Fig. 50 (pp. 216-17). Barley ripening in early March in terraced khet *fields at Jumla-Kalanga (2,330 m). © National Geographic Society.*

Fig. 51. Transplanting paddy near Jumla-Kalanga. The foreground plot is a seedbed from which the women are removing plants. In the background the winter barley will be harvested and paddy immediately planted.

During the late winter and spring the poorly decomposed fertilizer mix is carried to the fields in bell-shaped bamboo baskets (*dokas*), where it is distributed in piles 2-5 m apart, according to the amount that has been allocated (figures 52 and 53). The quantity applied depends on the location of the plot and the crop regime that is followed there. Those fields in which double cropping is practiced receive the greatest attention. A definite correlation exists between the amount of fertilizer used in a specific field and the distance of that field from the farmstead. Therefore a distance/decay factor, tied to the availability of human labor, is striking in use of composted manure as well as in other labor-intensive agricultural tasks such as weeding. Thus, the amount of prepared manure mix used decreases with the distance of the field from the home. In the case of *khet* plots that lie within an hour of the homestead and in which a sequence of paddy-barley is grown, the spring manuring rate may be anywhere between 5,000 and 20,000 kg per hectare. Similar fields two hours away receive only 1,500 to 4,000 kg of manure per hectare.

The other manuring system involves the widespread practice of grazing livestock in the fields during fallow periods and calls for the integration and timing of pastoral regimes with crop regimes. Highland *pakho*, in which a single crop is planted, is grazed once during the summer. Lower single- or double-cropped *pakho* plots, as well as *khet*, are usually grazed twice in the course of the annual circulation of cattle, buffalo, horses, sheep, and goats. While some households have enough animals to pursue independently this practice of raw manuring, most band together in village or kin groups. They carefully coordinate the movements of their combined herds to permit the agreed-upon allotment of grazing time in each field. Livestock-poor households arrange to have animals belonging to other families graze the stubble of their harvested fields. In some cases this fodder-dung exchange is an even one. More often, however, the animal owners, especially those with sheep and goats, also receive a small amount of grain for their manuring service.[19]

The vast majority of Karnali families employ a combination of both manuring systems described. But since most fail to obtain the amount they desire, they employ various compromise strategies to stretch their supply as far as possible. Some fertilize all of their fields, but at lighter rates than they would prefer. Others apply heavier dressings of raw manure and/or crude compost to only one-third to one-half of their arable land each year, in a manner that is best fitted to their current cropping calendars. One version of these rotations is the manuring of *rabi* and *kharif* fields on alternate years. And some will farm spatially and productively marginal or recently claimed *pakho* plots without manuring of any sort.

The varying degrees to which the peasants are able to maintain, or on occasion enhance, the fertility of their arable land by manuring is strikingly illustrated by the soil chemistry of four fields located close to the sites of my four weather stations (table 12). At Bumra (in the upper Sinja Valley, Asi Dara), the terraced *pakho* plot faces south, slopes at an angle of twenty degrees, and is located two minutes from the owner's home. The soil is a poorly developed, skeletal sandy loam only 10-30 cm in depth and is derived from a foliated gneiss that is highly susceptible to erosion. Claimed for agri-

---

[19] It is important to note in this context that a sheep or goat annually produces 450 to 650 kg of manure that contains approximately twice the quantities of nitrogen and potassium found in cattle dung. Agronomists believe that sheep and goats will supply a sufficient manure dressing to an area in a single night when corralled or penned at a density of 5,000/ha (Kurup 1967:41, 93).

TABLE 12. Soil chemistry of four fields in 2026 V.S. (1969-70).

Site	Sample depth (cm)	pH	Buffer pH	Lime required (kg/ha)	Phosphorus (kg/ha)	Potassium (kg/ha)	Calcium (kg/ha)	Magnesium (kg/ha)	Carbon (%)	Organic Material (approx. %)
Bumra (2,865 m)	5	6.5	7.0	1,121	363	565	9,074	1,488	5.1	8.7
	10	6.7	7.2	—	605	425	8,860	1,273	5.4	9.2
	16	6.8	—	—	285	293	7,168	968	3.8	6.5
	23	7.3	—	—	45	145	5,713	502	4.3	7.3
Dillikot (2,774 m)	8	5.1	6.4	12,329	98	1,858	5,713	986	3.9	6.6
	15	5.3	6.5	10,087	22	380	1,884	215	.9	1.5
	30	5.3	6.7	5,604	11	293	1,102	126	.7	1.2
	45	6.2	6.9	2,242	11	105	1,297	215	.5	.9
	60	6.0	6.7	5,604	19	67	2,279	143	.5	.9
	76	6.7	7.2	—	12	59	2,675	143	.4	.7
Gum (2,030 m)	8	6.2	6.9	2,242	77	242	1,297	233	1.4	2.4
	20	6.0	6.8	3,362	39	98	1,102	197	.9	1.5
	40	5.6	6.7	5,604	26	59	907	143	.7	1.2
	53	5.1	6.4	12,329	19	105	3,475	502	5.7	9.7
	79	6.0	7.0	1,121	24	59	713	126	.1	.2
	96	6.4	7.0	1,121	33	59	713	90	.1	.2
Jumla (2,387 m)	8	4.8	6.4	12,329	22	113	1,884	215	2.2	3.7
	15	4.8	6.4	12,329	24	129	2,279	215	1.9	3.2
	25	6.0	6.9	2,242	16	82	2,875	287	.7	1.2
	33	6.5	7.0	1,121	19	113	2,279	161	.7	1.2
	46	6.5	7.0	1,121	36	152	1,492	126	.4	.7

NOTE: Chemical analysis performed by the Department of Crop and Soil Sciences, Michigan State University.

culture only forty-five years ago, the field is cropped in a three-year sequence of winter wheat and summer buckwheat with a nine-month fallow period between the two crops. Because of both its location and its importance to the Matwali Chhetri owner's household economy, it is heavily manured, as indicated by the high percentage of organic matter, and thus has actually been enhanced to a relatively high level of fertility.

The Dillikot field (upper Tila Valley, Chaudhabisa Dara) is on a confined, north-south trending alluvial terrace. Its soil is a well-developed podsol 80 cm in depth. First tilled approximately 300 years ago, it was, until forty years ago, devoted to a single summer crop of finger millet. However, when the frequency and intensity of spring flooding increased with extended land reclamation and deforestation on the slopes of the catchment basin, the field became unsuitable for any grain crop and was allowed to revert to grass. Today it is used only as pasture. Although deficient in lime, it is fairly fertile and might well be suitable for growing a fodder crop such as alfalfa.

The field near Gum (Mugu Karnali Valley, Gum Dara) is a southeast-facing, well developed, and nearly horizontal *pakho* terrace in which the soil is micaceous and stony, sandy loam of undetermined depth. Farmed for the past 400-500 years, it currently produces a double crop each year of barley and transplanted finger millet. Although considered a first-grade unirrigated plot by the owner-cultivator, it does not receive adequate manuring, for it lies a half hour above his home. As the data indicate, it is in need of lime and is clearly low in organic material, and thus in nitrogen.[20]

The Jumla field (in the middle Tila Karnali Valley near Kalanga, Asi Dara) is vulnerable *khet* on a broad alluvial terrace on the north side of the river (figure 50). The soil is a heavy, silty clay-loam containing pebbles and cobbles that increase with depth; at 55-60 cm below the surface it is abruptly replaced by old flood-plain cobbles and boulders. But despite the fact that the field is only 100 m from the owner's home, it is insufficiently fertilized. Like the Gum field its soil chemistry reflects a long history of intensive cultivation (400-500 years) that has depleted it of plant nutrients. Critically acid near the surface, and low in phosphorus and potassium, it is in need of heavy liming and manuring. Although ample limestone deposits are found two days away in the Chaudhabisa Valley, they are not quarried for fertilizer. The higher pH values in the lower horizons of all four soil profiles no doubt reflect chemical weathering and decomposition of organic matter.[21]

---

[20] Note that the high value of carbon and organic matter at 53 cm in the profile reflects a thin and old root system.

[21] Tamhane et al. (1964:181-95) give a good explanation of the effects of lime on crop production, while Jenny and Raychaudhuri (1960) furnish valuable information on the interrelated effects of temperature, precipitation, elevation, and cultivation on nitrogen and organic matter reserves in Indian soils.

Fig. 52. Women carrying 30 kg loads of manure mix to the double-crop khet *fields in birch-bark baskets, or* dokas, *in February*

Terraces are the most prominent and visually dramatic feature of the agricultural landscape in Karnali Zone, as throughout the Himalaya. They constitute the chief means by which the mountaineers have modified, and continue to modify, their rugged habitat for permanent cultivation with the plow. Two basic types of terraces—*khet* and *pakho*—can be distinguished by location, function, form, and construction.

Fig. 53. Piles of manure mix in recently harvested barley plots awaiting spreading for plowing under

Khet terraces are designed to provide a field environment in which semiaquatic paddy can be grown. They are found on major valley flood plains and bordering natural terraces and alluvial fans where irrigation water can be diverted by weir or groin from the rivers and brought to them via extensive canals and channels (figure 54). *Khet* terraces are also found on perched benches and steep hillsides above the valleys where tributary streams can furnish water (figure 55). Hollowed logs are often used to bridge declivities that obstruct the course of irrigation channels (figure 56). In all cases *khet* terraces are carefully engineered networks of tiered, or stepped, and leveled plots in which water can be impounded and controlled by watertight mud bunds that rise 15-25 cm above the field surface. Although

Fig. 54. The extensive khet *plots and irrigation networks in Jumla-Kalanga (aerial photograph, December)*

the walls of some valley terraces may be made of earth, most are built of stone brought from a nearby watercourse or from the field itself. Where terraces have been carved from precipitous slopes—sometimes with an angle of over forty degrees—these stone walls must be strong enough to support considerable soil weight that is seasonally increased by flooding. They vary in height with slope angle and field width, and generally are 1-3 m high, but in extreme cases they may be as high as 5 m in order to permit a level plot surface wide enough to accommodate a bullock team.

The principal purpose of terracing dry-farmed *pakho* fields is to check or reduce erosion and soil loss. Once stripped of stabilizing natural vegetation the steep upland slopes, with their thin and light soils, are particularly susceptible to rapid late-spring runoff of snow-melt and intense summer rainstorms that follow long, dry winters (the characteristic monsoon pattern in Karnali Zone). As a result, sheetwash and gullying are serious problems with which the farmers must constantly contend. Where the natural slope is too steep for plowing, terracing also reduces it to an acceptable gradient, and on those slopes where the mantle is especially sparse, terracing redistributes the available soil in narrow plots of depths sufficient for cultivation.

Unlike *khet, pakho* terrace surfaces slope downhill and often undulate. Where they are well developed, the terraces may have surfaces that approach the horizontal and solid stone walls similar in height to those of hillside *khet* (see figure 55). Usually they slope markedly and have stone walls or stone-reinforced earthen walls of lesser height (figure 57). Thus *pakho* areas display a wider range of terrace morphology than do *khet*.

The stage of development of both *khet* and *pakho* terraces varies according to a number of interrelated physical and human factors. These include the location and elevation of the arable land, the agroecological conditions present, the length of time the land has been cultivated, and the amount of effort the cultivators, past and present, have exerted in improving and maintaining old plots and reclaiming new farmland. Many years, sometimes generations, are needed to develop terraces fully, particularly those on upland slopes. Construction work is carried out after the fall harvest and is undertaken at, and limited by, a considerable cost in time and labor. Terrace repairs are a yearly necessity for almost all landowners, and these too can be expensive.

However, terracing of both *khet* and *pakho* holdings on the steep slopes of Karnali produces agriculturally beneficial changes that extend beyond conservation of moisture and soil. Temperature regimes in the arable land are also altered with the reduction of field gradients. On north-facing hillsides terracing increases the incidence of solar radiation and heat absorption over the entire year. On south-facing hillsides terracing decreases these processes during the winter and increases them during the summer. The

Fig. 55. Well-developed terrace systems near Thirpu. Those below the village are khet; those on the hill flanks above the village, pakho.

overall effect of terraces is a general improvement in the heat budget of the arable soils.[22]

    Although the peasants' agricultural technology reflects a long history of generally shrewd human adjustment to and manipulation of their harsh

---

[22] A general discussion of agricultural terracing is furnished by Spencer and Hale (1961:1-40). For a valuable detailed analysis of terracing in central Himalaya of India, which close-ly resembles that in Karnali, the reader is referred to Andress (1966:141-78). Pant (1935:90-94) has some interesting observations on terraces and their importance in Kumaon.

Fig. 56. A log aqueduct bridging a defile conducts water from a tributary stream to khet *plots.*

environment, often by the processes of trial and error, it also reflects the severe locational, social, education, financial, and energy limitations with which they cope. When viewed by Western standards the agricultural technology is extremely backward. Tools and implements are a case in point.

Approximately a dozen different hand tools (hoes, mattocks, sickles, etc.) with wooden handles as shafts and iron blades or tips are used for various planting, cultivating, weeding, and harvesting tasks (see figure 58). However, wooden-tipped plows that differ little from those of the Middle East or Greece five thousand years ago are used almost universally in Karnali Zone (figure 59). Only a few random Pahari innovators in the lower Tila and Sinja valleys, as well as the Bhotia of upper Humla and Mugu, scratch the soil with iron-tipped plows such as are commonly used elsewhere in Nepal. Despite the fact that farmers may break five or six oak points in a day's plowing of rocky plots, and although they are aware of the iron-tipped plow and know that such an iron tip costs only two to four rupees (twenty to forty cents U.S.) they are loath to change, for they believe that it is easier for oxen to pull a wood-tipped plow. Yet they do plow with different weight implements according to the field condition. A fairly heavy plow of about 8-10 kg is used on *khet* fields to permit greater penetration of

Fig. 57. Upland pakho *terraces of immature development on a slope of twenty degrees in Gum Dara*

Fig. 58. A variety of iron-tipped or bladed agriculture implements. Scale is 50 cm.

the heavy clay loams, while a lighter plow is used on upland *pakho*.[23] Traction is usually supplied by teams of oxen, but a single ox, a cross-breed (from yak or cow), or even a horse may furnish traction on the light and dry soils in the Bhotia fringe areas.

During harvest times the food grains are cut, collected, and threshed by cattle teams, by flail (figure 60), or merely by beating the grain-bearing stems against the ground. In winnowing grains from chaff, families make good use of strong diurnal valley winds (figure 61). Once threshed and winnowed the grains are stored in a variety of containers in the home and, in many villages, in farmyard pits. Wooden chests called *katha* are large enough for a person to sleep on and hold 700-900 l (figure 62). Even larger, ceiling-high chests known as *bhakari*s hold as much as 2,200-2,500 l. Some

[23] For comparative densities and distributions of iron and wood plows in India, see Singh (1974:85-87).

Fig. 59. Plowman carrying wooden plow with oak tip used in khet *fields. © National Geographic Society.*

grain-rich households may devote entire rooms of their homes to grain storage after first sealing the walls with birch bark. Smaller containers such as clay pots (*dharos*) and woven bamboo vessels of 100-200 l in volume are also commonly used. All chests, pots, and bamboo vessels are carefully sealed with dung to obviate the ever present problem of loss to mice and rats. Storage pits often rival the wooden chests in size (figure 63). When grains are stored beneath the ground the pits are always lined with birch bark; but potato pits are not lined. However all are capped with a sheet of slate or schist and then covered with as much as a meter of soil to protect the foodstuffs from marauding animals.

Fig. 60. *Threshing with flails at Chhapru village, Rara Lake*

Cereal Yields and Total Production

The success or failure Karnali's peasant families have in producing enough food grain to meet their yearly requirements depends on the quality, quantity, and location of arable land at their disposal, the agricultural technology within their community, and the amount of labor they can marshall to apply that technology. With increasing elevation the range of crop combinations and associations that are possible narrows and the volume of cereal production decreases. Hence, at all spatial scales—household, village, panchayat, valley, economic subregion, and region—crop yields vary mar-

Fig. 61. Winnowing grain with help of a valley wind in khet fields in Asi Dara

kedly in response to the myriad of ecological and sociocultural conditions present. In addition, they fluctuate from year to year because of the vagaries of many of these conditions themselves. For example, in a good year some Tagadhari households produce a twenty-four-month food supply, while some Dum families are able to raise only a two-month supply on their own fields.

The 1969-70 (2026 V.S.) yields achieved in the thirty-five panchayats I surveyed are incorporated in table 13. These data indicate in striking fashion the wide range of yield values. They reflect not only the characteristic variation in productivity that exists among crops, but also the effect that varying combinations of spatial and temporal conditions have on each crop. Where improved varieties of wheat and maize seeds have been distributed by the government to a few families near Jumla-Kalanga (i.e., Jumla and Tibrikot districts), yields of four to ten times those obtained from indigenous varieties are reported, but only when recommended cultivation procedures have been adhered to.[24]

Fig. 62. Drying grain on a threshing floor roof for storage in a wooden chest, or katha

Throughout the zone, manure and seed rates (the amount of seed sown in a given plot or unit area) significantly affect yields, as do the cultivator's proficiency in agricultural pursuits and the amount of time invested in a field.

Other factors, over which the farmer has little or no control, further reduce potential crop productivity. Plant diseases and insects take their toll each year. So too do the vagaries of weather, such as unseasonable frosts, snow depth, flood, wind, and hail. For example, during the first week of October 1969, a single hailstorm that centered on the confluence of the Sinja and Tila rivers (economic region B) destroyed an estimated 20 percent of the

[24] Although the Panchayat Raj has established District Agricultural offices in Karnali Zone, as well as an agricultural experiment station at Jumla-Kalanga, use by the populace of better-yielding cereal varieties is, as yet, insignificant.

expected paddy production one week before harvest. For some households in its wake, this loss constituted 50 to 60 percent of the total grain yields they had expected in 2026 V.S.

Wild animals present a particularly serious problem to cereal production. Each year rhesus and langur monkeys, wild boars, Himalayan black bears, porcupines, jackals, and birds (especially crows) consume or destroy 10 to 25 percent of ripening grain crops in fields that fringe protective forests and rugged wastelands. I have watched, spellbound, a troop of twenty langurs eat their way through a finger millet field along the Mugu Karnali River like so many scythes. The people of nearby Rugu panchayat claim that such langur troops, totaling some 300 animals, deprive them of one-half their crops. Throughout the zone, but especially in upland *pakho* areas, concerned cultivators complain that this loss to wild animals has steadily increased since 1962 when the Panchayat Raj imposed restrictions on the possession and use of the ancient muzzle-loading muskets with which they previously had been able to hold in check or reduce such encroachments. Furthermore, labor demands prevent them from posting guards in all of their dispersed or scattered fields to scare away such intruders with noisemakers. And of the yields that are harvested, mice and rats, as well as insects such as rice weevils, often claim as much as 5 to 10 percent.

What then is the total annual cereal production of Karnali Zone? The Ministry of Agriculture estimates that the combined paddy, millets (including buckwheat), maize, wheat, and barley production totaled 30,200 metric tons in 2026 (Nepal 1972: table 11). However, field data on landholdings, crop regime, and yields indicate that this figure is highly questionable.[25] For example, the government estimate for Tibrikot District is grossly inflated, for it includes most of Tibrikot Dara, which is part of Dolpo District in Dhauligiri Zone, and (in 1969-70) not part of Karnali Zone. The field data suggest that a more plausible, albeit rough, estimate of food-grain production in 1969-79 is 24,600 metric tons. This figure is derived by applying the following assumptions, based on both informants and field observations, to the average kilogram per hectare yield figures in table 13: (1) of the *khet*, 95 percent is double cropped each year, while 5 percent is planted only in paddy; (2) of the *pakho*, 25 percent is double cropped and 75 percent is single cropped each year; (3) an additional 1,000 ha of recently reclaimed upland

---

[25] A recent regional development study by the Center for Economic Development and Administration supports this contention (CEDA 1975, pt. 2a, pp. 174-75): "No quantitative data on agricultural aspects such as total area of land cultivated, irrigated and nonirrigated land area under different crops, yields, etc. are available with the local agricultural office. The information in the 'Agricultural Statistics' published by EAPD [Economic Analysis and Planning Division, Ministry of Agriculture] is highly suspect and cannot be used for purposes of analysis."

Fig. 63. Pit storage of grain

and single-cropped *pakho* is unrecorded and thus not reflected in table 9; (4) of all *pakho* (both registered and unrecorded) 25 percent is fallow each year.

Accepting 24,600 metric tons as a fairly accurate approximation of total annual grain production, the question remains whether this quantity, equivalent to 132.3 kg per person, is sufficient for all the needs of Karnali's 186,000 population. Colin Clark and Margaret Haswell state that about 210 kg of grain per person per year is the minimum amount required for human

TABLE 13. Yields of important food crops for 2026 V.S. (1969-70) in kilograms per hectare.

| | Karnali Zone[a] | All Nepal[b] | |
	Range	Average	Average
Wheat (*Gahuñ*)	320-5,600	1,730	1,170
Barley (*Jau*)	200-4,350	1,450	930
Naked barley (*Uwā*)	150-2,570	660	N.A.
Paddy (*Dhān*)	750-8,750	2,120	1,910
Broadcast rice (*Buyā Dhān*)	190-2,730	680	N.A.
Maize (*Ghoga* or *Makai*)	190-2,940	1,170	1,840
Finger millet (*Kodo*)	260-5,600	2,050	1,110
Common millet (*Chinu*)	150-4,480	990	N.A.
Italian millet (*Kāguno*)	140-3,680	840	N.A.
Buckwheat (*Phaphar*)	200-3,200	1,230	N.A.
Beans (*Simi*)	70-2,210	700	N.A.
Potato (*Alu*)	150-4,600	1,190	5,770

[a]SOURCE: Bishop Panchayat Survey Data
[b]SOURCE: HMG Census of Agriculture, 1970-71

consumption in communities whose diet is primarily cereal (1970:59). By this measure, the zone produces only two-thirds of the grain required for human consumption. The following examination of diet and consumption permits both a clearer understanding of Karnali's agricultural deficit and a more realistic appraisal of its grain deficiency.

Diet and Consumption

Food grains constitute the major proportion of the diet throughout Karnali Zone. As has been emphasized, rice is the most important cereal for the Pahari, partially because of its status connotation and religious significance. It is called *chamal* once it has been dehusked with the use of a stone or wooden mortar and a heavy log pestle and *bhat* when it has been cooked (boiled) for consumption. The number of rice-based meals a family eats varies greatly with the availability of paddy. Some prosperous families are able to have rice for every meal each day; the least prosperous families, and especially the Dum, may enjoy a rice meal only once a month, usually at the time of a religious festival (i.e., the full-moon *purnimas*).

The other grains are similarly dehusked, ground to flour by either a hand-operated stone mill at home or by a water-powered communal *khatta*, and eaten in the form of fairly thin, round bread (*roti*) or thinner but larger *chapati*. A common practice is to stretch barley flour by mixing it with millet flour at a ratio between 1:1 and 5:1. Among the Bhotia, *tsampa* (barley that is roasted or popped on a bed of sand before milling) is mixed with water and eaten as a gruel or porridge. *Roti, chapati,* or *tsampa* often are the sole component of a meal, especially when people are working in the fields or traveling. However, most meals contain a portion of other foods that supplement the cereals. Protein-rich pulses are particularly important to the Pahari, who prepare them as a sauce known as *dhal* that is eaten with *bhat*. Vegetables are generally cooked as curries. Potatoes are usually treated as a curry ingredient, but among the Bhotia and poorer Pahari, they may be eaten, like the cereals, as a meal in themselves. Consumption of meat, milk products such as curd, and eggs and fowl varies with availability and caste precepts. In addition, all castes, particularly the Chhetri and Dum, make considerable use of edible wild plants to supplement kitchen garden foods. Overall the diet is bland and most dishes are augmented with spices, chili (*corsani*) and other condiments, often in the form of chutneys. Thus it is evident that in composition, quality, and variety, the diets of Karnali households display appreciable spatial, seasonal, and social (caste and ethnic group) variation.

The total amount of food grains eaten annually by Karnali's population is difficult to ascertain. The following information is based only on informants' responses to inquiries and direct observation of their eating habits, since actual measurement was beyond the scope of the field research.

The initial response of all adults questioned is always that they eat one *mana* (a volumetric measure equal to 0.568 l) of milled grain per meal, three meals a day. But, as James Fisher (1972:61) found in his study of Magar village in Dolpo, further questioning reveals that the number of daily meals and the amount of grain eaten at those meals currently falls short of this ideal. The standard of three *mana* of grain each day represents the amount adults may well have enjoyed prior to the population explosion that hit the zone in the early 1950s. While a few wealthy families still eat three large meals a day, the vast majority have only two major meals, plus a light half-meal or tiffin. Moreover, during preharvest periods when acute grain shortages occur, many families are forced to cut back to two or one and a half meals per day. Some Dum state that on such occasions they are able to eat only one daily meal.

The quantity of grain an individual consumes daily varies with such factors as age, sex, workload, size and body weight, time of year, and ambient temperature. My data reveal that the average daily grain consumption by an adult is only 2.0 *mana* or about 0.6 kg of flour (219.0 kg/year).[26] This is equivalent to 0.78 kg/day (284.7 kg/year) of harvested but unhusked cereal if we assume that an average weight loss of 30 percent occurs in dehusking and milling. The data also indicate that variations in consumption according to an individual's age are strikingly similar to those F. G. Bailey found in a multicaste village in the highlands of Orrisa State, India. Bailey states that he "considered all persons of fifteen years and over as full consumers, those from ten to fourteen as half consumers, those from two to nine as quarter consumers . . . [and] ignored those under two years old, since the amount of rice [cereals] they eat is negligible" (1957:277).[27]

If we take 284.7 kg/year of unhusked grain to be one consumption unit and apply Bailey's age/consumption multiplier to Karnali's population using the zonal age breakdown indicated in the 1971 Census of Population (vol. 1, table 6, pp. 63-64), we obtain a rough estimate of 37,700 metric tons of grains consumed by the population in 2026 V.S. This amount is 13,100 metric tons or 35 percent more than produced in the zone. Moreover, not all 24,600 metric tons produced in Karnali is available for household consumption, and storage and milling losses reduce the amount. In addition, every family uses some of its yields for trade and barter, as well as seeds for next year's planting. Some is also used by the Matwali Chhetri and Dum to make beer or liquor. Therefore as much as 40 to 45 percent of the total current grain requirements of the zone must come from surplus regions to the south.

The consumption figures above indicate the inescapable fact that in the face of increasing population pressure and limited resources at home and abroad most Karnali families are experiencing a gradual deterioration of their subsistence standard. The average daily adult consumption of prepared grains (0.6 kg) provides only about 1,911 calories and 49 g of protein.[28] If we accept 1,821 calories as the minimum caloric requirement for an adult male working eight hours a day (Clark and Haswell 1970:17), then this minimum is met. Grains and supplementary pulses and beans together probably are sufficient to meet more than the minimum protein requirement (Clark and Haswell 1970:6-7).

It must be remembered, however, that not all families are able to achieve even this level of consumption. The few health and nutrition stud-

---

[26] In order to compare grain consumption directly with yields and total production I have converted volumetric quantities to weight quantities according to the conversion tables included in Appendix B.

[27] It is noteworthy that Lionel Caplan (1970:77) in his study of Limbus in eastern Nepal, and Alan MacFarlane (1976:164) in his work with Gurung in central Nepal, also found that Bailey's formula fit the age/food consumption situation of their populations.

[28] Values obtained from Bernice K. Watt and Annabel L. Merrill, eds., *Composition of Foods*, Agriculture Handbook no. 8 (Washington, D.C.: U.S. Department of Agriculture, 1963).

ies that have been conducted in Nepal have found some degree of malnutrition in every section of the country surveyed, including Karnali Zone (Nepal Nutrition Status Survey, January-May, 1975).

Special Crops

In addition to the field and kitchen garden crops already discussed, a number of subsidiary fruit crops are grown on many homesteads throughout Karnali Zone. Walnuts, peaches, and apricots are the most important. These are raised between 1,000 and 3,000 m, but are more prevalent and productive in the temperate belt between 1,500 and 2,500 m. While all three crops, especially varieties of walnuts and peaches, are eaten in season, their seeds are usually of greater importance to the household economy, for these are a source of cooking oil, which supplements or sometimes replaces ghee or mustard oil. Families with a surplus sell or trade the fruits within their own village or panchayat. For those who live near Jumla-Kalanga, walnuts and peaches are particularly valuable trade commodities. In that bazaar twenty to fifty walnuts bring one rupee, depending on their size and quality. Similarly, fifteen to twenty peaches fetch one rupee in the market.

Below 1,000 m in the subtropical river valleys of economic region A, the villagers grow a variety of other fruits: bananas, mangos, guavas, rough lemons (*Citrus jambhiri*) and figs. A few villages, including Manma (a south-facing community at 1,150 m above the lower Tila River in Kalikot Dara) even boast a few mandarin orange trees, but their yields are reportedly low. In these lower reaches where walnut and peach trees are few or absent, ghee made from buffalo milk is the predominant cooking oil, although in some instances it is augmented with cottonseed oil.

The recent introduction of apple trees in the cool uplands has attracted considerable interest by both local farmers and government development planners. In 1953-54 a few Chhetri of Topla panchayat (Gum Dara) returned from winter work in the Naini Tal area of Kumaon with apples. Some seeds were planted in Toplagaon and nearby Raragaon, as well as at one village in Ludku panchayat, Sinja Dara. The few trees that grew to maturity in these villages each now bear 1,500-3,000 apples annually and provide their owners with a sizeable additional income, often as much as 700 rupees per tree. After harvest in Kartic (October/November) the apples are sold locally or in Jumla bazaar, where they have found a ready market at the rate of four to nine apples per rupee.

Recognizing the potential for arboriculture in Karnali Zone, the Panchayat Raj began an ambitious program of seedling distribution in 2025 and 2026 (1968-70) through the Remote Areas Development Board. Approximately 200,000 apple seedlings, as well as several thousand young walnut, apricot, and pear plants, were airlifted to Jumla for free distribution to

Karnali villages through the panchayat network. To date the success of this continuing assistance program has been limited because of slow distribution (many plants did not survive shipment), poor dissemination of cultivation instructions, inappropriate selection of planting sites, and inadequate watering and protection of the young saplings from animals. In the panchayats surveyed, the survival rate of these initial seedling shipments varies between 0 and 95 percent; overall it probably is no greater than 10-15 percent.

6

Animals, Extractive Industries, and Home Production

ANIMAL HUSBANDRY

A variety of domestic animals are kept by the people of Karnali Zone, principally water buffalo, hill cattle, yaks, yak–common cattle hybrids, sheep and goats, and horses. This husbandry is an essential ingredient not only in agriculture but also in home industry (handicrafts) and trade pursuits. For the vast majority of Pahari families livestock constitute a source of income and a capital investment second only to landholdings; but as crop productivity decreases with elevation, the importance of livestock in livelihood pursuits other than agriculture increases. For many Bhotia living in the highlands of economic regions C and D, as well as for some land-poor Pahari in regions A and B, animal husbandry supplants agriculture in importance. Therefore throughout the zone, possession of land or livestock determines and reflects both wealth and status.

The elevational zones within which these animals are found in Karnali are shown in table 14. The principal factor determining the elevation limits at which an animal can exist is the range of ambient temperatures it is able to tolerate. Hence, during the yearly round the seasonal movement of the more temperature-sensitive animals is critical to their survival.

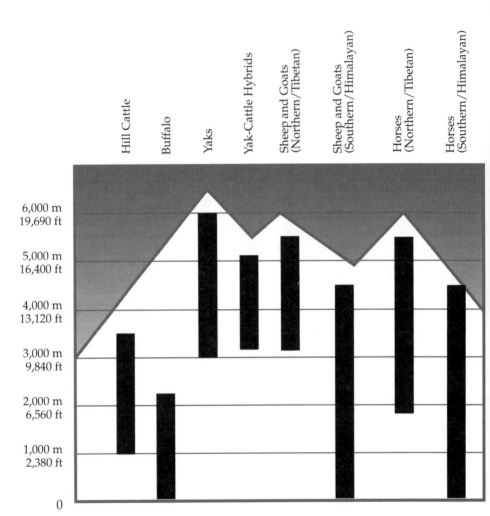

TABLE 14. Relative elevational zones of principal domestic animals in Karnali Zone.

The number and kind of animals a family is able to keep vary according to (1) its financial ability to acquire livestock; (2) the amount of time its labor force can devote to the care of animals, especially during the summer; (3) the capacity of its winter stabling facilities; (4) the location and ecological conditions of both its homestead and its grazing grounds; and (5) most important, the amount of fodder it can provide them from the fields, forests, and meadows to which it has access.

Unlike the quantitative information on landholding presented earlier, there exists a dearth of credible statistical data on livestock holdings in Karnali. On the basis of thirty of the thirty-five panchayats I surveyed (Appendix G, figure 99)[1] the estimated average family holding of livestock for 1969-70 is 2.5 cattle and buffalo, 0.05 yaks and yak-cattle hybrids, 6.7 sheep and goats, and 0.3 horses. The total number of these animals in the panchayat sample is about 104,000, or 9.6 per household and 1.63 per person. If these figures, which encompass one-third of Karnali's populace, are considered fairly representative of the zone as a whole, then the total current animal population of Karnali Zone is about 303,000. However, this very rough estimate must be accepted with caution, for it not only may reflect errors in informants' estimates in the panchayats surveyed but also may not account for large family holdings of sheep and goats, as well as yaks and yak-cattle hybrids, in unsurveyed highland panchayats on the Bhotia periphery. All available information leads to the belief that the figure may be on the low side by 5-10 percent at the most. Furthermore, such a gross family or per capita average obscures the great disparity in livestock ownership that exists not only among families but within and between the different castes or ethnic groups of Karnali. These differences in domestic animal holdings are illustrated by a sample of seventy-four households (table 15).

The Economic Roles of Domestic Animals

In order to better and more clearly understand not only the density and distribution of livestock in Karnali Zone but the roles the different animals play in the family economy (table 16), a brief discussion of each is called for.

Cattle and Buffalo. Karnali Zone cattle, which are small, nondescript hill breeds of poor genetic stock, are the most important animals for the Pahari farmers, for their roles are essential to their agricultural operations. The data indicate that hill cattle make up about 25 percent of the zone's livestock and

---

[1]   The following panchayats are not included because of insufficient or unreliable information on livestock holdings: Dhunge Dhara (Korana Dara), Seri (Khatyal Dara), Siuna (Raskot Dara), Mahadev (Rahala Dara), Gairogaon (Asi Dara).

TABLE 15. Animal holdings of seventy-four households by caste in 2026 V.S. (1969-70).

	Hill cattle	Buffalo	Yaks and hybrids	Sheep and goats	Horses	Total
A. Number (and percentage) of families owning animals						
Brahman	12	4		3	6	
	(100.0)	(33.3)	—	(25.0)	(50.0)	
Thakuri	7	5		4	5	
	(100.0)	(71.4)	—	(57.1)	(71.4)	
Chhetri	31	14		19	14	
	(91.1)	(41.1)	—	(55.8)	(41.1)	
Bhotia	4		4	3	2	
	(80.0)	—	(80.0)	(60.0)	(40.0)	
Dum	12	3		2		
	(75.0)	(18.8)	—	(40.0)	—	
B. Average number of animals per household						
Brahman (12)	11.9	0.3	—	0.8	2.2	15.2
Thakuri (7)	14.1	2.7	—	8.7	1.4	27.3
Chhetri (34)	6.5	1.0	—	18.2	1.7	28.8
Bhotia (5)	11.5	—	5.2	72.0	8.2	94.6
Dum (16)	2.5	0.3	—	1.0	—	3.8
Families (74)	7.4	0.4	0.4	14.4	1.8	24.8
C. Average number of animals per capita						
Brahman (102)	1.4	0.04	—	0.09	0.25	1.8
Thakuri (132)	0.8	0.14	—	0.46	0.08	1.4
Chhetri (289)	0.8	0.11	—	2.14	0.20	3.2
Bhotia (38)	1.2	—	0.68	9.47	1.08	12.5
Dum (104)	0.4	0.05	—	0.16	—	0.6
People (665)	0.8	0.09	—	1.6	0.20	2.8

85 percent of all its bovines. As is the case throughout South Asia, the cow is viewed as the mother of the bullock, which supplies the draught power in plowing, harrowing, and sometimes threshing. Although lighter and weaker than their counterparts on the plains to the south, hill bullocks are sure-footed and thus well suited for work in small plots on steeply terraced slopes. Ideally a family will own a sufficient number of bullock teams to handle all of its traction needs. Therefore the number of teams the more prosperous Pahari families possess is often an indicator of the amount of arable land they own. Those households with small landholdings or an insufficient number of bullocks must borrow or lease animals, or share them on a reciprocal and rotating basis; these cases often result in acute time binds during the critical planting seasons.

Cows and bullocks, like all livestock, are essential sources of manure. Although the cow's role as a milk producer is secondary to providing bullocks and dung, it is important for home consumption.

TABLE 16. Economic uses of principal domestic animals in Karnali Zone in 2026 V.S. (1969-70).

	Cattle	Buffalo	Yaks and crossbreeds	Sheep and goats	Horses
Manure	x	x	x	x	x
Meat		x	x	x	
Milk	x	x	x	x*	
Ghee, butter	x	x	x		
Yogurt, curds, whey, cheese	x	x		x*	
Plowing	x		x		
Transport			x	x	x
Sale	x	x	x	x	x
Sacrifice		x		x	x†
Hides, skin	x	x	x	x	
Hair			x	x	x

* Bhotia
† Only in Raku panchayat

Yields vary greatly according to the age and health of the milch cow, the time of its lactation period, the climatic conditions in which it lives, and the quality and quantity of fodder it receives. Throughout the zone yields are extremely low, averaging only about a liter per day. Maximum yields generally occur in July and August, when the cows feed on plentiful grasses in the grazing grounds, but even at that time they seldom exceed 2.5 l per day. Those families who produce a surplus of milk, curds, or ghee (clarified butter) will sell these items locally at about one rupee per *mana* (two rupees/l), 0.5 rupees per *mana* (one rupee/l), and five rupees per *mana* (10 rupees/l) respectively. Families living within a half day's walk of Jumla-Kalanga find a ready market for these products at the bazaar's hotels and teashops. There is little difference in the sales price of cows and bullocks. Values vary with the age of both, the milk yields of the cow, and the strength of the bullock. Adult animals bring between eighty and 400 rupees according to the village location and associated supply and demand; the average price in the zone is about 240 rupees.

Water buffalo constitute only about 3 percent of the total livestock population in the zone and 11 percent of all bovine, for they are generally ill-suited to the Karnali environment, Not only are they large, slow-moving, and clumsy, and hence unable to negotiate the rugged terrain as well as hill cattle, but neither do they tolerate the zone's cold winters. However, buffalo do accept stabling more readily than cattle. Thus buffalo are kept only by families living below about 2,400 m, with the greatest concentrations in the lower reaches of economic regions A and B. Because of their physical characteristics bull buffalo are never used for plowing, as they are on the plains. While a few are kept for breeding purposes, most males are disposed of. Some young are ritually sacrificed, chiefly during Dashain festivals, and their meat given to the Dum; most are sold or traded, again to the Dum, who have no sanctions against eating buffalo.

It is, then, the she-buffalo that is highly prized by the Pahari, for it produces more milk and manure than cows. Milch buffalo yield an average of 3 l of milk a day, three times that of cows. In addition, since their milk contains up to 50 percent more butterfat (Spate and Learmouth 1967:247), they are favored for ghee production.

For many buffalo-owning households ghee constitutes an important trade item for winter sale, chiefly in Nepalganj or Rajapur. Ghee, unlike milk, is generally measured by weight. One container (a kerosene tin) of ghee destined for export contains about 7.5 *dharni* (18 kg). Sold locally it brings 120 rupees; in the Tarai border market it fetches between 140 and 170 rupees, depending on its quality.[2] The difference in the economic roles milch and bull buffalo play is reflected in their rupee value. Adult females generally sell in Karnali Zone for 400 to 800 rupees, while a top milk producer may bring 1,000 rupees. Adult males, on the other hand, sell for only half the price of females.

When cattle and buffalo die from infectious diseases (cattle plague, or rinderpest, and foot-and-mouth disease are common and often take a heavy toll), they are buried. However, when they succumb to natural causes (including sacrifice), they are put to a number of uses. Dum eat the flesh of these animals, both male and female. Moreover both cattle and buffalo hides are used by Sarki for making shoes and in some instances bags for carrying grain. Damai also use ox hides in making their drums.[3]

Yaks and Yak–Common Cattle Hybrids. In Karnali Zone the long-haired, high-altitude yaks of central or inner-Asian origin and the yak–common cattle hybrids comprise about 0.5 percent of the total livestock population and about 2 percent of all bovines. As is the case throughout the Himalaya, these animals are associated with the Tibetan cultural tradition. Thus, their presence in Karnali coincides with the location of the Bhotia minority in northern Humla and Mugu (economic region C), as well as in the few scattered enclaves of Lum and Manisangu panchayats in economic region D.

---

[2] For a discussion of the importance of and constraints on ghee as a trade commodity in the hills to the south of Karnali Zone, see McDougal (1968:35, 47) and Caplan (1972:35-36).

[3] Marvin Harris (1966) provides an important analysis of the cultural ecology of India's sacred cow that is pertinent to Karnali Zone; so too is the treatise by Robert Hoffpauir (1974) on the water buffalo.

Purebred stock thrive best above 3,000 m; their greatest concentration is in Limi panchayat, upper Humla, where approximately 1,800 animals are maintained.[4] Yaks (male) and *dri* (female) serve a variety of economic functions: both furnish meat, manure, hides, and hair (which is woven into cloth for tents, ground cloths, etc.); males are important beasts of burden and plow animals (although in isolated villages that retain more relaxed non-Hindu precepts, females are also used); *dri* yield milk, much of which is converted into butter (especially for butter tea—comprised of Chinese brick tea, Tibetan salt, and butter—and votive butter lamps) and cheese.

However hybrids, which serve all the economic functions of the yaks except for supplying hair, are preferred by Bhotia living at lower elevations or in close proximity to the Pahari, for they have two important advantages. First, although the milk of the female hybrid contains less butterfat than *dri* milk, her yield is markedly higher in volume; hybrids produce approximately 2.5 l per day while a *dri* produces about 1.5 l per day. It should be noted that *dri* milk production exceeds that of milch cows and hybrid production approaches that of milch buffalo. The second important advantage of the yak–common cattle hybrid is that its temperature tolerances permit it to function well over a greater range of elevations. This attribute, plus the fact that hybrids are considered to be more tractable than yaks on the trail, makes the hybrid a more useful beast of burden.

The breeding of hybrids is the exclusive purview of Bhotia; most of the yaks and hybrids are owned by Bhotia families. However, a few Thakuri and Chhetri families in the cluster of polyethnic panchayats around Simikot in upper Humla do purchase hybrids from their Bhotia neighbors who deal in a brisk trade of these animals. In terms of sales values an adult yak or male hybrid may sell for 800 to 1,500 rupees, an adult *dri* with calf for 2,000 rupees, and yak–common cattle female hybrids for as much as 2,500 rupees.[5]

Sheep and Goats. Ovines comprise about 70 percent of Karnali's livestock population. The ratio of sheep to goats differs widely among households. Available data indicate no distinctive interregional patterns, but do show a general preference for sheep. At the zonal scale sheep outnumber goats two to one and reflect the suitability of Karnali's cool and fairly dry climate for sheep rearing.[6] Although goats are thought to be hardier than sheep, they are also more active and require greater attention in herding. Moreover, be-

---

[4]   Melvyn Goldstein, personal communication, Nov. 10, 1975.

[5]   Palmieri (1976) furnishes an exhaustive explanation of the ecological, functional, and cultural roles yaks and yak–common cattle hybrids play in the Nepal Himalaya and Tibet.

[6]   This condition contrasts with that in the lower hills south of Karnali Zone, where goats predominate over sheep primarily because they can tolerate greater rainfall and humidity.

cause of their browsing habits, goats require more human help in feeding (i.e., the lopping of green foliage from trees and large bushes for fodder). Family holdings of sheep and/or goats vary more widely than that of other principal domestic animals. Some Thakuri, Chhetri, and Bhotia households heavily engaged in trade keep flocks of 200 to 300; among the Bhotia of Limi panchayat 7,000 ovines, principally sheep, are husbanded and some rich families have 500 or more animals in their flocks.[7]

The sheep and goats found throughout most of the zone are light, small-framed, long-legged hill breeds with short, coarse hair, which tolerate a wide range of temperature (that is, elevational zones). In addition these animals are ideally suited for carrying loads over steep, rocky trails and weak, narrow suspension bridges that larger transport animals (the bovines already discussed, as well as horses) have difficulty on or cannot negotiate. The hill sheep of Karnali resemble the *barowal* breeds of Kumaon. When used for transporting loads they are known locally as *jaknas*. Similar distinctions are made with hill goats. High-altitude Tibetan sheep and goats, whose wool or hair is longer, thicker, and finer than the hill or southern varieties, are currently kept only by the Bhotia of Limi and Muchu panchayats in northwestern Humla. Since the tolerance of these northern varieties for warm weather is low, they are not suitable for long-distance transport to the south; hence they are used as beasts of burden only in the trans-Himalayan regions.

Thus, great differences exist between Tibetan and Himalayan (hill) sheep and goats, not only in their ability as pack animals but in the quality and quantity of wool or hair they yield. For example, Himalayan sheep, which are generally shorn twice a year—once in the spring (February or March) and once in the fall (September or October)—yield a total of between 0.5 and 1.5 kg, depending on the sex, size, and physical condition of the animal.[8] Their poorer-grade raw wool is normally converted to cloth, clothing, and knitted items that are used at home. When the wool of these southern sheep is sold, it brings only about seven to eight rupees per kg. Tibetan sheep, on the other hand, are shorn once a year—during the summer—and yield 2-3.5 kg of higher-quality, long-fibered raw wool that commands ten to twelve rupees per kg. This superior and preferred wool is used to make better-grade cloth, blankets, and knitted goods that are more often used for trade and export than for home consumption. A similar distinction is made in the quality of hair from hill and Tibetan goats, which is woven into blan-

---

[7] Melvyn Goldstein, personal communication, April 20, 1977.

[8] Both sheep and goats, like cattle, are subject to many ailments: liver flukes and eye infections are common; rinderpest and foot-and-mouth disease frequently reduce the size of flocks. Moreover informants report that 20 to 50 percent of newly dropped lambs and kids do not survive.

kets and rugs. In some Matwali Chhetri households goat hair is also tied into nets that are used to capture wild fowl.

As can be seen from table 16, the usefulness of sheep and goats extends beyond load carrying and wool or hair yields. For the Pahari, hill stock are not only the principal sacrificed animals but the chief source of meat. In the case of young animals, their skin is eaten along with their flesh. The skins of adult animals are used for rugs and, like bovine hides, for grain-carrying bags. However, neither ewes nor she-goats are milked by clean-caste Hindus, or by Bhotia who live in close proximity, apparently because of the Pahari sanction against consuming milk of animals whose meat is eaten.[9]

Only the more remote Bhotia (in Muchu and Limi panchayats) milk their sheep and goats. But, interestingly, the Bhotia of Mugugaon milk no animals of any kind, for they believe that milking reduces the strength of their livestock.

The rupee value of sheep and goats is generally similar and varies primarily according to age. Among the Pahari, lambs and kids intended for sacrifice bring twenty to forty rupees, while adult animals are valued between sixty and 150 rupees. A high-grade adult male Tibetan sheep in Limi commands 250 rupees because of its superior wool.[10]

Horses. Horses currently constitute about 3 percent of Karnali's livestock. They are used to some extent for riding and load carrying, and even for pulling the plow in remote Bhotia villages of northwest Humla. Their mane and tail hair is a valued fiber for woven ropes. And in at least one panchayat (Raku, in Sanni Dara) a young male is sacrificed yearly to the land god Bhumiaj. However, throughout the zone horses are raised principally for sale, either locally during the summer or, more important, at trade marts or fairs to the south and west (chiefly the Dang Valley, Rajapur, and Jouljibi) during the winter. While some Pahari and Bhotia households raise and breed horses, many more engage in this brisk seasonal trade by buying and reselling animals for a quick profit.

This horse trade is based on a deeply entrenched tradition. For many centuries the horses from what is today Karnali Zone have been renowned throughout western Nepal for their strength and stamina. One factor that has not only permitted the rearing of superior horses but has also contributed to their reputation has been the availability of extensive summer grazing grounds, or *patans*, between 3,000 and 4,500 m everywhere in the zone except its lower southwestern reaches (the trans-Karnali region of Sanni and Raskot *daras*). These subalpine and alpine meadows (see figure 18) are be-

---

9   Andress (1966:209) mentions that this belief exists among the Pahari of Garhwal.

10   Melvyn Goldstein, personal communication, April 20, 1977.

lieved to provide grasses and herbs during the monsoon season that are especially good for the animals' health and strength.

Two basic types or breeds are recognized: the small, wiry, long-haired, high-altitude (i.e., northern) horse and the larger and generally stronger, shorter-haired, southern Jumla horse. By crossing Jumla mares with Tibetan stallions, Pahari breeders achieve a cross-breed that blends the more desirable qualities of each. Informants concede that over the past decade the horse population of Karnali, and with it the volume of horse trade, has decreased because of both the difficulty in obtaining Tibetan stallions for stud and the increase of roads and mechanized transport in the Tarai. However, Jumla horses remain in great demand throughout the western hills of Nepal and even in the eastern Himalaya of India.

The rupee values of Karnali horses vary more than any other domestic animal. Within the zone Jumla horses or Jumla-Tibetan mixed breeds sell for from 100 to 300 rupees as yearlings, from 200 to 600 rupees as two-year-olds, and from 500 to 1,500 as adults, depending on their characteristics. When sold outside the zone the same stock will bring 50 to 100 percent more. And a high-quality Tibetan stallion from Limi panchayat may cost as much as 4,000 to 5,000 rupees.

Other Domestic Animals. Although mules are an important load-carrying animal in the lower hills of western Nepal as well as along the Kali Gandaki trade route between the Pokhara Valley and Mustang to the east, they are currently an insignificant beast of burden in Karnali Zone. The panchayat survey revealed only one donkey and eight mules in the Bhotia village of Mandara (Lum panchayat, Chaudhabisa Dara) and one donkey and fourteen mules owned by a shopkeeper in Jumla Kalanga (Chhinasim panchayat, Asi Dara). Whereas Karnali traders recognize the suitability of mules for transporting goods between the southern parts of the zone and the lower hills and the Tarai, recent efforts to form "mule cooperatives" have, to date, been unsuccessful. At present adult Jumla mules are sold to Byansi from Dharchula District (Mahakali Zone) for 800 to 1,200 rupees depending on their size.[11]

Poultry and pigs are also insignificant livestock in Karnali. Because of Hindu religious sanctions, high-caste families (thread-wearing Brahmans, Thakuri, and Chhetri) do not eat chickens or eggs, although they are permitted to eat wild fowl such as pheasant. Thus chickens are raised only by Matwali Chhetri and Dum, as well as by some Bhotia living in adjacent niches such Mangri village (Karan Dara) and Dillikot (Chaudhabisa Dara). Their current value is ten to twelve rupees. On the other hand, pigs are kept

---

[11] Mules from Tibetan mares are reported to be larger than those from local mares.

solely by a few Dum families as a source of meat and manure. Their sales value varies between thirty and ninety rupees, according to their size. Dogs are used by the Bhotia of Karnali Zone to guard the homestead or tent, as well as to help herd sheep and goats along the trail. Especially prized are hunting dogs trained to run musk deer to ground; these may sell for as much as 2,500 to 3,500 rupees.

Pastoral Regimes

Despite its long history of human occupance with associated alteration or destruction of its floral cover, Karnali Zone still contains extensive though rapidly deteriorating forest, grasslands, and meadows (table 6). The botanical composition of these areas varies with site (altitude, latitude, and longitude) and situation—in particular bioclimatological and edaphic conditions, and orientation and angle of slope (see chapter 2). Hence, a number of tiered and ecologically diverse belts and niches are present in the intermontane basin complex of the zone, as well as in the lower or outer midland Himalaya to the south: (1) subtropical, from 1,000 to 2,000 m (present in the zone only in the major incised river valleys, principally in economic region A); (2) temperate, from 2,000 to 3,000 m; (3) subalpine, from 3,000 to 4,000 m, which is generally the tree line in the zone; (4) alpine, from 4,000 to 5,000 m, approximately the lowest level of the zone's perpetual snow line (see figure 13).

The availability of sufficient wild vegetation for livestock fodder from these ecological belts and niches not only is essential for the husbandry of domestic animals per se, but is vital for agropastoral trade activities as well. By pursuing pastoral patterns of transhumance,[12] which span two or more ecological belts or niches, Karnali families owning livestock significantly expand the resource base of their household economies. These transhumant strategies permit them to devote all of their meager arable land to crops for human consumption or trade; no fodder crops are cultivated. Thus, humans and their livestock generally do not compete for food from the same land, as is usually the case on the plains, since most available pastureland is ill-suited for crops. Instead animal husbandry is not only seasonally and symbiotically intermeshed with crop production and trade, but furnishes an important linkage between humans and wild vegetation at their disposal.

Village membership determines a family's access to grazing grounds in nearby subtropical, temperate, and subalpine forests and grasslands (from

---

12 Winick defines transhumance as "seasonal movements of domestic animals from one area to another in which different climatic conditions prevail. This usually refers to mountainous regions, where such climatic differences in a fairly small area are common. Transhumance means also a kind of nomadism in which villages migrate annually with the herds to upland pastures during the summer months" (1956: 544).

a few minutes to one to two days away from the homestead), as well as the right to exploit other natural resources of those areas. Unlike cropland, which is privately owned, uncultivated land is communally controlled. Although all nonarable lands are the de jure property of the Government of Nepal, each village continues to exercise traditional de facto usufructuary authority over those in its immediate area and limits their exploitation to village residents. The adequacy of community forests and grassland pastures differs among neighboring villages because of variations not only in ecological conditions but in cultural history and associated settlement patterns. Such disparities or inequities may cause heated disputes between villages within a panchayat. More widely spread alpine meadows above the tree line on the *lekhs* (ridges) and mountain flanks lie from several hours' to four to five days' travel distance from the villages. Many of these highland *patans* (pastures) are shared during the summer by several communities from one or more panchayats (often from different valleys), again on the basis of long-standing tradition. Foreigners on the move with livestock are customarily granted reciprocal transit and limited grazing rights through any village or panchayat domain. They are not, however, permitted to use most of the lower grazing grounds close to villages, nor are they allowed to pasture their herds and flocks in higher *patans* for more than a few days.

Four distinctive though often interdependent or overlapping forms of transhumance are followed by the people of Karnali. These pastoral cycles represent adaptive strategies (i.e., human adjustments) motivated primarily by a combination of environmental conditions and economic considerations. Thus, according to its uses, each animal species occupies its own appropriate ecological niche, which varies with the time of year.

Ninety-nine percent of the zone's villages—all Pahari and most Bhotia communities below 3,000-3,300 m—pursue a pattern of transhumance that both supports and supplements sedentary agriculture (table 17,[13] and diagram A of figure 64). While examples in table 17 reveal expected spatial and temporal variations in the movement of livestock, they all display some common features.

In the spring (late March to early May) large flocks of sheep and goats, which have been pastured and used to carry trade goods south of Karnali Zone during the winter, are shepherded back to their home villages. There, for a few days to several weeks, they are grazed in nearby pastures or corralled briefly on fallow cropland for their manure. Then the ovines, along with horses, are sent uphill for four to six months to graze first through lower forests and grasslands, which early in the spring have been burned

---

[13] Note that the crop calendars of these villages are presented in table 11. The pastoral regime of Yari village, Muchu panchayat, in upper Humla is omitted, since its transhumance pattern is similar to that of Simikot.

over to foster a more succulent growth of summer grass (see figure 17), and then through higher and more distant alpine meadows. During the summer castrated male ovines (the transport animals) are also employed in northward-oriented or Tibetan trade trips.

About a month after the ovines and horses have been sent to summer pastures, the bovines follow. In the majority of villages these animals have been stabled on the farmstead during the winter and fed both hay residue from the grain crops and wild fodder collected from terrace bunds and hedgerows and nearby forests and grasslands during the previous fall.[14] By May or June this stock has been depleted but the wild vegetation of the grazing grounds is again available. For three to five months the bovines circulate through the lower forest and grassland pastures that the ovines and horses have vacated (frontispiece and figure 65). When draft animals are required for planting they are taken to the fields and then returned to the pastures.

Each summer those family members responsible for shepherding livestock build or reoccupy temporary *goths* (animal shelters) and *kharaks* (human habitations) in the grazing grounds. At lower temperate and subalpine forest and grassland camps they sometimes plant a supplementary and usually poor-yielding crop of buckwheat or, less often, potatoes, with village sanction. Cows, milch buffalo, and female yak-cattle hybrids must be milked daily and from time to time milk curds and ghee are brought down to the village. It is during these months when livestock can graze green herbage that they are the healthiest.

In September and October, with the end of the rainy season and with the exhaustion of fodder in the higher or more distant grazing grounds, the bovines are brought down to the village area, followed a few days to several weeks later by the sheep, goats, and horses. As in the spring, the return of the livestock in the fall is carefully coordinated with the agricultural calendar—the harvest of *kharif* crops, the planting of *rabi* crops, and the availability of stubble that can be grazed in the fallow fields. During the winter most families keep their bovines on the homestead. If a household has only a few ovines or horses that are not destined for transport or sale on trade trips to the lowlands, these animals are also wintered on or near the farmstead.

---

14 Among the grasses cut for fodder are *Chrysopogon* sp. (also used as a roofing material), *Helictotrichon* sp., *Pennisetum floccidum griseb.*, *Echinochloa crusyalli L. Bean,* and *Koeleria cristata.* Other herbage commonly lopped for animal food includes: *Caragona brevispina Royle (Balu kaldo,* or blackthorn), which is fed to livestock after the thorns have been removed; *Desmodium floribundum (D. Don),* a large shrub common in hedgerows and known locally as *chumlo;* and *Philadephus tomentosus Wall.,* a shrub found in temperate forest undergrowth. The foliage of many trees is also lopped for fodder; of these the oaks (*Quercus incana, Q. dilatata,* and *Q. semecarpifolia),* wherever they survive after many centuries of human destruction, remain an important source of wild fodder.

TABLE 17. Animal movement calendars for selected villages.

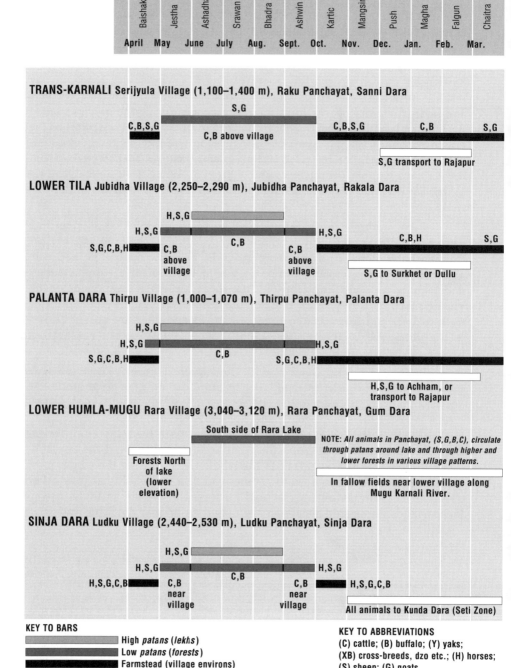

	Baishakh	Jestha	Ashadha	Srawan	Bhadra	Ashwin	Kartic	Mangsir	Push	Magha	Falgun	Chaitra
	April	May	June	July	Aug.	Sept.	Oct.	Nov.	Dec.	Jan.	Feb.	Mar.

TRANS-KARNALI Serijyula Village (1,100–1,400 m), Raku Panchayat, Sanni Dara

S,G

C,B,S,G   C,B,S,G   C,B   S,G

C,B above village

S,G transport to Rajapur

LOWER TILA Jubidha Village (2,250–2,290 m), Jubidha Panchayat, Rakala Dara

H,S,G

H,S,G   H,S,G   C,B,H   S,G

S,G,C,B,H   C,B   C,B   C,B
            above   above
            village   village   S,G to Surkhet or Dullu

PALANTA DARA Thirpu Village (1,000–1,070 m), Thirpu Panchayat, Palanta Dara

H,S,G

H,S,G   H,S,G

S,G,C,B,H   C,B   S,G,C,B,H

H,S,G to Achham, or
transport to Rajapur

LOWER HUMLA-MUGU Rara Village (3,040–3,120 m), Rara Panchayat, Gum Dara

South side of Rara Lake

NOTE: All animals in Panchayat, (S,G,B,C), circulate
through patans around lake and through higher and
lower forests in various village patterns.

Forests North
of lake
(lower   In fallow fields near lower village along
elevation)   Mugu Karnali River.

SINJA DARA Ludku Village (2,440–2,530 m), Ludku Panchayat, Sinja Dara

H,S,G

H,S,G   H,S,G

H,S,G,C,B   C,B   C,B   H,S,G,C,B
            near   near
            village   village

All animals to Kunda Dara (Seti Zone)

KEY TO BARS

High *patans* (*lekhs*)
Low *patans* (*forests*)
Farmstead (village environs)
Lowlands (within or south of Karnali)

KEY TO ABBREVIATIONS
(C) cattle; (B) buffalo; (Y) yaks;
(XB) cross-breeds, dzo etc.; (H) horses;
(S) sheep; (G) goats

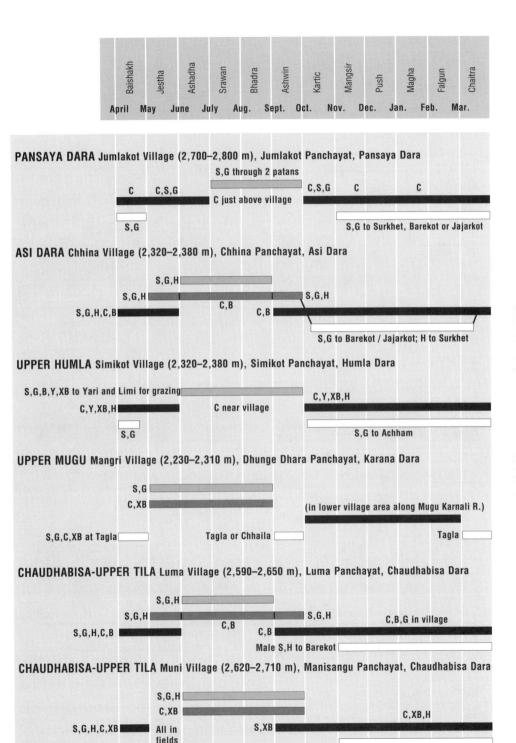

PANSAYA DARA Jumlakot Village (2,700–2,800 m), Jumlakot Panchayat, Pansaya Dara

S,G through 2 patans
C   C,S,G   C,S,G   C   C
C just above village

S,G   S,G to Surkhet, Barekot or Jajarkot

ASI DARA Chhina Village (2,320–2,380 m), Chhina Panchayat, Asi Dara

S,G,H
S,G,H   S,G,H
              C,B
S,G,H,C,B   C,B
S,G to Barekot / Jajarkot; H to Surkhet

UPPER HUMLA Simikot Village (2,320–2,380 m), Simikot Panchayat, Humla Dara

S,G,B,Y,XB to Yari and Limi for grazing   C,Y,XB,H
C,Y,XB,H   C near village

S,G   S,G to Achham

UPPER MUGU Mangri Village (2,230–2,310 m), Dhunge Dhara Panchayat, Karana Dara

S,G
C,XB
(in lower village area along Mugu Karnali R.)

S,G,C,XB at Tagla   Tagla or Chhaila   Tagla

CHAUDHABISA-UPPER TILA Luma Village (2,590–2,650 m), Luma Panchayat, Chaudhabisa Dara

S,G,H
S,G,H   S,G,H   C,B,G in village
              C,B
S,G,H,C,B   C,B
Male S,H to Barekot

CHAUDHABISA-UPPER TILA Muni Village (2,620–2,710 m), Manisangu Panchayat, Chaudhabisa Dara

S,G,H
C,XB
                                                              C,XB,H
S,G,H,C,XB   All in   S,XB
               fields
               above village
S,G in Barekot area

TYPE A—Dominant Pattern: All Parari and most Bhotia villages (from 1,100 to 3,200 m)

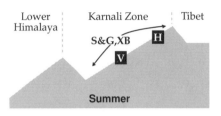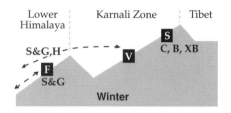

TYPE B—Limi Panchayat Bhotia of Upper Humla (villages at 3,700 to 3,900 m)

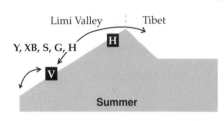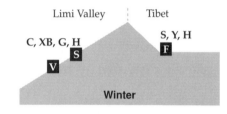

TYPE C—Mugu Panchayat Bhotia of Upper Mugu (village at 3,650 m)

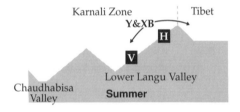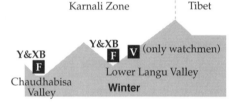

TYPE D—Mandara Bhotia of Lum Panchayat, Chaudhabisa Dara (village at 3,300 m)

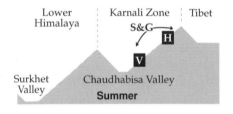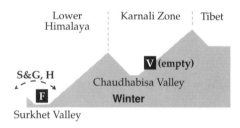

KEY

H Home village or Panchayat grazing grounds

S Homesteads stables and/or nearby village pastures

F Other (foreign) grazing grounds

V Village

C=common cattle/ **B**=buffalo/
Y=yaks/ **XB**=yak-common
cattle hybrids/ **S**=sheep/
G=goats/ **H**=horses

———— Transport animals to Upper Humla, Upper Mugu, or Tibetan border, grazing en route

- - - - Transport animals to Lower Himalaya, Tarai or Indian border, grazing en route

Fig. 64. Transhumance patterns of Karnali villagers in 2026 v.s.

Fig. 65. Pahari boy shepherding cattle in temperate forest. Note terressette caused by heavy grazing of bovines.

Families keeping large numbers of sheep and goats for long-distance transport, as well as those with horses for winter sale, permit the animals to graze briefly (several days to one or two weeks) on crop residue in vacant fields or in pastures near their villages. Then in late October or November they drive the animals south to lower, warmer, and snow-free areas in Achham District (Seti Zone) or Surkhet, Dailekh, or Jajarkot Districts (Bheri Zone).

During the winter Karnali transport and trade animals on the move are allowed to graze along the way on crop stubble in fallow fields, usually without charge, in return for the manure they deposit. However, when Karnali flocks are grazed for an extended period (three to five months) on the naturally cured wild vegetation in foreign pasture lands, the owners are generally required to pay a grazing fee to the village or panchayat having jurisdiction over these forests and grasslands. With the coming of spring, the hot, dry, premonsoon season, the yearly cycle begins once more.

Thus, as the examples in table 17 strikingly show, two spatially and temporally different pastoral patterns are followed by the majority of Karnali villagers—one involving bovines, the other large flocks of ovines. The bovine pattern (summer in the upland grazing grounds and winter on or near the homestead) closely resembles the seasonal bovine migration pattern of the European Alps; as such it might better be termed *alpage* (French) or *Almwirstschaft* (German). On the other hand, the ovine pattern just described is a true form of transhumance, for it involves both summer and winter pastorage far from the owner's farmstead. Three other distinctive patterns are followed by Bhotia whose villages are in peripheral or more isolated locations in Karnali Zone (see diagrams B, C, and D of figure 64).

Melvyn C. Goldstein (1975, 1980) discusses in detail the pastoral regimes of Limi panchayat (upper Humla) and the importance of these regimes to the panchayat's agriculturally based but grain-deficient economy.[15] Limi's three Bhotia villages (Til, 3,870 m; Alzhi, 3,690 m; and Tsang, 3,930 m) are the most northern, and possibly the most remote in all Nepal; they are also the highest in Karnali Zone. Because of a combination of environmental factors, winter snows block trails to the south and east, isolating Limi from the rest of Nepal for five months (mid-November to mid-April); routes to Tibet, on the other hand, are usually passable throughout the year. Therefore, while Limi lies within Nepal, its diverse economic pursuits, and especially its animal husbandry, display a strong year-round northward or Tibetan orientation.

---

[15] Since neither I nor my field assistant was able to visit Limi panchayat in the course of my fieldwork, the information presented on Limi is drawn from both Goldstein's publications and personal communications with him.

The Limi Bhotia control a number of extensive alpine meadows above timberline that lie within one or at most two days' travel north, south, and east of their villages. For four summer months (mid-May to mid-September) all panchayat livestock—yaks and *dri*, common cattle, yak-cattle hybrids, Tibetan sheep and goats, and Tibetan horses—circulate and graze through these communal pastures, managed by herders who live in yak-hair tents traditional to Tibetan and inner-Asian nomads. The highest-ranging animals are horses, which graze to about 5,200 m, and yaks, which may graze as high as 5,500 m or more on some south-facing, snow-free meadowlands. Each year families draw lots to determine which *patans* each may use, and in what order. Moreover, no livestock may be grazed close to the villages where grassy areas are the source of fodder that is cut and later fed to stabled animals during the winter. Families with small numbers of livestock sometimes attach these animals to large herds and flocks to conserve their limited labor force.

During the winter all Limi families stable their few common cattle and yak-cattle hybrids, and in some cases their horses, in the home. When weather permits they also allow these animals to graze on nearby slopes in order to supplement the limited store of cut fodder. In addition families of Til village, which has more adjacent pastures that are snow-free in winter, keep from ten to thirty yaks and *dri* and as many as thirty to forty goats at home throughout the winter. This seasonal pastoral regime of grazing livestock in upland pasture in summer and stabling them in the home in winter with supplementary grazing nearby conforms with the *alpage* pattern found elsewhere in Karnali Zone.

However, those few Limi families (about two dozen, principally from Tsang village) who husband large flocks of Tibetan sheep (often over 500) and herds of yaks and *dri* must seek extensive snow-free winter pastures outside the panchayat's domain. These they find to the north in Tibet (see diagram B, figure 65). In mid-October these animals, along with some horses and a few goats, are driven over the Lapcha Pass (approximately 5,600 m) to an area east of Lake Manosarowar that is as high in elevation as many of the summer grazing grounds in Limi. There on the treeless, cold, and windy Tibetan Plateau these vast flocks and herds graze naturally crude, arid, alpine steppe vegetation for eight months; not until the end of May will they return to Limi. For successful winter grazing a combination of light snowfall and high-velocity winds that sweep the snow into drifts and expose the grass is essential. When heavy snowstorms or light winds occur there is high animal mortality.

Those family members who manage the flocks and herds are often assisted by hired hands or relatives. These herders and shepherds continue to live in their yak-hair tents through the Tibetan winter. Thus, this segment of the Limi population leads a life of true pastoral nomadism, moving with the season between the Limi and Tibetan econiches.

Until a decade ago many Nepalese Bhotia groups with villages close to the Tibetan border were able to engage in this nomadic form of transhumance. However, in the early 1960s the Chinese closed Tibetan grazing grounds to all Nepalese Bhotia except those of Limi. By a unique agreement with the Chinese the Limi Bhotia continue this traditional pastoral regime and thus are able to maintain their large and lucrative herds and flocks. But for all other Bhotia groups in Nepal the loss of access to winter plateau pastures has been economically devastating. Lacking suitable winter grazing grounds in the Nepal Himalaya, they have been forced to drastically reduce their animal holdings and readjust their pastoral practices. In Karnali Zone the villagers of Mugu are a case in point.

Possessing scant and poorly producing arable land, the Bhotia of Mugu village (figure 66), at 3,650 m in the upper Mugu Karnali Valley only 15 km from the Tibetan border, have always depended on trade and associated animal husbandry for their livelihood. Until 1962 these Mugali enjoyed a profitable entrepôt or middleman position (a virtual monopoly) in the salt-grain exchange trade between eastern Karnali Zone and Tibet.[16] Their livestock—Tibetan sheep, yaks, and *dri,* and a few yak–common cattle hybrids—were used primarily for transporting loads and for wool and hair. The Mugali milked no female animals, because of their curious belief that the practice would reduce the animals' strength. Neither would they use any bovines for draft animals. Instead, they cultivated their meager fields by hoe or by pulling the plow themselves.

During the summer (June through September) large Mugali caravans shuttled back and forth between Cheptu, just on the north side of the Namja Pass (5,600 m). The distance between Mugu and Cheptu was three days' travel with animals, which would graze the alpine meadows along the way. In Cheptu the Mugali exchanged food grains obtained from Gum, Sinja, and Asi *dara*s the previous fall and stored in Mugu over the winter for salt and wool supplied by Drogpas (Tibetan pastoral nomads referred to as Chopas by the Mugali).[17] In October the Mugali drove their sheep unladen to Cheptu, where their Chopa trading partners were hired, at a rate of about 1 kg of food grain per animal, to shepherd the flocks in Tibetan winter pastures until the following June, when the Namja Pass was snow-free and summer trade could recommence. However, the Mugali pastured their bovines through the winter (from November through February) in the lower Langu Valley

---

[16] In this volume the term "Mugali" denotes only Bhotia of Mugu village and not all Bhotia of upper Mugu (i.e., economic subregion 9). Also note that Mugu panchayat consists of only one village (Mugu).

[17] A detailed discussion of the salt-grain trade appears in a later section.

one day's journey south of Mugugaon. These pastures belong to Bhotia villages in Karan Dara who exact a grazing fee of three rupees per animal for the use of their pastures. Leaving usually only one family member to look after the home and herders to tend the bovine in the Langu Valley, all other Mugali spend the winter months trading or working further south, primarily in the Pahari villages of Gum, Sinja, and Asi *daras*.

When the Chinese closed Tibetan pastures to the Mugali in 1962, they also imposed restrictions such as price-fixing on Mugali-Chopa trade. Subsequently, in 1968, they closed the Cheptu trade mart in favor of one they themselves supervised at Pongdzu, an additional three days' travel into Tibet (six days from Mugugaon). In the face of these changes the Mugali were forced to modify as best they could the pastoral regime just described. Lacking access to sufficient winter pasture for sheep, they no longer could maintain flocks. To compensate for the loss of this important animal, the more prosperous families actually increased the number of yaks they kept; but severed from their Chopa source of these animals, the Mugali can now replenish their herds only by obtaining yaks from Limi. Moreover, they no longer breed yak–common cattle hybrids, for they can no longer sell them to Chopa trade partners. Those few hybrids that the Mugali kept are acquired from other Bhotia in upper Mugu or, more often, upper Humla.

Since 1962, when some Mugali began to enlarge their yak herds, the winter snow-free grazing areas (open, wind-blown slopes with a southern exposure) in the lower Langu Valley have been insufficient.[18] Today over half the herds are pastured for six months (October through March) in the Chaudhabisa Valley six days' journey south of Mugugaon. There the Mugali pay a similar grazing fee to the Matwali Chhetri villages that control these *patans*. Hence the current Mugu Bhotia pattern of transhumance involves summer grazing of bovines (used chiefly as pack animals) along the route between Mugugaon and Pongdzu and winter pastorage of these herds in both the Langu and Chaudhabisa valleys. This regime is illustrated in diagram C, figure 64.

A third distinctive Bhotia pattern of transhumance is followed by the families of both Mandara village at approximately 3,300 m in Lum panchayat (Chaudhabisa Dara) and Dandakhet at about the same elevation in Jhakot panchayat (Gum Dara) and 10 km north of Mandara. Since the settlement history, pastoral regime, and seasonal migration routine of these two intermarrying Bhotia groups are virtually identical, only Mandara is discussed here.

About seventy-five to 100 years ago these Bhotia migrated from Mustang to Karnali. Owning no land or permanent homes, they were no-

---

[18] In 1969 twenty-one Mugu families maintained 700 yaks.

nomadic herder-traders whose livelihood depended primarily on their role as middlemen in the northern (or Tibetan) trade during the summer and the southern (Nepal lowlands and India) trade during the winter. But in 1951 the government granted them ownership of some subalpine cropland on the northern fringe of the Chaudhabisa Valley on which they subsequently built permanent summer homes.

Today the Mandara Bhotia (nineteen families and eighty-five people) raise barely a two-month supply of food (winter barley or wheat, summer buckwheat, potatoes, and radishes). Furthermore, they own no bovines, but do lease draft bullocks each year from their Matwali Chhetri neighbors for one *dharni* of wool or twenty-five rupees per team. Thus their livelihood remains dependent on the profits they accrue from trade, which in turn de-

Fig. 66. Bhotia village of Mugu at 3,650 m. Since 1966, Chinese restrictions on trade with Tibet coupled with a poor agricultural base have forced a permanent out-migration of forty-four families to the southern reaches of Karnali Zone, to Kathmandu, or to India (Darjeeling, Kalimpong, and the Kulu Valley).

pends on the husbandry of transport animals (in 1969-70 they owned 300 sheep, 220 goats, fifty horses, nine mules, and one donkey). As such the Mandara Bhotia are now seminomadic agropastoralists whose transhumant regime is illustrated in diagram D, figure 65.

For a month in the late spring (mid-May to mid-June) all livestock are grazed on or near the Mandara homesteads. Then animals not used on trade trips to Mugu circulate through three alpine meadow areas until mid-September, when all animals return to the village area for another month. In mid-October the entire population abandon the village and as a group drive their livestock (carrying trade goods) south to the Surkhet Valley in the inner Tarai. This migration takes four to six weeks. For the next four months (mid-November through mid-March) the Mandara Bhotia dwell in temporary shelters erected on fallow fields 3-4 km east of the Surkhet airfield and graze their animals first on crop residue in those fields and then on the wild vegetation of nearby subtropical forests and grasslands. Each family pays the host households one rupee for sitting rights; each also pays the host village a grazing fee of 0.5 rupees per horse or mule and 0.15 rupees per sheep or goat. From their winter base members of each family make several trade trips to Nepalganj, usually using their transport animals. Then with the coming of spring and the hot season (April) they regroup to begin the return migration to their Chaudhabisa homesteads.

In sum, these are two basic traditional systems of transhumance in Karnali—the dominant system pursued by 99 percent of the population (all Pahari and most Bhotia) and the subordinate, and today unique, system of the Limi Bhotia, whose viability depends on access to Tibetan pastures. Each has, in turn, a Bhotia variant. One is that of the Mandara Bhotia, relatively recent immigrants who were formerly landless but now own some arable land; their system is evidently in transition from a true pastoral form to one more closely resembling the dominant Pahari/Bhotia system. The Limi variant is that of the Mugali, whose traditional transhumance was recently truncated by the loss of Tibetan grazing grounds and whose current form appears to be the least viable. Their life style seems to be on its way to extinction. Furthermore, while it is true that in the past the distance animals were taken in search of food during the rhythmical pastoral cycles was usually directly proportional to the severity of the environment at the home village, it now appears that social, political, and economic concerns have so modified transhumance that distance is no longer an independent variable.[19]

Beekeeping

Beekeeping is an ancillary aspect of animal husbandry that is extensively, if not intensively, practiced throughout the zone below 3,000 m. Families living in upland villages, where nearby plant cover furnishes a better supply of pollen and nectar, maintain more hives than those living in lower and more denuded valleys. The most notable beekeeping regions are the upper Sinja Valley, where Had Sinja panchayat alone has 1,075 hives, and the Chaudhabisa and upper Tila valleys, where Lum and Manisangu panchayats boast 864 and 259 hives respectively. The most northern extent

---

[19] Uhlig (1976) models and describes for comparative purposes the various elevationally and ethnically stratified or graded transhumance systems followed by mountain farmers and shepherds of the Himalaya. Pant (1935:49-60; 165-74; 175-86) describes forms of transhumance as they existed in Kumaon prior to World War II; these forms are similar to those followed in Karnali Zone today. Other valuable discussions of Himalayan transhumance include those provided by: Nitzberg (1970:22-30) for Chamba in the western Himalaya of India; Andress (1966:236-49) for the lower Himalaya (i.e., the Mussoorie Ridge) in Tehri Garhwal; Fisher (1972) for a Magar village in Dolpo District; and Messerschmidt (in Goldstein and Messerschmidt 1980) on the Gurung of central Nepal.

of beekeeping is found in the Simikot area of upper Humla, 431 hives. Although most beekeeping families maintain only one to three hives, a few have as many as thirty-five or forty.

Karnali's populace is unaware of the valuable role bees perform in the pollination of their economically significant plants, particularly their fruit trees and kitchen garden (horticultural) crops, and many of their major field crops as well (see Kurup 1967:585-86). Those families who keep bees do so solely for honey. As a substitute for sugar, which must be imported from the Tarai or India, honey is used primarily in tea and sweets; it is often spread on breads (*roti*) or pancakes (*chapati*). It is also a key ingredient in a number of home remedies and in Hindu rites, especially the marriage ceremony. Thus, honey has both economic and religious importance for the Pahari who predominate in the regions of the zone where beekeeping is practiced. On the other hand, no such importance is attached to apiculture in the exclusively Buddhist Bhotia areas of upper Humla and Mugu where honey cannot be produced and thus must be imported.

Husbandry techniques are relatively unskilled and honey yields are correspondingly modest. Hollowed sections of logs 25-40 cm in diameter and 50-100 cm in length, or roughly constructed wooden boxes of similar volume (figure 67) are used as hives and placed in shaded homestead sites. Such single-chambered hives make the removal of honey awkward and that which is harvested is often impure, because it contains bee larvae. Moreover, the crowded conditions in many hives frequently cause colonies to swarm and at lower elevations the bees are ill-tempered and prone to migrate.[20]

Recent attempts by a government-sponsored Cottage Industries Program at Jumla-Kalanga to introduce an improved design of hive with moveable frames have been unsuccessful, apparently because the thin-walled construction of the new hive did not provide sufficient insulation for local conditions.

Honey is usually harvested once each year in Kartic (October/ November). Yields range between 0.5 and 25.0 kg per hive, but average only about 4.2 kg per hive. On the basis of my panchayat survey, I estimate that the total annual production in Karnali Zone is about 70,000 kg.

All honey is consumed locally. Those beekeeping families who produce a surplus exchange honey for cash, grains, or ghee. Its cash value varies from region to region, ranging between three and twelve rupees per kg and averaging seven rupees per kg.

---

[20] Although I did not identify the species of *Apis* kept in Karnali, these characteristics would seem to indicate that *A. dorsata* are common in the lower areas, while *A. indica* are more widespread and predominate at higher elevations (see Kurup 1967:575-82).

Fig. 67. Newly constructed beehives, Gum Dara

OTHER USES OF AVAILABLE RESOURCES

Timber and Firewood

Over the centuries Karnali households have not only cleared the forested slopes for settlement, farmland, and grazing grounds but have also derived a variety of useful and needed products from the remaining forests. Besides fodder for livestock these include: lumber for bridges, homes, furniture, plows, and other agricultural implements, tools, and containers (*katha* and beehives); scores of edible wild plants and medicinal herbs for both home consumption and trade; and, most important, firewood for cooking, heating, and processing various products.

As they exploited their forests the villagers altered, and in many instances destroyed, the original forest cover. Especially hard hit over time have been the oak species of the subtropical, temperate, and subalpine ecological belts where the vast majority of the zone's settlements (both permanent and temporary) are located. On the lower subtropical valley flanks below 2,000 m the oaks have been succeeded by either *Pinus roxburghii* (Chir pine) or, more often, grass and scrub species. In higher temperate environments the fast-regenerating blue pine (*Pinus excelsa* or *salo*) has colonized areas where oaks and other trees have been destroyed.

Another notable species that over the years has suffered even greater decimation than the oaks is the Himalayan cedar (*Cedrus deodara*). Deodar beams are reported to last for seventy-five to 100 years and hence are prized for construction. Furthermore, in the past cedar was the only tree of sufficient commercial value to warrant its difficult export to India. Village elders in Asi and Sinja *daras* recount that as recently as the 1930s huge cedar logs were floated down the Karnali River system to the railhead at Katorian Ghat, southeast of the Tarai border bazaar or Rajapur. Today mature deodar grow only in isolated niches or as sacred village trees, generally associated with Masta shrines (see figures 36 and 67). Some have a diameter of 3-4 m. In addition large trunks still bridge many rivers in economic region B. In those panchayats where a few deodar are still felled today, twenty planks (approximately 0.5 m wide and 3-4 m long) are worth twenty-five rupees, while an entire mature blue pine fetches only nine rupees.

Because of their proximity to Tibet and their access to nearby subalpine and temperate forests in upper Humla, the Bhotia of Limi have for many generations engaged in a profitable export of two forest products to Purang and the trade town of Taklakot: birch (*Betula utilis*) and pine (*P. excelsa*) beams for building construction on the treeless plateau; and lathed wooden bowls, for which Limi craftsmen are famous throughout Tibet. Bowls of lower quality are made of birch, while high-quality and preferred ones with striking grain are fashioned from maple burls cut from live trees.[21] In recent years the increasing scarcity of such burls in Humla has made it necessary for Limi Bhotia to travel during the winter to northern Kumaon and procure them from Indian foresters. Limi panchayat's command of these products in all probability has contributed to its continued right to use winter grazing grounds in Tibet.

During the Rana regime the government attempted to impose laws designed to regulate village exploitation of the forests. In most parts of Karnali these "foreign" sanctions were largely ignored or circumvented. Indeed the population had not reached a size that overtaxed the forest resource capacity—a capacity due in part to the regenerative characteristics of blue pine, which by then had become the most commonly used species for both lumber and firewood. With a seemingly inexhaustible amount of forest available for their basic needs, Karnali households were generally both lavish and wasteful in their use of wood. For example, the use of only crude

---

21 This practice does not kill the tree.

axes and adzes for felling trees and shaping beams and planks sacrificed a high proportion of the tree. During the clearing of forests for cropland, "unneeded" trees were indiscriminately burned (figure 17). In many areas field-trail boundaries were fenced with an excessive amount of timber.

Since the 1950s, however, escalated population growth has triggered a marked increase in forest deterioration—one that is approaching critical proportions. The cumulative and combined effects of continued forest clearance for cultivation, heavy interforest grazing of livestock, uncontrolled burning of forest undergrowth and grasslands, lopping for additional fodder, and timber and firewood extraction are contributing to the accelerated degradation and destruction of the delicate ecology of the upper Karnali intermontane basins. Most alarming is the dwindling availability of lumber and firewood. In response to this condition the Panchayat Raj has imposed a more stringent forest management policy. In order to fell trees for lumber a household head must procure a special permit from the district government officials in return for a fee. In the case of firewood, only dry or dead timber can be collected. But with the exhaustion of this store, live trees are continually felled, often after their trunks have been ringed to kill the tree and so conform to the deadwood sanction. Thus, as in Rana times, most forest foragers, particularly those from villages far from government scrutiny, continue to disregard Kathmandu's dictates.

The amount of wood collected from Karnali forests solely for cooking and heating is staggering, as it is throughout Nepal.[22] On the basis of panchayat and household interviews, as well as personal observations and limited measurements, I estimate that in 1969-70 (2026 v.s.) the average Karnali household of six persons cut, collected, and consumed 6,100 kg of wood for fuel and heating. At this rate the population of the zone currently requires about 191,000 metric tons of fuel wood annually. Although this rough approximation may overestimate somewhat Karnali's fuel wood consumption, it does indicate its order of magnitude.[23] S. P. Mauch's (1976:125) estimate of fuel wood consumption in the Jiri region of the eastern Nepal Himalaya is of a similar magnitude.

Another striking measure of the escalating population's impact on the zone's forest cover is suggested by available maps and satellite data. A comparison of maps (1:50,000 and 1:250,000 scales) based on 1950 informa-

---

[22] The Energy Research and Development Group (1976) estimates that 95 percent of all wood removed from the forests and scrublands is consumed for fuel.

[23] It must be noted that because of insufficient data this present annual fuel consumption calculation (191,000 metric tons) does not reflect the portion of the populace who use dung as fuel in alpine grazing grounds above tree line, those Karnali residents who travel or reside outside the zone for extended periods (for trade trips, seasonal work in the lower Himalaya or India, etc.), or those foreigners who travel through or temporarily reside in the zone (e.g., traders, trekkers, and government employees).

tion and 1972 Landsat imagery indicates that approximately 50 percent of the zone's forests were destroyed in two decades (about one generation), leaving less than 20 percent of Karnali Zone still under forest cover.[24]

These recent trends are causing increasingly serious time and labor binds for most Karnali households, particularly those in the longer and more densely populated lower valleys of economic regions A and B. There the collection of a load of firewood now commonly requires a one-day trip from the farmstead. A generation ago such a trip would have required only an hour or two. Projecting this current rate of deforestation, the fuel wood supply for many communities will be so distant that the villagers will not be able to afford the increased time required for obtaining wood. They will then be forced to burn dung, at the expense of their fertilizer needs, as is now done in the lower, more denuded regions of Nepal. Thus, a negative chain reaction (i.e., positive feedback) in the energy flow will be set in motion.[25]

Although His Majesty's Government has recognized, belatedly, the severity of deforestation on the steep Himalayan slopes, it has to date in Karnali Zone initiated no effective measures to counteract the problem, such as much-needed village or panchayat programs to develop sustained-yield tree farming for wood fuel. Although most Karnali families are ever more aware of their dilemma, they have as yet been unable to abandon traditional exploitive practices in favor of cooperative communal efforts to develop an adequate, self-sustaining, and nearby source of firewood.[26]

Only in Phoi village of Mahadev panchayat (lower Sinja Valley) has an attempt been made at tree farming. This successful innovation was initiated by a village leader who was a representative of the Farmer's Organization to the National Panchayat.

Plants and Medicinal Herbs

Exploitation of the flora in Karnali Zone extends beyond fodder for livestock, timber for construction, and firewood for the hearth. From the time humans first penetrated this inner-montane region over a millen-

---

[24] Here again these estimates must be viewed with some caution. The extent of forest cover indicated on the maps (see table 6) in all probability overestimated the extent of forests in 1950; the Landsat data (figure 19) on the other hand presents a more accurate measure of the 1972 extent of forest, although some errors in interpretation could have been caused by the fact that the imagery was recorded in November and deciduous forest areas are difficult to discern. Therefore, the 1972 amount of forest area (20 percent) may be an underestimation.

[25] Eckholm (1976:74-113) presents a cogent discussion of deteriorating mountain environments and the alarming energy/firewood crisis that the developing nations face. The subject of positive feedback systems is dealt with in chapter 8.

[26] Rieger (1977:539-45) furnishes a brief but perceptive insight on the social problems associated with and contributing to deforestation in the Himalaya.

nium ago, they have derived a variety of other benefits from the wild vegetation at their disposal. In the course of our fieldwork my wife and I collected only a limited sample of 225 plants; but of these, 107 serve one or
more useful purposes. They range from edible berries, fruits, nuts, and leafy
wild vegetables to pigments for dying cloth (*Rubia cordifolia*), fiber for twine
and paper (*Daphne papyracea*), conifer cones for ink (*Abies spectabilis*), and
aromatic oil for both cooking and anointing the heads of newborn babies to
protect them from the cold (*Prinsepia utilis*).

Most of the beneficial species we collected are important for their
healing properties and are used to treat human or animal maladies. The following examples further illustrate the keen ethnobotanical knowledge displayed by Karnali families:[27]

Aesculus indicus Hiern. (horse chestnut): a large, moist, temperate-
forest deciduous tree between 1,200 and 3,000 m whose fruit is not only fed
to horses suffering colic but is also ground into a powder applied to humans' boils.

Anemone elongata D. Dom (vernacular: *congrate phul*): an alpine
flower used to remove leeches in the noses of sheep by making them snuff
its juice.

Anemone rupicola camb. (vernacular: *magramul*): a flowering plant
found in alpine meadows between 3,500 and 4,200 m; the uncooked juice
from its roots kills worms on vegetables and meat.

Argyreia ventusta Chaisy: a vine in low river valleys used to treat
both humans and horses with sudden stomach pain; part of the flower is
mixed with garlic and taken internally.

Arisaema tortuosum (Wall.) Shatt.: a tuberous herb that looks like a
large jack-in-the-pulpit, found between 900 and 2,700 m; is used as an animal medicine: the seeds with salt are fed to sheep to cure colic, and the roots
are fed to cattle with worms; is also used as an ingredient in making *rakshi*
(a native liquor).

Litsea umbrosa Nees. (vernacular: *kaule*): a small evergreen tree
found in moist, shady draws between 1,500 and 2,500 m; its bark is ground to
a powder and added to bread (*roti*) as a baking powder; its seeds are dried and
pressed for oil to treat skin diseases and abrasions.

Origanum vulgar Linn. (oregano): a small herb of the mint family
common throughout Karnali between 2,000 and 3,700 m; yields a pungent
aromatic oil that is applied externally on toothache, earache, and rheuma-
tisms; is also dried, ground to a powder, and used as incense.

---

[27] A more extensive list of useful wild flora of Karnali Zone is provided by Shrestha
(1977:71-72).

Potentilla fruticosa Linn.: a shrub found between 2,200 and 4,800 m; its dried leaves are burned in some religious rites, used as an astringent, and boiled as a tea substitute.

Punica granatum Linn. (pomegranate): the fruit is eaten and cooked as an ingredient in chutney; the juice is a pickling agent. All parts of the plant are used as medicine.

Pyrus pashia Ham.: a species of wild pear that is eaten, added to tobacco, and cooked with water for sick cattle.

Rhamnus minuta Crub.: a shrub, used as an eye medicine (the juice of the wood is cooked).

Rheum specitorme Royle (rhubarb): grows in subalpine and alpine pastures up to 4,200 m; its roots are a strong astringent used to stop diarrhea.

Rhus semialata (sumac): found in shrub form below 1800 m in the warm valleys; its berries are mashed to a paste, mixed with honey, and taken for dysentery.

Thymus serphyllum (wild thyme): common in alpine meadows; its leaves and flowers are cooked in water and eaten as a vegetable. The preparation is also used as a horse medicine.

Several dozen medicinal herbs that grow in the zone are of commercial value. They are in demand not only by practioners of ayurvedic medicine in Nepal and India but by pharmaceutical firms in India and other countries.[28] These plants provide many families with an important supplementary source of income. They are collected from the temperate and subalpine forests and alpine meadows during the rainy season and early fall by members of generally poorer Chhetri, Matwali Chhetri, Bhotia, and Dum households who use them as trade items, either within the zone or, more often, at the Tarai border markets of Nepalganj or Rajapur during the winter. Table 18 indicates the dried or cured 1969-70 values of the three most important medicinal herbs exported from Karnali Zone—*hattijaro (Orchis stracheyi)*, *attis (Ascontitum heterophyllum Wall.)*, and *katuko (Picrorhiza scrophulariae)*.

Karnali plant collectors report a marked decrease in availability of all species, and especially those of trade value, in recent years. This trend they universally ascribe to the environmental degradation already discussed. Many collectors now find it more profitable to pursue other strategies for supplementary income such as porterage, seasonal (winter) work in India, or panchayat development projects that pay a wage.

---

[28] The Nepal Himalaya contains a wealth of medicinal plants that are exported. For a comprehensive country-wide enumeration and description of this resource see Nepal (1970). In addition, Dobremez (1976:97-107) furnishes a brief discussion of the exploitation and prospects of medicinal plants in eastern Nepal.

TABLE 18. Value of three important medicinal herbs in 2026 V.S. (1969-70).

Herb	Within Karnali Zone Rupees/*dharni* (rupees/kg)	Tarai border markets Rupees/*dharni* (rupees/kg)
Hattijaro	50-70 (21-29)	100-150 (42-63)
Attis	8-12 (3-5)	20-30 (8-13)
Katuko	4-5 (1.7-2)	10-20 (4-8)

Cannabis sativa, from which *ganja* (marijuana) and *charas* (hashish) are obtained, is today an even more valuable trade item than the herbs just mentioned. The cultivation of *Cannabis* by some households has already been noted. However, wild *Cannabis* is ubiquitous throughout the zone's temperate regions, between 2,000 and 3,000 m (see figure 68). It is this feral variety that furnishes the bulk of the *charas* produced in the zone. Three to four hundred plants yield one *tola* (11.664 g) of the resinous hashish after about one hour of laborious hand rubbing by a skilled old woman.

Although *Cannabis* has been used in Nepal as an ayurvedic medicine and as a hallucinogen for centuries, it was the demand by westerners for hashish, both in Nepal and elsewhere,[29] that greatly inflated its value during the 1960s (see Fisher 1975:247-55). In response to this demand the Panchayat Raj has attempted since 1961 to regulate the production and traffic of *Cannabis* in all forms and confine its sale to licensed dealers within the country. These events are reflected in the current 1969-70 values of Karnali *charas.* Within the zone it sells for a half rupee per *tola* (forty-three rupees/kg). When sold to licensed dealers in Nepalganj or Rajapur it brings two to three rupees per *tola* (172-258 rupees/kg), but when sold illegally in northern India it fetches about five rupees per *tola* or 429 rupees per kg. Informants estimate that over half the *charas* exported from Karnali Zone (and the rest of western Nepal as well) is smuggled into India.[30]

---

[29] Reliable sources state that the 1970 street value of pure, high-grade hashish in Western Europe or the United States was about $3,500-$3,900 per kg.

[30] It is important to point out that in 1973 His Majesty's Government bowed to pressures exerted by many countries and the United Nations and banned the cultivation, purchase, or sale of *Cannabis* in Nepal; however the possession and traditional uses by Nepalese citizens were not outlawed. Insufficient information precludes appraisal of the effects these new laws have had on the collection, processing, and illegal traffic of *Cannabis* in Karnali Zone.

Fig. 68. Wild Cannabis sativa *at 2,400 m in Gum Dara.* © *National Geographic Society.*

Hunting and Fishing

Until about 1960, the hunting of noncarnivorous mammals for food was an important pursuit of many Karnali households, Pahari (Brahman and Dum excepted) and Bhotia alike.[31] The chief herbivorous meat-yielding species were wild boar, or *badal* (*Sus scrofa*), barking deer, or *ratua* (*Muntiacus muntjak*), gray goral (*Nemorhaedus goral*), himalayan *thar* or *jharal* (*Hemitragus jemlahicus*), and serow, or *thar* (*Capricornis sumatraensis*). For Bhotia near the Tibetan border, blue sheep or *bharal* (*Pseudois nayaur*) was the most important species hunted. Goldstein[32] reports that Limi Bhotia sometimes shot for food great Tibetan sheep, or *nayan* (*Ovis amon hodgsoni*) and wild yak (*Bos grunniens*) in the vicinity of their winter grazing grounds in Tibet. Animals that destroyed crops or preyed on livestock were also hunted. Thus such hunting, along with the degradation or destruction of the animals' natural habitats, drastically reduced the zone's wildlife populations.

However since the early 1960s, when the Panchayat Raj imposed not only rules governing the use of firearms in hunting but regulations intended to restrict the exploitation of forest and forest animals, the hunting of large animals for these purposes has become insignificant in most panchayats, particularly in the more densely settled lower areas of economic regions A and B. Only in more remote and higher areas far from government eyes and ears is clandestine and now illegal shooting of wildlife continued by a few hunters. Hence government sanctions on hunting have slowed the rate at which most wildlife species are shrinking. Exceptions to this trend are two animals that furnish products of great trade value: the snow leopard, or *chitwa* (*Panthera uncia*) for its pelt, and the musk deer, or *kasturi* (*Moschus moschiferus*) for its musk. The killing of these animals continues unabated and they now face extinction in Karnali Zone, as well as throughout the Himalaya.

The habitat of the rare snow leopard is the treeless alpine and subalpine wilds of upper Humla and Mugu. In Humla, Bhotia pit-trap them near their village in winter when they attempt to prey on livestock. In the Langu Valley of upper Mugu, Bhotia kill the cat with poison-tipped bamboo spears, which they drive into the ground along rocky game trails during the December-January hunting season (Jackson 1979:63-72).[33]

The musk deer, whose habitat is the subalpine birch forests, produce the most valuable single trade item obtained from the zone's wild biota.

---

[31] The major wildlife species and their habitats are discussed in chapter 2. It should be noted that carnivores and omnivores (animals that themselves eat flesh) are not eaten by either Pahari or Bhotia because of religiously based dietary prohibition.

[32] Personal communication, Oct. 15, 1979.

[33] Jackson, who observed the annual winter hunt of the Bhotia of Dalphu and Wangri in 1976-77, reports that since international prohibitions on the traffic of snow leopard pelts were imposed in the early 1970s its trade value has dropped drastically; however, the cat is still killed in order to demonstrate the hunter's skill.

Musk, a pungent substance obtained from a subcutaneous abdominal sac found only in males, is in great demand throughout the world as a perfume fixative and, in Asia, as an ingredient in some oriental medicines.[34]

A single gland contains from one to five *tola* (12-60 g) of musk. When sold in the Tarai or India each *tola* of the dried secretion in 1969-70 brought about 500 rupees (43,000 rupees/kg).[35] With such economic rewards to be had, Pahari and Bhotia hunters ignore 1962 government bans on killing musk deer in Karnali Zone and poach intensively using techniques that vary regionally.

In the birch forests of Humla and those further south in economic regions B and D the hunters drive the deer between ever narrowing brush barriers toward snare traps. Others employ specially trained hunting dogs to run down the deer. These dogs, which resemble a Shetland in size and shape, are bred by Tibetan refugees now living in Humla and sell for 2,000 to 3,000 rupees. A buyer can usually cover this cost with the capture of only one or two male musk deer. The Bhotia of the Langu Valley (upper Mugu) do not use snares, barricades, or dogs. Instead they hold to their traditional hunting technique and use poison-tipped bamboo spear traps. When hunting musk deer, they place their spears in forest locations frequented by the animal and often drive their prey toward the traps by setting fire to the forests.

Small game is still hunted legally throughout the zone and continues to provide many households with additional food. For example, in many Pahari panchayats villagers use snares or nets to capture various pheasants for home consumption or local trade. However, Pahari hunters no longer engage in trapping and training falcons for export to India. With the end of the British Raj in 1947, the demand for these hunting raptors—for which Karnali was a famous source—ceased.

The fish that abound in Karnali Zone rivers and streams below 300 m, as well as those in Rara Lake, are another important food resource, one that is primarily exploited by Pahari and Dum of economic regions A, B, and D. Although families of all castes are free to fish within their village or panchayat domain, it is the Dum who most frequently engage in this supplementary livelihood pursuit. Nevertheless, some exceptions to this general

---

[34] Local legend in Karnali attributes the formation of the musk sac to the male deer eating many poisonous snakes and in the process developing an immunity. Thus it is taken internally as an antidote for snake bites. Moreover it is believed that musk contains medicinal properties that protect people not only from malaria (*aul*) when they travel in the lowlands in summer but from the cold of severe highland winters.

[35] Foreign importers report that the 1969-70 value of first-quality musk was approximately $H.K. 17,800/kg and $U.S. 5,000/kg. (personal communication with importers on May 20, 1970).

rule do exist. In a few panchayats the traditional practice of contracting out fishing rights to foreigners from other panchayats still prevails. When poachers are caught fishing these privileged streams, they are fined as much as forty rupees per violation by the controlling panchayat.

The most commonly consumed species is the snow trout, or *asla* (*Oreinus richardsonii*), which grow to 45 or 50 cm in length and 8-10 cm in diameter. Species of carp (*Barbus*), which grow no longer than 15 cm, are also eaten. Fishing techniques vary according to ecological conditions or local custom: hook and line, spear, net, and bamboo trap (figure 69). Fish that are not eaten immediately are either sun-dried or smoked for future home consumption, and any surplus is traded within the village or panchayat generally for food grains. The current rate of exchange is one *dharni* (2.393 kg) of dried or smoked *asla* for four to eight *mana* (2-4 kg) of grain, depending on which cereal is procured. Fish caught in the Tila River or its tributaries near Jumla-Kalanga are often sold in the bazaar for four rupees per *dharni* (about two rupees/kg).

Mining and Quarrying

Karnali villagers put stone, clay, and earth from nearby rock outcrops and wastelands to a number of uses. Metasediments, principally schists but in a few locations slate, furnish building material for homes, terrace walls, trail steps, etc. Ochre and white clays and earths provide plaster and paint for the walls and floors of homes. Some earths are also used as fixatives to prevent natural vegetable pigments from running when cloth is dyed. Others are themselves used as fabric dyes. A few informants report that in the past, when they could hunt with muskets, they sometimes pried garnet crystals of the correct caliber from schists and used them as a substitute for lead shot.

However, within the zone only limestone and copper have been found in sufficient quantity or quality to warrant mining. The largest exploitable deposits of limestone are located near Mandara in the Chaudhabisa drainage. These outcrops constitute a readily available source of lime that could provide much-needed fertilizer; but, as has already been mentioned, they have not as yet been put to this use. At present the Chaudhabisa limestone deposits are quarried only to supply cement, plaster, and whitewash for new government buildings, two days away in Jumla-Kalanga. There, one maund (37.324 kg) fetches fourteen rupees.

Until recently, a workable copper mine near the villages of Dalphu and Wangri in the Langu Valley provided many Bhotia families an important source of income. During the Rana regime each family was required to pay the government an annual contract fee of forty-five rupees for the right to use the mine. High-quality ore was collected from scree slopes below the ore-bearing outcrop and extracted from the outcrop itself. In the latter case

Fig. 69. Dum trapping fish in Tila Karnali River near Jumla-Kalanga

horizontal shafts were dug into the bedrock as far as 10 m in order to remove a seam of ore that contained solid copper nodules sometimes as large
as 50 cm in diameter. After smelting the ore using small-scale and primitive
methods, the mining families not only fashioned the metal into vessels and
utensils for household use locally but traded it regionally. However, the
great amount of charcoal required in the crude smelting process (about 222
kg of wood—*Pinus excelsa*—for every kilogram of pure copper produced)
was causing such forest destruction that the government banned this Langu
industry in 1950. At present only surreptitious mining and processing continues for home needs. The loss of this trade commodity, along with more
recent Chinese restrictions on Tibetan trade, has contributed to the increased
emphasis the families of Dalphu and Wangri are currently placing on hunting activities already described. Thus we have in this instance an example
where government conservation policies are, in fact, a double-edged sword.

Even though no exploitable iron deposits have as yet been discovered in Karnali Zone itself, several working mines are found to the south in Jajarkot District (Bheri Zone). These mines are the closest source of iron for agricultural implements in Karnali; hence, the import of pig iron from Jajarkot remains an important feature of interregional trade. In Jajarkot the locally produced iron currently has a cash value of twelve rupees per *dharni* (five rupees/kg); in Karnali Zone it sells for twice this amount. More often, however, Jajarkot iron is exchanged for Karnali medicinal herbs.

Today only one geological resource, *silagit*, is exported from Karnali Zone. *Silagit* is a sticky black hydrocarbon similar to tar that oozes from a few rock outcrops in Sinja and Gum *dara*s. It is in demand in India for use as an ayurvedic medicine and aphrodisiac. Karnali informants claim that when this substance is mixed with milk and drunk it "cleans out the insides and makes you pure and strong." Every few years (twelve to fifteen years in Sinja Dara) the Pahari families who control access to this "renewable" resource collect, boil down, and shape the substance into pancakes, which they sell in Nepalganj for two to three rupees per *tola* (172-258 rupees/kg).

HOME INDUSTRIES

As in most agriculturally oriented subsistence economies throughout the Himalaya, home industry of one type or another is an essential livelihood component for the great majority of households in Karnali Zone. The less productive the agricultural or animal husbandry components of a family's economy, the more important is its home manufacture of basic necessities. Thus, while those wealthy Pahari and Bhotia households possess the purchasing power to obtain, either locally or abroad, not only these articles but luxury items as well, most must produce for themselves as many items as possible if they are to make ends meet. Moreover, for many families the production each year of these items for sale or barter is critical.

The principal homemade products of the zone are wool and cotton cloth for clothing, woolen knit goods such as sweaters and mufflers, and woven wool, goat-hair, and yak-hair blankets and rugs. A family's ability to engage in these handicrafts, as well as its volume of production, depends on a number of factors. These include the family's access to the requisite raw materials, the size and composition of its labor force, the traditional or newly acquired skills of that labor force, and the amount of time the family can devote to home industry.

Cotton and Woolen Cloth

Cotton homespun, known in Karnali as *tetuwa*, is produced only by Pahari villagers who live in or near the lower valleys of economic region A, where the fiber crop has long been cultivated. Most carding and spinning, and all weaving, of *tetuwa* is performed by men (figure 70), and all dying or printing is done by women (figure 71). These tasks are not caste-specific; instead they are undertaken by all ranks, Brahmans and Thakuri included. However, tailoring of Pahari clothing is, with few exceptions, caste-specific, for this task is performed by occupational Damai specialists who work within the *jajmani* system or are hired for piecemeal sewing.[36]

Some families who do not grow cotton themselves purchase raw cotton from neighbors for either five rupees per *dharni* (two rupees/kg) or for tobacco at an equal exchange rate by weight. Other households that no longer grow or have access to Karnali cotton but continue to produce homespun use Indian yarn, which in Tarai market towns sells for forty to sixty rupees per bundle. Most *tetuwa* is consumed at home, but a few families do produce a surplus, which they sell, usually in their village or panchayat, by the roll for fifteen to twenty rupees. The fabric in a roll measures one *hat*, 45-50 cm in width (the standard loom width for not only cotton but also most woolen goods) and twenty-four *hat*, or about 12 m in length. Hence the value of cotton homespun in Karnali is two to four rupees per m^2.

Although Karnali zone may well have been self-sufficient in cotton at some time in the past, it is not today. The *tetuwa* currently produced satisfies the needs of only a small portion of the populace. In the face of the fast-growing population, the availability of cheaper and preferred machine-loomed cotton cloth from India, and recent changes in the styles of dress which reflect both Indian and Western influences, less and less cotton is grown in Karnali each year. Thus, the vast majority of households import Indian cotton fabric from Tarai markets where it sells for 0.75-12.0 rupees per meter, depending on the type, quality, and width of goods. In Jumla Bazaar these goods are twice as expensive.

Woolen homespun is produced throughout the zone in Pahari, Bhotia, and Dum households. But while wool from Karnali sheep is used, this source falls far short of meeting the zone's needs for both clothing and other products. Hence most households must depend on the flow of imported wool from Tibet. Wool, unlike cotton, is always spun on a hand spindle (figure 72). This technique allows men mobility and the opportunity to spin yarn during their leisure time (of which they have much more than women) or when they are away from their homestead performing tasks not requiring the use of hands (e.g., carrying loads, tending animals). In order to

---

[36] A few enterprising Damai now work with hand-powered sewing machines they have imported from India and charge six rupees to sew a set of clothes. With the increased speed that their machines provide, they can earn much more per day working by the job than by time (i.e., eight rupees/day). Although their clients prefer to have machine-sewn clothes (a status symbol), they concede that hand-sewn apparel lasts longer.

Fig. 70. Matwali Chhetri man weaving cotton cloth, or tetuwa. Such pit looms are commonly used in the Mugu Karnali Valley.

meet some of their own needs, Dum often spin for Pahari in return for raw wool. Men on the move are able to spin as much as 0.5 kg per day; when stationary they double this output. If woolen yarn, unlike *tetuwa*, is to be dyed, this female operation is usually performed prior to weaving. Between seven and nine *dharni* (3-4 kg) of yarn can be dyed in one day. In Pahari households only men weave; but in Bhotia homes it is the women who weave (figure 73).

Fig. 71. Pahari woman printing hand-loomed cotton cloth with natural dyes

The production of both woolen and cotton hand-loomed cloth, as well as other woven woolen items, is a winter activity. Only the elderly family members, who no longer can perform strenuous physical labor, have the time to weave during the agricultural seasons. Women weavers of Bhotia households from upper Humla and Mugu who winter in Pahari areas further south (i.e., the Simikot area of Humla and Gum, Sinja, and Asi *daras*) often weave for high-caste Pahari in return for six rupees per day (in cash or grain). The daily output of either wool or cotton on the crude shuttle looms varies between four and eight *hat* (1-2 m^2) per day, depending on the weaver's skill and the type of item being woven. While almost all *tetuwa* is consumed within the zone, woolen hand-loomed cloth for clothing is important for both home consumption and trade. Many Karnali households produce a surplus which they sell within the zone in the lower hills, and in

Fig. 72. Matwali Chhetri man spinning wool on a hand spindle

the Tarai. In all three areas first-quality dyed fabric sells for about 2.5 rupees per *hat* (ten rupees/m^2).

Clothing costs constitute the highest yearly manufactured commodity expenditure for all but the most wealthy Karnali families. Among the Pahari, women's apparel is less expensive than that of men, who wear a greater number of woolen items. A set of men's woolen clothes (i.e., coat and pants cut to the current fashion) costs sixty to seventy rupees in materials and dye, and thirty to forty rupees in labor. If sold locally, this set fetches 120 to 160 rupees and may last through two or three years of hard wear, whereas a set of Pahari woman's wear is approximately half as expensive, but must be replaced more often. Among the Bhotia, both men and women

Fig. 73. Bhotia woman weaving woolen cloth at her homestead. Note that the warp is cotton yarn while the woof is woolen yarn.

wear wool garments in styles that require more material than those of the Pahari.[37] Thus clothing expenditures vary according to caste and status. These conditions are apparent from a sample of seventy-four households (table 19). Note that the strikingly low Dum clothing expenditure reflects not only these occupational castes' meager purchasing power but also the fact that they are not expected, required, or encouraged to be au courant in dress.

---

[37] It should be noted that the Bhotia of upper Humla also make sheepskin coats for greater warmth during the harsh winters. Melvyn Goldstein (personal communication, Oct. 15, 1979) reports that those of superior quality are made from forty to fifty lambskins for an adult's garment and are covered with Chinese corduroy cotton cloth obtained from Tibet. These lightweight but warm garments sell for about 1,000 rupees. Inferior and heavier coats are made from seven to eight mature sheep and sell for 500 rupees.

TABLE 19. Clothing and total commodity expenditures for seventy-four families in 2026 V.S. (1969-70).

Caste	Average expenditure on clothing (in rupees)[a]	Average total expenditures on all commodities (in rupees)[b]	Average clothing expenditure as percentage of total
Brahman	10,659	26,760	
per family (12)	888	2,230	40.5%
per person (102)	106	262	
Thakuri	16,410	34,878	
per family (7)[c]	2,344	4,938	47.0%
per person (132)	124	264	
Chhetri	21,503	42,132	
per family (34)	632	1,239	50.7%
per person (289)	74	146	
Bhotia	4,715	9,758	
per family (5)	943	1,952	48.2%
per person (38)	124	257	
Dum	4,136	8,167	
per family (16)	259	510	50.6%
per person (104)	40	79	
Total	57,423	121,695	
per family (74)	776	1,645	48.1%
per person (665)	88	183	

[a] Both local and foreign-made items; values include all costs (e.g., raw materials, tailoring, sewing) except family labor inputs.

[b] All local and foreign products except home-produced foodstuffs and family labor inputs.

[c] Note that this sample includes one extended family with sixty-four members.

Indeed many Dum families must depend on the largess of high-caste Pahari clients for their clothing.

Knitted Garments

Hand-knitted woolen sweaters, mufflers, socks, gloves, and hats are also important for both home consumption and trade. In Karnali Zone these articles are knitted only by men, Pahari and Bhotia alike. Elderly informants state that knitting is a recently acquired skill, one that has developed only since the 1930s.[38] The importance of this significant innovation lies in

[38] Evidently this is the case throughout most sectors of the Himalaya. Nitzberg (1970:94-95) notes that the knitting skill was first introduced in Chamba (the Indian Himalaya) in the 1930s. Pant (1935), in his detailed descriptions of both Pahari and Bhotia handicrafts in Kumaon, does not mention the production of any knitted items; his field observations were made prior to 1932. James Fisher (personal communication, Mar. 18, 1969) believes that knitting is a recently introduced handicraft in the Magar village of Tarangpur (Dolpo District).

the fact that, like spinning with a hand spindle but unlike weaving with a throw-shuttle loom, it is a mobile or footloose activity that can be done anywhere at any time one's hands are free.

In Karnali only natural (i.e., undyed) wool is knitted, usually with homemade needles or imported wire or with metal struts cannibalized from machine-made umbrellas of Indian manufacture. The knitted items produced, particularly sweaters and mufflers from the superior wool of Tibetan sheep, are in great demand not only in the zone but also in the lower hills and Tarai as well. The material and labor costs and trade values of the principal garments knitted in Karnali are presented in table 20.

TABLE 20. Principal knitted garments for home use and trade in 2026 V.S. (1969-70).

	Sweater	Sleeveless sweater	Muffler
Amount of wool (avg. weight)	1.8 kg	1.2 kg	0.6 kg
Cost of wool (in rupees)	13-22	8-14	4-7
Spinning time (in hours)	23-40	10-16	5-8
Weaving time (in hours)	30-34	23-25	7-9
Rupee value, within zone	30-40	15-20	8-10
Rupee value, south of zone	40-60	20-35	10-20

Blankets, Rugs, and Other Woven Goods

Of the limited variety of blankets and rugs produced in Karnali, most are made from the same woolen fabrics that are woven for clothing. These generally are a single, solid, natural color (i.e., white, brown, or black). Others, however, are woven specifically for use as blankets or rugs. Families in some villages or valleys produce distinctively striped items with dyed wool that identifies their source. For example, the Bhotia and Matwali Chhetri of economic region D (Chaudhabisa Dara) produce finely woven blankets or wraps of alternating red, white, and black bands (see figure 31), or red and black bands.

Bhotia and Pahari alike weave undyed goat hair (cut from their animals only every other year in order to have sufficiently long fibers) for a rug known as *pheruwa*. In addition, Bhotia of economic region C (upper Humla and Mugu) also weave yak-hair blankets and tent material for household use and local trade. Notably absent from Bhotia woven goods are thick-piled "Tibetan" rugs and carpets of intricate designs, many colors and great width

---

There, as in Karnali Zone to the west, only men knit. For a discussion of the important function of knitted goods in Tarangpur trade see Fisher (1972:109-16).

(up to 1 m) such as the Sherpas of eastern Nepal produce; these the Karnali Bhotia have traditionally obtained from Tibet itself. Indeed, throughout Karnali all wide woven items are made by joining strips of fabric produced on the standard loom with one *hat*, or 0.5 m, capacity.

For many households woolen and goat-hair blankets and rugs are, like woolen cloth for clothing, important trade items, which they export to the lower hills and the Tarai in winter. The value of these items varies greatly with quality of wool or hair and workmanship, and with supply and demand. First-grade *pheruwa* sell for about twenty-five rupees per m², while high-quality, light woolen blankets bring as much as thirty-five rupees per m².

A number of other woven wool items are produced in Karnali solely for home use or local trade. Among the Bhotia tightly woven striped aprons and knee-length cloth boots with leather soles are important products. The former sell locally for 120 to 140 rupees; the latter, known as *lam*, are sold for fifteen to thirty rupees to Pahari neighbors, among whom they are in great demand during winter. Both Bhotia and Pahari make cloth sacks of several sizes for carrying food commodities as well as saddlebags in which salt and grain are transported by animals. These tightly woven woolen containers, some reinforced with deerskin, sell for between twenty rupees (small saddlebags for sheep and goats) and eighty rupees (large food sacks).

Additional Handicrafts

Karnali families of all castes and ethnic groups, but especially the poorer Chhetri and Dum, make other household necessities from local materials in an effort to promote self-sufficiency by reducing expenditures or to augment their incomes by selling or trading the items within their villages, panchayats, or valleys. Most important are different types of split-bamboo mats and baskets (figure 74) designed for a variety of uses. For example one type of mat is circular in shape, folds through the middle, sells for two rupees, and when lined with leaves or birchbark serves as both a sleeping mat and an umbrella (figure 75). Another plant from which many items are made is *Cannabis*. Its long fibers are woven into supple and rollable mats and braided into rope; tumplines with which people carry loads are produced by a combination of weaving and braiding (see figure 52).

Fig. 74. Dum making bamboo basket

Fig. 75. Pahari traveling with a homemade mat-umbrella and a machine-made umbrella of Indian manufacture

7
Trade, Migrations, and Markets

TRADING PURSUITS

During the year most Karnali Zone families engage in a variety of rhythmical trading activities, both within the zone and with surrounding regions. Lightly interwoven and carefully scheduled with the components of their economies already discussed, these activities are keyed primarily to the supply and demand of food grains, as well as to the households' requirements for other necessities that are either not found or produced within the zone (e.g., salt, iron, spices, tea, sugar, aluminum and plastic utensils and containers) or, like food grains, are not produced in sufficient quantities (e.g., wool, cotton cloth and clothing, tobacco products, and cooking oils). The expenditures on such imported commodities by seventy-four Karnali families during 2026 V.S. (1969-70) are shown by caste in table 21.

Trading activities are also keyed, of necessity, to the seasonal and locational availability of these commodities and to the travel and transport conditions that themselves regulate the acquisition of household needs. Thus, the trading pursuits of Karnali families exhibit distinctive multidimensional time-space patterns that link the diverse ecological belts and niches of the zone, western Nepal, and neighboring Tibet and India (see figure 5). At the same time, these trade networks link two major cultural belts whose people display dissimilar racial origins, mother tongues, religion, and social organization: (1) that of the Buddhist Tibetans and the Bhotia in the high or

TABLE 21. Family Expenditures on imported commodities in rupees during 2026 V.S. (1969-70).

Caste	Salt[a]	Wool[b]	Kerosene[e]	Cooking oil (ghee and mustard)[d]	Sugar[c]	Tea[c]	Spices[c]	Tobacco[e]	Paper[f]	Soap[c]	Cloth and ready-made clothes[e]	Pig iron and iron implements[g]	Misc.[c]	Total
Brahman	2,277	363	327	2,579	1,451	467	1,110	1,898	498	737	9,558	257	2,428	23,957
Avg./family (12)	190	31	27	215	121	39	93	158	42	61	797	22	202	1,996
Avg./person (102)	22	4	3	25	14	5	11	19	5	7	94	3	24	235
(% of total)	(9.5)	(1.5)	(1.4)	(10.8)	(6.1)	(1.9)	(4.6)	(7.9)	(2.1)	(3.1)	(39.9)	(1.1)	(10.1)	(100.0)
Thakuri	4,080	278	1,480	1,095	3,292	221	1,168	3,345	499	558	13,430	252	993	30,691
Avg./family (7)	583	40	211	156	470	32	167	478	71	80	1,919	36	142	4,384
Avg./person (132)	31	2	11	8	25	2	9	25	4	4	102	2	8	233
(% of total)	(13.3)	(0.9)	(4.8)	(3.6)	(10.7)	(0.7)	(3.8)	(10.9)	(1.6)	(1.8)	(43.8)	(0.8)	(3.2)	(100.0)
Chhetri	5,406	2,330	442	3,224	1,440	407	976	1,891	594	596	17,038	609	1,152	36,105
Avg./family (34)	159	69	13	95	42	12	29	56	18	18	501	18	34	1,062
Avg./person (289)	19	8	2	11	5	1	3	7	2	2	59	2	4	125
(% of total)	(15.0)	(6.5)	(1.2)	(8.9)	(4.0)	(1.1)	(2.7)	(5.2)	(1.6)	(1.6)	(47.2)	(1.7)	(3.2)	(100.0)
Bhotia	1,935	1,825	100	1,098	55	177	251	490	15	77	2,600	105	328	9,056
Avg./family (5)	387	365	20	220	11	35	50	98	3	15	520	21	66	1,811
Avg./person (38)	51	48	3	29	1	5	7	13	—	2	68	3	9	238
(% of total)	(21.4)	(20.2)	(1.1)	(12.1)	(0.6)	(2.0)	(2.8)	(5.4)	(0.2)	(0.9)	(28.7)	(1.2)	(3.6)	(100.0)
Dum	1,431	245	30	748	53	57	131	301	7	80	3,393	98	720	7,294
Avg./family (16)	89	15	2	47	3	4	8	19	—	5	212	6	45	456
Avg./person (104)	14	2	—	7	1	1	1	3	—	1	33	1	7	70
(% of total)	(19.6)	(3.4)	(0.4)	(10.3)	(0.7)	(0.8)	(1.8)	(4.1)	(0.1)	(1.1)	(46.5)	(1.3)	(9.9)	(100.0)
Total	15,130	5,046	2,379	8,744	6,291	1,329	3,636	7,925	1,613	2,048	46,019	1,323	5,621	107,104
Avg./family (74)	204	68	32	118	85	18	49	107	22	28	622	18	76	1,447
Avg./person (665)	23	8	4	13	10	2	6	12	2	3	69	2	9	161
(% of total)	(14.1)	(4.7)	(2.2)	(8.2)	(5.9)	(1.2)	(3.4)	(7.4)	(1.5)	(1.9)	(43.0)	(1.2)	(5.3)	(100.0)

Origins of commodities:
a Tibet and India
b Tibet and within Karnali Zone
c India
d Within Karnali Zone; Lower Nepal Himalaya
e Within Karnali Zone; Lower Nepal Himalaya; India
f Within Karnali Zone; India
g Lower Nepal Himalaya; India

NOTE: 1 rupee Nepalese Currency is equal to approximately 0.10 $U.S.

northern border regions of Karnali Zone; and (2) that of the Hindu Pahari in the lower or southern reaches of Karnali Zone and the outer hills, as well as the more orthodox Hindus in the Nepal lowlands and India (see chapters 3 and 4).

In a pragmatic effort to facilitate their trade movements and negotiations within and between areas of the two great cultural traditions, family members from different castes or ethnic groups and far-flung geographical locations enter into two special types of friendship relations known respectively as *mit* and *ista*. The former are ritually formalized "blood-brother" pacts based on fictitious kinship that usually endure throughout the brothers' lives and may be perpetuated between two households for many generations (see Okada 1957). The latter are casual friendships that can be more easily terminated. Although both types serve a number of noneconomic social functions, they stem primarily from the desire for preferential trading partners and the need to reduce the barriers to such partnerships imposed by Hindu social and religious caste hierarchies. For many centuries *mit* and *ista* relationships have been common between Tibetans or Bhotia and Pahari, between Pahari of different castes, and even between Pahari and Dum (a facet of the *jajmani* system). Apart from trade intercourse per se, all call for one or both partners to furnish shelter and food, supply storage facilities for goods, and lend a helping hand and share resources in hard times. Hence these friendship ties are cohesive bonds that are tightly intertwined with trade networks.[1]

Marriage ties also facilitate trading activities and are similarly intertwined with trade networks. My panchayat survey indicates that most Pahari caste marriages, as well as those of the Bhotia and Dum, are between families living within two days' travel of one another.[2] These ties are aids in local trade. However, Thakuri marriage ties in Karnali Zone and western Nepal are exceptional, for they span much greater distances. Since their widespread distribution during the Baisi era (ca. the fifteenth and sixteenth centuries), these "ruling Rajput" families of Karnali have continued to maintain distant marriage contacts, not only throughout the territory of their former feudal domain but with neighboring regions in the lower Himalaya two to three weeks' travel away. Such current kinship contacts are an additional boon to the Thakuri, for they provide them with the support and succor of relatives when they travel south on long-distance trade trips (see Ross 1980).

---

1   Campbell (1978:92-94) elaborates on the noneconomic aspects of *mit* and *ista* in economic region B of Karnali Zone, while Fisher (1972:92-94) furnishes valuable information on the economic importance of these friendship bonds to the Magar of Tarakot (Tarangpur) in Dolpo.

2   Such areally prescribed or limited marriage networks are typical of most clan-kinship groups throughout the Himalaya; this is especially true in Pahari regions. For an example of Pahari marriage contacts in the Indian Himalaya of Garhwal see Berreman (1972:159-60).

When Bhotia of Karnali trade with Pahari, either on their own home ground or in southern parts of the zone and the lower Himalaya, they encounter relatively few obstacles to economic interaction, for in the traditionally flexible hill-Hindu caste system of western Nepal they enjoy clean-caste status. When Bhotia travel further south to the more orthodox Hindu regions of the inner Tarai, Tarai, and India they must contend with a more rigid caste system in which they are ranked as untouchables. Saddled with this stigma, they are at a considerable disadvantage compared to the Pahari traders who travel to the lowlands. A common ruse the Bhotia use to avoid the stigma and so trade in the lowlands on a par with the Pahari is to assume the identity of clean-caste Matwali Chhetri. By adopting appropriate clan names, speaking Nepali, wearing Pahari-style clothing, and observing the necessary Hindu dietary restrictions and religious practices, they successfully pass themselves off as Matwali Chhetri when it is to their social or economic advantage. However, once they return home, they reassume their original identity and associated cultural beliefs and practices. Therefore, this deception is a form of economically motivated seasonal Sanskritization.[3]

The commodity circuits currently followed by Karnali families are outlined in figure 76. In essence, the diagram indicates how the exchange of goods creates the prevailing trade system. It also indicates the temporal-spatial manner by which the trade flows serve to collect and redistribute goods at both intraregional and interregional scales. In the process, these commodity circuits even out the striking disparities in the environmental and economic gradients both within Karnali Zone itself and in the lower southern regions of Nepal and of Tibet. As can be seen, Karnali trade movements are oriented northward to Tibet or the Bhotia border regions in summer and fall, to the southern reaches of the zone and neighboring regions of the lower Himalaya (the Midlands) throughout the year, and to the southern lowlands of Nepal (the inner Tarai and Tarai) and India in winter and spring.

The travel times required for the movement of commodities are mapped in figure 77. Note that the number of days indicated is for a strong man carrying a one-maund (37.3 kg) load under optimal trail conditions. Unencumbered by a heavy load he generally requires only half the indicated times; when journeying with loaded transport animals or with animals for sale, he usually requires between 50 and 100 percent more time than that indicated, for he must graze his livestock along the way.

Especially evident from figure 77 is the fact that the time required to cover a given distance is directly proportional to the elevation and relief of

---

[3]   For a more detailed discussion of identity manipulation by Bhotia, see Fisher (1972:97-99).

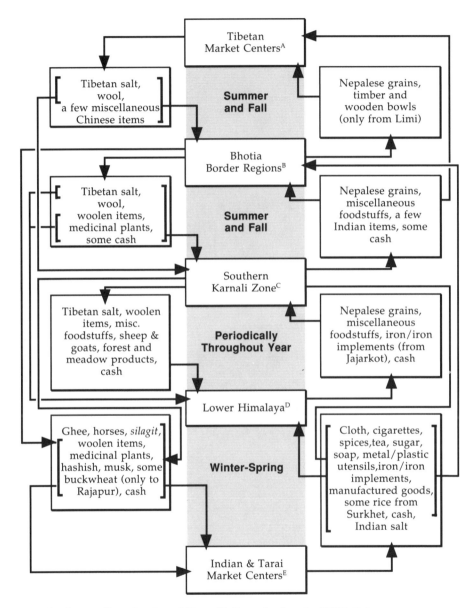

Fig. 76. Commodity circuits of Karnali Zone traders in 2026 v.s.

A: Taklakot and Pongdzu. B: Upper Humla, upper Mugu, and northeast Dolpo. C: Also the Bheri River corridor in southern Dolpo District. D: Bajura and Achham districts of Seti Zone; Dailekh and Jajarkot districts of Bheri Zone. E: Also the Surkhet and Dang valleys of the inner Tarai

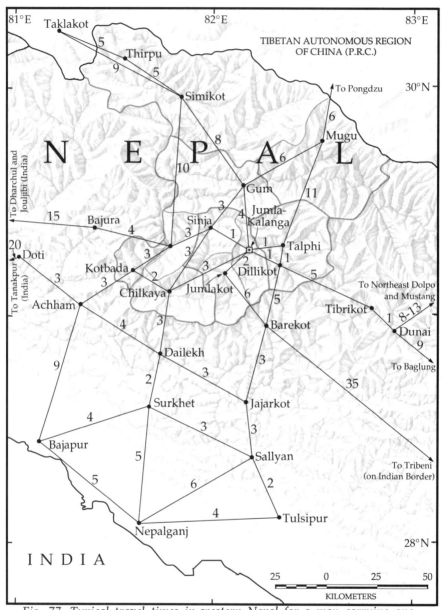

Fig. 77. Typical travel times in western Nepal for a man carrying one maund (37.3 kg), in days

the terrain encountered. Hence, winter and spring travel in the relatively flat lowlands is less arduous and, under normal trail conditions, takes fewer days than summer and fall travel through the rugged northern highlands.

The transport animals used by Karnali trading households are castrated adult male sheep and goats, castrated yaks, *dri* (female yaks), neuter and female yak-cattle hybrids and, to a very minor extent, horses and mules.

Fig. 78. Sheep caravan carrying Tibetan salt en route from upper Mugu to Sinja. Each ovine can carry up to 13 or 14 kg evenly distributed in two small saddlebags. © National Geographic Society.

Sheep and goats can carry up to 13 or 14 kg evenly distributed in two small saddlebags (figure 78), or about one-third the load of a strong man. When on the move, one shepherd is required for every thirty to forty ovines in a caravan. Bovines (figure 79) and equines usually carry about 75 kg, or twice a human load; one herder is needed for every six to ten animals, depending on their kind and irascibility.

In practice, the weight transport animals are required to carry varies considerably with the age, strength, and health of the individual beast. The weight is also a function of the number of animals and the volume of goods its owner has to transport and the distance and duration of the trip. Moreover, the suitability of different species for carrying loads varies with trail conditions and time of year, as well as with the bulkiness of the commodities carried. For example, bovines and equines can negotiate thinly snow-covered trails on which ovines would flounder. Conversely, sheep and goats, which are generally used to carry only grains, salt, wool, and other durable items easy to package compactly, can traverse narrow and confined paths that would be impossible for larger and more heavily laden animals.

The trade movement calendars followed in representative villages of Karnali Zone's ten economic subregions are illustrated in table 22. Differences in timing, duration, and destination of trade trips that are exhibited among these villages reflect not only the influence of village location and seasonal trail conditions but also regional variations in both crop and pastoral regimes with which trading activities are closely coordinated and scheduled.[4]

A number of factors combine to determine the degree to which a Karnali family is able to engage in trade. These include the size and age and sex composition of its labor force, the location of its homestead, its access to and command of exchangeable commodities or cash that can be allocated for trade purposes, its ability to keep and maintain transport animals, and the suitability of the trail network between home and trading destinations for using transport animals. Furthermore, for all but large or wealthy families, the late spring to early fall is a period when trading activities compete with other livelihood pursuits, especially agriculture, for labor inputs. In the face of these time binds, all farming-season activities directly or indirectly tied to trade must be carefully weighed against all other alternatives for achieving the family's subsistence requirements. Hence, choices, which are usually compromises, must be made. Only those few households with considerable purchasing power, a large labor force, and many transport animals can engage in profitable large-scale and long-range trade that contributes to the family's economic well-being beyond merely supplying basic yearly needs.

The Grain-Salt Exchange

In order to understand more fully how Karnali Zone's economy is articulated by the movement of people, animals and goods, and by trading activities in particular, one must keep in mind two basic facts of life that have

---

[4]   The crop and animal movement calendars for these villages are presented in tables 11 and 17, respectively.

Fig. 79. Yak–common cattle hybrids carrying grain to Mugugaon. Each bovine can carry up to 75 kg in three large sacks.

existed in the mountains of western Nepal since humans first settled there. First are the disparities in food production from household to household, village to village, valley to valley, region to region. Second, Karnali Zone and western Nepal, like all sectors of the Himalaya, possess no indigenous source of salt, a mineral that is essential for the maintenance of all plant and animal life. As discussed in chapter 5, some areas within Karnali (principally the double-cropped *khet* farmlands of the Pahari in economic regions A and B), as well as some areas of the lower Himalaya to the south and west, produce a food-grain surplus. The higher or more northern single-cropped *pakho* areas of the Pahari in Karnali, and especially the Bhotia fringe areas of economic region C (upper Humla and Mugu), produce a grain deficit. However, a few households in almost all grain-deficient areas, even on the Bhotia fringe, raise a cereal surplus. The absence of salt shows no such regional variation; it is universal throughout the zone.

TABLE 22. Trade movement calendars for selected Karnali villages.

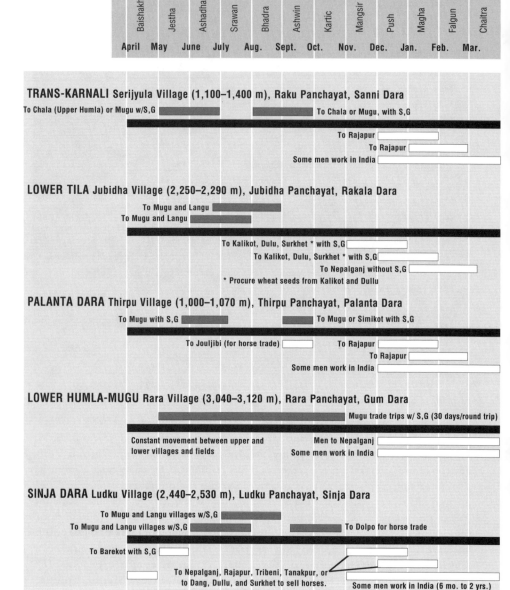

TRANS-KARNALI Serijyula Village (1,100–1,400 m), Raku Panchayat, Sanni Dara

To Chala (Upper Humla) or Mugu w/S,G ▪▪▪▪▪   ▪▪▪▪▪ To Chala or Mugu, with S,G

To Rajapur ▭

To Rajapur ▭

Some men work in India ▭

LOWER TILA Jubidha Village (2,250–2,290 m), Jubidha Panchayat, Rakala Dara

To Mugu and Langu ▪▪▪▪

To Mugu and Langu ▪▪▪▪

To Kalikot, Dulu, Surkhet * with S,G ▭

To Kalikot, Dulu, Surkhet * with S,G ▭

To Nepalganj without S,G ▭

* Procure wheat seeds from Kalikot and Dullu

PALANTA DARA Thirpu Village (1,000–1,070 m), Thirpu Panchayat, Palanta Dara

To Mugu with S,G ▪▪▪▪   ▪▪▪▪ To Mugu or Simikot with S,G

To Jouljibi (for horse trade) ▭   To Rajapur ▭

To Rajapur ▭

Some men work in India ▭

LOWER HUMLA-MUGU Rara Village (3,040–3,120 m), Rara Panchayat, Gum Dara

▪▪▪▪▪▪ Mugu trade trips w/ S,G (30 days/round trip)

Constant movement between upper and   Men to Nepalganj ▭
lower villages and fields   Some men work in India ▭

SINJA DARA Ludku Village (2,440–2,530 m), Ludku Panchayat, Sinja Dara

To Mugu and Langu villages w/S,G ▪▪▪▪

To Mugu and Langu villages w/S,G ▪▪▪▪   ▪▪▪▪ To Dolpo for horse trade

To Barekot with S,G ▭

▭   To Nepalganj, Rajapur, Tribeni, Tanakpur, or ▭
to Dang, Dullu, and Surkhet to sell horses.   Some men work in India (6 mo. to 2 yrs.)

KEY TO BARS

▪▪▪▪▪ Summer Trade (oriented northward and/or with Tibet)

▬▬▬▬ People at home

▭ Winter trade (oriented southward and/or with the Tarai and India)

KEY TO ABBREVIATIONS

(C) cattle; (B) buffalo; (Y) yaks;

(XB) cross-breeds, dzo, etc.; (H) horses;

(S) sheep; (G) goats

Baishakh	Jestha	Ashadha	Srawan	Bhadra	Ashwin	Kartic	Mangsir	Push	Magha	Falgun	Chaitra
April	May	June	July	Aug.	Sept.	Oct.	Nov.	Dec.	Jan.	Feb.	Mar.

PANSAYA DARA Jumlakot Village (2,700–2,800 m), Jumlakot Panchayat, Pansaya Dara

To Langu (w/S&G; 2 mo. round trip)
To Mugu w/S,G
To Surkhet, Barekot or Janakpur w/S&G
To Nepalganj
Some work in Indian hills.

ASI DARA Chhina Village (2,320–2,380 m), Chhina Panchayat, Asi Dara

With S to Langu or Dolpo
To Jouljibi or Dang Valley (for horse trade)
To Barekot, Jajarkot with S,G; To Surkhet with H
To Nepalganj

UPPER HUMLA Simikot Village (2,320–2,380 m), Simikot Panchayat, Humla Dara

With H,S,G to Limi or Taklakot   With H,S,G to Limi or Taklakot
To Darma with S,G   To Darma with S,G   Without animals to Rajapur

UPPER MUGU Mangri Village (2,230–2,310 m), Dhunge Dhara Panchayat, Karana Dara

To Mugu
Only a few old people in Village
To Gum
To Gum
Without animals to Sinja or Jumla, then to Nepalganj

CHAUDHABISA-UPPER TILA Luma Village (2,590–2,650 m), Luma Panchayat, Chaudhabisa Dara

To Mugu and Langu with H,S,G
To Mugu and Langu with H,S,G
To Barekot with S,G
To Nepalganj without animals
Some to work in India

CHAUDHABISA-UPPER TILA Muni Village (2,620–2,710 m), Manisangu Panchayat, Chaudhabisa Dara

To Langu or Dolpo with S,G   Some collect medicinal herbs in patans
To Barekot for grain with S,G
To Barekot or Jumla for grain with S,G
To Dang with H, then without animals to Nepalganj

Isaac Asimov (1977) points out that all herbivorous animals require more salt than the amount present in the plant tissue of their fodder. Similarly, whereas omnivorous humans whose diet includes large quantities of roasted meat and milk products get sufficient salt from their food, those whose diet is primarily grain do not; they also require supplementary salt. The closest sources of salt for the people of the Himalaya were, and continue to be, Tibet and India. In Tibet, salt was obtained from internally drained playa lakes on the plateau north of the Tsangpo River and east of Lake Manosarowar and Mount Kailas; Indian salt was procured from the sea, deep wells, or surface salt beds. Of the two, Tibetan salt has been, until recently, more readily obtainable. It has supplied all the human and livestock needs in Karnali Zone and western Nepal; indeed such was generally the case throughout the entire Nepal Himalaya.

In western Nepal, the patterns and processes by which this indispensable commodity, along with wool, animals, and other goods of Tibetan and Chinese origin, flowed southward, and by which equally indispensable grains, as well as other items of Nepalese or Indian origin, flowed northward, were well established by the twelfth century when the western Malla kingdom controlled trade routes through the Himalaya—a control that was the basis of their power. The most important routes were those that led to the trading entrepôt of Taklakot, especially those that followed the Humla Karnali Valley. Of the other routes—those crossing the Tibetan border range to the north and east—the one through Mugugaon became the most important (see figure 20).

Although subsequent sociopolitical events and associated power shifts caused minor perturbations and realignments in these trade networks, the basic system remained unchanged and viable until the end of the Rana regime in 1951. Grains continued to be markedly more valuable than salt in Tibet and the northern reaches of Karnali, while salt remained significantly more dear than grain in the predominantly agricultural regions of southern Karnali and the lower (outer) hills. By engaging in one or more linkages or stages in the Nepalese grain–Tibetan salt exchange during the course of the year, both Pahari and Bhotia, along with Drogpa (pastoral nomads) and other Tibetans, were able to turn a profit that enabled them to satisfy their salt requirements and eliminate their food-grain deficit. Thus the transfer of these commodities triggered, and continues to trigger, all trade in the subsistence economy of Karnali Zone. Indeed, it constitutes the cornerstone on which the other trading activities hinge.

As a backdrop against which to examine the current trade mechanisms and networks, a brief description of the traditional ones as they existed in late Rana times (ca. 1920-50) can be reconstructed from interviews. The Tibetan salt consumed in Karnali and the lower Himalaya entered western Nepal by the way of three Bhotia border regions. These were, in order of importance, upper Humla, upper Mugu, and northeast Dolpo (see figure 43). Subsequently, the salt was distributed throughout Karnali and the lower hills via two trade networks. One included upper Mugu (and to a lesser extent Dolpo) in the north, and Jajarkot and Dailekh districts in the south. The other stretched from upper Humla in the north to Bajura and Achham in the southern hills. These networks exhibited many common and often overlapping or interlocking features. They also displayed some significant and unique differences. Therefore, for clarity and ease of presentation they are traced in turn.

The Upper Mugu Network. Owing to the location of their villages in the upper Mugu Karnali drainage within three to five days of the border, the Bhotia of Mugu and Karan *daras* (economic subregion 9) were in a position to control the initial phase of trade-goods traffic between Tibet and south-central and eastern Karnali Zone. This was particularly true for Mugugaon, which lay astride the trail to Tibet. Only the Bhotia dealt directly with Drogpa trading partners who brought salt, wool, animals (sheep, goats, and yaks), and miscellaneous Tibetan and Chinese goods to the summer trade mart at Cheptu, near the Namja Pass (approximately 4,900 m), but who did not venture south into upper Mugu.

This monopolistic intermediary role of the Bhotia was vitally important to the 150 or so families of Mugugaon who, unlike their neighbors, had to depend almost entirely on the grain-salt exchange for their livelihood. For a period of five or six years in the 1940s they even forcibly blocked the passage of other Bhotia to Cheptu, just north of the Tibetan border, requiring them to trade instead in Mugugaon. Only by obtaining a government order that forbade the Mugali from continuing their total monopoly were the Tihar and Dhunge Dhara panchayat Bhotia able to break the stranglehold and again have direct access to Tibet and the Drogpa.

During the summer and fall (June to November), when the route was free of snow, the Bhotia traveled to Cheptu with bovines and ovines laden with grain, almost all of which they had obtained from Pahari. There they bartered the grain for salt and wool. The grain-salt exchange was measured by volume, while that involving grain and wool was computed by weight. The rates of exchange fluctuated considerably with the seasonal supply and demand of goods, the type of grain (e.g., rice was three to five times more valuable than other grains), and the form of the cereals. For example, barley and wheat flour brought a higher price than the unground grains. Hence, one unit of grain brought three to six units of salt by volume. In the grain-wool exchange, two to four units of grain got one unit of wool by weight.

During the mental machinations that their bartering entailed, the participants translated from kind to cash values and then back to kind, for their economy had for centuries been partially monetized. In some instances Bhotia who had acquired cash from other trade or work in the south purchased salt or wool from Drogpa who had already acquired their yearly grain needs. Such nonbarter transactions permitted poorer Bhotia, without transport animals, to obtain salt and wool, which they themselves carried home; they also gave the Drogpa needed cash for other trade pursuits. Nepalese paper currency was seldom used; Indian silver rupees were the more common and popular tender.

The number of trips the Bhotia made to Cheptu during the Tibetan trading season varied with importance of that trade to their household economies. Those from Tihar and Dhunge Dhara villages (in Karan Dara south of Mugu), which enjoyed a relatively more viable agricultural base, made one to three trips; those from Mugugaon shuttled back and forth between their village and Cheptu many times. In addition, those Mugali with sufficient labor or transport animals also shuttled between Cheptu and their homes and Pahari villages in Gum, Sinja, and Asi *daras*, where they exchanged salt and wool for grains.

The Pahari of southern Karnali, who were oriented to upper Mugu because of the location of their villages, procured salt and wool in two ways. Those with transport sheep and goats (along with some petty traders without animals but with the time to be content with obtaining only their own needs by what they could carry on their backs) made one or two trips to either Mugugaon or the Bhotia villages in the Langu Valley (Tihar panchayat), which were two days closer. There they bartered their grain for salt and wool approximately twice as expensive as in Cheptu, to which they had no access. Other Pahari households—those who lacked the time or transport animals to travel north and those with minimal needs—bartered for or bought salt and wool from Pahari or other Bhotia who came to the villages with their surplus. In these agriculturally more productive regions of the zone, the exchange rates were approximately the inverse ratio of those in Cheptu (five to nine grain for one salt; three to six grain for one wool).

A relatively small amount of Tibetan salt flowed into Karnali from adjacent Dolpo to the east. The Matwali Chhetri villages of Manisangu panchayat, and especially the Bhotia enclave villages of Dillikot, Chutra, and Naphukona, in the headwaters of the Tila Karnali River lay on or near the major route leading to Tibrikot Dara and the upper Bheri River corridor.[5] Families of both groups who kept yak-cattle hybrids or sheep and goats for transport made a single summer journey with grain-laden animals to the Bhotia village of Ringmo (on Phoksumdo Lake, Tibrikot Dara) or to Bhotia villages such as Saldang in inner Dolpo, several days further away. There

---

5   Note that during the Rana regime Tibrikot Dara included the upper Bheri River corridor as far east as Tarakot and was part of "old" Jumla District (see figure 38).

they exchanged the grain for salt their trading partners had brought from Tibet. Other Manisangu families bartered or bought "Dolpo" salt from these trader neighbors upon their return or from Dolpo Bhotia who traveled as far west as Asi and Chaudhabisa *daras* with salt-carrying animals to obtain grain.

The northward flow of grains in the phases of the salt-grain trade just described—the Drogpa-Bhotia exchange, the Bhotia-Pahari exchanges, and the Pahari-Pahari exchange—depleted the grain supply in the lower regions where overall production was marginal at best. The deficiencies caused by limited production, and added to by the grain flow northward, had to be overcome by trade with the lower Himalaya. Animal-owning Pahari who had amassed a large salt surplus often journeyed south once during the summer to the grain surplus area of Barekot in Jajarkot District (see figure 20), where the exchange rates were about the same as those in southern Karnali. Others with surplus salt bartered at home with Barekot traders who drove their own grain-laden animals north to Asi and Chaudhabisa *daras*.

A final phase in the Mugu-initiated grain-salt circuit took place in the late fall. Pahari families from villages throughout economic regions B and D, who wintered their large flocks of sheep and goats in Jajarkot and Dailekh districts, loaded their transport animals once more with Tibetan salt, which they exchanged for grain in the lower hills. If and when these Karnali Pahari traveled further south to the Tarai border market of Nepalganj, either with or without transport animals, to procure products of Indian origin, most did not barter for or buy Indian salt. Indian salt, however, was in general use throughout the Tarai and parts of the inner Tarai (the Dang Valley); moreover, since World War I it had begun to penetrate the southern fringe of the lower Himalaya (see Field 1959). Those few Pahari from Karnali who did obtain Indian salt exchanged it for grains in these lower regions.

It is important to note that with the exception of the Mandara villagers who wintered with their animals in the Surkhet Valley, and those of Manisangu panchayat who took their livestock to the Barekot area, the Bhotia of eastern Karnali (and of Dolpo) did not winter their animals in the lower hills. Thus they did not engage in the dry-season phase of the salt-grain exchange. However, some Bhotia men from Mugu and Karan *daras*, as well as male members of many Pahari and Dum households in eastern Karnali, did travel south in winter, without transport animals, to work in India or obtain from the Tarai border markets or India commodities needed for either home consumption or petty trade.

The Upper Humla Network. The Humla-oriented trade network was significantly more important than that through Mugu and eastern Karnali, for it contained the zone's most densely populated regions (see figure 44). Hence a much greater volume of Tibetan salt and Nepalese grains circulated through this western circuit. A number of physical and cultural factors also combined to make the Humla trade network both spatially and temporally more complex.

Because of the topographic grain and relief of the Karnali catchment basin, a number of routes connected the lower reaches of western Karnali Zone (economic region A) with upper Humla, and upper Humla with Tibet (see figure 20). Two minor routes led from upper Humla to seasonal trade marts north of the Tibetan border range. These transversed the high and difficult Takhu and Tanke passes, about 4,800 m and 5,500 m respectively. But by far the most important route to Tibet was that which followed along the Humla River, then cut cross-country over Nara Pass (4,800 m), regained the river, and again followed it upstream to the major trade center of Taklakot. Other routes from regions west of Karnali also converged on Taklakot by way of passes in the Zaskar range, all above 5,000 m: from Kumaon via Lipu Pass; from Mahakali Zone via Tinkar Pass; from Seti Zone via Urai Pass. Hence, during the summer and fall Bhotia and Byansi traders from these regions had commercial contact with Karnali traders in the Taklakot area (Purang).

For most Bhotia of Humla Dara trade was not the primary livelihood pursuit as it was for all those of Mugu Dara and many of those in Karan Dara. Instead, it was an important adjunct to agriculture and animal husbandry. With a smaller grain deficit to overcome, the Bhotia traders of Humla achieved a much higher level of prosperity. Their superior agricultural base is evidenced by land reform data showing that as a group Humla Bhotia possessed over two and one-half times as much arable land per person as the Mugu Bhotia (see table 9). As a result, the Humla Bhotia invested more time and effort in farming and, in turn, had need to coordinate more closely their trading activities with their crop calendars.

A singularly striking difference between the two networks was that Pahari often traded directly with Tibetans, either in Tibet or in upper Humla. Although the most northerly Bhotia villages in Humla (those of Limi and Muchu panchayats) were located on or near the major route to Tibet and Taklakot, they did not have, nor did they need, exclusive command of the first phase or stage in the grain-salt exchange process. Many Pahari families of upper Humla, (especially Thakuri, but also Brahmans, Chhetri, and Matwali Chhetri), as well as many from villages further south in economic region A, traveled north with their transport animals during the snow-free monsoon and postmonsoon seasons to trade with Drogpa or settled Tibetans (Purangba) at Taklakot, or with Purangba who entered upper Humla with goods-laden animals. Other Pahari households followed the Takhu Pass or Tanke Pass trails to deal with Drogpa trade partners on the Tibetan side of the border.

These parallel Bhotia and Pahari trade movements were unique in the Himalaya, the outgrowth of early Khasa and Thakuri settlement far up the Humla Karnali drainage during the Malla and Jumla Baisi eras and the accompanying sociopolitical dominance in the feudal order they introduced.

Focusing on the important Taklakot-oriented trade, the following phases or linkages in the Humla network took place in the course of a year and involved fluctuating exchange rates similar to those of the Mugu network.

While Limi Bhotia collected salt from playa lakes on the Tibetan Plateau in return for a fee paid to local officials (Goldstein 1975:97), most Bhotia of Muchu panchayat traded for salt and wool in Taklakot. During the summer they made numerous trips between their villages and the Tibetan entrepôt, primarily with bovines but also with some ovines and a few horses. Some households from both all-Bhotia groups of villages also drove their carrying animals down the Humla Valley to the mixed Bhotia and Pahari panchayats around Simikot, the present-day headquarters for Humla District.[6] There they exchanged salt, wool, and miscellaneous Tibetan and Chinese items for grains and other commodities. One of these was butter, which they used in quantities beyond their own supply for votive butter-lamps and for butter-tea.

The Bhotia and Pahari families from these lower villages who kept transport animals made one or two trips to Taklakot or to Limi and Muchu panchayats for salt and wool during the summer. Many preferred to deal with the latter sources, despite the fact that salt was twice as expensive there as in Tibet; Limi and Muchu panchayats were not only nearer but had more fodder for their animals then did the Taklakot area. For the Limi households who kept large flocks of Tibetan sheep themselves, the sale of wool to these visitors was particularly lucrative.

Many long-distance trading families from the Simikot area—Bhotia and Pahari alike—also made a single summer trip with their transport sheep and goats (usually the Himalayan breeds) as far south as Sanni and Raskot *daras* (economic subregion 1, trans-Karnali) or Bajura and Achham (Seti Zone), where they exchanged salt and some surplus wool for grains. The Bhotia of Limi and Muchu, however did not engage in this southern phase of summer trade.

One aspect of the trade network in upper Humla that was not present in upper Mugu was the *mela,* or trade fair. Two such fairs, each lasting about a month, were held in the area of Muchu panchayat after the harvest of crops in the fall and before winter snows impeded travel. The larger of the two was held during Kartic (mid-October to mid-November) at Chala, a high

---

6 These panchayats are Khorchi, Dandaphaya, Simikot, Baragaon, Chhipra, and Yanchu.

(4,000 m) and relatively isolated Bhotia village on the trail that followed the western border of Karnali Zone into the Humla River drainage by way of the Sankha Pass (4,500 m). It attracted Purangba from Tibet and Pahari from as far away as southwestern Karnali and Achham who gathered with their Chala hosts to exchange or purchase a spectrum of commodities, but especially salt, wool, and grains. The other *mela* took place at the Bhotia village of Yalbang (3,200 m) in the Humla River valley during Mangsir (mid-November to mid-December). It was attended by both Bhotia and Pahari from throughout upper Humla, as well as by some Purangba.

Unlike the final phase of the Mugu grain-salt circuit, which was almost exclusively in the hands of Pahari, that of Humla also involved many Bhotia. Pahari of economic region A, along with Pahari and Bhotia of upper Humla, wintered their sheep and goats in the lower Himalaya of Bajura, Achham, and Dailekh. They brought Tibetan salt on their transport ovines and exchanged it for grain in the southern hills during their winter grazing regime. The Bhotia of Limi and most of those in Muchu were the exception. They, like the Bhotia of Mugu and Karan *dara*s, did not winter livestock in the south and hence did not take part in this phase of the salt-grain trade. Furthermore, and unlike the less prosperous Bhotia of upper Mugu, they had no need at this time to engage in other far-flung winter trading pursuits without transport animals; they confined themselves exclusively to trade with Tibet and within upper Humla.

With these exceptions, the dry-season work and petty trade of all castes or ethnic groups from western Karnali were the same as those from the zone's eastern regions. However, owing to the pattern of trails that led from the southwestern corner of Karnali to the lower hills and beyond, the border market of Rajapur was as often frequented as Nepalganj.

Several additional points concerning the movements and mechanics of the traditional salt-grain trade of Karnali Zone households are important. South of the Mugu Karnali River the two trail networks interlocked. Therefore there was considerable crossover by Pahari of economic regions A and B who journeyed north for salt. Some from the *dara*s in the southwest (see figure 43) dealt with upper Mugu, while some from Pansaya, Sinja, and Asi *dara*s travelled to Taklakot or upper Humla. Often flooding and bridge destruction in the Mugu and main Karnali rivers (figures 80 and 81), the time available to delay a trip or follow alternate routes, and slight regional differences in exchange rates dictated which northern source of salt was sought.

All traders who trafficked in salt (and wool) and grains at any stage in the circuits, either with or without animals, were faced with a sometimes serious and often time-consuming transport problem imposed by both the exchange ratios of these commodities and by their different density. A trader exchanging one unit of grain for five of salt in the north or, conversely, one unit of salt for five of grain in the south, ostensibly required five times the number of transport animals on one leg of his trip as on the reverse leg. The problem was exacerbated by the fact that the average weight per unit volume of unground grains is about 60 percent that of Tibetan salt, which weighed approximately 1.2 kg/l; the average weight of grains in flour form is only 40 percent that of salt. These conditions, coupled with the number of human or animal carriers and the amount of time a trader had at his disposal, placed logistical limits on the volume of his salt-grain exchange. A trader with sufficient transport animals was able to obviate the problem by including unladen animals in his caravan. More often, however, he was required to store a portion of his profit at the point of transaction and make two or more shuttles, deadheading on one leg, to transfer it all.

Fig. 80. High water in the Mugu Karnali River near Mangri. Flood conditions often make low valley trails impassable during the monsoon.

The common practice of extending credit in transactions within and between southern Karnali Zone and the lower hills (the grain-producing regions) also called for considerable shuttling and deadheading. These deal-

Fig. 81. A major washed-out cantilever bridge at Gum. On August 6, 1969, monsoon floodwaters destroyed all spans across the Mugu Karnali River, severing traffic between Humla District and the south for six weeks.

ings, which were not only between trade partners but between casual acquaintances and even strangers, called for credit periods of from several months to as much as a year. They involved the barter or purchase of various commodities, generally foodstuffs and especially grains. In some cases, they were an accommodation the visiting buyer extended to the sedentary seller when the timing of the buyer's trade trip did not or could not correspond to the availability of the seller's commodity. For example, traders from Chaudhabisa Dara took salt to the Barekot area in the late summer which they exchanged for *kharif* grains that had yet to be harvested. Later they would return to collect their due. In other cases, sedentary sellers extended credit to needy buyers; in the early summer Chaudhabisa traders without sufficient grain for immediate home consumption or trade journeyed to Barekot to buy on credit their needs from the seller's *rabi* harvest; after a subsequent grain-salt exchange in Mugu they returned to Barekot with salt and repaid their debt. Hence these credit transactions were predicated by regional differences in crop calendars and production and by differences between trade and harvest times.

In contrast to Sherpa families in the Mount Everest area of northeastern Nepal or to Thakali families in the upper Kali Gandaki Valley of central Nepal, no Bhotia households in northern Karnali Zone were able to amass huge fortunes from trade, or trade-related activities such as the collection of customs, during the Rana regime.[7] Although the Bhotia of upper Mugu had exclusive control of the Tibetan salt and wool that flowed south over Namja Pass, the volume of that flow was insufficient to produce large profits. Nor did their long-range dry-season trade in other commodities (including some luxury items) without the use of transport animals contribute to a markedly high living standard.

---

[7] In an important work on Himalayan traders of Nepal, Christoph von Fürer-Haimendorf (1975) describes the trans-Himalayan activities, both traditional and contemporary, of the Sherpas, Thakali, and Humla-Mugu Bhotia. In it he presents some detailed case studies of individual Karnali traders.

Fürer-Haimendorf also espouses the questionable theory that of the groups engaged in trans-Himalayan trade, those belonging to the Buddhist/Tibetan cultural sphere are better suited for and more successful in such trade; in essence, their socioeconomic structures and flexible adaptive attitudes give them a distinct advantage over Hindu traders whose activities are constrained by caste rules. Furthermore, he believes that the atypical case of Karnali, where Bhotia and Pahari engage in trans-Himalayan trade on par, does not negate his argument because both groups are small-scale petty traders, while the Sherpas and Thakali are large-scale entrepreneurs. These contentions have been justifiably challenged by other Himalayan anthropologists (Goldstein 1976; Manzardo 1977). Indeed, the basic stimuli for members of both groups are more ecological than cultural; both respond to need in regions where agropastoral resources are inadequate for survival. The degree of success a group attains is not so much a function of its social outlook as it is of the degree of freedom it is permitted by the mix of geographical position, environmental conditions, transport facilities, and external political forces.

In upper Humla, through which a larger volume of salt, wool, and other products flowed from Taklakot, the Bhotia held no trade monopolies; instead, they shared the initial phase of the salt-grain exchange with Pahari. Except for a few Limi households whose trading activities were tied to their exceptionally large animal holdings, neither group garnered appreciable wealth from trade. Such was also the case in the all-Pahari regions further south. Viewed as a whole, Karnali Zone was an economic backwater where intraregional and interregional trafficking in Tibetan salt and Nepalese grain, and petty trade generally, was essential for making ends meet but was not conducive to the acquisition of great wealth.

Disruptions and Adjustments in the Grain-Salt Circuits

My panchayat survey data indicate that the current yearly per capita consumption of salt in those thirty-five panchayats averages approximately 4.9 kg. If this figure seems high to the Western reader, it is important to note that food contractors for the military and police personnel stationed in Jumla-Kalanga are required to supply one ounce (28.3 g) of salt per day per man, or 10.4 kg per year (over twice the amount consumed by the local population).[8] My data also indicate that livestock are currently given a yearly average of 1.7 kg of salt per animal. If one accepts these amounts to be representative of the zone as a whole, and also accepts an estimate of the current Karnali livestock population, a rough approximation of the zonal salt consumption of 2026 V.S. (1969-70) is about 1,417 metric tons: 912 metric tons (64 percent) by humans; 505 metric tons (36 percent) by livestock.

Just how much of this amount is from Tibet and how much is from India is difficult to ascertain because of insufficient or unreliable information. Although His Majesty's Government maintains customs posts at Yari (Muchu panchayat, upper Humla) and at Mugugaon and levies duty on all Tibetan imports that pass through check posts, the duty records for 2026 V.S. were unavailable to me. Customs information on the amount of Indian salt entering Nepal through Nepalganj and Rajapur was available, but gave no clue to the amount that ultimately reached Karnali Zone.

However, the Nepal Salt Corporation, which controls most of the sale of Indian salt throughout the country, estimates that 1,000 metric tons were consumed in Karnali Zone in 2026 V.S.[9] Assuming that this estimate is fairly accurate, it not only indicates that over 400 metric tons of Tibetan salt were consumed in Karnali Zone in that year, but that Indian salt comprises over 70 percent of the zone's total consumption.

---

[8]   All salt provided by the contractors is of Indian origin.

[9]   Personal communications with the corporation's account officer, Mar. 10, 1970.

These rough estimates suggest the degree to which Indian salt has captured the Karnali market and the current magnitude of salt consumption in the zone. However, the actual quantities of Tibetan and Indian salt that Karnali traders transfer far exceeds the quantities consumed in the zone, for the traders exchange both salts in the lower Himalaya in order to partially offset the zone's food-grain deficit—a deficit compounded by the export of grains to Tibet. While a dearth of data unfortunately precludes any attempt to estimate this amount, this quantity of salt must be appreciable.

Within this context of a large, continuous, and growing demand for salt, we can now look at the effects on the overall ecological pattern of recent disruptions and adjustments in the grain-salt circuits.

As long as salt was readily available in Tibet, and as long as the hill peoples' fear of prolonged excursions through the malaria-infested tropical lowlands and their preference for Tibetan salt deterred appreciable penetration of Indian salt into the southern hills, Karnali traders were able to supply themselves and the rest of the zone's population with adequate Tibetan salt and Nepalese grains. However, events that followed the Chinese annexation of Tibet, coupled with transportation improvements in the Tarai and inner Tarai and a successful malaria eradication program in those lowlands, had deleterious effects on not only those households engaged in phases of the grain-salt exchange, but on the entire population's subsistence economy.

For the first few years of their control in Tibet, the Chinese allowed the traditional trade circuits to operate as before. But when the Tibetans arose in an abortive armed revolt in 1959, the Chinese curtailed commerce with Nepal and the southward flow of salt diminished to a trickle. The Bhotia and Pahari were forced to seek Indian salt to partially fill the void. After the Chinese reopened the border in 1963, not only did Tibetan salt (and wool) remain in short supply, but the Chinese imposed numerous restrictions that altered the manner in which trade with Tibet was conducted. The Tibetan salt monopoly in Karnali Zone and the lower hills, as throughout the Nepal Himalaya, was irrevocably broken, to the economic detriment of most mountain dwellers.

Today Karnali traders are not permitted to trade directly with their traditional Tibetan partners. Instead they must deal through Chinese officials who stipulate what Nepalese commodities will be accepted in trade and at which rates of exchange. These commodities are almost exclusively grains, which in order of importance to the Chinese (and Tibetans) are rice, wheat, barley, naked barley, millets, and buckwheat. The Chinese insist on carefully inspecting each load for quality and on measuring all grain, whether it is to be exchanged for salt or wool, by weight rather than by volume, a procedure that apparently creates some confusion for the Nepalese in understanding what the current exchange rates actually are. Upon deposit of his loads at the inspection point, the trader is given two chits, one a receipt for his grain that he is obliged to exchange for Chinese currency at a bank in the mart, the other a ration slip indicating what items he may buy with his Chinese cash from the Tibetans in the market.[10]

Fewer Tibetan markets are now available to Karnali traders, for the Chinese have closed the minor marts north of Takhu and Tanke passes in order to channel Humla trade through Taklakot. And, as previously discussed, they have moved the mart used by the Bhotia of upper Mugu from Cheptu to Pongdzu, a less convenient site three days further into Tibet. Moreover, present-day shortages of salt and wool are more acute in Pongdzu than in Taklakot; during the summer of 1969, many Pahari who traveled to upper Mugu with grain were unable to obtain any of their needs.

Of the Karnali Zone Bhotia, those of Mugugaon have been most seriously affected by the Chinese trading (and grazing) policies, for they lack sufficiently productive farmland and other resources to fall back on. As a result, from 1966 to 1969 forty-four families were forced to abandon their homesteads and migrate to Jumla-Kalanga, Kathmandu, or the Indian foothills of Kumaon and Garhwal to seek a new life. The number is increasing each year. The Bhotia of both Karan and Humla *daras* have been less affected by the Tibetan trade restrictions because of their better agropastoral and biotic resources; to date, few families have been forced to leave their villages permanently. However, many families in Limi and Muchu panchayats now find it necessary to engage in long-distance, southern-oriented trade in miscellaneous commodities during the winter, as those from Karan have done for decades.

Another factor that has made participation in any phase of the Nepalese grain–Tibetan salt traffic less profitable than before is the change in exchange ratios of these commodities. While Chinese price-fixing has intentionally prevented the cost of Tibetan salt and wool from rising appreciably, such has not been the case with grains in southern Karnali and the lower Himalaya. In these regions agricultural production has not kept pace with the population explosion. As a result, grain values have doubled or tripled since 1950. These increases are reflected in the current exchange rates shown in table 23.

All of these events and changes have made it impossible for Karnali Zone's population to rely solely on trade in Tibetan salt to overcome their grain deficiencies and to satisfy their own salt requirements. Since 1959, trade in Indian salt has become an essential dry-season, lowland-oriented phase of the grain-salt circuits. Those Pahari and Bhotia traders, with large

---

[10] Although the Chinese permitted some Purangba to journey as before into upper Humla for trade, this permission was not granted after 1972 (Ross 1980).

TABLE 23. Volumetric exchange rates for Tibetan salt and Nepalese grains in 2026 v.s. (1969-70).

Grain for salt		Salt for grain
Tibet[1]	Bhotia border regions[2]	Southern Karnali Zone[3] and lower Himalaya[4]
1 wheat : 1.5 - 4.0 salt	1 wheat : 1.0 - 2.0 salt	1 salt : 1.0 - 2.0 wheat
1 barley : 1.5 - 4.0 salt	1 barley : 0.5 - 2.0 salt	1 salt : 2.0 - 3.0 barley
1 naked barley : 1.5 - 3.0 salt	1 naked barley : 0.8 - 2.0 salt	1 salt : 2.0 - 3.0 naked barley
1 rice (husked) : 3.0 - 5.0 salt	1 rice (husked) : 1.0 - 3.0 salt	1 salt : 1.0 - 2.0 rice (husked)
maize[5] :	maize[5] :	1 salt : 1.5 - 3.0 maize
1 millet[6] : 1.5 - 2.0 salt	1 millet[6] : 1.0 - 2.0 salt	1 salt : 1.5 - 2.0 millet
1 buckwheat[6] : 1.0 - 1.5 salt	1 buckwheat[6] : 1.0 salt	1 salt : 1.0 - 1.5 buckwheat

1   Taklakot and Pongdzu.
2   Limi and Muchu panchayats, Upper Humla; Mugu and Tihar (Langu Valley) panchayats, Upper Mugu.
3   Economic regions A, B, and D.
4   Bajura and Achham districts, Seti Zone; Dailekh and Jajarkot Districts, Bheri Zone.
5   Maize is not exchanged for salt in Tibet nor, generally, in the Bhotia border regions. However, maize flour, along with wheat flour, is exchanged for Tibetan wool at Pongdzu and Upper Mugu.
6   Millets (common, Italian and finger) and buckwheat are less often exchanged for salt in the Bhotia regions, and seldom in Tibet.

flocks of sheep and goats that they winter in the lower hills, now take their transport animals, usually unladen, to the Dang or Surkhet valleys, or, more often, to Nepalganj or Rajapur, where they buy Indian salt. The current price in the border bazaars is 0.25 rupees per kilogram. With one exception, grain from the hills is not exchanged in the lowland breadbasket. Some traders from the higher reaches of western Karnali take buckwheat to Rajapur, where it is in demand by people from the Seti Zone hills. There one unit of buckwheat brings one unit of salt, by volume.

On their return trip with their laden ovines the Karnali traders barter Indian salt for grains (preferably rice) in the lower Himalaya and in southern Karnali Zone. Many traders from the latter region must also retain some Indian salt for their own consumption. The changing distribution and values of Tibetan and Indian salt are diagrammed in figure 82.

The greatest penetration of Indian salt in Karnali Zone is in the southwestern parts of economic region A (i.e., the main Karnali and lower Tila valleys) and in economic region B (the Sinja and middle Tila valleys). While some families in these regions now use only Indian salt, most use both; but as is strikingly evident from diagram C, figure 82, Indian salt is significantly cheaper not only in the lower Himalaya but in southern Karnali. Why then is Tibetan salt still in great demand?

The peoples of Karnali and the lower Himalaya universally prefer Tibetan salt, believing that it is more healthful for their livestock. They also choose it over Indian salt for its taste. Moreover, many informants report that when they first started consuming Indian salt it made them itch, but that this condition abated with time. Today most families in the two-salt regions reserve Tibetan salt for their animals, while they consume a combination of both or, if necessary, only Indian salt. In order to follow this strategy, they are willing to ignore the difference in costs.

However, if and when a motor road is finally completed from Nepalganj to the Dailekh area in the lower Himalaya, or if the supply of Tibetan salt becomes further reduced, the price differential between Indian and Tibetan salt will widen even more as the former penetrates further north. More and more Karnali families will forsake preference for practicality until the two-salt trade system collapses entirely. At such a time the most seriously affected segment of the population will be those traders, Bhotia and Pahari alike, whose traffic in Tibetan salt is critical for their livelihood.[11]

---

[11]   This has already occurred in the Kali Gandaki watershed of central Nepal, where a few wealthy Thakali families of Tukche controlled the profitable movement of Tibetan salt to the lower hills and the Pokhara Valley. In January 1968, the price of Indian salt in Pokhara bazaar was .092 rupees/kg (Schroeder and Sisler 1970:51). In May, when a highway connecting Pokhara with the Tarai and India was opened to public trucking, the price dropped to 0.46 rupees/kg. Virtually overnight the viability of Thakali trade in Tibetan salt ended.

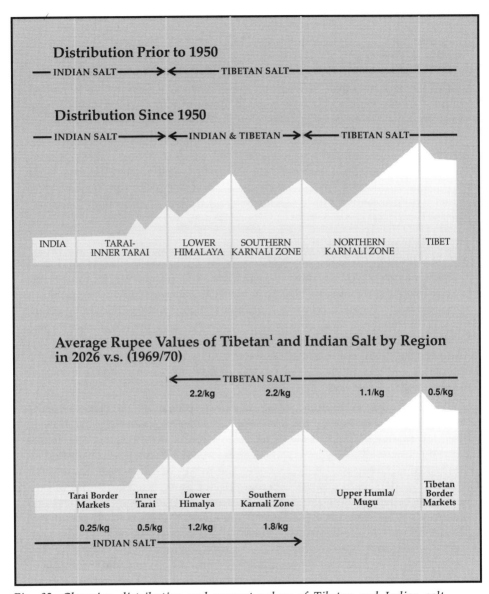

Fig. 82. Changing distribution and current values of Tibetan and Indian salt

[1]The rupee values for Tibetan salt are derived from the average southern Karnali Zone and lower Himalaya prices of the grains that are exchanged for salt.

Even now the Chinese policies governing commerce with Tibet, the perennial shortage of Tibetan salt, and the corresponding importance of Indian salt in southern Karnali and the lower Himalaya are eroding key cogs in the traditional trade mechanisms. *Mit* and *ista* relations between the Nepalese and Tibetans have been severed. With the reduced importance of Bhotia salt traders to Pahari in the lower hills, the friendship bonds that have cemented this symbiotic interregional trade are also beginning to break down. So too are those between high and low castes within the Pahari regions. For the Bhotia, their strategy of identity manipulation during long-range trading activities in the Hindu cultural belts is waxing in importance.

Other signs of stress are in evidence. Transactions involving the extension of short or long-term credit, while still common, are becoming more difficult to consummate. Fewer Pahari from the lower Himalaya come north into southern Karnali to exchange grain for Tibetan salt; instead, most now barter randomly with those Karnali salt traders who come to them.

Miscellaneous Petty Trade

Although the salt-grain exchange is far and away the largest and most important type of trade transaction in Karnali Zone, there are innumerable exchanges or purchases of other commodities. These involve the numerous necessities of a peasant household economy, such as other foodstuffs, condiments, implements and containers for cultivating, cooking, and eating, cloth and clothing, as well as luxury items like cigarettes and cosmetics, that cannot be grown, collected, or manufactured by the individual household. Some idea of the diversity and volume of trade in these goods is indicated in Appendix H, table 36.

With the exception of the northern phase of the Tibetan salt–Nepalese grain exchange, the spatial and temporal patterning and flow of this miscellaneous petty trade is virtually identical to the salt-grain circuits already described. In some instances these sundry items are transported simultaneously with salt and grain. For the most part, however, these other items provide separate exchanges that are not transported by beasts of burden, but rather by household members themselves. Such intraregional and interregional petty trade links Karnali Zone with the Bheri River corridor of Dolpo and the lower Himalaya of Bheri and Seti zones throughout the year, and Karnali Zone with the lowlands during the winter and spring according to the spatial and temporal availability of commodities and the trading families' free time to transport them. (It should be noted that traders put no monetary value on the time they expend in these endeavors).

A few examples illustrate the symbiotic interaction of this sundry trade, which further evens out regional inequalities. Many families who raise a grain deficit, who possess few, if any, transport animals, and who do not engage in the transfer and trade of salt, substitute other commodities in order to obtain grain. Those Pahari families of Gum Dara who raise a surplus of chilis (*corsani*) will, after harvest in November, take them to the Sinja and Tila valleys, or to Jajarkot District further south, where they exchange them for grains. One unit of chili brings one unit of rice or 1.5 units of other grains by volume. Some poorer families exploit the wild biota for items that they can exchange for grain. A number of households in Chaudhabisa Dara collect birch bark or a wild vegetable known locally as *ruga sag* (*Megacarpoea ployandra*) from subalpine and lower alpine regions during the summer (June to August) which they take to the Barekot area of Jajarkot District. There one load of dried *ruga sag* fetches approximately one load of barley or one-half load of other grains; birch bark brings twice these amounts.

Families from economic regions A and B buy mandarin oranges in the Dullu-Dailekh region of the lower Himalaya for one rupee per hundred fruit in October, carry them to the Jumla-Kalanga area, and sell them for one rupee per ten fruit—a tenfold profit. Similarly, some families from southern Karnali buy peanuts in Jajarkot during August for about one rupee per 1.5 l and sell them at home for a sixfold profit. In this way families generate cash that can be used to secure the spectrum of their subsistence needs.

Several generalizations can be made about Karnali Zone traders. Like petty traders everywhere they attempt to eliminate as many intermediaries as possible. In order to be successful and show a profit they must have significant business acumen, especially a keen awareness of seasonal and regional price differences and fluctuations. The farther they can travel (a function of their available time), the more phases or stages they can either bypass or, at their option, engage in themselves. Only those from families with a sizeable economic surplus can afford to buy low, stockpile, and sell high. They also are the only ones who can engage in high-risk, high-gain trade such as raising or buying and selling livestock. The majority of Karnali traders, however, have little surplus capital with which to work; thus they can engage only in low-risk, low-gain trade in volumes that meet only their subsistence requirements.

WINTER EXODUS TO LOWER REGIONS

During the nonagricultural season (November through March), three types of seasonal migrations take place that shift a sizeable proportion of Karnali's population southward. One involves Bhotia from the high northern fringe of upper Humla and upper Mugu who do not take part in long-distance dry-season trade. Entire families from Limi and Muchu panchayats descend to the Simikot area, where they work as weavers; those from Mugugaon, as already mentioned, descend to Gum, Sinja, and Asi *daras* where

Fig. 83. The seasonal border market of Rajapur at about 180 m on the Karnali River in Bardia District, Bheri Zone. Its 450 shack shops are erected each November and dismantled each July at the beginning of the wet season. The only permanent structures in the bazaar are a police station, a customs post, a few government-owned storehouses in which merchants keep goods during the monsoon, five Hindu shrines, and one mosque.

they are employed as weavers, or, in some instances, construction workers.

While Karnali Bhotia men and women seldom hire out as porters, similarly economically marginal Matwali Chhetri and Dum men commonly work as carriers at this time. They earn six to eight rupees per day transporting one-maund (37.3 kg) loads for up to 20 km.[12] Some transport the goods of others within the zone; many more carry between Karnali and the lower reaches of western Nepal.

However, the impact of tourism, including the demand for porters by trekkers and mountaineering expeditions, has yet to be felt in Karnali Zone. Although the number of adventure travelers who visit Nepal each year is steadily increasing, these trekkers and climbers come to experience the big peaks—particularly the Annapurna region of the upper Kali Gandaki drainage and Mount Everest (Sagarmatha) National Park further to the east. Karnali is seldom visited, and tourist porterage remains undeveloped.

The second type of seasonal migration is the winter trade trip to the lowlands by male members of Pahari and Bhotia households, both those with sizeable flocks of sheep and goats, which they winter in the lower hills of the Surkhet Valley (i.e., those for whom trade is intertwined with animal husbandry) and those without such livestock (those who trade without

---

[12] During the agricultural season, when their efforts are required in their own and others' fields, porters often demand up to twice the winter rates (12-25 rupees per day).

transport animals). While a few of the latter travel as far as Kanpur, Lucknow, and other large Indian cities, the vast majority frequent the Nepalese border bazaars of Nepalganj and Rajapur.

Today Nepalganj is a bustling and burgeoning permanent market center with a population (1969-70) of about 22,500 and some 1,000 shops, a sizeable proportion of which are operated by Indian merchants or Mawari. By contrast Rajapur, which was founded by the Rana regime in 1890, functions as a major market for only eight months each year (mid-November through mid-July). It has about 450 shops, of which only 25 percent are operated by Nepalese (figure 83). Twice, in 1920 and again in 1955, rampant flood waters of the Karnali River have not only destroyed the bazaar's *godowns*, or summer storage sheds, but altered the braided channels and course of the river itself, requiring the market site to be shifted.

Because of the dominance of Indian merchants in these Nepalese border markets, less cash and fewer commodities remain and circulate within western Nepal than flow out to India. Likewise an unfavorable balance of trade exists between India and the Nepalese lowlands on the one hand, and the Nepalese highlands on the other. Given Karnali's limited resources, the value and volume of the zone's imports far exceed those of its exports. Considerably more Karnali families engage in the southern phases of the trade circuits than in the northward oriented phases with Tibet or the Bhotia fringe. For example, of the seventy-four families whose household economies I studied in detail, thirty-five (47.4 percent) sent family members

to the lowlands, and another five (6.8 percent) sent money with neighbors, to purchase needed commodities during the dry season of 2026 V.S. (see figure 76). On the other hand, only nineteen (25.7 percent) of these households engaged in summer trade with Tibet or the Bhotia fringe. My panchayat-scale survey information indicates that most households make the southern trip either every year or every other year. Only those few agriculturally rich families can afford to purchase their needs locally.

The chief items exported to the south are: ghee from economic subregions 1, 2, and 3 in the southwestern corner of the zone (see figure 43);[13] animals, chiefly sheep and goats, which are usually sold in the lower Himalaya

---

[13] The greatest quantity of exported Karnali ghee comes from Raskot Dara. Informants estimate that in 2026 V.S., 2,400 rupees (5,743 kg) were sold in Nepalganj for approximately 55,200 rupees. It must be emphasized that precise or reliable quantitative data at panchayat, *dara*, district, or zonal scales on either exports or imports are not available. Nor is it usually possible to make even gross approximations.

Fig. 84. The all-weather Bheri River suspension bridge at Rong Ghat (439 m), one day south of the Surkhet Valley. En route to Nepalganj in January, a Karnali caravan of transport ovines carrying rice from the Inner Tarai crosses the bridge. Tolls are 0.10 rupees per animal and 0.25 rupees per person and are levied by the local panchayat that maintains the span. This caravan also must carry feed for its sheep and goats because of inadequate forage in the Tarai. © National Geographic Society.

en route to the lowlands, but also horses, which are sold at winter horse fairs, or *melas*, in Tribeni, the Dang Valley, Dharchula, Jouljibi, and Tanakpur (see figure 77); low-volume but high-density and high-value items such as knitted garments, homespun, medicinal herbs, *silagit*, hashish, musk, and cash from throughout the zone, which are exchanged in the lowlands for cloth, cigarettes, spices, tea, sugar, soap, metal and plastic utensils, and a variety of other manufactured goods. Of these imports only some brands of cigarettes, *bidi*s (cruder and cheaper cigarettes), and soap are manufactured in Nepal; the rest are of Indian origin. As has already been discussed, only those high-volume traders with transport ovines procure great amounts of Indian salt (figure 84). The vast majority of Karnali families are limited to bartering or buying commodities that they themselves can carry or, in rare instances, can hire porters or muleteers to transport.

As is the case throughout the Nepal Himalaya, Karnali Bhotia are noted for ranging far afield during their long-distance winter trade trips.

Some from Limi panchayat carry loads of the wooden bowls for which they are famous to both the Indian Himalaya and the Kathmandu Valley. Other Bhotia from enclaves in Chaudhabisa Dara engage in the lucrative traffic of musk from their home region and coral, turquoise, and amber that they obtain in Calcutta. Still other Bhotia from the Langu Valley and the upper Mugu who formerly traded directly with Drogpa in Tibet for both necessity and luxury items during the summer now follow a more indirect and time-consuming winter circuit in order to obtain these goods. They carry medicinal herbs, rare skins, and musk to Nepalganj. If these items fetch only an average price they content themselves with buying cotton cloth and other household goods and returning directly home. If, on the other hand, their export items bring a higher than average price, they first cross the border to the nearby railhead in India; second, travel by train and truck (often hitchhiking) 1,100 km to Kalimpong, a bazaar town 20 km east of Darjeeling and on a major trade route to Tibet; third, purchase from Tibetan refugees there man-loads consisting of such items as Tibetan brick tea, snuff, leather boots, and *bakkhus*, (the traditional Tibetan woolen robe); fourth, return to upper Mugu, where these goods are in great demand and bring two to three times their cost; and fifth, make a second trip to Nepalganj to buy their own ordinary household needs.

Prior to the imposition of trade restrictions by the Chinese, their summer circuit required only two weeks of travel. Now their alternative winter circuit requires two months and a journey of over 3,000 km. In the face of the deteriorating economic viability of this way of life a few Langu traders are now using some of their profits to buy farmland in the Surkhet Valley (figure 85), where they plan to settle and farm as soon as they can acquire sufficient property. However, informants report that Surkhet land values are rising faster than they can generate savings for this purpose.

For both Pahari and Bhotia throughout the zone, when a family has an atypical cash surplus after obtaining their imported needs it commonly buys silver and gold jewelry for its womenfolk in the border bazaars or in India. The most common Chhetri jewelry is "Company," solid silver Indian rupee coins that date back to the British East Indian, or "John" Company issue (figure 86). Wealthier Brahmans and Thakuri tend to invest more in gold items (figure 87). Such jewelry constitutes a walking family savings account that is a buffer against bad years. The women seldom object to parting with their jewelry in hard times, for "our stomachs tell us to."

A third type of migration involves families, principally Pahari and Dum, who have generated neither goods nor cash for their winter buying trip. Young men of these households seek work in the Tarai and inner Tarai or, more often, in India. The extent to which a family engages in such dry-season wage labor varies according to the viability of its other livelihood pursuits, especially farming. Thus in drought years, when food production falls, the number of families whose members work abroad increases.

Most migrant workers of Karnali Zone prefer to work in the cool, lower Himalaya of Kumaon and Garhwal (i.e., the Almora and Naini Tal areas) as unskilled laborers on road construction or in timber cutting. Daily wages currently are between 2.5 and 4.0 Indian rupees (equivalent to 3.3 and

Fig. 85. View southwest over the Surkhet Valley (ca. 600 m) and the Churia range beyond. With the recent eradication of malaria in the lowlands of western Nepal, His Majesty's Government is engaged in clearing tracts of subtropical forests for agriculture and resettlement by hill families. Note the overgrazed slope in the foreground.

5.3 Nepalese rupees, respectively).[14] Usually these laborers are able to subsist on about half their earnings. With the cash they save they purchase their families' needs in India or the Nepalese border bazaars on their way home in the spring. Young men of other Karnali families, usually those with a

---

[14] In translating Indian currency to Nepalese currency, 7.5 Indian rupees equal 10.25 Nepalese rupees.

Fig. 86. Chhetri woman wearing "Company" jewelry, solid silver Indian rupees that can be readily converted to cash in times of family need.

large labor force or with small labor demands in agriculture, engage in long-term work in India for one or more years before returning home.

These seasonal and long-term, but nonpermanent, migrations constitute a pressure-valve strategy that relieves to some degree the economic stress caused by accelerating population and degenerating resources in Karnali Zone. The importance of these work migrations is increasing each year. As yet no credible estimates have been made of the number of Karnali

Fig. 87. Wealthy Thakuri maiden with a traditional gold headband, modern gold earrings, and cultured pearls for a festival at Jumla-Kalanga. When she marries, this jewelry will be part of her dowry.

residents so employed. A common figure given by zone officials is 25 to 33 percent. Of the seventy-four households I studied for 2026 V.S., only three (4.1 percent) had members working in India for one to three months, and seven (9.5 percent) for one or more years. However, this sample fails to show the importance of temporary work in India to the Karnali economy.[15]

---

[15] McDougal (1968:57-76) and Rana (1971:56-74) discuss with some supporting survey data the importance of seasonal and long-term labor migrations to the economies of other regions in

Unlike those Magar, Gurung, Sunwar, Limbu, and Rai tribal areas of Nepal where mercenary service in Indian or British Ghurka regiments is a significant economic pressure valve, this form of migratory labor has never been open to the predominantly Pahari Karnali Zone. The panchayat data also indicate that service in the Nepalese army is rare.

Finally, travel between Karnali Zone and the lowlands during the dry season is not without some danger. Lone travelers are often robbed when trekking isolated stretches of trail. One young Chhetri informant reported that on his journey home to Gum Dara the previous March after working near Almora for a year, he was beaten and relieved of his load of Indian imports and 700 rupees (N.C.). Given this danger, more prudent travelers move in groups. Despite the fact that emergency rest shelters have been built on the major routes over the Chakhure-Mabu Lekh, death from exposure and hypothermia is not uncommon when travelers are trapped in the open by unseasonable or unusually heavy snowstorms. In 1946, when shelters were less numerous, such a sudden and severe November storm caught a number of parties in the open on the Mabu Lekh. Unable to move to safety, twenty-five people perished that night.

JUMLA-KALANGA AND ITS BAZAAR

If we discount those larger villages in which petty entrepreneurs sell goods such as cigarettes, matches, batteries, and other low-bulk items from boxes in their homes, Karnali Zone has only a single urban place of commercial note—Jumla-Kalanga, the zonal capital. Its site in the upper Tila Valley was most conducive to the growth of a relatively large town or, in fact, a complex of towns. There settlement and subsequent growth followed the collapse of the western Malla kingdom and the shift of power from Sinja, which had been a commercial node, to Chhinasim (Jumla-Kalanga) by the Kalyal kings of the Jumla Baisi in the early fifteenth century (see chapter 4). After Jumla's annexation by the House of Gorkha in the late eighteenth century this center experienced gradual though limited growth during the Rana regime. It was the headquarters of the Ranas' representative from Kathmandu as well as the site of a military garrison, a revenue office, a post office, a district court, and a jail. Because of its remote location, considerable de facto autonomy was held by the Ranas' representative in league with key local landlords and headmen. Throughout this final period of feudal exploitation of the general population there was little need for development of a major market in Jumla-Kalanga. Those in power imported goods not available within the zone from abroad. The peasant majority did without.

---

far western Nepal (i.e., Rapti, Bheri, Seti, and Mahakali zones). Rana points out that members of some hill households journey to the Tarai each winter to supervise or live on farmsteads they own there; such is also the case for a very few Karnali Brahmans and Thakuri.

The 1969-70 size of Chhinasim was 734 households and 4,100 people. Of these, only about 24 percent (176 families and 1,210 people) lived in Chhinasim village proper, the zonal headquarters and the site of the only bazaar of any consequence in all Karnali Zone.

Between eighty and a hundred years ago several Newars, who had previously served in the area as civil servants, opened shops in Jumla-Kalanga, thus forming the nucleus of a permanent bazaar. Their clientele were the civil and military personnel posted there. Seeing the success of the Newars and the accelerated growth of the zonal capital since the end of the Rana era in 1951, a number of local landed Pahari also opened shops. This resulted in a division of the limited market and forced the Newars, who previously did not farm, to buy land to make ends meet.

In 1970 there were twenty-nine shops, along with eighteen tea shops and five hotels[16] in both the old and new bazaar areas (figure 88). Collectively they now stock over 250 different items for sale primarily to the government servants. The indigenous population has been slow to use the bazaar principally because of the cost of the goods. Merchants feel they must average a 50 percent profit on their wares in order to remain viable. Transfer costs for one maund, or porter load (37.3 kg), from Nepalganj to Jumla-Kalanga are 100 rupees (2.68 rupees/kg). These transport costs account for an average of 13.6 percent of the lowland cost for their goods, which are then sold at prices 50 to 100 percent higher than in Nepalganj. The local peasants' relative lack of cash or kind for such purchases makes it more economical for them to continue their annual winter trade trips to the lowlands.

Viewed at a larger zonal or regional scale, Jumla-Kalanga does not function as a major market center. In Karnali Zone the major trails are, as one would suspect, the major trade routes. These tend to conform to or follow the dendritic drainage pattern of the upper Karnali River system, which trends generally west or southwest. There are relatively few major trails that cross from one drainage basin to another. Therefore, Jumla-Kalanga with its site on the upper Tila River has an extended hinterland of about 31 percent of the zone's population—the 52,000 villagers of economic region B (Sinja, Pansaya, and Asi *dara*s) and economic region D (Chaudhabisa Dara), all of whom live within an easy two days' travel distance.

Four major trails lead into Jumla-Kalanga: the trail from Dolpo District to the east, the trail down the Chaudhabisa Khola, which enters the Tila River a half hour's walk east of Jumla-Kalanga at Dansangu; the trail entering Jumla-Kalanga from the north over the Dori Lekh; and the major Tila River trail, which enters the zonal capital from the west (see figure 20). In 2026 V.S., 4,982 informants were questioned as they passed into or

---

[16] Of these, only one can be considered a true hotel.

through Jumla-Kalanga by way of these four trails. Of these, 2,152 (43 percent) were traveling alone; the remainder represented groups totaling 10,190 people (average group size was 3.6). Of the total number of informants only 1,100 stated that they or their party had Jumla-Kalanga as a final destination for the purpose of trade (an additional 408 were on trading trips to other des-

Fig. 88. December aerial view of Jumla-Kalanga looking west. Shops of the old bazaar flank the plaza in the middle ground, which is oriented north-south. Partially completed buldings of the new bazaar, where three of the zonal capital's twenty-nine shops are now located, are in the left background.

tinations). An almost equal number, 1,027, were coming to the capital for social reasons, and 981 on legal or government business (847 for court cases, 84 for government business). Animal husbandry (grazing), pilgrimages, and other seasonal or permanent migrations account for the rest. For all of these, informants with a final destination of Jumla-Kalanga totaled 3,229 (65 percent), but the 1,100 going for purposes of trade constituted only 22 percent. Even adding the service functions of government to the figure totals only 42 percent of informants with Jumla-Kalanga as their final destination.[17]

---

[17] See Appendix H, table 33. These figures must be used with caution. Owing to a misunderstanding by my enumerators, no individual informant was counted more than once during the year. Thus, if an individual lived in the immediate Jumla-Kalanga area and came into town

Until the early 1970s, Candan Nath and Bhairan Nath shrines in Jumla-Kalanga drew both Indian and Nepalese pilgrims off the direct Karnali River route to sacred Lake Manosarowar and Mount Kailas in Tibet. Today such pilgrim traffic has stopped, owing to border restrictions imposed by the Chinese. However, during late September and early October, a slack period for the hinterland farmers before they harvest their *kharif* crops, the celebration of Lord Krishna's birthday (a festival introduced by the Newars of the bazaar) and of Durga Puja or Dasai (known as Desera in India) attracts thousands of villagers from round about. They briefly swell the population of Jumla-Kalanga fivefold (figure 89). Bazaar shopkeepers estimate that they

Fig. 89. Celebration of Lord Krishna's birthday in Jumla-Kalanga. In early September, a throng of villagers from the surrounding area attend the two-day festival pageant of Lord Krishna's birthday in the old bazaar. Women and most children watch from the rooftops, while men line the plaza. Shopkeepers' daily average sales increase fourfold with the influx of an estimated 10,000 visitors during the celebration. © National Geographic Society.

four or five times in 2026 V.S., he was enumerated only once. This represents a serious under-counting of local trips by villagers from Sinja, Pansaya, Asi, and Chaudhabisa *daras*. All are within two days' walk of Jumla-Kalanga and are referred to here as its extended hinterland.

TABLE 24. Importance of items sold by Jumla bazaar shopkeepers in 2026 V.S.

Item	Percentage of sales	Item	Percentage of sales
Cloth	26.9	Cooking oils	2.0
Cigarettes	13.0	Soap	1.6
Ready-made clothes	9.5	Kerosene	1.6
Shoes	8.0	Batteries, flashlights	1.5
Foodstuffs	7.2	Tea	1.4
Cosmetics, toiletries	5.7	Medicines	1.0
Paper, stationery	5.1	Alcoholic beverages	0.9
Spices	4.2	Salt (Tibetan and Indian)	0.9
Miscellaneous	3.5	Matches	0.6
Sugar	3.3	Metal and plastic utensils	0.5
Hardware	3.0	Schoolbooks	0.3

they do four times their average daily sales during these festivals.

Such trade as does take place in Jumla-Kalanga bazaar is highly varied in nature (table 24). It should be noted, however, that the first five categories—cloth, cigarettes, ready-made clothes, shoes, and foodstuffs—account for almost 65 percent of all sales (in rupee volume); the other 35 percent is divided among seventeen minor categories.

Customers fall into four broad groups. There are the urban dwellers employed by the government in various capacities, who constitute two categories, the military detachment (128) and the armed police personnel (25), whose food is supplied by government-contracted commissaries but who purchase sundries and luxury items in the bazaar; the rest are the government-service personnel (389), who are almost totally reliant on the local economy (including the bazaar) for their daily needs. A third category is the local rural, agricultural people, who tend to establish long-term customer loyalty to a shopkeeper in order to facilitate buying on credit. Finally, there are the travelers from beyond the extended hinterland, who spread their custom among various shops and who, in attempting to minimize dealings with intermediaries, are a shifting and ephemeral source of custom.

A detailed breakdown of the bazaar shopkeepers' activities for 2026 V.S. is given in table 25. As indicated, of a potential 328 shop-months during which the twenty-nine Jumla-Kalanga merchants could have been open for business, they were in fact open only 261 months, or 80 percent of the potential time. Only ten shops remained open throughout the year.[18] Moreover,

---

[18] Those who closed for part of the year did so during the winter months. It was then that they, like their local rural customers, went south on buying trips.

only eight shopkeepers (28 percent) depended on their shops as a primary source of livelihood. Farming remained the essential pursuit for the other twenty-one. Excluding foodstuffs procured locally, the combined weight of goods imported from the lowlands in that year by all twenty-nine shopkeepers was only 472 loads (17,606 kg).

Although transportation costs per se account for only 13.6 percent of the cost of goods imported from the lowlands or, in four instances (160 kg) from Kathmandu, transportation problems remain the single greatest deterrent to individual commercial expansion.[19] Some shopkeepers expected the 1968 introduction of STOL aircraft connecting Jumla-Kalanga with Nepalganj and Surkhet to the south and Kathmandu to the east to relieve this problem. Hearing of this, the porters who in previous years transported for most of the shopkeepers did not show up. In the event, air transportation from Nepalganj to Jumla-Kalanga this year proved to be exceedingly unreliable, and all of the shopkeepers were caught between technologies, having neither new air transportation nor traditional porters. They were therefore forced to turn to more expensive porters contracted for in Nepalganj. As can be seen from table 25, they were forced to rely primarily on their traditional methods of transporting imports from the lowlands—porters and/or pack equines. But these costs were higher than anticipated, and averaged 3.00 rupees/kg rather than 2.68 rupees/kg. This reduced the hoped-for average profit of 50 percent to an actual average profit of 38 percent.

The technological change that caused this temporary economic embarrassment is only one of a number of incipient structural shifts occurring in Jumla-Kalanga. At the end of the Rana period (1951) there had been only five government services provided; in 1970 there were twenty-four, staffed by 247 outsiders and 295 locals (see table 26). In 1951 only six shops were in operation; in 1970, as we know, there were twenty-nine. In 1967 a branch of the state-owned National Commercial Bank opened. In 1970 it did a business of two to three *lahks* (one *lahk* equals 100,000 rupees) per year in bank drafts for individuals traveling to Nepalganj alone. This was double the 1-1.5 *lahk* business per year in bank drafts generated by merchants from the bazaar. Bank use by the government for payrolls and development projects ran to a further eighteen *lahks* per year. Although local reliance on this banking facility is growing slowly, it is growing.

The impact of government payrolls and projects is also felt in increasing rates of inflation owing to more money being available for limited

---

19 The 13.6 percent figure is derived by dividing the rupee cost of imported goods (table 25) by the product of the sum of loads multiplied by an average cost factor of 3.0 rupees/kg. Further, it should be noted that the two apparent anomolies in lines 6 and 12 (in the "Months closed" column) represent one shopkeeper with serious illness in the family which prevented him from opening his shop that year; the other shopkeeper who did not open was in jail.

TABLE 25. Jumla bazaar shopkeepers' activities in 2026 v.s. (1969-70).

Shop	Caste of shopkeeper[1]	Size of family	Years operated	Principle occupation[2]	Owns shop	Months closed in 2026 V.S.	Chief items imported[3]	Where bought[4]	Yearly buying trips	Method of transport[5]	Number of loads[6]	Rupee cost of imported goods (includes transport and tariffs)	Shop sales in 2026 V.S. (includes local foodstuffs)	Average sales/day	Business trend[7]
1.	T	7	1	F	no	3	Clo, Cos	N,I	1	H,P	12	20,000	27,000	100	S
2.	C	15	1	F	yes	3	Clo, Sho	N,I	1*	P	—	—	18,250	68	S
3.	C	5	1	F	no	7	Sho, Cig	N	1*	P	—	—	4,500	30	D
4.	T	3	3	Sh	no	—	Cig, Sho	N	1	P	5	9,000	14,600	41	I
5.	Nr	10	80	F	yes	—	Cig, Pap	N,K	2	P,A	23	14,800	26,800	74	I
6.	B	9	2	F	no	12	Clo, Cig	N	1*	P	—	—	—	—	—
7.	C	19	4	F	no	1	Clo, Rea	N	1	P	12	12,000	18,300	55	S
8.	C	11	5	F	no	1	Clo, Cig	N	1	P	10	10,000	41,900	127	S
9.	C	9	1 mo.	F	yes	—	Clo, Cig	N	1	P	7	6,000	?	?	?
10.	C	25	3	F	no	—	Clo, Sho	N	1	P	12	8,000	3,400	10	D
11.	B	11	1	F	no	4	Clo, Cig	N,I	1	H,P	8	6,000	8,200	34	I
12.	B	15	3	F	yes	12	Clo, Cig	N	1*	P	13	10,000	—	—	—
13.	C	21	16	F	yes	3	Clo, Sho	N,K	2	P,A	21	30,000	33,700	125	I
14.	B	7	16	F	no	3	Clo, Sho	N,I	1	P	38	31,000	21,100	78	I
15.	C	15	18	F	no	5	Clo, Alc	N,K	2*	P,A	—	—	12,800	61	I
16.	Nr	8	4	Sh	yes	4	Sho, Cig	N,I	1	M,P	10	8,200	13,200	55	I
17.	Nr	32	100	F	yes	—	Clo, Cig	N,I	1	M,P	70	40,000	30,700	85	D
18.	C	8	14	F	no	—	Clo, Cig	N,I	1	H,P	13	20,000	16,700	46	I

19.	C	10	3	F	no	1	Clo, Spi	N,I	1	M,P	20	20,000	26,600	81	I
20.	Nr	10	3	Sh,Ho	yes	—	Cos,Rea	N,I	1	M,P	12	12,500	15,500	43	D
21.	TL	6	24	Sh	yes	4	Cig,Sug	N,Sr	2	M,P	34	19,000	11,600	48	I
22.	Nr	6	28	F	yes	1	Clo,Cig	N	1	M,P	11	6,000	6,500	20	S
23.	C	4	3	F	no	—	Cig, Har	N	1*	P	—	—	4,100	11	S
24.	B	18	1	F	no	—	Cig,Cos	N	1	P	10	8,000	5,800	16	S
25.	B	15	6	Sh	no	—	Clo, Rea	N,I,K	2	M,P,A	56	31,000	60,100	167	I
26.	C	42	17	Sh	yes	2	Clo, Rea	N,I	1	M,P	38	37,400	64,300	214	I
27.	Nr	8	25	Sh	yes	1	Clo, Sho	N	1	P	15	12,000	21,500	65	I
28.	Nr	13	80	Sh	yes	—	Cig, Spi	N,I	1	P	17	13,000	30,200	84	S
29.	C	45	3 mos.	F	yes	—	Cig, Sho	N	1	P	5	6,000	10,700	119	S
Total												390,000	538,155		

a B - Brahman
   T - Thakuri
   C - Chhetri
   Nr - Newar
   TL - Thakali

b F - farming
   Sh - shop
   Ho - hotel

c Alc - alcoholic beverage
   Cig - cigarettes (and *Bidi*)
   Clo - cloth
   Cos - cosmetics, toiletries
   Har - hardware
   Pap - paper, stationery
   Rea - ready-made clothes
   Sho - shoes
   Spi - spices
   Sug - sugar

d I - India
   K - Kathmandu
   N - Nepalganj
   Sr - Surkhet

e P - porter
   H - horse
   M - mule
   A - aircraft

f 1 load = 1 maund = 37.3 kg

g D - Decreasing
   I - Increasing
   S - Stationary

* Shopkeeper did not make winter buying trip.

TABLE 26. Government services and personnel in Jumla-Kalanga in 2026 V.S. (1969-70).

Services	Local personnel	Foreign personnel[†]	Total personnel
1. Zonal Commissioner's Office*	52	16	68
2. Cottage Industry Training Center	35	4	39
3. Jumla District Panchayat Office	29	5	34
4. Land Reform Office	26	3	29
5. Jumla District Court*	22	3	25
6. Zonal Court	15	4	19
7. Public Buildings Office	13	4	17
8. Revenue Office*	15	—	15
9. Hospital	12	2	14
10. Candan Nath Multi-Purpose High School	12	—	12
11. National Commercial Bank	8	3	11
12. Chief Zonal Post Office*	8	2	10
13. Zonal School Inspection Office	8	1	9
14. Veterinary Hospital	5	3	8
15. Zonal Postal Control Office	5	2	7
16. Tele-Communications Office	4	—	4
17. Public Service Commission	3	1	4
18. Jumla District Panchayat, Education Branch	3	1	4
19. Farmers' and Women's Organizations Office	2	—	2
20. Superintendent of Police	5	15	20
21. Jumla District Police	8	25	33
22. Armed Police	—	25	25
23. Military Detachment*	—	128	128
24. Jail*	5	—	5
Total personnel	295	247	542

[*]   Service existing at the end of the Rana regime (1951); number of personnel unknown.
[†]   From elsewhere in Nepal.

goods. This local inflation rate, imbedded in the growing national inflation rate, is similarly reflected in the increased cost of portering. If the STOL aircraft service becomes more reliable, and the subsequent increasing volume of freight shipped by plane lowers air freight rates, the new transportation will replace the ever more comparatively expensive and time-consuming portering. A greater flow of goods at lower prices into Jumla-Kalanga will make the local market system more attractive and the rural residents of the extended hinterland will begin to utilize it not only to sell their own surplus, as they do now, but to purchase a greater proportion of their necessities and luxuries. The structural shifts and the direction of development of the urban functions of Jumla-Kalanga seem evident.

8
Summary and Conclusions

THE SUBSISTENCE SYSTEM MODELED

The preceding explanatory description, while by no means complete, touches upon the salient processes that have produced, and continue to produce, both the physical and cultural landscapes of Karnali Zone. As such, it has focused upon the components of the peasants' cultural-ecological system, both historical and contemporary. A unifying explanatory analysis of their ways of life is more difficult, because their multidimensional character exhibits great inherent complexity of processes in relation to scale, place, and time. On the basis of field investigations it is possible, however, to construct a simplified model of the Karnali Zone subsistence cultural-ecological system (figure 90).

The data used represent actual figures taken from one of seventy-four individual household questionnaires, that of a Matwali Chhetri family of Septi village (at approximately 2,900 m in Chhinasim panchayat, Asi Dara). The name of the household head has been changed to preserve anonymity (this family is, however, the top line of the Septi village Chhetri, Appendix G, table 32. Using information from a single family has the advantage of tying the lowest unit of observation, the household, to the most abstract unit of analysis, the model. This approach also allows full use of the aggregate data presented in table 27, as well as that in Appendix G.

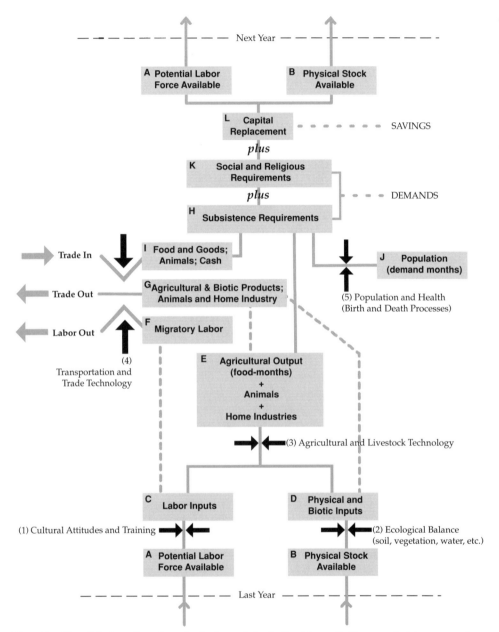

Fig. 90. Simplified cultural-ecological model of the Karnali Zone subsistence system
NOTE: Quantifiable components (cells) of the system are lettered. Constraints on the system are numbered and underlined, and their pressure points are indicated by double arrows.

TABLE 27. Family economies by caste for 2026 V.S. (1969-70).

	Brahman	Thakuri	Chhetri	Bhotia	Dum	Total
1. Number of families[a]	12	7	34	5	16	74
(Number of people)	(102)	(132)	(289)	(38)	(104)	(665)
2. Producers (P)[b]	57.3	81.8	154.5	23.8	59.8	377.0
(Avg. number P/family)	(4.8)	(11.7)	(4.5)	(4.8)	(3.7)	(5.1)
3. Consumers (C)[c]	68.0	92.5	185.5	27.0	72.3	445.3
(Avg. number C/family)	(5.7)	(13.2)	(5.5)	(5.4)	(4.5)	(6.0)
4. Producer/consumer ratio	1:1.2	1:1.1	1:1.2	1:1.1	1:1.2	1:1.2
5. Number of *khet* fields[d]	361	259	664	2	36	1,302
(Avg. number/family)	(30.1)	(37.0)	(18.9)	(0.4)	(2.3)	(17.6)
6. Number of *pakho* fields	74	329	864	545	202	2,014
(Avg. number/family)	(6.2)	(47.0)	(25.4)	(109.0)	(12.6)	(27.2)
7. Mean maximum distance to fields (in hours)	1.3	6.6	1.8	1.9	0.9	2.0
8. Mean minimum distance to fields (in minutes)	3.5	0.5	3.5	2.0	1.5	2.7
9. Average distance to fields (in hours)	0.5	0.7	0.7	0.7	0.6	0.6
10. Hectares of *khet*	7.2	7.4	5.9	(nil)	0.5	21.1
(Average per family)	(0.6)	(1.1)	(0.2)	(nil)	(nil)	(0.3)
11. Hectares of *pakho*	18.9	33.6	59.3	6.0	9.7	127.5
(Average per family)	(1.6)	(4.8)	(1.7)	(1.2)	(0.6)	(1.7)
12. Percentage of *khet*	27.6	18.1	9.1	0.7	4.7	14.2
(Percentage of *pakho*)	(72.4)	(81.9)	(90.9)	(99.3)	(95.3)	(85.8)
13. Total farmland (in ha)	26.1	41.1	65.2	6.1	10.2	148.6
(Average per family)	(2.2)	(5.9)	(1.9)	(1.2)	(0.6)	(2.0)
14. Average ha/P	0.5	0.5	0.4	0.3	0.2	0.4
15. Average ha/C	0.4	0.4	0.4	0.2	0.1	0.3
16. Number of bovines	149	188	251	72	47	637
(Average number/CU)[e]	(2.2)	(1.3)	(1.4)	(2.7)	(0.7)	(1.4)
17. Number of ovines	9	103	559	360	17	1,048
(Average number/CU)	(0.1)	(1.1)	(3.0)	(13.3)	(0.2)	(2.4)
18. Number of equines	26	10	56	41	—	133
(Average number/CU)	(0.4)	(0.1)	(0.3)	(1.5)		(0.3)

[a] The family is considered a household, whether nuclear or extended, that uses (that is, eats from) a common hearth. Note that the data on Thakuri households reflect one extended family of 64 members.

[b] Producers (P): family members under age 10 = 0.00 P; aged 10 to 14 = 0.50 P; aged 15 to 50 = 1.00 P; over age 50 = 0.25 P.

[c] Consumers (C): family members under age 2 = 0.00 C; aged 2 to 9 = 0.25 C; aged 10 to 14 = 0.50 C; aged 15 and over = 1.00 C.

[d] Fields are discrete plots.

[e] A consumer unit (CU) is one day of consumption by a consumer (C) in the family: similarly, a producer unit (PU) is one day of work by a producer (P) in the family.

(TABLE 27 *continued*)

	Brahman	Thakuri	Chhetri	Bhotia	Dum	Total
19. Total number of animals	184	231	866	473	64	1,818
(Average number/CU)	(2.7)	(2.5)	(4.7)	(17.5)	(0.9)	(4.1)
20. PU in agriculture	5,717	954	14,003	1,811	2,294	24,779
(Average PU/family)	(476.4)	(136.3)	(411.9)	(362.2)	(143.4)	(334.9)
Percentage of total PU expended (item 27)	40.8	8.0	39.4	30.2	18.2	30.9
21. PU in animal husbandry	457	610	2,358	500	166	4,091
(Average PU/family)	(38.1)	(87.1)	(69.4)	(100.0)	(10.4)	(55.3)
Percentage of total PU expended (item 27)	3.3	5.1	6.6	8.3	1.3	5.1
22. PU in handicrafts[f]	40	405	1,354	908	176	2,883
(Average PU/family)	(3.3)	(57.9)	(39.8)	(181.6)	(11.0)	(39.0)
Percentage of total PU expended (item 27)	0.3	3.4	3.8	15.1	1.4	3.6
23. PU in trade	1,109	1,275	2,075	479	135	5,073
(Average PU/family)	(92.4)	(182.1)	(61.0)	(95.8)	(8.4)	(68.6)
Percentage of total PU expended (item 27)	7.9	10.7	5.8	8.0	1.1	6.3
24. PU in misc. labor[g]	996	1,827	737	20	3,000	6,580
(Average PU/family)	(83.0)	(261.0)	(21.7)	(4.0)	(187.5)	(88.9)
Percentage of total PU expended (item 27)	7.1	15.3	2.1	0.3	23.8	8.2
25. PU in housework	4,512	5,505	11,782	1,857	5,715	29,371
(Average PU/family)	(376.0)	(786.4)	(346.5)	(371.4)	(357.2)	(396.9)
Percentage of total PU expended (item 27)	32.2	46.1	33.2	30.9	45.3	36.7
26. PU in religious activity[h]	1,189	1,378	3,222	429	1,128	7,346
(Average PU/family)	(99.1)	(196.9)	(94.8)	(85.8)	(70.5)	(99.3)
Percentage of total PU expended (item 27)	8.5	11.5	9.1	7.1	8.9	9.2
27. Total PU expended	14,020	11,954	35,531	6,004	12,614	80,123
(Average PU/family)	(1,168.3)	(1,707.7)	(1,045.0)	(1,200.8)	(788.3)	(1,082.7)
28. Total PU available[i]	20,900	29,840	56,395	8.670	21,813	137,618

[f] For both home consumption and trade. Such products that are traded are included in item 31 (total income in rupees).

[g] *Jajmani* labor, hired agricultural labor, migrant labor, miscellaneous exploitation of the biota, teaching, or government service. Note that reciprocal exchange labor is not included.

[h] Religious activities are included as a PU input because they are an inextricable facet of the peasant household's way of life and its way of coping with economic stress (see Wolf 1966: 96-106).

[i] The sum of the family's PU x 365 days; total yearly CU are similarly derived.

	Brahman	Thakuri	Chhetri	Bhotia	Dum	Total
29. PU not used	6,880	17,886	20,864	2,666	9.199	57,495
(Percentage of total PU expended [item 27])	(33.0)	(60.0)	(37.0)	(31.0)	(42.0)	(42.0)
30. PU away from home: Social activities[j]	1,833	498	4,482	366	714	7,893
(Average per family)	(152.8)	(71.1)	(131.8)	(73.2)	(44.6)	(106.7)
31. Total income in rupees	99,252	175,096	107,015	21,380	21,870	424,613
(Average per family)	(8,271)	(25,014)	(3,148)	(4,276)	(1,367)	(5,738)
32. Average income/P	1,734	2,142	693	900	366	1,126
33. Income in cash	62,535	121,849	28,475	8,679	10,550	232,088
(Average per C)	(920)	(1,317)	(154)	(321)	(146)	(521)
34, Percentage in cash	63	70	27	41	48	55
35. Income in kind[k]	36,717	53,247	78,564	12,701	11,320	192,525
(Average per C)	(540)	(576)	(424)	(470)	(157)	(432)
36. Percentage in kind	37	30	73	59	52	45
37. Total expenditures	55,973	93,546	71,620	18,742	12,502	252,383
(Average per family)	(4,664)	(13,364)	(2,106)	(3,748)	(781)	(3,411)
38. Average expenditure/P	978	1,144	464	789	209	669
37. Average expenditure/C	823	1,011	386	694	173	567
38. Surplus[l]	43,279	81,550	35,395	2,638	9,368	172,230
(Average per family)	(3,607)	(11,650)	(1,041)	(528)	(586)	(2,327)
39. Surplus per C	636	882	191	98	130	387

[j] Visiting relatives or friends; Pahari women often spend appreciable time at their natal homes.

[k] When peasants exchange (barter for) commodities, they place a monetary value on the items; these values are reflected here.

[l] What appears to be a large surplus in reality must be allocated for seed, animals, or other costs during the coming year. For most families, this apparent surplus corresponds to what Wolf (1966: 6) refers to as the peasant's "replacement fund." Note the great variation in surplus among the families of all castes (table 32).

Obviously no single household or year is typical. However, using data from a single family circumvents the methodological problems inherent in a Weberian ideal-type approach, and avoids problems inherent in the application of statistical analysis and measurement to a situation in which the complexity of unmeasurables provides as many penetrating insights as the presentation of measurements. Although the quantities presented here and elsewhere in this work represent hard-won battles against the intransigent realities of field research, and whereas these measures and observations are closer to the reality of Karnali Zone life than any elsewhere available, it is the interaction of people and places and things that is under consideration, and this ecological interaction is as much felt as measured. The journey of Ram Batta Kathayat and his family through an entire year should be viewed as an instruction manual on how to use the model as well as an analysis of the system applied to a single household. The interested reader can then go on to use the model at the family or the caste level and thereby perhaps get the feel as well as the fact of this Himalayan segment of the world's people.

With mid-April, or Chaitra, 2026 V.S. (1969-70), as the starting point, we enter the schematic at the bottom left-hand side. Ram's household contained a potential labor force of 4.75 producers from a total resident family of eleven individuals (the eldest son had migrated to the Almora area of India six years before; he had not returned in this time, nor had he sent any earnings home; and he is therefore not included in this analysis). The consumers in the household totaled 6.5, and the producer/consumer ratio was therefore 1:1.37 (for definitions of producer, consumer, producer/consumer ratio and other terms used below, see table 27).

Ram's farm totaled 1.04 ha consisting of fifty-one plots located in three separate areas. The farthest field was two hours away; the nearest was the kitchen garden at his doorstep. The average distance of his plots from home was one hour. None of these were *khet* (irrigated land); all were undulating, terraced *pakho* plots. In addition he had use of village grazing grounds for his twenty-four head of livestock and access to village forest and meadowlands for the collection of fuel and exploitation of other biota.

The total family labor input for 2026 was 1,087 producer units; this represented 63 percent of the total of 1,734 potentially available producer units. This input was broken down as follows: agriculture, 44.3 percent; housework (including cooking and obtaining water and fuel wood), 31.2 percent; religious activities (including daily family *pujas*, monthly observances, and occasional large festivals and celebrations), 9.5 percent; animal husbandry, 5.6 percent; handicrafts, 4.5 percent; trade, 4.0 percent; miscellaneous labor (portering locally), 0.9 percent.

The physical and biotic inputs represented extraction from the land and, in addition to the wood, fuel, and water already mentioned, included the gathering and processing of biota for cooking oil. This involved collecting an average of one maund (37.3 kg) of firewood per day, an activity requiring two hours of travel, round trip. Ram's family also produced 50 percent, or 4.5 l, of its yearly cooking oil requirements by processing walnuts, *dantelo* (*Prinsepia utilis*) and marijuana (*Cannabis sativa*); the other 50 percent of the family cooking oil requirement was met by importing mustard oil from the Surkhet Valley. This year no biotic inputs to the household economy were used as barter items in trade; all were consumed at home.

There was no labor migration as such this year, the eldest son having been discounted, but Ram did work within Asi Dara as a porter for Jumla-Kalanga officials for ten days, earning 120 rupees.

Home industry this year consisted only of processing wool and knitting garments for family use; none were used for trade purposes. Of the twenty-four household animals, one was a bullock (in order to make up a plow team, Ram reciprocally shared with a neighbor who also had only a single bullock), two were milch cows, each of which produced a liter per day during the monsoon season and virtually nothing during the dry winter. The total milk production was consumed at home. There was also one male calf being raised for future use as the other half of Ram's plow team. The remaining twenty animals were ovines: thirteen sheep and seven goats, of which eight were transport animals (castrated males). Ram sold one sheep for 80 rupees and one goat for 100 rupees in the month of Aswin (early October); he butchered a sheep valued at 100 rupees for home consumption during Durga Puja or Dasai the same month. This was the only meat the family consumed during the year.

Agricultural outputs were primarily winter or *rabi* grains; this year production totaled 1,885 kg (1,674 of barley, 109 of buckwheat, 102 of wheat). In addition, 156 kg of potatoes and 342 kg of radishes, beans, and miscellaneous vegetables were produced. The grain production represented a value of 3,038 rupees and, because of unusually beneficial rainfall, constituted what was considered, after deducting grain required for trade and seed, to represent a thirteen months' supply for the home. In normal years only a similarly derived ten-month supply is produced, the two-month deficit being purchased with monies acquired from some combination of additional labor by Ram as a porter, increased exploitation of wild biota for sale, selling of more animals, or, in years of extreme need, cashing in jewelry of one or both of his wives. Another common strategy would be cutting back on the amount of food consumed during the lean weeks just prior to harvest.

As can be gathered from the analysis thus far, trading activities during the year were quite limited. They consisted of only three trips and a total of forty-three days. The first, in July, involved a twenty-four-day round trip to Mugugaon by Ram with his eight transport animals loaded with 100 kg of barley. This grain was exchanged, at almost a 1:1 ratio for salt (104 kg). Of this salt, obtained at such an unfavorably low exchange because of a temporary oversupply of grain in Mugugaon, 60 kg were reserved for home use (34 kg by the family; 26 kg by livestock), while the remaining 40 kg surplus provided the basis for the second trade trip. This two-day round trip was in October, when Ram and a friend portered the salt to Luma village in the Chaudhabisa Valley. There they exchanged it for 80 kg of maize to be used for home consumption. (It should be noted that Ram and his family ate rice on only four or five festival days during 2026; it was obtained by bartering barley with passing travelers).

Finally in December, having earned 120 rupees portering the previous month, and having 180 rupees from the two animals he sold, Ram borrowed an additional 100 rupees from a Brahman in Had Sinja and took the total 400 rupees to the Surkhet Valley. On this fifteen-day round-trip journey he purchased two rupees of spices, four rupees of paper (for his eleven-year-old son, who attended school), forty rupees of mustard oil, and 300 rupees of factory-made cotton cloth from India—all for family consumption or use. The remaining fifty-four rupees were spent for food and bridge tolls on the trip. Ram went to Surkhet, where he was forced to pay slightly higher prices, rather than continue on to Nepalganj, because he did not want to leave his family without an adult male at home for the additional seven or eight days this would have taken. It is equally noteworthy that he did not buy those other most commonly sought goods: tea, soap, sugar, and cigarettes. Substitutes were supplied from his kitchen garden (tobacco) or from additional exploitation of the wild biota (especially honey).

After all trade and exchange were taken into account the family consumed about 1,365 kg of grain, 498 kg of potatoes, radishes, beans, and miscellaneous vegetables, and one sheep. This left a grain surplus of around 500 kg, with a value of about 750 rupees. From this surplus, 107 kg (value 161 rupees) was bartered for goods and services: 45 rupees for shoes, 25 for wool, 24 for school expenses, 21 for six days of hired field labor, 20 for tailoring, 16 for tool repair, and 10 for miscellaneous. An additional 110 rupees' worth of grain (73 kg) went to repay the 100-rupee loan plus interest. The family, then, was left with an unusual grain surplus of roughly 320 kg, valued at about 480 rupees. Their grain consumption of 1,365 is very close to the projected population demand of 1,425.5 kg (obtained by multiplying the average 219.3 kg per consumer by the 6.5 consumers in the family).

During 2026, Ram's outlay for social and religious requirements was minimal. There occurred none of those major life-cycle events such as marriages or deaths that require relatively large cash and kind expenditures. The total family costs in this category consisted of the consumption of the sheep, worth about 100 rupees, plus only six rupees for sacrificial grains used in pujas.

Similarly, needed capital replacements were very limited this year; 204 kg (396 rupees value) of grain were set aside for seed for the following year, and, as already mentioned, sixteen rupees were spent for tool repairs. Here again there were none of those periodic large expenses such as house rebuilding or major terracing that generally require hired labor. When all was said and done, Ram and his family entered the next year (2027 V.S.) with a 116 kg grain surplus valued at 174 rupees. This amount was equivalent to a one-month food supply. In 2027, however, the youngest daughter would move into the consumer category (from age one to age two) and add 0.25 to that set. The family makeup would thus be 4.75 producers and 6.75 consumers, and the producer/consumer ratio would be 1:1.42, less favorable than the earlier year's 1:1.37.

A few caveats on Ram's 2026 household economy are in order. First, the sheep consumed at Dasai was, it is true, a 100-rupees loss of the family's livestock, but is also constituted a caloric input into the family diet. Second, it should be noted that an easement on the consumption demands was brought about by the number of producer units spent away from home (Appendix G, table 32). For the year the figure was 108 producer units, which reduced grain consumption by 65 kg. This plus factor was, however, offset by the minus factor of an unknown number of visitors (producer units away from *their* homes) who were fed from Ram's household stores.

THE SUBSISTENCE SYSTEM CONSTRAINED

Impinging on the flow of activities and goods through this model are five major constraining forces. These must, of course, be recognized as a part of the subsistence system and not something external to it. Nonetheless, it is in the makeup of these constraints that elements both distant and near in time and space combine to cause great change in the manner and direction in which the system moves. Put another way, the flow of energy through the system must pass through these five constrictions, and the degree of pressure exerted by these constrictions is in part a reflection of forces external to the cultural-ecological system itself. The five constraining forces are: (1) cultural attitudes and training, (2) the ecological balance, (3) agricultural and animal technology, (4) transportation and trade technology, (5) population and health.

Today these forces no longer regulate and maintain a homeostatic system; instead they are restrictors that impede the peasants' livelihood pursuits and prevent harmonious use of the environment. Collectively they destroy the long-standing way of life, for they act as a positive feedback mechanism.

Cultural Attitudes and Training

A variety of beliefs, practices, and attitudes, exhibited primarily by the Pahari (hill Hindu) majority, but to a lesser extent by the Bhotia Buddhist minority, conspires to constrain the livelihood system of Karnali Zone. Interwoven in the sociopolitical fabric of the region, all are manifestations of traditionalism and varying degrees of orthodoxy. Two important contributing factors to this conservatism are the remote and isolated location of the region and the political history of the region and the nation. Historically, the region hosted a series of in-migrations and conquests; petty hill kingdoms have risen and fallen, and the Pahari have predominated. They occupy the better agricultural lands in the valley bottoms and adjacent slopes, pushing or confining the Bhotia to higher, agriculturally less productive terrain along the northern border fringe and isolated enclaves farther south. An exploitative feudal system was imposed in the region, many vestiges of which are still present, such as *jajmani* practices. The rugged, and in many respects inhospitable, physical landscape contributed to an insular cultural landscape characterized by the complex symbioses previously discussed.

Annexation of Jumla and the other Baisi and Chaubisi princedoms by the House of Gorkha at the end of the eighteenth century not only served to intensify the existing economic exploitation, but shifted the focus of power to Kathmandu. The ensuing 105-year period of Rana repression, which ended only in 1951, further contributed to the insularism of the region.

All these factors combined to encapsulate the population, who were, and still are, suspicious and distrustful of outsiders and foreign influences. It is not surprising that until recently most of the population had either no concept of nation-state or were unable to think in terms of Nepal as a whole. Even today one meets an occasional traveler on the trail who, when asked where he is from and where he is going, replies that he is from *aul* ("malaria"), meaning the Tarai, or that he is on his way to "Nepal," meaning the Kathmandu Valley. Since 1951, when Rana isolationism ended and Nepal opened its doors to the outside world, thus entering the twentieth century, the government has been struggling to build a politically, socially, and economically viable nation.

Prior to the establishment of the panchayat governmental system in 1962, local village government was of the traditional headman or village elders' council type. In general these leadership positions were held by men from affluent and influential families. In Pahari areas, they were usually of high caste and were key men in the local social and economic framework of the communities. Because such families produced an economic surplus they were less constricted by the common household labor bind. This, in turn, permitted them to give their male children traditional education, either by Brahman tutors or in Brahmanical schools (in Jumla, in the Tarai, or in

India). It was only natural that members of this same, small, educated elite group were elected to the village panchayats.[1]

On the other hand, the vast majority of the population were, and still are, uneducated and politically unsophisticated. Even though they now increasingly aspire to a better way of life, they are conditioned to a subservient role. Although the government's efforts in education are beginning to break down this condition, the majority of people still suffer from what can be termed the "vested interest syndrome," a common attitude of frustrated acceptance of their second-class role, manifested by general apathy and lack of initiative. Despite efforts in land reform, as well as the potential of the panchayat system, very few examples can be cited where the wide gap between the power-elite minority and vast, less affluent majority has been narrowed.

In general, the civil servants posted in Karnali Zone are confronted by a local population not only suspicious but steeped in traditional parochial attitudes. These outsiders are usually unhappy in their isolated, relatively primitive posts and miss the amenities of the Kathmandu Valley. Moreover, they feel that they have been ostracized from the mainstream of civil service and that their chances for advancement in government are seriously jeopardized (an appraisal that is essentially correct). The resulting state of mind in turn affects their ability to develop good rapport with some local leaders and the population as a whole.

To the factionalism among Karnali's population and their distrust of governmental officials, factors that generally deter cooperation at all scales— village, panchayat, district, and zone—must be added a number of additional roadblocks caused by the dearth of education and training. One is the almost total lack of managerial skills. Another is lack of any large-scale coordinated home industry in the form of cooperatives.

Finally, inheritance practices contribute to the seemingly insurmountable problem of ever increasing land fragmentation. Although the people recognize this to be a paramount problem, they accept it, for they perceive no way within their own social system that such fragmentation can be stopped.

---

1 With the advent of the Panchayat Raj in 1962, the traditional high-caste control of and exclusive access to education was technically broken; universal education (i.e., the opportunity for education regardless of sex or caste) was introduced. By 1969-70, 115 primary schools had been established in Karnali Zone (Nepal, *Statistical Pocket Book*, 1975). Most of these, however, did not furnish totally free public education, for the students' families were required to contribute some financial support. The 1971 National Census reports that by 1969-70 literacy in Karnali Zone had risen to 6.1 percent. However, it must be noted that in spite of this educational reform, the actual distribution of education in the zone's population was closely correlated with caste rank. For an insightful discussion of cultural barriers to educational innovations, see Reed and Reed (1968). Especially relevant to the case of Karnali are pp. 151-69.

Ecological Balance

The relation of people to the biota of their habitat has been discussed earlier. Throughout most of Karnali Zone, principally below 3,800 m, humans, the dominant species in the ecosystem, alter and often destructively exploit the other components of the system, creating an ecological imbalance. Natural erosion has always been considerable in the upper Karnali watershed because of the high volume and speed of water runoff caused by climatic, topographic, and geological factors. Today the increasingly large human population and the behavior of that population are factors contributing to that erosion (figure 91). It has been calculated that the entire Karnali River catchment basin, of which the zone is a part, now removes $75 \times 10^6 \, m^3$ of silt annually, a volume equivalent to the removal of 1.7 mm of topsoil from the entire area each year (Nepal and Nippon Koei Co. 1970:7).

Timber extraction for construction, forest clearance for cultivation, overgrazing, uncontrolled burning of undergrowth and grasslands, and lopping for fodder are all contributing to the accelerated degradation and destruction of the delicate ecology of the upper Karnali drainage basins (figure 92). The population's need for firewood is anther important contributing factor. A conservative estimate of the average yearly household consumption of dry wood for fuel and heating dung is 6,000 kg. At this rate the population of the zone now consumes 200,000 metric tons annually.

In the central and southern parts of the zone the collection of a load of firewood now often requires a one-day trip from the farmstead. A generation ago such a trip would have required only an hour or two. Projecting this rate of deforestation, the fuel-wood supply for most villages soon will be so distant that the villagers will not be able to afford the increased time required for obtaining wood. They will then revert to burning dung, as is now done in the lower, more denuded regions of Nepal, at the expense of their fertilizer needs. Thus, another negative chain reaction (i.e., positive feedback) will be set in motion. To date no effective measures have been taken to counteract this process; if it continues, the zone is likely to be totally denuded before the end of the century.

One government project to provide an alternative industry, which at the same time would help stabilize recently deforested areas in the cool montane basins, is a large-scale program instituted in 1968 to plant 200,000 apple seedlings. It has had mixed success; the survival rate has varied from 0 to 95 percent depending on protection from browsing animals. However, the region is ideally suited for arboriculture and a viable apple industry could result if given sufficient care and if transfer and market facilities were developed.

Near the Bhotia town of Wangri in upper Mugu, high-grade copper deposits had long provided the people with an economic base that offset

Fig. 91. Landslide in Gum Dara, the result of deforestation and overgrazing on a steep and unstable slope

their marginal agriculture. However, the charcoal requirements of this industry (222 kg of wood for every kg of copper processed) was causing such forest destruction that the industry was banned. Examples of this double-edged sword are prevalent throughout the zone. Because of the increasing Chinese demands for construction timber as well as for wooden bowls, the people of Limi panchayat are accelerating deforestation in that area.

Fig. 92. Lopping of sal forest for animal fodder above Dailekh in the Himalaya. Here humans and livestock compete for the biota. Trees are kept alive as long as they produce foliage for fodder; they then are cut for firewood. With the total destruction of this forest, dung needed for manure will be burned for fuel. This negative chain reaction will soon penetrate Karnali Zone, where forests used for fodder and fuel wood are already as much as a day's distance from the farmstead. © National Geographic Society.

Many home industries that traditionally exploited the wild biota for trading purposes or household use are now either declining as a result of ecological alteration and deterioration or are curtailed by government law. Medicinal herbs, as well as dozens of other useful wild species of vegetation, are becoming increasingly scarce. And since 1974 the government has been cracking down on the *charas* (hashish) trade.

Despite government laws prohibiting the killing of musk deer (*Moschus moschiferus*), this species faces extinction by poachers because of the high price the musk gland brings for aphrodisiacs and perfumes. Conversely, gun restriction measures imposed on the population by the central government since 1960 have caused an increase in the number of monkeys, Himalayan black bears, wild boars, and porcupines. These four species constitute an increasing problem, for in the higher and peripheral agricultural areas of the watershed cultivators estimate that they now consume as much as 25 percent of the potential food-grain yield.

Agricultural and Livestock Technology

A major constraint on the agriculturally based economy of Karnali Zone is the current state of agricultural and animal technology, which, while well adjusted to the traditional production system, is unable to cope with the pressure of contemporary change.

With few exceptions the wood-tipped plow, the wooden barrow and leveler, and about a dozen iron-tipped digging and cutting tools constitute the farmer's inventory of field equipment. The fields themselves—numerous, small, fragmented, and dispersed terraced plots on steep slopes with a fragile soil structure (figure 93)—do not lend themselves to more technologically elaborate plowing, weeding, and harvesting methods. Under increasing population pressure, the area under cultivation is expanding into peripheral forest or grass-covered upland slopes that are ill-suited for agriculture and can at best yield only marginal returns. Fields have been carved from hillsides that have an angle of slope of more than 40° at elevations as high as 3,700 m. Here erosion is especially rampant, since it can be held in check only by difficult terracing for which the farmer has diminishing time. Moreover, these fields can rarely be irrigated. In fact, as has been noted in chapter 5, in the last 100 years *khet* lands have been extended by 54.9 percent. But during that same period the spiraling population has risen 159 percent, reducing the per capita *khet* holdings by 50 percent (from 0.02 ha/person to 0.01 ha/person).

The steadily increasing land fragmentation is another major deterrent to efficient farming, for it places added time binds on the family labor force. Today it is common to find a peasant's holdings made up of fifty or more discontinuous plots widely dispersed over distances of several hours, or even days, of travel. Because of the time-distance factor that these discontinuous locations present, the amount of labor invested in a field is inversely proportional to its distance from the farmstead. This is reflected in both the type of crop grown and the yields of that crop.

Other agricultural time-labor binds are occurring. The *jajmani* system is currently breaking down at an increasingly rapid rate as a result of the growing monetarization of the economy, the increasing availability of consumer or ready-made goods in the border bazaars, and the acquisition of their own land by the occupational Dum castes.

The recent introduction of improved seeds (wheat and rice) has been sporadic and quite limited. Where introduced, these seeds have had varying, but sometimes spectacular, success. A tenfold increase in wheat yield was obtained in 1970 at a test plot in the upper Tila Valley. The viability, and indeed the desirability, of high-yield varieties remain to be proven, given the often elaborate and finely honed fertilizer, labor, and irrigation inputs required. In any event, government efforts in agricultural experiment stations and in farm extension services to date have been confined to the area immediately around Jumla-Kalanga.

A stressed state of animal husbandry parallels that of agriculture: good pasture land is rapidly diminishing, overgrazing of the *patans* is rampant, lopping for fodder is accelerating, and winter fodder is scarce. Fodder crops are rare because all fields must be planted in food crops for human consumption. Animals are grazed or fed on wild grasses and during brief periods are allowed to graze on the stubble of harvested fields. Yet the peasants are reluctant to reduce the number of animals they keep. For the Pahari majority, cattle are the most important source of fertilizer. However, all livestock combined furnish most families only about 50 percent of what they perceive to be minimum requirements. Because of its scarcity, manure is mixed with pine needles and leaves, also in diminishing supply, at a ratio that varies from 1:1 to 1:3. Moreover, many fields are fertilized only every other year and some fields never receive fertilizer. There is a definite correlation between the amount of fertilizer used on a specific field and the distance of that field from the farmstead. While a few farmers recently attempted to use compost pits, recognizing the advantage of this technique, they stopped the practice because of the ever present time-labor bind. During the short, critical, spring harvest and planting period, the farmers found that they had insufficient time and labor to move great amounts of fertilizer from the farmsteads' compost pits to their widely dispersed fields.

Bullocks are used for plowing and cows provide milk for home consumption, but excessive inbreeding and poor nutrition have reduced their strength and yield. Cows now yield an average of about 1.0 l per day during lactation (that is, about .25 kg per day during the winter and 1.0 kg during the summer months). Water buffalo are kept for milk and for the produc-

Fig. 93. The traditional agricultural technology in a time bind as winter barley is harvested and summer paddy is transplanted in khet plots near Jumla-Kalanga (2,340 m). In order to permit acceptable maturation of the paddy crop, these activities must be accomplished during a critically short period in late May. © National Geographic Society.

tion of ghee. However, as with milch cows, milk yields are low, averaging about 3.0 l per day. During winter the average milch buffalo gives approximately 1-2 kg per day, with the maximum seldom above 6 kg per day. The production of milk and ghee is, therefore, generally sufficient for home consumption and occasional local sale. Only in the southwestern reaches of economic region A is milk a significant export item. Although in 1972 the Nepalese government established a livestock experiment station near Jumla for the purpose of improving livestock production through selective reduction of the population and improvement of both genetic stock and fodder availability, significant results have yet to be felt.

On the northern periphery of the intermontane basins, Chinese restrictions now prevent the Bhotia of upper Humla and Mugu from taking their herds of yaks, sheep, goats, and horses to traditional winter grazing grounds in Tibet. Not only have most families been forced to reduce their herds, but those remaining are placing greater stress on new winter sites within Nepal. As discussed in chapter 4, one notable exception is found in Limi panchayat in the northwest corner of Humla, where the people have been able to maintain a way of life based on animals and trade because of special grazing-ground agreements with the Chinese that allow them to winter their animals in Tibet.

Transportation and Trade Technology

Transport technology, and thus trade, are intimately linked to the rugged landscape of Karnali Zone. Travel throughout the region is limited to the topographically controlled network of trails. Moreover, the closest motorable roadheads are Nepalganj on the Indian border, 190 km south of Jumla-Kalanga, and Taklakot in Tibet, 200 km northwest of Jumla-Kalanga. Not until the east-west highway now under construction across the Tarai is completed will western Nepal have any internal road connections with the eastern parts of the country.

Within the zone itself, climatic factors impose seasonal restrictions on the movement of people, animals, and goods. From December through April, deep snows on the high passes and forested slopes make travel difficult and often impossible (figure 94). During the July-through-September monsoon, floods and landslides restrict and sometimes prevent summer travel. Often key bridges are washed away, isolating large areas of the zone for weeks or even months. This is particularly true for Humla District, north of the Mugu Karnali, and for that part of Jumla District (economic subregion 1) lying west of the main Karnali River.

Horses and mules, commonly employed as a more efficient means of transportation in other roadless parts of Nepal, can be used on only a few trails from Karnali Zone to the lower Himalaya to the south. A decade ago,

Fig. 94. Construction of a cantiliver bridge in Chaudhabisa Dara. When completed, the bridge will permit access to the trail on the south-facing slope in the background, which becomes snow-free earlier in the spring.

an attempt by Jumla merchants to establish a mule train failed because of the inability of the shopkeepers to cooperate in this endeavor. The transfer of consumer goods from Nepalganj to Jumla by STOL aircraft is as yet insignificant, primarily because of undependable service.

Finally, Chinese price-fixing and other regulations on trade with Tibet since 1963 have restricted the food-grain/salt and wool exchange in the entire central and northern parts of the zone. Wool is in short supply and Indian salt is spreading northward into the Karnali basin. Traditional trading agreements (mits and istas) between Bhotia and Pahari, and among Pahari, are breaking down. A general disruption of the economic symbioses previously described is taking place.

Those Bhotia families who depended almost entirely on trade have been most seriously hurt. A permanent out-migration from Mugu panchayat began in 1966. Some of the families were able to resettle in the Surkhet Valley of the inner Tarai, where a successful malaria eradication program has permitted the opening of sal forests for agriculture.

Population and Health

The demographic picture in Karnali Zone is extremely serious, and population trends are similar to those throughout the rest of Nepal (figure 40). Available data indicate that the crude birthrate is approximately 56/1,000 and holding steady, while the crude death rate is approximately 27/1,000 and dropping. These figures portend a doubling of the population in the next thirty years.[2]

The burgeoning population of Karnali Zone, increasing more then 2 percent per year over the past three decades, continues to be the catalyst for the deterioration of the people's standard of living. Today, although it has reached 186,000 (in 1968), its density in the zone is only 14.1 km²; but this statistic obscures reality, for only 1.1 percent of the area is under cultivation. Much more pertinent is the staggeringly high density of 1,243 persons per km² of tilled land. The average household's landholding is extremely small; whereas a few large extended families of high caste may have 4.5 ha or more, the average occupational caste has only 0.24 ha. The average holding per capita in Karnali Zone is less than 0.08 ha (800 m²).

Families require a large labor force, and if they are to achieve the ideal size of four or five children who survive beyond the age of five, the wife or wives must have many pregnancies as insurance against the high rate of infant mortality; only one out of three children lives beyond the age of four (Worth and Shah 1969:27). Because of these family labor requirements, they are unwilling or reluctant to adopt contraceptive practices. There are no religious restraints or cultural taboos against such practices, but only after infant and child mortality rates have been drastically lowered by health education, care by midwives, and formal medical attention, could birth control programs be successful.

Health problems in the Karnali Zone are like those in other areas of Nepal and further constrain the economic system. Prasanna C. Gautam, the energetic doctor stationed at the zonal hospital in Jumla-Kalanga during the

---

[2] While in the field I undertook no demographic survey. These figures are based on the 1961 and 1971 Censuses of Nepal as well as the work of Worth and Shah (1969), who carried out a sample health survey in 1965-66 that included Talichaur village near Jumla-Kalanga in Asi Dara. For a country-scale analysis of the structure and change in the population of Nepal, using 1952-54, 1961, and 1971 census data, see Tuladhar, Gubhaju, and Soeckel (1977).

period of my field study, reports a broad spectrum of illness and injuries. Dysentery, diarrhea, and associated dehydration caused by worms and parasites (especially from foul farmstead conditions and impure water) are a major cause of infant and child mortality. Despite malaria "eradication," cases of the disease are frequently reported in the low southwestern corner of the zone. Of the communicable childhood diseases, whooping cough and diphtheria are common killers. A high level of malnutrition is also common especially among children. Respiratory disorders, exacerbated by the smoky conditions in the home, are ubiquitous. Everywhere there is also a high frequency of occupational injuries such as broken bones, cutting-tool wounds, and burns. Because of improper or delayed treatment (or no treatment at all) the injured commonly are crippled and often die.

Fig. 95. A Bhotia woman from Mangri in Upper Mugu with a severe goiter receives iodine tablets.

Owing to the fact that Tibetan salt, as well as most Indian salt, is un-iodized, goiter is one of the primary health problems in the area (figure 95). Almost 90 percent of the population suffers from an iodine deficiency (Worth and Shah 1969:53).

Today, the region is almost totally without medical services. A fifteen-bed hospital at Jumla built only a few years ago is already in serious disrepair. Only one doctor serves the largest of the nation's zones. A critical shortage of medicines at Jumla and at district dispensaries in Humla and Mugu, as well as a lack of trained assistants, further restrict medical services. Although the people are anxious to have medical help and they received the government's initial efforts in this area with enthusiasm, many soon became disillusioned. They often found that after making a long journey from their homestead to the district dispensary or to the zonal hospital, the compounders or the doctors were unavailable or that medicine was non-existent. Because of this, they fail to take advantage of even the minimal medical help available. They feel their work schedule will not permit them to take the time, and many believe that medical attention will be too costly.

KARNALI'S FATE

Over the past one and a half millennia, the intermontane basins of the upper Karnali River drainage in the western Nepal Himalaya have witnessed successive waves of settlement by peoples from the west, the most important being the Caucasoid Khasa, the progenitors of the present-day Pahari of the eastern Indian Himalaya (Garhwal and Kumaon) and Nepal. Indigenous Mongoloid Kirati were either biologically absorbed or pushed to peripheral and less agriculturally productive higher reaches. Under the Khasa Malla kings (twelfth through fifteenth centuries), Karnali was the core of a vast feudal kingdom that grew, expanded, and then suddenly crumbled when its spatial extent, equal in area to that of present-day Nepal, exceeded that which could be firmly controlled. Malla power was based upon the allegiance of an array of vassal lords. In league, the royalty exploited the limited, though at that time adequate, agricultural, pastoral, and other biotic resources with the subservient labor force at their disposal and, equally important, commanded the lucrative trade routes between Tibet and India that traversed their domain. Throughout the Malla era and the following four centuries of domination by princely Rajput interlopers (the Kalyal kings of Jumla who had fled to Karnali in the wake of Muslim invasions of the subcontinent and had deposed the Malla dynasty), Hindu religious and political institutions were introduced, developed, and modified to produce a distinctive regional culture with special brands of social and economic stratification. Modeled after the orthodox systems of northern India, they were perforce ameliorated by local environmental conditions. Within these social institutions an elite high-caste minority of Thakuri and Brahmans prospered by controlling both Karnali environmental and human resources.

The 1788 forcible annexation of the Jumla (Kalyal) princedom into the incipient state of Nepal by the House of Gorkha caused great loss of life and much permanent out-migration and therefore postponed what might have proven to be overpopulation for over 130 years. The fact of Jumla's marginal and isolated position within this new nation-state assured that local social institutions and traditions would become increasingly entrenched. The Karnali region (now old Jumla District) ceased to be a relatively autonomous political and economic entity and became instead a peripheral appendage of a larger state centered in the Kathmandu Valley.

Throughout the subsequent Rana regime (1846-1951) Jumla's role as an economically unimportant backwater buffer region became even more firmly established. So too did the Rana-fostered, intermeshed, and oppressive social, political, and economic systems. A period of stagnation set in, which saw both the exploitation and the regulation of Karnali's Pahari populace and resources from Kathmandu. The gap between the landed elite and the tenant or serf commoners widened as the latter majority became more bound to the former through debt and taxation. Less adversely affected were the Bhotia of Tibetan origin who had settled the upper Humla and Mugu valleys, and with whom a variety of economic symbioses were important. Thus two distinct though overlapping cultures, one with a Buddhist Tibetan tradition, the other with a hill-Hindu Pahari tradition, were areally arranged in elevational belts and characterized the multiethnic composition of the region. During the Rana regime the increase in Karnali's population was gradual, as it was generally throughout Nepal. Only in the twentieth century did it begin to accelerate, portending the end of over a century during which livelihood activities in Jumla were in a homeostatic state.

The period since 1951 (the end of the Rana family oligarchy), and particularly since the introduction of the Panchayat Raj in 1962, was a time when external events and developments, both national and international, combined with an accelerating population explosion to destroy the homeostatic state of life in the insular upper Karnali basin and propel the populace into the twentieth century. These events and developments brought or forecast changes. Most were positive, such as administrative, educational, legal, tax, land, and labor reforms for the promotion of social and economic growth; some were negative, such as the Chinese trade restrictions in Tibet. Other negative developments were internally generated. In the face of the new egalitarian ideals of Kathmandu that were manifested in reform measures, the high-caste Pahari elite lost much of the political and economic leverage they had long enjoyed over the lower castes and Dum. To counter these developments they intensified their remaining source of power—religious sanctions—in an effort to maintain the status quo. A "hardening of the caste arteries" resulted, similar to that experienced in the Indian Himalaya in the wake of liberalized British administration after 1815. It was during this post-Rana modern period of political, social, economic, and psychological readjustment that my research on the cultural ecology of Karnali Zone was undertaken.

The world's high mountain environments provide fragile ecosystems for people. The extremities of slope, range of temperature, thinness and poverty of soil, paucity of water, and delicate and easily disturbed biota provide a poor resource base for humans dependent primarily upon such bases for their existence. A livelihood with traditional or slowly changing technology is possible, however, provided that population pressure does not increase and access to widely dispersed resources is not limited by political or environmental barriers. Thus in earlier centuries Nepal and Karnali Zone were able to provide support for a people, not richly but adequately, in the face of a poverty of natural resources and a wealth of human exploitation. These populations were able to sustain themselves by a combination of livelihood strategies of a social, spatial, and temporal nature.

The social procedures were as much inadvertent as planned and consisted, until the 1920s, mainly of Malthusian checks on population growth. Not until the first quarter of the twentieth century, or even the midpoint of this century, did modest inputs of health technology (an overflow from British efforts in India) and relative civil peace drive the demographic curve upward on what we now recognize as the self-sustaining population explosion typical of most developing nations. Trapped in the cultural attitudes and practices appropriate to a society with high rates of infant and child mortality (and, given the nature of the life, relatively high accidental mortality rates in the adult population), even slight reductions in death rates set into motion the positive feedback mechanism of population expansion.

The constraints of space, particularly space containing a dearth of resources, are inhibiting to all populations but are particularly pressing on an isolated agrarian population in such a harsh mountain environment as Karnali. This particular population in this particular environment copes with the problem by extending its spatial resource base in a number of divergent ways, taking full advantage of all three dimensions of the Himalayan habitat. In spite of the terrain-imposed difficulty of transportation, Karnali Zone was long tied by elaborate trade networks to both the relatively rich reaches of southern Nepal and adjacent India, from which a variety of imports (food, as well as other commodities) were obtained, and to the even more harsh and limited environment of the Tibetan Plateau, which supplied specialized dietary inputs, particularly salt, as well as raw materials, especially wool, for the local home production of goods. With little of great value to introduce into this wide-spreading net, the people of Karnali Zone were nonetheless able to barter and trade, buy and sell, make or produce enough of a range of items to provide an adequate resource base within which they could subsist.

They were able to extend the spatial range of their activities because of the severe seasonality of their environment. In other words, they were able to substitute time for value of goods; having little else to do in their home areas during the winter, they sought to use otherwise idle time in wide-ranging but marginally profitable trading activities and migratory labor that would not have been viable had the time been productive elsewhere.

It is precisely this temporal buffer, crucial for the continued satisfactory operation of the three-dimensional spatial activities, that is currently being destroyed. The forces of destruction, while set in motion by people and events external to Karnali Zone, are in the process of irrevocably changing the local environment and way of life. Hence, decisions made by Peking restrict and alter traditional Nepal-Tibet trade. What had been a two-week summer trip of 100 km to Tibet for a Mugu Bhotia is now a two-month winter trip of 3,000 km to west Bengal and back. Local population increases, themselves the result of externally introduced health measures, and the need for the basics of shelter and fuel mean that a daily trip of two hours for wood has become an all-day venture for many villagers.

Such restrictions have meant that the buffer time available has been cut back severely. Work that was marginally productive before must now be undertaken because the return on time inputs has dropped; alternative trading activities may be reduced either because of increased competition from imported goods or simply because of a lack of readily available outlets. The ever expanding population must turn to more and more restricted activities into which they put increasingly time-inefficient labor.

It is only one of the many ironies of modern life that efforts, for the most part undertaken with good intent, to modernize and develop backward regions often destroy a delicate and already endangered way of life. Karnali Zone is one such region in which the aims and the results of a central government's development efforts are often far apart. Improvements in the transportation system, designed admittedly to tie the region more closely to other regions and the capital and to provide commercial, health, and communications links both within the country and with the outside world, prove to be insufficient in these goals but effective enough to topple the marginal but vital trade patterns of the local population. The establishment of a national park (figure 96), aiming to bring much needed foreign currency

---

Fig. 96 (pp. 362-63). View from high patans *northwest over Rara Lake, with the Saipal Himal (7,000 m) in the distance. In 1974, His Majesty's Government declared the lake and its surroundings a national park, and the villagers of Chhapru and Raragaon have since been obliged to resettle in the western inner Tarai. In addition to removing land from cultivation, the establishment of this park is expected to increase tourism and recreational trekking in Karnali Zone. Increase in these latter activities elsewhere in Nepal (such as in Mount Everest National Park) have had a markedly negative impact on the fragile mountain ecosystems.*

into both the national and local economy, serves instead to remove desperately needed land from cultivation, introduce sudden and extreme stresses on both local food supply and forests, and provide precious little cash for the pockets of the local cultivator, as opposed to the urban-based (most frequently from Kathmandu) entrepreneur and the national government. Health measures themselves, unaccompanied by the widespread economic and social pressure-valve opportunities necessary to permanently siphon off the resultant increase in population, are another two-edged sword. An increase in life expectancy quickly enhances the quality of life; it may just as quickly erode its quality.

There is no place in the modern world for journeys whose length is measured in pipefuls of tobacco. Time does become money and, unfortunately, a lack of money can cause a lack of time. But time had been a buffer and friend here in Karnali Zone—life had been difficult but tolerable so long as the richness of options for trade and movement could be substituted for the poverty of immediate resources. Now the options are rapidly disappearing, and the cultural ecological subsistence system may be locked onto an ever increasing, downward spiral of degradation.

Appendixes

Appendix A
Glossary of Selected Nepali Words in Common Use in Karnali Zone

abal	First grade *khet* land (for tax assessment)
adhikari	Chief judicial minister
adhiyã	System of produce Sharing
alika	Lush, fertile
ālu	Potatoes
anāj	Grain
attar	Marijuana
attim or *kaṭus*	Chestnut
aul	Malarious, hot, and level area
Baḍā Hakim	Governor (in late Rana times)
bancharo	Axe
bāsā	Subgroup within *thar*
besī	River or valley bottom land in the hill districts
bhānjyāng	Mountain pass or gap
bhāt	Boiled rice
bhaṭṭa	Soybean
bhitri madesh	"Flat ground on the inside"
Bhoṭ	Trans-Himalayan or Tibetan region
bīj	Seed
bījan	A system of tax assessment based on the quantity of maize estimated to be needed for sowing

NOTE: The transliteration method employed above is the same as that used by Turner (1965).

bingāre	One who levels the field at the time of transplanting
birtā	Royal tax-free land grant
buḍhā gahū̃	Wheat that can be harvested after fourteen months
chahār	Fourth-grade *khet* land (for tax assessment)
chāmal	Rice
chhu	River
chilgāḍi	Airplane
chino	Common millet
crore	10,000,000
daha	Lake
damāi	Tailor (Dum caste)
ḍā̃:ḍā	Spur hill
ḍā̃phe	Peasant
darā	Crack; old administrative division
Dasaĩ	Festival celebrated on the tenth day of the bright half of the moon in the month of Asoj of Kartic (October-November)
debdār	*Cedrus deodar*
dekhā jā̃chā	System of land survey under which the land is not actually measured, but the area, the size, or the amount of seeds needed for sowing is extimated
dhāmi	Oracle (shaman)
dhān	Paddy
dhaniyā	Coriander
ḍharo	Clay pot made to store food grain
ḍhik	Terrace
dhupī	Fir tree
dhurī	Mountain; house
ḍhwang	House
dochā	A kind of men's shoe made by Bhotias
doyam	Second-grade *khet* land (for tax assessment)
dumsī	Porcupine
fal chindu	Wooden water vessel
feruwā	Carpet made from goat's hair
gāḍ	Stream
gahū̃	Wheat
gangrī	Mountain
gāū̃	Village
gauruwan	Servant

ghar	House
ghārā	Beehive
ghāṭ	Ferry or ford; cremation site
ghaṭṭa	Water mill
ghee	Clarified butter
girī	Mountain
gompā	Tibetan shrine
goṭh	Fieldhouse; animal shelter
gotra	Sanskritic kin grouping
guṭhī	Land alienated by the state or by individuals for the performance of charitable, religious, or philanthropic functions
hākim	Head of a government office
hal	Ox team
hale	*Pakho* holding that can be plowed by an ox team in one day (in hill districts)
halebīj	Land capable of being plowed by an ox team for purpose of tax assessment under Bijan system
halī	One who plows the field
hāt	Bazaar
hāttijarā, or *pāch-aūle*	A very valuable medicinal herb
himal	Mountain; massif
hule	Plow unit
jāgnā	Sheep
janai	Sacred thread
jāti (jāt, jāts)	Caste; clan
jau	Barley
jhãkri	Witchdoctor or shaman
jhārā	Compulsory labor system
jhil	Lake
jhopā	Crossbreeds of yak and cow, male breed
jhul	Shelter under the trees
jimmāwāl	Tax collector (*khet* area)
johar	Immolation of females
jyulo	Farm
kaddu	Pumpkin
kāguno	Indian millet
kãcho	Tobacco plant
karkya	Matches
kasturī	Musk deer

kaṭero	Temporary house in grazing land or *patans*
kawāse or *kāṭh*	Wooden box for storing grain
khalangā	Administrative center
kharcharī	Tax on pasture land (in the hill districts)
kholā	Stream
kodo	Millet
koṭ	Old fortress
Kriṣṇāṣṭamī	Birthday of Lord Krishna, hero in the epic Mahābhārat
kulo	Irrigation channel
kuriyā	House
kuṭo	Hoe
la	Mountain pass
lakh	100,000
Lal-Mohar	"Red Seal" official state order
lām	A kind of shoe for women
lekh	Ridge
liu	A kind of thin carpet
lungpā	Stream, valley
makai	Maize
māl,	
or *Māl Aḍḍā*	Revenue office
malsāpro	Marten
mānṭha	Man
mārse	Amaranth
mat	Liquor
māṭo	Soil
mauja	Basic revenue unit (village or group of villages)
mhāgo	Marijuana plant
moṭh lagat	Tax assessment register
mukhiyā	Generic term used to denote land tax collectors
mukhuja	Tax collector (*pakho* area)
mulā	Radish
nadī	River
nambarī	Taxable land listed in the assessment register
nathani	Nose ring
odār	Gorge
okhar	Walnut
pāhāḍ	Mountain
pahāḍā	Sunny place

pākho	Unirrigated land on which only maize, millet, or other dry crops can be grown
panchāyat	Village council; a village or group of villages
paharā	Dry, steep land
pāṭan	Open grazing land or meadows on the *lekhs*
paṭṭi	To side with (e.g., Hitanpatti, Bramanpatti)
phaṭke	Wooden bridge
potā	Land tax
raikar	Crown landholdings
sāgpāt	Green vegetables
sāg̃hu	Wooden bridge
sāune fāgu	Homestead tax
sermā	Tax on unmeasured *pakho* land
silājit	Tarlike hydrocarbon extracted from sedimentary or metamorphic rocks
sim	Third-grade *khet* land (for tax assessment)
sipa	Clay pipe
siyānlā	Shady place
soto	Stream
tāl	Lake
tālukdār	Generic term used to denote land tax collectors
tamākhu	Tobacco
ṭāri	Terraced hillside (rain irrigated)
taulos	Copper pots
ṭhākura	Chief, man of rank
Thapale	Bhote and Tamang are called *Thapale* in Humla
thar	Subcaste
ṭhek tiro	Tax on *khet* land
ṭhetuwā	Homemade cotton cloth
til	Sesame
Topītale	Excluding *Thapale*, the rest of the people are called *Topitale* in Humla
tuin	Bridge made by a single rope

Appendix B
Weights and Measures Used in Karnali Zone
(with Metric Equivalents)

In Karnali Zone, as throughout Nepal, a number of measurement systems or schemes are employed. All are of great antiquity. Because of considerable local or regional variation in both their use or unit value, they are complex and can be confusing. This is particularly true of area and yield measurements involving landholdings and agricultural production. Therefore, all data in this study have been converted to the metric system for the sake of simplicity, clarity, and comparativeness. Only the most commonly used or important units employed in Karnali are presented here. For information on weights and measures throughout Nepal see chapter 18 in *Agricultural Statistics of Nepal* (1972).

THE CALENDAR YEAR

Two calendars, one lunar for religious and ceremonial purposes and one solar for all other aspects of life, are employed today in Nepal. The solar calendar is of Indian origin, is based on the Vikrama or Bikian era (*samvat*) beginning in 57 B.C., and came into use during the Gorkha period. Much of my field study is based on the official Nepalese solar calendar year 2026 V.S. (Vikrama Samvat), which corresponds to mid-April 1969 to mid-April 1970 of the Gregorian calendar as follows:

Nepalese			Gregorian		
Chaitra	30	2025	April	12	1969
Baishakh	1	2026		13	
	31		May	13	
Jestha	1			14	
	32		June	14	
Ashadha	1			15	
	31		July	15	
Srawan	1			16	
	32		August	16	
Bhadra	1			17	
	31		September	16	
Ashwin	1			17	
	30		October	16	
Kartic	1			17	
	30		November	15	
Mashir	1			16	
	30		December	15	
Push	1			16	
	17		January	1	1970
	29			13	
Magha	1			14	
	29		February	11	
Falgun	1			12	
	30		March	13	
Chaitra	1			14	
	31		April	13	

For a detailed explanation of Nepalese calendars and eras see Slusser (1982).

LENGTH

> 1 cubit = 45.72 centimeters
> 1 *kos* = 8,000 cubits or 3.658 kilometers

The linear distance measurement of the *kos,* or "postman's mile," is not generally used by Karnali's indigenous population. Instead, they log distances on the basis of *sipa* (clay pipe) smokes—the distance one can walk in the forty-five minutes or so one pipeful of tobacco lasts. Although this method is highly imprecise because of the number of environmental and human variables it involves, "*sipa* time" is functional and easily under-stood by the population who travel in this mountainous terrain on foot.

AREA

$$1 \ khet \ muri = 100 \ mato \ muri$$
$$4 \ mato \ muri = 1 \ ropani$$

1 *khet muri* = 1.2718 hectare	1 hectare = 0.7863 *khet muri*
1 *mato muri* = 0.0127 hectare	1 hectare = 78.6257 *mato muri*
1 *ropani* = 0.0509 hectare	1 hectare = 19.6564 *ropani*

This system is applied whenever farmland has actually been surveyed and chained, as is the case for all *khet* (irrigated fields on which paddy can be grown). However, in upland *pakho* (unirrigated) areas measurement is an estimate based on the *hule* or plow unit—the amount of land a bullock can plow in one day. This method is imprecise because of the variability of slope, quality, and condition of both team and soil, skill of plower, etc. In Karnali Zone I found the average *hule* unit to equal 0.128 ha (approximately 2.5 *ropanis*).

WEIGHT

$$1 \ maund = 15.595 \ dharni$$
$$1 \ dharni = 3 \ seer \ (\text{hill})^1$$
$$1 \ seer \ (\text{hill}) = 4 \ pau$$

1 maund = 37.324 kilograms	1 kilogram = 0.027 maund
1 *dharni* = 2.393 kilograms	1 kilogram = 0.418 *dharni*
1 *seer* (hill) = 0.798 kilograms	1 kilogram = 1.253 *seer* (hill)
1 *pau* = 0.200 kilograms	1 kilogram = 6.014 *pau*

VOLUME

$$1 \ muri = 20 \ pathi$$
$$1 \ pathi = 8 \ mana^2$$

1 *muri* = 90.909 liters	1 liter = 0.011 *muri*
1 *pathi* = 4.545 liters	1 liter = 0.220 *pathi*
1 *mana* = 0.568 liters	1 liter = 1.760 *mana*

---

[1] In the Tarai of Nepal a *seer* has a different value (i.e., 0.933 kg).

[2] The 8-*mana pathi* is the standard throughout Nepal. However, in Karnali Zone a 4-*mana pathi* (i.e., 1/2 standard value) is commonly used and in some areas of Humla a 2-*mana pathi* (1/4 standard value) is employed.

VOLUME-TO-WEIGHT CONVERSION (DENSITY) OF MAJOR AGRICULTURAL COMMODITIES

Commodity	Kg per *mana*	Kg per *pathi*	Kg per *muri*
Wheat	0.425	3.40	68.04
Barley	0.327	2.62	52.32
Oats	0.283	2.27	45.36
Paddy (rough rice in husk)	0.305	2.44	48.77
Rice (husk removed)	0.439	3.52	70.31
Maize	0.392	3.14	62.72
Millets	0.411	3.29	65.77
Buckwheat	0.340	2.72	54.43
Grams and pulses	0.454	3.63	72.58
Soybean	0.397	3.18	63.50
Beans	0.366	2.93	58.51
Kidney Beans	0.425	3.40	68.04
Peas	0.425	3.40	68.04
Mustard	0.354	2.84	56.70

VOLUME-TO-WEIGHT CONVERSION (DENSITY) OF PROCESSED AGRICULTURAL COMMODITIES

Commodity	Kg per *mana*
Wheat flour	0.279
Barley flour	0.196
Rice flour	0.320
Rice flour, beaten	0.227
Maize flour	0.303
Millet flour	0.309
Buckwheat flour	0.196
Black Gram, broken (*mas*)	0.397
Yellow Gram, broken (*mugi*)	0.397
Musuro, broken (*Lens esculenta*)	0.431
Peas, broken (*kala*)	0.411

IMPORTANT MISCELLANEOUS MEASURES

- 1 *hat* = approximately 45 centimeters. (This unit of length is determined by the distance between a person's elbow and fingertips and is most commonly used in measuring cloth.)
- Homemade paper in the hills (paper size is usually about 60 x 60 cm or 60 x 120 cm):

Fig. 97. The lal, *or crabs eye plant*

$$1\ pau\ =\ 1\ \text{sheet}$$
$$1\ dhep\ =\ 12\ \text{sheets}$$
$$12\ dhep\ =\ 1\ kori\ (\text{i.e., 1 gross or 144 sheets})$$

- 1 *tola* = 11.664 grams. The *tola* weight/mass unit is used to measure items of high value such as gold and silver, musk, and hashish. To determine weights less than one *tola* the berries of the crabs eye plant (*Arbus precatorius Linn.*) are commonly used, for 100 berries inevitably weigh 1 *tola* (see figure 97).

Appendix C
Supplementary Climate Information for Selected Stations in Nepal

TABLE 28. Average climatic water balance data for figure 13.

Nepalganj, 1 year: 1970 (181 m; 28°06'N / 81°37'E; WHC* = 300 mm)

	J	F	M	A	M	J	J	A	S	O	N	D	Total
PE[†]	19	29	71	151	197	181	170	176	158	115	43	19	1,329
P	46	16	12	0	36	364	344	197	179	70	0	0	1,264
ST	242	232	190	114	66	249	300	300	300	266	230	215	
AE	19	26	54	76	84	181	170	176	158	113	36	15	1,108
D	0	3	17	75	113	0	0	0	0	2	7	4	221
S	0	0	0	0	0	0	123	21	12	0	0	0	156

Chisapani, 4 years: 1968-70 (225 m; 28°39'N / 81°16'E; WHC = 300 mm)

	J	F	M	A	M	J	J	A	S	O	N	D	Total
PE	22	37	96	167	204	191	186	173	155	115	56	24	1,426
P	53	12	27	13	32	347	732	522	367	29	0	14	2,148
ST	211	194	154	92	51	207	300	300	300	225	186	180	
AE	22	29	67	75	73	191	186	173	155	104	39	20	1,134
D	0	8	29	92	131	0	0	0	0	11	17	4	292
S	0	0	0	0	0	0	453	349	212	0	0	0	1,014

Thirpu, 6 years: 1961-62, 1964, 1967-69 (1,030 m; 29°19'N / 81°46'E; WHC = 300 mm)

	J	F	M	A	M	J	J	A	S	O	N	D	Total
PE	19	21	43	77	112	150	161	139	111	62	37	21	953
P	53	32	32	20	26	40	73	94	65	22	0	13	470
ST	43	54	52	43	32	22	17	14	12	11	9	9	
AE	19	21	34	29	37	50	78	97	67	23	2	13	470
D	0	0	9	48	75	100	83	42	44	39	35	8	483
S	0	0	0	0	0	0	0	0	0	0	0	0	0

Dailekh, 8 years: 1959, 1963-68, 1970 (1,304 m; 28°51'N / 81°43'E; WHC = 300 mm)

	J	F	M	A	M	J	J	A	S	O	N	D	Total
PE	16	29	56	93	130	129	121	115	99	71	43	24	926
P	31	21	32	21	49	265	447	495	154	48	7	10	1,580
ST	250	244	225	176	134	270	300	300	300	278	246	235	
AE	16	27	51	70	91	129	121	115	99	70	39	21	849
D	0	2	5	23	39	0	0	0	0	1	4	3	77
S	0	0	0	0	0	0	296	380	55	0	0	0	731

Bijapur, 5 years: 1961-62, 1964, 1966, 1970 (1,823 m; 29°14'N / 81°38'E; WHC = 300 mm)

	J	F	M	A	M	J	J	A	S	O	N	D	Total
PE	14	16	37	64	91	115	121	108	90	50	32	16	754
P	59	63	29	20	72	145	207	211	105	49	2	7	969
ST	300	300	292	252	236	266	300	300	300	299	270	262	
AE	14	16	37	60	88	115	121	108	90	50	31	15	745
D	0	0	0	4	3	0	0	0	0	0	1	1	9
S	7	47	0	0	0	0	52	103	15	0	0	0	224

---

* WHC = Water holding capacity
† Monthly averages. PE = Potential evapotranspiration; P = Precipitation; ST = Storage of moisture in the soil; AE = Actual evapotranspiration; D = Water deficit; S = Water surplus

Gum, 1 year: 1969-70 (2,103 m; 29°33'N / 82°10'E; WHC = 300 mm)

	J	F	M	A	M	J	J	A	S	O	N	D	Total
PE	16	23	46	91	110	130	119	109	83	56	37	24	844
P	30	30	10	20	60	60	200	270	170	20	0	10	880
ST	238	245	217	171	145	114	195	300	300	266	235	224	
AE	16	23	38	66	86	91	119	109	83	54	31	21	737
D	0	0	8	25	24	39	0	0	0	2	6	3	107
S	0	0	0	0	0	0	0	56	87	0	0	0	143

Jumla, 10 years: 1961-70 (2,387 m; 29°16'N / 82°11'E; WHC = 300 mm)

	J	F	M	A	M	J	J	A	S	O	N	D	Total
PE	11	13	34	61	84	104	111	98	80	47	29	13	685
P	27	41	41	27	31	61	171	152	79	28	1	6	665
ST	265	293	300	268	224	194	254	300	299	280	255	249	
AE	11	13	34	59	75	91	111	98	80	47	26	12	657
D	0	0	0	2	9	13	0	0	0	0	3	1	28
S	0	0	0	0	0	0	0	8	0	0	0	0	8

Dillikot, 1 year: 1969-70 (2,774 m; 29°12'N / 82°22'E; WHC = 300 mm)

	J	F	M	A	M	J	J	A	S	O	N	D	Total
PE	5	8	31	58	81	94	100	95	71	44	32	16	635
P	60	40	0	35	40	80	225	320	180	30	0	0	1,010
ST	299	300	270	250	218	208	300	300	300	286	257	244	
AE	5	8	30	55	72	90	100	95	71	44	29	13	612
D	0	0	1	3	9	4	0	0	0	0	3	3	23
S	0	31	0	0	0	0	33	225	109	0	0	0	398

Mugu, 1 year: 1969 (3,658 m; 29°45'N / 82°33'E; WHC = 300 mm)

	J	F	M	A	M	J	J	A	S	O	N	D	Total
PE	0	0	12	42	64	81	86	75	62	29	11	0	462
P	18	7	35	60	62	55	140	172	122	12	0	2	685
ST	293	300	300	300	298	273	300	300	300	283	273	275	
AE	0	0	12	42	64	80	86	75	62	29	10	0	460
D	0	0	0	0	0	1	0	0	0	0	1	0	2
S	0	0	23	18	0	0	27	97	60	0	0	0	225

Bumra, 1 year: 1969-70 (2,865 m; 29°24'N / 82°08'E; WHC = 300 mm)

	J	F	M	A	M	J	J	A	S	O	N	D	Total
PE	5	8	25	58	70	87	96	92	71	44	32	19	607
P	60	60	20	43	42	50	340	350	210	30	0	20	1,225
ST	300	300	295	280	255	225	300	300	300	286	257	258	
AE	5	8	25	58	67	80	96	92	71	44	29	19	594
D	0	0	0	0	3	7	0	0	0	0	3	0	13
S	13	52	0	0	0	0	169	258	139	0	0	0	631

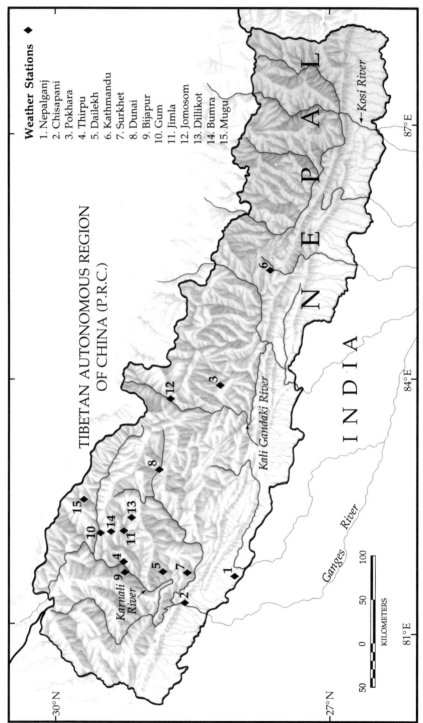

Weather Stations ◆

1. Nepalganj
2. Chisapani
3. Pokhara
4. Thirpu
5. Dailekh
6. Kathmandu
7. Surkhet
8. Dunai
9. Bijapur
10. Gum
11. Jimla
12. Jomosom
13. Dillikot
14. Bumra
15. Mugu

TIBETAN AUTONOMOUS REGION
OF CHINA (P.R.C.)

N E P A L

I N D I A

Kali Gandaki River

Karnali River

Ganges River

← Kosi River

30°N

27°N

81°E   84°E   87°E

KILOMETERS

50   0   50   100

Fig. 98. Map of weather station locations

TABLE 29. Climate classifications for selected stations.

	Thornthwaite[a]		Ecological life zones[b]
Nepalganj 181 m	C_1 A' d a'	Dry, subhumid Megathermal Little or no water surplus Summer concentration, less than 48%	Subtropical, premontane dry forest, subhumid
Chisipani 225 m	B_2 A' w_2 a'	Humid Megathermal Large winter water deficiency Summer concentration, less than 48%	Subtropical, premontane moist forest, humid
Pokhara 855 m	A A' r a'	Perhumid Megathermal Little or no water deficiency Summer concentration, less than 48%	Subtropical, premontane wet forest, perhumid
Thirpu 1,030 m	D_1 C'_2 d a'	Semiarid Microthermal Little or no water surplus Summer concentration, less than 48%	Subtropical, premontane thorn woodland, semiarid
Dailekh 1,304 m	B_3 A' r a'	Humid Megathermal Little or no water deficiency Summer concentration, less than 48%	Subtropical, premontane moist forest, humid
Kathmandu 1,323 m	B_1 A' r a'	Humid Megathermal Little or no water deficiency Summer concentration, less than 48%	Subtropical, premontane moist forest, humid
Surkhet 1,396 m			Subtropical, premontane moist forest, humid
Dunai 1,768 m	C_1 B'_1 d a'	Dry/subhumid Mesothermal Little or no water surplus Summer concentration, less than 48%	Warm, temperate, lower montane, very dry forest, semiarid
Bijapur 1,823 m	B_1 B'_3 r a'	Humid Mesothermal Little or no water deficiency Summer concentration, less than 48%	Warm, temperate, lower montane dry forest, subhumid

[a] Based on Thornthwaite (1948).
[b] Based on L. R. Holdridge (1967).

(TABLE 29 *continued*)

	Thornthwaite		Ecological life zones
Gum 2,103 m	C_2 B'_3 w a'	Moist/subhumid Mesothermal Moderate winter water deficiency Summer concentration, less than 48%	Warm, temperate, lower montane dry forest, subhumid
Jumla 2,387 m	C_2 B'_2 w a'	Moist/subhumid Mesothermal Moderate winter water deficiency Summer concentration, less than 48%	Cool, temperate, montane dry forest, subhumid
Jomosom 2,615 m	D D' d a'	Semiarid Tundra Little or no water surplus Summer concentration, less than 48%	Cool, temperate, lower montane desert scrub, arid
Dillikot 2,774 m	B_2 B'_4 r a'	Humid Mesothermal Little or no water deficiency Summer concentration, less than 48%	Cool, temperate, montane dry forest, subhumid
Bumra 2,865 m	B_4 A' r a'	Humid Megathermal Little or no water deficiency Summer concentration, less than 48%	Cool, temperate, montane dry forest, subhumid
Mugu 3,658 m	B_2 B'_1 r b'_3	Humid Mesothermal Little or no water deficiency More than 52% in the summer	Boreal, subalpine, very dry forest, semiarid

Appendix D
Indigenous Castes of Karnali

BRAMAN: *Upadhaya* (of higher status; plains origin) and *Jaisi* (of lower status; Khasa origin). Honorific form of address is "Thani" (a village-level revenue functionary).

Thar (clan) names:

Acharya or Acharja	Kharel
Adhikari	Koirala
Baral	Kumai
Baskota	Nyupane
Bhat (only Jaisi)	Pande
Bhatta	Pandit
Bhattarai	Panta
Bista	Pokharyal
Chaulagaiñ	Regmi
Debkota	Samal
Dhitai	Sanjyal
Debkota	Samal

SANYASI: Religious hermits or ascetics who have returned to the real world and married; of nebulous but high Tagadhari status.

Thar names:

Bharati	Nath
Giri	Yogi

THAKURI: (of Rajput or Khasa origin). Honorific form of address is "Anse Babusahib" (a royal family member).

Thar names:

Bam	Khati
Chan	Malla
Chhatyal	Rakal
Hamal	Saha
Hitan	Sahi
Kalyal	Sing

CHHETRI: Both twice-born sacred thread (*jamai*) wearers and liquor-drinkers (Matwali) who are not twice-born. It is generally impossible to differentiate between Chhetri and Matwali Chhetri on the basis of Thar name alone. Honorific form of address is "Kaji Sahib" (a king's minister).

Thar names:

Adhikari (may be Brahman too)	Kawar
Aidi	Khadka
Baduwal	Khatri
Baniya	Lampal
Basnet	Lamsal
Bhadari	Mahari
Bhakri	Mahat
Bham	Mahatara
Bista	Rana
Bogati	Raul
Bohara	Raut
Budha	Rokaya
Budha Thapa	Samal
Budhatheki	Saud
Dhami	Sejuwal
Dharala	Swar
Karki	Thami
Kasera	Thapa
Kathayat	Thyait
	Gharti Chhetri (ex-slaves)

MAGAR: Only a few families of the Thapa Thar.

NEWAR: Originally from Kathmandu; in Jumla bazaar.
Thar names:

Nagarkoti   Shrestha

THAKALI: Originally from Thak Khola (upper Kali Gandaki River); in Jumla bazaar.
Thar names:

Bhattachan   Serchan

SUNUWAR: A few families.

TAMANG: Predominantly Bhotia who are attempting to move upward in caste (i.e., the process of sanskritization).

BHOTIA:
Thar names:

Amdu   Khamba

DUM: Unclean occupationals
- Kami (metalworkers)
    - Sunar (goldsmiths)
    - Tamatto (coppersmiths)
    - Lohar or Luwar (ironsmiths)
    - Tiruwar (vessel makers)
- Sarki (leatherworkers)
    - Kulal
    - Bhul
- Damai (tailors)
- Badi (itinerant dancers)

Appendix E
Jumla Administrative Regulations of 1796

From King Ran Bahadur Shah,
To Bhayaharan Thapa, son of Subba Prashram Thapa.

We hereby issue the following regulations regarding the work to be done by you in Jumla:—

1. Religious ceremonies during Dashain, Fagu and other festivals shall be conducted as usual. The *Kachahari* building [here the Kalyal court in Chhinasim] shall be repaired as done by previous *Subbas* [chief district administration officers]. Clothes shall be given to maid-servants and other menials at the palace during the Dashain festival.

2. Salaries in cash and in kind according to the revenue collected there shall be paid to the personnel of 18 military companies according to regulations, and receipts shall be obtained against such payments. Offenses committed by *Subedars* [company commanders] and *Jamadars* [military officers] shall be reported to us, and action shall be taken as ordered.

3. In the event of attack by enemies from any quarter, additional troops shall be recruited for repulsing them. Such troops shall be paid reasonable remunerations [*sic*] and dismissed after the enemy is repulsed.

4. Appropriate expenses for correspondence with foreign countries shall be incurred. Presents received from foreign countries shall be submitted to us.

5. Rs 30 each shall be paid as monthly salaries to the *Munshi* [government scribe] and the *Peshkar* [judicial functionary]. The *Munshi* shall scrutinize [whether collections have been made] according to the tax assessment records. Appropriate expenses shall be incurred for repairing forts, manufacturing gunpowder and cannon balls, maintaining reserves thereof and constructing wooden bridges.

6. Arrangements shall be made to operate mines. Income therefrom shall be collected and expenses incurred as prescribed. After making arrangements for operating mines, report the matter and dies for minting *Paisa* coins [of copper] shall be supplied. Stamps for weights and measures have been sent. Revenue from fees in consideration thereof shall be submitted to us.

7. *Birta* and *Fakirana* [tax-free grants to members of religious orders] land grants made by former *Rajas* during their reign, or *Birta* lands purchased from others, shall be scrutinized. Such grants, if valid, shall be confirmed when the matter is represented to us. *Salami* [fees or levies] shall be collected in consideration of such confirmation. *Birta* or *Fakirana* land grants made by persons other than reigning *Rajas* shall be confiscated.

8. People of all the 36 castes in Jumla shall display their loyalty to us by complying with the orders of the *Subba*. Cases of disobedience shall be judged by *Panchas* [members of village councils] and punishment shall be awarded according to caste status. Men guilty of treason and rebellion shall be beheaded if their caste status so warrants and if they are above 12 years of age. The members of their families shall not be enslaved but shall be sent to a distant place. Those who cannot be beheaded shall be punished with loss of caste or exile.

9. Persons guilty of immoral offenses shall be granted expiation in accordance with local usage and in consultation with a representative of the *Dharmadhikar* [chief religious authority of the kingdom].

10. The previous land tax assessment rates, as well as those now introduced in Jumla, shall be reported to us. The schedule of rates sanctioned by us shall then be enforced.

11. The land tax assessment system on the basis of blocks, which is customary in Jumla, shall be abolished and assessment shall be made on the basis of individual holdings. Reliable and honest persons shall be appointed as officials and frequently transferred.

12. Counterfeiters shall be punished with amputation or otherwise according to their caste status as ordered by us in offenses committed after the region was annexed by us.

13. Allowances shall be given to *Jagirdars* [government employees who are beneficiaries of land assignments] and military personnel according to regulations.

14. You have been deputed far from the palace. You shall remain there as long as our favor lasts. In case any evil person submits complaints against you, we shall award justice after hearing both sides. We shall not hear only one side.

Ashadh Sudi 4, 1853
(July 1796)

SOURCE: M. C. Regmi (1971:215-16)

Appendix F
Representative Crop Calendars for the Midlands,
Inner Tarai, and Tarai of Western Nepal

TABLE 30.   Representative crop, animal, and trade movement calendars for

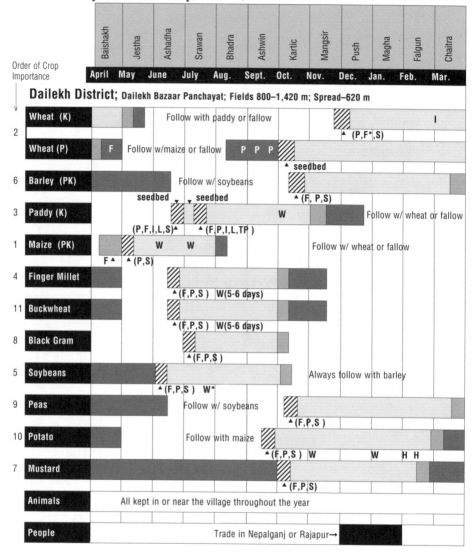

KEY TO BARS

Plant	Grow	Harvest	Fallow

KEY TO LETTER CODES

(**V**)=village; (**P**)=panchayat; (**B**)=burn; (**C&B**)=cut & bend maize plants; (**D**)=dig; (**F**)=fertilize; (**FG**)=force germinate paddy; (**H**)=harvest; (**I**)=irrigate; (**K**)=*khet* fields; (**L**)=level (smooth or harrow); (**P**)=plow; (**PK**)=*pakho* fields; (**S**)=sew; (**SB**)=sew bed; (**TP**)=transplant; (**W**)=weed; (*)=when necessary

the Midlands, inner Tarai, and Tarai of Western Nepal.

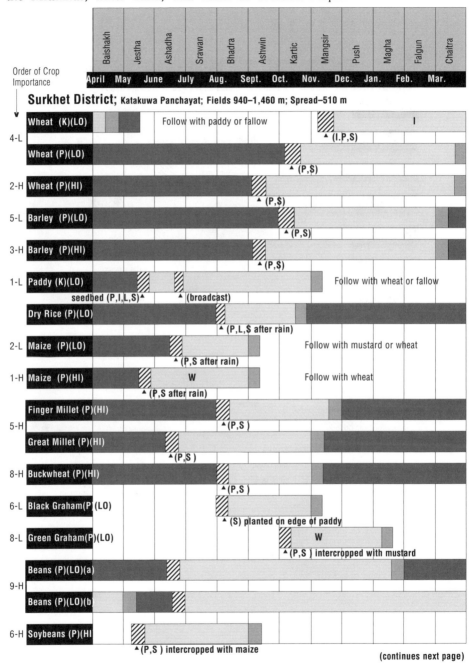

Surkhet District; Katakuwa Panchayat; Fields 940–1,460 m; Spread–510 m

(continues next page)

(continued from previous page)

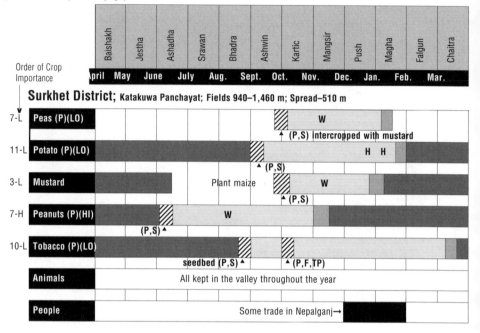

Surkhet District; Katakuwa Panchayat; Fields 940–1,460 m; Spread–510 m

	Baishakh	Jestha	Ashadha	Srawan	Bhadra	Ashwin	Kartic	Mangsir	Push	Magha	Falgun	Chaitra
Order of Crop Importance	April	May	June	July	Aug.	Sept.	Oct.	Nov.	Dec.	Jan.	Feb.	Mar.

7-L **Peas (P)(LO)** — W — (P,S) intercropped with mustard

11-L **Potato (P)(LO)** — ▲ (P,S) — H H

3-L **Mustard** — Plant maize — W — ▲ (P,S)

7-H **Peanuts (P)(HI)** — (P,S) ▲ — W

10-L **Tobacco (P)(LO)** — seedbed (P,S) ▲ — ▲ (P,F,TP)

Animals — All kept in the valley throughout the year

People — Some trade in Nepalganj→

KEY TO BARS

Plant	Grow	Harvest	Fallow

KEY TO LETTER CODES

(**V**)=village; (**P**)=panchayat; (**B**)=burn; (**C&B**)=cut & bend maize plants; (**D**)=dig; (**F**)=fertilize; (**FG**)=force germinate paddy; (**H**)=harvest; (**I**)=irrigate; (**K**)=*khet* fields; (**L**)=level (smooth or harrow); (**P**)=plow; (**PK**)=*pakho* fields; (**S**)=sew; (**SB**)=sew bed; (**TP**)=transplant; (**W**)=weed; (*)=when necessary

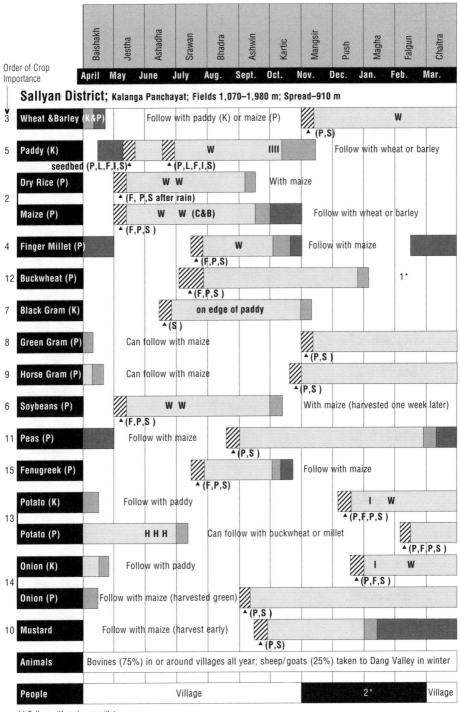

Sallyan District; Kalanga Panchayat; Fields 1,070–1,980 m; Spread–910 m

1* Follow with maize or millet
2* S&G to Dang Valley where some have land, trade in Nepalganj
Notes   1. Intercropping: Maize-Broadcast rice and maize—soybean, black gram
          2. Other crops: chili, garlic, ginger

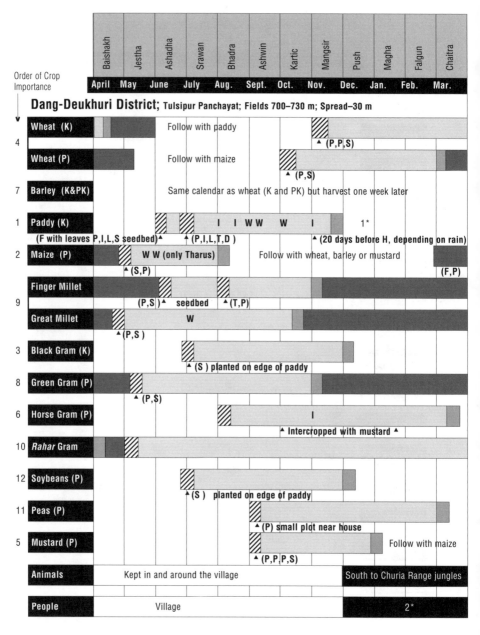

Dang-Deukhuri District; Tulsipur Panchayat; Fields 700–730 m; Spread–30 m

1* Follow with wheat, barley or gram
2* With animals to Churia range. Approx 8% trade in Nepalganj

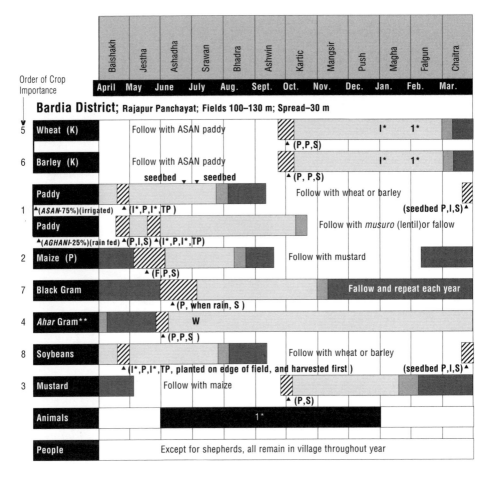

1* Families with many animals take livestock to Churia Range jungle to graze.

KEY TO BARS

Plant   Grow   Harvest   Fallow

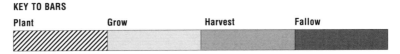

KEY TO LETTER CODES

(**V**)=village; (**P**)=panchayat; (**B**)=burn; (**C&B**)=cut & bend maize plants; (**D**)=dig; (**F**)=fertilize; (**FG**)=force germinate paddy; (**H**)=harvest; (**I**)=irrigate; (**K**)=*khet* fields; (**L**)=level (smooth or harrow); (**P**)=plow; (**PK**)=*pakho* fields; (**S**)=sew; (**SB**)=sew bed; (**TP**)=transplant; (**W**)=weed; (***)=when necessary

Appendix G
Seventy-four Karnali Family Economies for 2026 v.s. (1969-70)

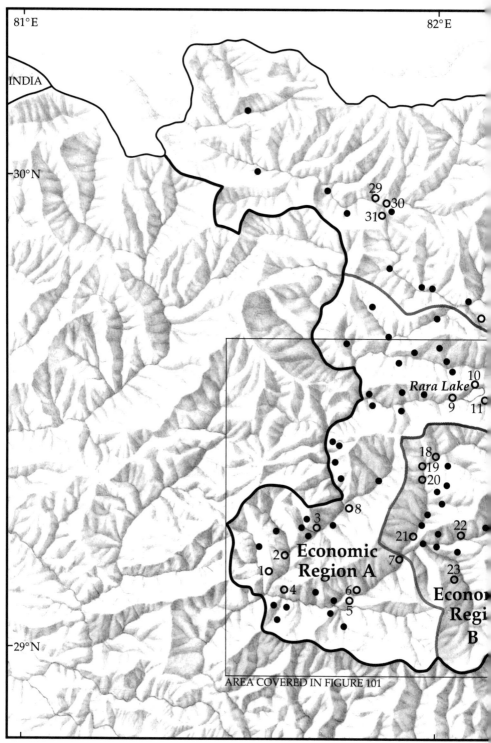

Fig. 99. Map of Karnali Zone panchayats surveyed

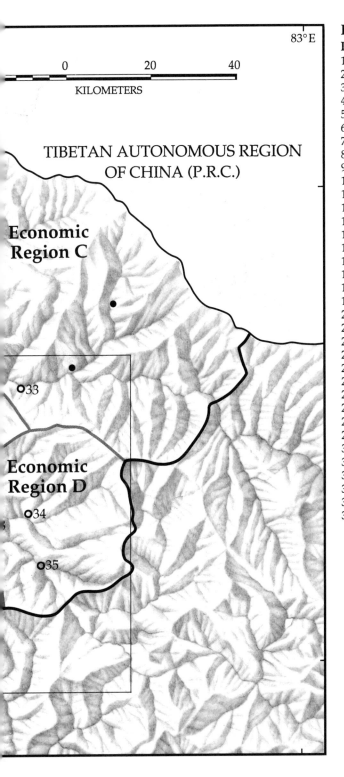

83°E

0 20 40
KILOMETERS

TIBETAN AUTONOMOUS REGION
OF CHINA (P.R.C.)

Economic
Region C

○33

Economic
Region D

○34

○35

Panchayats Surveyed

Panchayat	Dara
1 Kotbada	Sanni
2 Raku	Sanni
3 Siuna	Raskot
4 Manma	Kalikot
5 Chilkhaya	Barabisa
6 Jibitha	Rakala
7 Mahadev	Rakala
8 Thirpu	Palanta
9 Seri	Khatyad
10 Rara	Gama
11 Topla	Gama
12 Pina	Gama
13 Rugu	Gama
14 Karki Bada	Gama
15 Srinagar	Gama
16 Jhakot	Gama
17 Rowa	Gama
18 Had Sinja	Sinja
19 Ludku	Sinja
20 Dhapa	Sinja
21 Chiudi	Sinja
22 Jarmi	Pansaya
23 Jumlakot	Pansaya
24 Gairagaon	Asi
25 Depalgaon	Asi
26 Chhinasim	Asi
27 Chhina	Asi
28 Dasaundi	Asi
29 Simikot	Humla
30 Baragaon	Humla
31 Yanchu	Humla
32 Darma	Humla
33 Dhunge Dhara	Karana
34 Lum	Chaudhabisa
35 Manisangu	Chaudhabisa

TABLE 31. Agricultural labor inputs for seventy-four selected families in 2026 V.S. (1969-70).

Village and caste of family* (Economic subregion)		Holdings (in ha)	Labor inputs on family holdings (in producer units)					Intensity in PU/ha/year	Family labor on other holdings (in producer units)			
			Family	Exchange	Hired	Jajmani	Total		Exchange	Hired	Jajmani	Total
Region A												
Rara	T	8.97	—	—	—	835	835	93	—	—	—	—
(4)	T	3.98	291	—	—	330	621	156	—	—	—	—
	C	3.37	236	—	—	54	290	86	—	—	—	—
	C	1.98	258	—	—	—	258	130	—	—	—	—
Chhapru	C	3.72	386	—	—	26	412	111	—	—	—	—
(4)	C	1.60	290	8	—	—	298	185	8	—	—	8
	C	1.84	229	4	—	—	233	127	4	—	—	4
	DK	0.26	51	1	—	—	52	200	21	46	67	134
Topla	T	7.89	360	—	—	153	513	65	—	—	—	—
(4)	T	1.16	157	—	70	—	227	196	—	20	—	20
	DK	1.30	209	10	—	—	219	168	10	59	—	69
	DD	0.78	94	—	—	—	94	121	—	94	—	94
Srinagar	T	16.45	—	—	—	2,200	2,200	134	—	—	—	—
(4)	C	4.20	347	—	—	225	572	136	—	—	—	—
	C	2.75	537	—	—	141	678	247	—	—	—	—
	DD	0.40	97	6	—	—	103	258	6	108	42	156
Lumsa	C	2.23	350	—	214	—	564	253	—	—	—	—
(4)	C	1.57	421	10	105	—	536	341	10	—	—	10
	C	1.76	305	12	217	—	534	303	12	—	—	12
	DK	1.04	237	—	—	—	237	228	—	150	10	160

Region B												
Had Sinja (5)	B	1.30	304	—	30	—	334	257	—	—	—	—
	T	1.05	—	—	—	695	695	662	—	—	—	—
	T	1.56	146	—	652	—	798	512	—	—	—	—
	DD	1.54	283	43	—	—	326	212	—	—	91	91
Ranukbana (5)	B	3.55	861	—	690	—	1,551	437	—	—	—	—
	B	0.90	453	—	111	—	564	627	—	—	—	—
	B	0.78	464	60	200	—	724	928	60	—	—	60
	DK	0.23	41	10	—	—	51	222	10	—	—	10
Jarmi (6)	C	0.82	295	39	—	471	805	982	30	—	—	30
	C	0.91	353	38	50	26	467	513	38	—	—	38
	C	0.82	338	15	5	6	364	444	15	130	—	15
	DS	0.36	14	2	—	—	16	44	2		10	142
Litakot (6)	B	1.05	442	9	240	23	696	663	9	—	—	9
	B	0.94	345	8	254	24	631	671	8	—	—	8
	B	0.53	243	14	185	10	452	853	14	—	—	14
	C	0.38	173	—	—	4	177	466	—	—	—	—
Mahatbada (7)	C	3.83	429	48	—	512	989	258	48	—	—	48
	C	0.81	197	47	—	26	270	333	47	—	—	47
	C	1.43	365	25	16	21	427	299	25	—	—	25
	C	0.63	139	30	—	—	169	268	30	—	—	30
Bohoragaon (7)	B	2.10	746	130	—	628	1,504	716	130	—	—	130
	B	0.84	379	70	195	84	728	867	70	—	—	70
	C	1.50	557	59	91	12	719	479	59	—	—	59
	DS	0.76	118	12	—	—	130	171	12	16	—	28
	DS	0.35	128	14	—	—	142	406	14	—	41	55

* B = Brahman; T = Thakuri; C = Chhetri; Bh = Bhotia; DK = Kami; DS = Sarki; DD = Damai

(TABLE 31 continued)

Village and caste of family (Economic subregion)		Holdings (in ha)	Labor inputs on family holdings (in producer units)						Family labor on other holdings (in producer units)			
			Family	Exchange	Hired	Jajmani	Total	Intensity in PU/ha/year	Exchange	Hired	Jajmani	Total
Septi (7)	C	1.04	482	3	6	—	491	472	3	—	—	3
	C	0.92	412	3	2	—	417	453	3	—	—	3
	C	0.52	107	—	—	—	107	206	—	—	—	—
	C	0.26	44	—	—	—	44	169	7	—	—	7
Bhandari-Bada (7)	C	2.34	660	24	28	21	733	313	24	—	—	24
	C	1.95	1,011	203	145	9	1,368	702	203	—	—	203
	C	1.52	522	79	—	45	646	425	79	—	—	79
	DK	0.69	229	9	—	—	238	345	9	—	—	9
Acharya-Bada (7)	B	0.91	817	199	—	—	1,016	1,116	164	—	—	164
	B	0.84	380	45	9	69	503	599	45	—	—	45
	B	0.62	283	67	24	52	426	687	67	—	—	67
	DS	0.38	204	—	—	—	204	537	—	102	—	102
Region C												
Mangri (9)	Bh	2.62	910	—	355	—	1,265	483	—	—	—	—
	Bh	0.92	299	—	120	—	419	455	—	—	—	—
	DK	0.12	69	1	—	—	70	583	1	90	—	91
	DK	0.40	90	3	—	—	93	233	3	374	—	377
Region D												
Luma (10)	C	8.97	1,079	18	—	4	1,101	123	18	—	—	18
	C	9.64	1,183	20	—	4	1,207	260	20	—	—	20
	C	3.57	629	—	—	—	629	176	—	4	—	4
	DK	1.44	384	—	—	—	384	267	—	10	8	18
Mandara (10)	Bh	1.30	125	2	10	—	137	105	2	—	—	2

Dillikot (10)	C	0.20	49	8	—	—	57	285	8	60	—	68
	Bh	1.08	391	23	59	—	473	438	23	4	—	27
	Bh	0.16	86	2	—	—	88	550	2	—	—	2
	DK	0.18	47									
Kudigaon (10)	C	1.24	451	32	—	—	483	390	32	—	—	32
	C	0.72	465	8	—	—	473	657	8	—	—	8
	C	0.62	437	12	—	—	449	724	12	—	—	12
	C	0.52	267	2	—	—	269	517	2	—	—	2

TABLE 32. Seventy-four family economies for 2026 V.S. (1969-70).

Village and caste of family* (Economic subregion)		Family population	Producers (P)	Consumers (C)	P/C ratio	Number of *khet* fields	Number of *pakho* fields	Max. distance to fields (in hours)	Min. distance to fields (in hours)	Avg. distance to fields (in hours)
Region A										
Rara	T	19	10.0	12.0	1.20	60	102	12.0	0	1.0
(4)	T	17	11.0	13.0	1.18	5	4	5.0	0	0.3
	C	8	4.5	5.5	1.22	5	48	4.5	0	0.3
	C	11	5.3	6.8	1.29	—	19	1.0	0	0.5
Chhapru	C	9	5.0	6.0	1.20	—	33	1.5	0	0.8
(4)	C	3	1.8	2.0	1.14	16	34	6.0	0	0.3
	C	5	2.5	3.0	1.20	—	25	1.0	0	0.5
	DK	4	3.3	3.3	1.00	—	4	2.0	1.0	1.5
Topla	T	12	9.0	9.5	1.06	12	60	1.0	0	0.3
(4)	T	5	4.0	4.0	1.00	—	40	1.0	0	0.1
	DK	8	4.5	3.8	1.28	—	8	0.5	0.3	0.5
	DD	9	4.5	3.5	1.22	—	14	2.0	0	0.3
Srinigar	T	64	38.5	43.5	1.13	120	90	2.0	0	1.5
(4)	C	8	4.8	5.3	1.11	20	30	3.0	0	0.8
	C	9	6.3	7.0	1.12	9	11	1.0	0.3	0.3
	DD	3	2.8	2.8	1.00	—	9	0.3	0.3	0.3
Lumsa	C	8	3.3	4.0	1.23	16	50	1.0	0	0.5
(4)	C	14	7.0	7.8	1.11	16	24	2.0	0	1.0
	C	5	2.8	3.3	1.18	11	66	0.2	0	0.3
	DK	6	4.0	4.5	1.13	—	45	0.5	0	0.3
Region B										
Had Sinja	B	11	5.8	7.0	1.22	7	16	1.0	0	0.5
(5)	T	11	7.5	7.8	1.03	50	25	1.0	0	0.5
	T	4	1.8	2.8	1.57	12	8	24.0	0	1.0
	DD	7	3.5	4.8	1.36	11	29	1.5	0	0.5

*B = Brahman; T = Thakuri; C = Chhetri; Bh = Bhotia; DK = Kami; DS = Sarki; DD = Damai

Amount of *khet* (in hectares)	Amount of *pakho* (in ha)	Percentage of *pakho*	Total farmland	Hectares/P	Hectares/C	Number of bovines	Number of ovines	Number of equines	Total number of animals	Animals per CU	PU in farming
0.29	8.68	97	8.97	0.90	0.75	11	32	1	44	3.7	—
0.04	3.94	99	3.98	0.36	0.31	16	8	2	26	2.0	291
0.01	3.36	99	3.37	0.75	0.61	7	2	—	9	1.6	236
—	1.98	100	1.98	0.38	0.29	5	25	—	30	4.4	258
—	3.72	100	3.72	0.74	0.62	8	60	—	68	11.3	386
0.04	1.56	98	1.60	0.91	0.80	2	—	—	2	1.0	290
—	1.84	100	1.84	0.74	0.61	4	3	—	7	2.3	229
—	0.26	100	0.26	0.08	0.08	—	—	—	—	—	51
0.10	7.88	100	7.89	0.88	0.83	12	17	5	34	3.6	360
—	1.16	100	1.16	0.29	0.29	4	—	—	4	1.0	157
—	1.30	100	1.30	0.29	0.23	7	—	—	7	1.2	209
—	0.78	100	0.78	0.17	0.14	1	—	—	1	0.2	94
6.57	9.88	60	16.45	0.43	0.38	34	—	1	35	0.8	—
0.26	3.94	94	4.20	0.88	0.80	15	5	3	23	4.4	347
0.13	2.62	95	2.75	0.44	0.39	6	—	5	11	1.6	537
—	0.40	100	0.40	0.15	0.15	2	—	—	2	0.7	97
0.13	2.01	94	2.23	0.69	0.56	8	20	—	28	7.0	350
0.13	1.44	92	1.57	0.22	0.20	9	—	—	9	1.2	421
0.06	1.70	97	1.76	0.64	0.54	7	—	—	7	2.2	305
—	1.04	100	1.04	0.26	0.23	6	7	—	13	2.9	237
0.12	1.18	91	1.30	0.23	0.19	11	—	—	11	1.6	304
0.27	0.78	74	1.05	0.14	0.14	21	46	1	68	8.8	—
0.26	1.30	83	1.56	0.89	0.57	20	—	—	20	7.3	146
0.10	1.44	94	1.54	0.44	0.32	8	—	—	8	1.7	282

(TABLE 32 *continued*)

Village and caste of family* (Economic subregion)		Family population	Producers (P)	Consumers (C)	P/C ratio	Number of *khet* fields	Number of *pakho* fields	Max. distance to fields (in hours)	Min. distance to fields (in hours)	Avg. distance to fields (in hours)
Ranukbana	B	15	8.8	9.8	1.11	110	11	1.0	0	0.3
(5)	B	7	4.8	5.0	1.05	22	4	1.0	0	0.2
	B	8	3.8	4.5	1.20	21	5	0.8	0	0.2
	DK	5	1.8	2.5	1.43	1	3	1.0	0	0.2
Jarmi	C	6	2.3	3.3	1.44	18	8	1.5	0	0.8
(6)	C	7	4.3	5.0	1.18	40	15	2.0	0	1.5
	C	4	2.3	2.5	1.11	19	10	0.5	0	0.3
	DS	4	3.5	3.5	1.00	—	5	0.2	0	0.1
Litakot	B	7	5.5	6.3	1.14	40	7	3.0	0.5	0.5
(6)	B	9	5.5	6.0	1.09	31	7	0.5	0.3	0.3
	B	6	4.0	4.5	1.13	22	3	1.5	0	1.5
	C	4	2.8	2.8	1.00	7	3	1.0	0	0.5
Mahatbada	C	16	6.5	10.5	1.62	45	25	0.3	0.3	0.3
(7)	C	4	1.8	2.5	1.43	7	12	0.5	0	0.3
	C	10	3.3	4.8	1.46	7	5	1.5	0.3	0.5
	C	4	2.3	2.5	1.11	7	11	1.0	0.5	0.8
Bohoragaon	B	8	5.5	6.0	1.09	25	7	2.5	0	0.2
(7)	B	6	2.8	3.8	1.36	18	5	3.0	0	1.0
	C	6	2.8	3.8	1.36	47	10	0.5	0	0.3
	DS	7	2.3	3.5	1.56	9	7	0.5	0	0.3
	DS	3	1.8	2.0	1.14	7	2	0.3	0.3	0.3
Septi	C	11	4.8	6.5	1.37	—	51	2.0	0	1.0
(7)	C	7	3.3	4.0	1.23	—	45	6.0	0	0.8
	C	3	1.8	2.0	1.14	—	16	0.5	0	0.3
	C	5	3.0	3.3	1.08	—	30	6.0	0.2	6.0

Amount of *khet* (in hectares)	Amount of *pakho* (in ha)	Percentage of *pakho*	Total farmland	Hectares/P	Hectares/C	Number of bovines	Number of ovines	Number of equines	Total number of animals	Animals per CU	PU in farming
0.93	2.62	74	3.55	0.41	0.36	21	—	4	25	2.6	861
0.26	0.64	71	0.90	0.19	0.18	8	—	1	9	1.8	453
0.14	0.64	82	0.78	0.21	0.17	12	—	—	12	2.7	464
0.03	0.20	81	0.23	0.13	0.09	2	—	—	2	0.8	41
0.31	0.52	63	0.82	0.36	0.25	5	2	3	10	3.1	295
0.27	0.64	70	0.91	0.21	0.04	12	4	—	16	3.2	353
0.18	0.64	78	0.82	0.36	0.33	7	—	2	9	3.6	338
—	0.36	100	0.36	0.10	0.10	—	—	—	—	—	14
0.65	0.40	38	1.05	0.19	0.17	12	2	1	15	2.4	442
0.68	0.26	28	0.94	0.17	0.16	13	—	—	13	2.2	345
0.27	0.26	49	0.53	0.13	0.12	8	1	—	9	2.0	243
0.12	0.26	68	0.38	0.14	0.14	1	—	—	1	0.4	173
1.47	2.36	62	3.83	0.59	0.36	19	15	—	34	3.2	429
0.17	0.64	77	0.81	0.46	0.32	4	—	—	4	1.6	197
0.13	1.30	91	1.43	0.44	0.30	5	—	—	5	1.1	365
0.11	0.52	83	0.63	0.28	0.25	3	—	1	4	1.6	139
2.51	11.30	82	13.81	2.51	2.30	17	—	11	28	4.7	746
0.32	0.52	62	0.84	0.31	0.22	7	—	—	7	1.9	379
0.72	0.78	52	1.50	0.55	0.40	12	—	2	14	3.7	557
0.12	0.64	84	0.76	0.34	0.22	2	—	—	2	0.6	118
0.09	0.26	74	0.35	0.20	0.18	6	—	—	6	3.0	128
—	1.04	100	1.04	0.22	0.16	4	20	—	24	3.7	482
—	0.92	100	0.92	0.28	0.23	1	17	—	18	4.5	412
—	0.52	100	0.52	0.30	0.26	—	—-	—	—	—	107
—	0.26	100	0.26	0.09	0.08	—	8	—	8	2.5	44

(TABLE 32 *continued*)

Village and caste of family* (Economic subregion)		Family population	Producers (P)	Consumers (C)	P/C ratio	Number of *khet* fields	Number of *pakho* fields	Max. distance to fields (in hours)	Min. distance to fields (in hours)	Avg. distance to fields (in hours)
Bhandari-	C	11	7.3	8.3	1.14	30	6	2.0	0.5	0.8
Bada	C	18	12.3	13.3	1.08	11	4	1.5	0	0.3
(7)	C	7	2.8	3.5	1.27	30	15	1.0	0.2	0.5
	DK	6	4.5	5.0	1.11	5	8	2.0	0	2.0
Acharya-	B	13	6.0	7.5	1.30	20	2	0.2	0	0.2
Bada	B	8	2.5	5.0	2.00	9	4	0.5	0	0.5
(7)	B	4	2.5	2.8	1.10	36	3	1.0	0	0.3
	DS	6	2.3	3.3	1.44	3	5	0.3	0	0.3
Region C										
Mangri	B h	15	9.3	10.5	1.14	—	320	3.0	0	2.0
(9)	B h	6	3.5	4.5	1.29	—	154	2.0	0	1.0
	DK	4	1.8	3.0	1.71	—	15	1.0	1.0	1.0
	DK	5	3.5	4.0	1.14	—	30	1.0	0.5	0.8
Region D										
Luma	C	12	8.5	9.0	1.06	2	12	2.0	0	0.5
(10)	C	15	8.8	10.0	1.14	8	47	1.0	0	0.5
	C	16	9.5	11.0	1.16	3	19	1.0	0	0.5
	DK	17	11.5	12.5	1.09	—	11	1.5	0	1.0
Mandara	B h	6	3.5	4.0	1.14	—	10	0.2	0.2	0.2
(10)										
Dillikot	C	6	4.0	4.5	1.13	—	5	0.5	0.5	0.5
(10)	B h	5	4.0	4.0	1.00	2	51	1.5	0	0.3
	B h	6	3.5	4.0	1.14	—	10	0.3	0	0.2
	DK	10	4.5	6.5	1.44	—	7	0.3	0	0.3
Kudigaon	C	13	5.5	7.0	1.27	—	40	1.0	0	0.5
(10)	C	10	5.0	6.3	1.30	—	30	2.0	0	0.5
	C	9	5.0	6.3	1.30	—	31	1.5	0	0.5
	C	3	2.3	2.8	1.22	—	74	2.0	0	0.5

Amount of *khet* (in hectares)	Amount of *pakho* (in ha)	Percentage of *pakho*	Total farmland	Hectares/P	Hectares/C	Number of bovines	Number of ovines	Number of equines	Total number of animals	Animals per CU	PU in farming
0.64	1.70	73	2.34	0.32	0.28	18	—	12	30	3.6	660
0.59	1.36	70	1.95	0.16	0.15	10	184	12	206	15.5	1,011
0.36	1.16	76	1.52	0.55	0.43	9	—	—	9	2.6	522
0.05	0.64	93	0.69	0.15	0.14	6	4	—	10	2.0	229
0.65	0.26	29	0.91	0.15	0.12	22	6	2	30	4.0	817
0.32	0.52	64	0.84	0.34	0.17	13	—	7	20	4.0	380
0.36	0.26	42	0.62	0.25	0.23	5	—	—	5	1.8	283
0.12	0.26	68	0.38	0.17	0.12	—	—	—	—	—	204
—	2.62	100	2.62	0.28	0.25	41	260	19	320	30.5	910
—	0.92	100	0.92	0.26	0.20	7	20	—	27	6.0	299
—	0.12	100	0.12	0.07	0.04	1	—	—	1	0.3	69
—	0.40	100	0.40	0.11	0.10	—	6	—	6	1.5	90
0.03	8.94	97	8.97	1.06	1.00	20	10	2	32	3.6	1,079
0.04	4.60	99	4.64	0.53	0.46	14	34	5	53	5.3	1,183
0.01	3.56	97	3.57	0.38	0.32	12	30	6	48	16.0	629
—	1.44	100	1.44	0.13	0.12	5	—	—	5	1.3	384
—	1.30	100	1.30	0.37	0.33	—	80	6	86	21.5	125
—	0.20	100	0.20	0.05	0.04	—	—	—	—	—	49
0.04	1.04	96	1.08	0.27	0.27	17	—	16	33	7.3	391
—	0.16	100	0.16	0.05	0.04	7	—	—	7	1.8	86
—	0.18	100	0.18	0.04	0.03	1	—	—	1	0.2	47
—	1.24	100	1.24	0.23	0.18	9	50	2	61	8.7	451
—	0.72	100	0.72	0.14	0.12	7	23	1	31	5.0	465
—	0.62	100	0.62	0.12	0.10	4	47	—	51	8.2	437
—	0.52	100	0.52	0.23	0.19	4	—	—	4	1.5	267

(TABLE 32 *continued*)

Village and caste of family* (Economic subregion)		PU in animal husbandry	PU in handicrafts	PU in trade	PU in misc. labor	PU in housework	PU in religious activities	Total PU expended	Total PU available	PU not used
Region A										
Rara	T	—	106	182	—	631	176	1,095	3,650	2,555
(4)	T	150	160	182	—	513	190	1,486	4,015	2,529
	C	77	154	—	—	291	80	838	1,643	805
	C	149	129	30	—	340	90	996	1,916	920
Chhapru	C	240	150	60	—	510	42	1,388	1,825	437
(4)	C	—	49	—	—	234	35	608	639	31
	C	—	90	30	—	453	47	849	913	64
	DK	—	57	—	88	458	58	712	1,186	474
Topla	T	180	80	180	—	564	148	1,512	3,285	1,773
(4)	T	—	59	—	147	443	70	876	1,460	584
	DK	—	49	—	363	449	78	1,148	1,643	495
	DD	—	—	—	153	448	77	772	1,643	871
Srinagar	T	—	—	446	1,680	2,605	603	5,334	14,053	8,619
(4)	C	119	—	29	—	326	96	917	1,734	817
	C	59	30	45	—	326	121	1,118	2,281	1,163
	DD	—	—	—	182	333	50	662	1,004	342
Lumsa	C	60	112	112	—	258	68	960	1,186	226
(4)	C	15	103	46	—	361	129	1,075	2,555	1,480
	C	15	61	22	—	258	62	723	1,004	281
	BK	46	38	61	175	261	72	890	1,460	570
Region B										
Had Sinja	B	21	30	76	—	540	100	1,071	2,099	1,028
(5)	T	280	—	148	—	527	140	1,095	2,738	1,643
	T	—	—	137	—	222	51	556	639	83
	DD	—	—	—	168	408	63	921	1,278	357

Percentage PU not used	PU away from home (social activities)	Income/family (in rupees)	Income/P (in rupees)	Income in cash	Percentage in cash	Income in kind (rupee equivalent)	Percentage in kind	Family expenditures (in rupees)	Expenditures per P	Expenditures per C	Surplus (+) or deficit (-) per family
70	42	15,245	1,525	12,200	80	3,045	20	11,615	1,162	968	+3,630
63	132	6,958	633	5,125	74	1,833	26	4,781	435	368	+2,177
49	—	992	220	15	1	977	99	916	204	167	+76
48	—	1,225	233	—	—	1,225	100	1,161	221	172	+64
24	12	2,470	494	587	28	1,883	72	1,597	319	266	+873
5	—	854	488	80	9	774	91	398	227	199	+456
7	60	1,059	424	472	45	587	55	892	357	297	+267
40	43	746	230	355	47	391	53	110	34	34	+636
54	—	3,368	374	326	10	3,042	90	2,762	307	291	+606
40	—	1,009	252	433	43	576	57	758	190	190	+251
30	16	2,006	446	1,095	55	891	45	800	178	139	+1,206
53	—	1,883	418	1,298	70	585	30	638	142	116	+1,245
61	—	108,680	2,823	72,600	67	36,080	33	57,510	1,494	1,322	+51,170
47	—	6,297	1,326	720	11	3,577	89	2,552	537	486	+3,745
51	—	9,162	1,466	1,690	17	7,472	83	3,260	522	466	+5,902
34	—	1,286	468	784	61	502	39	326	119	119	+860
19	17	2,104	647	84	4	2,020	96	2,196	676	549	-92
58	14	1,258	180	400	32	858	68	1,852	265	239	-594
28	4	1,488	541	80	5	1,408	95	1,664	605	512	-176
39	—	489	122	225	46	264	54	581	145	129	-92
49	325	2,780	483	250	9	2,230	91	2,640	459	377	+140
60	244	34,715	4,629	30,015	87	4,701	13	10,360	1,381	1,337	+24,355
13	80	5,121	2,926	1,150	22	3,971	88	5,760	3,291	2,094	-639
28	—	2,549	728	739	29	1,810	71	2,586	739	544	-37

(TABLE 32 *continued*)

Village and caste of family* (Economic subregion)		PU in animal husbandry	PU in handicrafts	PU in trade	PU in misc. labor	PU in housework	PU in religious activities	Total PU expended	Total PU available	PU not used
Ranukbana	B	121	—	273	—	534	160	1,949	3,194	1,245
(5)	B	30	—	90	20	302	93	988	1,734	746
	B	20	—	91	—	307	78	960	1,369	409
	DK	—	—	—	34	293	35	403	639	236
Jarmi	C	—	—	36	—	223	62	616	821	205
(6)	C	19	—	—	59	282	93	806	1,551	745
	C	19	—	9	—	224	58	648	821	173
	DS	—	—	—	136	332	69	551	1,278	727
Litakot	B	—	—	128	270	436	117	1,394	2,008	614
(6)	B	—	—	40	—	441	118	944	2,008	1,064
	B	9	—	32	—	416	91	791	1,460	669
	C	—	—	40	10	441	68	732	1,004	262
Mahatbada	C	—	—	91	214	553	140	1,427	2,373	946
(7)	C	—	—	—	—	307	39	543	639	96
	C	—	—	—	—	380	76	821	1,186	365
	C	—	—	—	—	307	47	493	821	328
Bohoragaon	B	—	—	272	272	369	121	1,780	2,008	228
(7)	B	—	—	61	41	233	68	782	1,004	222
	C	—	—	26	—	232	68	883	1,004	121
	DS	—	—	—	292	222	59	691	821	130
	DS	—	10	—	204	221	39	602	639	37
Septi	C	61	49	43	10	339	103	1,087	1,734	643
(7)	C	41	46	—	2	290	64	855	1,186	331
	C	—	20	29	10	221	39	426	639	213
	C	—	21	30	7	284	60	446	1,095	649

Percentage PU not used	PU away from home (social activities)	Income/family (in rupees)	Income/P (in rupees)	Income in cash	Percentage in cash	Income in kind (rupee equivalent)	Percentage in kind	Family expenditures (in rupees)	Expenditures per P	Expenditures per C	Surplus (+) or deficit (-) per family
39	270	35,991	4,113	32,151	90	3,841	10	16,811	1,921	1,724	+19,180
43	162	4,657	980	189	4	4,468	96	1,175	247	235	+3,482
30	90	3,710	989	760	20	2,950	80	2,248	599	500	+1,462
37	—	656	375	—	—	656	100	110	63	44	+546
25	90	4,981	2,214	1,800	36	3,182	64	4,675	2,078	1,438	+306
48	74	2,618	616	2,290	88	328	12	2,519	593	504	+99
21	9	2,052	912	1,200	58	852	42	1,972	876	789	+80
57	461	858	245	576	67	282	33	230	66	66	+628
31	186	6,149	1,118	2,000	33	4,149	67	4,288	780	686	+1,861
53	351	3,558	647	1,834	50	1,804	50	3,047	554	508	+511
46	—	3,562	891	856	24	2,706	76	2,736	684	608	+826
26	373	1,624	591	462	28	1,162	72	1,770	644	644	-146
40	93	18,363	2,826	5,412	30	12,956	70	11,151	1,716	1,062	+7,217
15	59	1,328	759	846	63	488	37	859	1,191	344	+469
31	345	1,994	614	1,396	70	598	30	2,540	782	535	-546
40	93	1,207	536	380	31	827	69	468	208	197	+739
11	94	24,822	4,513	17,380	70	7,442	30	13,415	2,439	2,236	+11,407
22	108	3,043	1,100	535	18	2,508	82	1,759	640	469	+1,284
12	46	3,043	1,100	535	18	1,508	82	1,673	608	446	+1,284
16	67	2,409	1,071	686	29	1,723	71	2,164	962	618	+245
6	—	2,754	1,574	2,043	74	711	26	946	541	473	+1,808
37	108	3,128	659	300	10	2,828	90	2,648	557	407	+408
28	26	1,965	605	60	3	1,905	97	1,510	465	378	+455
33	30	661	378	100	15	561	85	582	333	291	+79
59	2	694	231	85	12	609	88	420	140	129	+274

(TABLE 32 *continued*)

Village and caste of family* (Economic subregion)		PU in animal husbandry	PU in handicrafts	PU in trade	PU in misc. labor	PU in housework	PU in religious activities	Total PU expended	Total PU available	PU not used
Bhandari-	C	122	—	—	—	366	149	1,297	2,646	1,349
Bada	C	444	21	40	—	574	237	2,327	4,471	2,144
(7)	C	—	—	59	72	225	68	946	1,004	58
	DK	—	—	—	188	302	87	806	1,643	837
Acharya-	B	246	—	—	393	419	126	2,001	2,190	189
Bada	B	10	10	46	—	287	53	786	913	127
(7)	B	—	—	—	—	228	64	575	913	338
	DS	—	—	—	54	278	47	583	821	238
Region C										
Mangri	B h	239	218	126	—	452	151	2,096	3,376	1,280
(9)	B h	58	102	38	—	334	64	895	1,278	383
	DK	—	19	44	117	334	36	619	639	20
	DK	29	3	—	409	275	61	867	1,278	411
Region D										
Luma	C	122	20	35	50	550	317	2,173	3,103	930
(10)	C	179	88	614	40	569	171	2,844	3,194	350
	C	159	60	332	19	555	184	1,938	3,468	1,530
	DK	91	—	30	301	660	213	1,679	4,198	2,519
Mandara	B h	101	318	58	—	347	62	1,011	1,278	267
(10)										
Dillikot	C	—	—	—	82	246	76	453	1,460	1,007
(10)	B h	102	103	183	—	222	78	1,079	1,460	381
	B h	—	167	74	20	502	74	923	1,278	355
	DK	—	—	—	136	441	84	708	1,643	935
Kudigaon	C	200	43	85	20	443	105	1,347	2,008	661
(10)	C	121	16	99	67	286	97	1,151	1,825	674
	C	137	76	79	26	305	84	1,144	1,825	681
	C	—	16	54	49	223	47	656	821	165

Percentage PU not used	PU away from home (social activities)	Income/family (in rupees)	Income/P (in rupees)	Income in cash	Percentage in cash	Income in kind (rupee equivalent)	Percentage in kind	Family expenditures (in rupees)	Expenditures per P	Expenditures per C	Surplus (+) or deficit (-) per family
51	—	5,179	714	2,026	39	3,153	61	4,200	579	509	+979
48	701	3,274	267	700	21	2,574	79	5,107	417	385	-1,833
6	46	2,720	989	725	27	1,995	73	684	249	195	+2,036
51	11	1,648	366	464	28	1,184	72	714	159	143	+934
9	152	5,344	891	4,400	82	994	18	4,310	718	575	+1,034
14	65	4,209	1,684	2,000	48	2,209	52	2,335	934	849	+1,874
37	30	1,427	571	180	13	1,247	87	1,209	484	440	+218
29	12	1,370	609	750	55	620	45	1,289	573	397	+81
38	104	8,980	971	4,211	48	4,769	52	7,680	830	731	+1,300
30	—	2,508	717	—	—	2,508	100	2,352	672	523	+156
3	—	276	158	243	88	33	12	237	135	79	+39
32	—	278	79	—	—	278	100	268	77	67	+10
30	80	5,194	611	2,140	41	3,054	59	2,317	273	257	+2,877
11	616	9,821	1,122	1,408	14	8,413	86	2,353	269	235	+7,468
44	602	3,254	343	396	12	2,858	88	1,160	122	105	+2,094
60	88	1,990	173	987	49	1,003	51	1,178	102	94	+812
21	—	1,638	468	16	1	1,622	99	2,699	771	675	-1,061
69	295	142	36	50	35	92	65	130	33	29	+12
26	187	6,762	1,691	3,500	52	3,262	48	5,157	1,289	1,289	+1,605
28	75	1,192	341	952	80	240	20	854	244	214	+338
57	16	672	149	305	45	362	55	325	72	50	+347
33	90	3,786	688	732	19	3,054	81	1,978	360	282	+1,808
37	60	868	174	210	24	658	76	1,254	251	201	-386
37	525	1,403	281	690	49	713	51	2,282	456	365	-879
20	112	802	356	410	51	392	49	880	391	320	-78

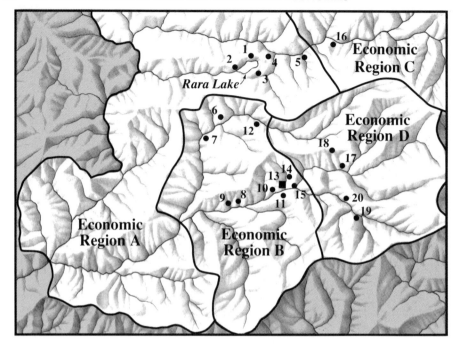

Village	Panchayat
1. Rara	Rara
2. Chhapru	Rara
3. Topla	Topla
4. Srinagar	Srinagar
5. Lumsa	Rowa
6. Had Sinja	Had Sinja
7. Ranukbada	Dhapa
8. Jarmigaon	Jarmi
9. Litakot	Jarmi
10. Mahatbada	Chhina
11. Bohoragaon	Gairagaon
12. Sipti	Chhinasim
13. Jumla Bazaar	Chhinasim
14. Bhandaribada	Chhinasim
15. Acharyabada	Dasaundi
16. Mangri	Dhunge Dhara
17. Luma	Lum
18. Mandara	Lum
19. Dillikot	Manisangu
20. Kudigaon	Manisangu

Fig. 100. Map of household survey villages

Appendix H
**Movement of People, Animals, and Goods to and through
Jumla-Kalanga in 2026 V.S. (1969-70)**

TABLE 33. Parties of travelers to or through Jumla-Kalanga by month in 2026

Home region	Baishakh	Jestha	Ashadha	Srawan	Bhadra	Ashwin	Kartic
	Apr.	May	June	July	Aug.	Sept.	Oct.
Trans-Karnali	7	16	4	10	8	2	
Lower Tila	28	39	32	26	45	21	
Palanta Dara	29	38	20	10	34	32	
Lower Humla-Mugu	41	31	11	31	22	36	
Sinja Dara	73	75	55	73	79	55	
Pansaya Dara	72	64	49	86	107	40	
Asi Dara–Kalanga	205	217	55	96	88	41	
Upper Humla	16	12	9	1	9	4	
Upper Mugu	34	39	13	21	1	4	
Chaudhabisa/Tila	83	112	64	45	52	25	
West Dolpo	15	28	4	8	6	2	
East Dolpo	6	2	5	4	4	—	
Jajarkot District	17	40	29	63	81	45	
Sallyan District	—	—	3	—	1	—	
Dang Valley	—	—	—	—	—	1	
Dailekh District	6	12	8	5	27	12	
Surkhet Valley	2	—	1	1	4	1	
Nepalganj	3	1	—	—	—	—	
Seti and Mahakali zones	4	2	4	3	5	1	
Kathmandu	3	2	6	2	4	—	
Elsewhere in Nepal	2	7	3	4	4	8	
Totals by month	646	737	375	489	581	330	
(%)	(13)	(15)	(7)	(10)	(12)	(7)	

v.s. (1969-70).

Kartic	Mangsir	Push	Magha	Falgun	Chaitra	Totals by home region	Percentage
Oct.	Nov.	Dec.	Jan.	Feb.	Mar.	Apr.	
4	10	6	—	1	20	88	1.8
23	24	20	26	6	19	309	6.2
7	24	20	8	6	32	260	5.2
6	32	54	7	28	44	343	6.9
55	54	49	15	20	37	640	12.9
60	82	65	35	24	12	696	14.0
51	94	75	56	61	31	1,070	21.5
4	8	15	1	12	5	96	1.9
5	18	13	12	12	12	184	3.7
55	33	55	30	21	21	596	12.0
3	7	8	4	3	2	90	1.8
—	1	1	—	1	4	28	0.6
18	40	6	—	—	15	354	7.1
—	—	—	—	—	—	4	0.1
—	—	—	—	—	1	2	0.0
7	3	5	2	3	6	96	1.9
—	1	—	—	—	—	10	0.2
—	1	—	—	—	—	5	0.1
3	—	7	2	—	1	32	0.6
2	1	1	2	2	2	27	0.5
4	8	6	2	2	2	52	1.0
307	441	406	202	204	266	4,982	100.0
(6)	(9)	(8)	(4)	(4)	(5)		

TABLE 34. Homes and destinations of travelers to and through Jumla-Kalanga in

Destinations of travelers	Homes of travelers									
	Trans-Karnali	Lower Tila	Palanta Dara	Lower Humla-Mugu	Sinja Dara	Pansaya Dara	Asi Dara–Kalanga	Upper Humla	Upper Mugu	Chaudhabisa/Tila
Trans-Karnali	—	—	—	—	—	—	4	—	—	1
Lower Tila	—	1	1	1	—	—	15	2	—	2
Palanta Dara	—	—	—	—	—	—	1	—	1	1
Lower Humla-Mugu	—	2	1	1	—	2	27	—	—	2
Sinja Dara	—	—	—	1	2	2	32	—	1	8
Pansaya Dara	—	—	—	1	3	3	86	1	6	48
Asi Dara–Kalanga	88	243	239	319	553	542	392	78	154	442
Upper Humla	—	—	—	—	—	3	13	—	—	—
Upper Mugu	—	—	—	—	—	5	9	—	—	1
Chaudhabisa/Tila	—	9	2	3	46	84	285	1	7	23
West Dolpo	—	38	2	—	21	12	14	—	—	1
East Dolpo	—	16	15	—	1	10	6	—	—	—
Jajarkot District	—	—	—	6	4	7	35	10	1	5
Sallyan District	—	—	—	—	—	—	—	1	—	3
Dang Valley	—	—	—	—	1	—	2	—	—	—
Dailekh District	—	—	—	—	—	—	12	—	1	7
Surkhet Valley	—	—	—	5	1	2	14	—	—	28
Nepalganj	—	—	—	4	—	1	101	2	3	22
Seti and Mahakali zones	—	—	—	—	—	—	3	—	—	—
Kathmandu	—	—	—	1	2	—	6	1	7	—
Elsewhere in Nepal	—	—	—	1	6	23	13	—	3	2
India	—	—	—	—	—	—	—	—	—	—
Totals	88	309	260	343	640	696	1,070	96	184	596

2026 V.S. (1969-70).

| | | | | | | | Homes of travelers | | | | | |
West Dolpo	East Dolpo	Jajarkot District	Sallyan District	Dang Valley	Dailekh District	Surkhet Valley	Nepalganj	Seti and Mahakali zones	Kathmandu	Elsewhere in Nepal	India	Totals
—	—	—	—	—	—	—	—	—	—	1	—	6
6	1	—	—	—	—	—	—	—	—	—	—	29
—	—	—	—	—	—	—	—	—	—	1	—	4
—	—	7	—	—	3	—	—	—	1	4	—	50
20	2	7	—	—	—	—	—	1	—	4	—	80
4	1	6	—	—	—	—	—	—	—	1	—	160
55	18	298	4	2	73	5	4	30	19	31	—	3,589
—	—	23	—	—	1	—	—	—	4	—	—	44
2	1	1	—	—	4	—	1	—	2	—	—	26
—	2	10	—	—	13	3	—	1	—	2	—	491
—	—	1	—	—	1	1	—	—	—	—	—	91
—	—	—	—	—	—	—	—	—	—	1	—	49
—	—	—	—	—	1	—	—	—	—	1	—	70
—	—	—	—	—	—	—	—	—	—	—	—	4
—	—	—	—	—	—	—	—	—	—	1	—	4
—	1	—	—	—	—	—	—	—	—	—	—	21
—	—	1	—	—	—	—	—	—	—	—	—	51
3	1	—	—	—	—	—	—	—	—	3	—	140
—	—	—	—	—	—	—	—	—	—	1	—	4
—	—	—	—	—	—	—	—	—	—	1	—	18
—	1	—	—	—	—	1	—	—	1	—	—	51
—	—	—	—	—	—	—	—	—	—	—	—	—
90	28	354	4	2	96	10	5	32	27	52	—	4,982

TABLE 35. Homes and destinations of parties with animals to and through Jumla-

Homes of parties with animals

Destinations of parties with animals	Trans-Karnali	Lower Tila	Palanta Dara	Lower Humla-Mugu	Sinja Dara	Pansaya Dara	Asi Dara-Kalanga	Upper Humla	Upper Mugu	Chaudhabisa/Tila
Trans-Karnali	—	—	—	—	—	—	1	—	—	—
Lower Tila	—	—	—	—	—	—	4	—	—	1
Palanta Dara	—	—	—	—	—	—	—	—	—	—
Lower Humla-Mugu	—	1	—	1	—	—	1	—	—	1
Sinja Dara	—	—	—	—	2	—	7	—	—	2
Pansaya Dara	—	—	—	—	—	1	13	—	3	3
Asi Dara–Kalanga	5	11	16	12	16	42	98	13	29	19
Upper Humla	—	—	—	—	—	1	3	—	—	—
Upper Mugu	—	—	—	—	—	—	2	—	2	—
Chaudhabisa/Tila	—	1	—	1	7	7	68	—	2	20
West Dolpo	—	12	—	—	4	1	4	—	—	—
East Dolpo	—	5	4	—	1	9	3	—	—	—
Jajarkot District	—	—	—	—	—	5	29	1	1	5
Sallyan District	—	—	—	—	—	—	—	—	—	—
Dang Valley	—	—	—	—	1	—	2	—	—	—
Dailekh District	—	—	—	—	—	—	3	—	—	6
Surkhet Valley	—	—	—	5	1	—	5	—	—	21
Nepalganj	—	—	—	—	—	—	1	—	—	—
Seti and Mahakali zones	—	—	—	—	—	—	2	—	—	—
Kathmandu	—	—	—	—	—	—	—	—	—	—
Elsewhere in Nepal	—	—	—	—	2	23	5	—	—	—
India	—	—	—	—	—	—	—	—	—	—
Totals	5	30	20	19	34	89	251	14	37	78

Kalanga in 2026 V.S. (1969-70).

| | | | | | Homes of parties with animals | | | | | | | |
West Dolpo	East Dolpo	Jajarkot District	Sallyan District	Dang Valley	Dailekh District	Surkhet Valley	Nepalganj	Seti and Mahakali zones	Kathmandu	Elsewhere in Nepal	India	Totals
—	—	—	—	—	—	—	—	—	—	—	—	1
—	1	—	—	—	—	—	—	—	—	—	—	6
—	—	—	—	—	—	—	—	—	—	—	—	—
—	—	—	—	—	1	—	—	—	—	1	—	6
11	2	—	—	—	—	—	—	—	—	—	—	24
—	—	—	—	—	—	—	—	—	—	—	—	20
9	1	24	1	1	—	—	—	—	—	—	—	297
—	—	—	—	—	—	—	—	—	—	—	—	4
—	—	—	—	—	—	—	—	—	—	—	—	4
—	1	1	—	—	—	—	—	—	—	—	—	108
—	—	—	—	—	—	—	—	—	—	—	—	21
—	—	—	—	—	—	—	—	—	—	—	—	22
—	—	—	—	—	—	—	—	—	—	—	—	41
—	—	—	—	—	—	—	—	—	—	—	—	—
—	—	—	—	—	—	—	—	—	—	—	—	3
—	—	—	—	—	—	—	—	—	—	—	—	9
—	—	1	—	—	—	—	—	—	—	—	—	33
—	—	—	—	—	—	—	—	—	—	—	—	1
—	—	—	—	—	—	—	—	—	—	—	—	2
—	—	—	—	—	—	—	—	—	—	—	—	—
—	—	—	—	—	—	—	—	—	—	—	—	30
—	—	—	—	—	—	—	—	—	—	—	—	—
20	5	26	1	1	1	—	—	—	—	1	—	632

TABLE 36. Movement of travelers, animals, and goods to and through Jumla-Kalanga in

				Home region				
	Trans-Karnali	Lower Tila	Palanta Dara	Lower Humla-Mugu	Sinja Dara	Pansaya Dara	Asi Dara–Kalanga	Upper Humla
Number of informants	88	309	260	343	640	696	1,070	96
Parties with destination of Kalanga	88	232	234	284	518	456	284	70
Travelers alone	31	120	123	195	317	266	505	46
Travelers in groups	174	619	723	704	1,019	1,693	2,061	156
Parties with animals	5	30	20	19	34	89	251	14
Travelers' castes: Brahman	38	102	159	67	325	119	516	1
Thakuri	96	443	365	142	226	280	74	71
Chhetri	58	99	263	550	684	1,227	1,298	73
Bhotia	—	—	—	—	—	—	—	7
Dum	13	95	57	113	101	333	628	22
Magar	—	—	—	—	—	—	—	10
Gurung	—	—	—	8	—	—	10	1
Newar	—	—	—	1	—	—	39	1
Sunuwar	—	—	—	9	—	—	—	—
Tamang	—	—	—	8	—	—	1	16
Tibetan refugees	—	—	2	1	—	—	—	—
Informants owning land	88	301	257	333	623	676	980	78
Amount of *khet* owned (hectares)	23	49	40	24	89	62	174	5
Amount of *pakho* owned (hectares)	28	40	42	65	89	88	111	16
Purpose of travel:								
Trade: in Jumla-Kalanga	20	46	54	44	104	244	115	11
in Nepalganj	—	—	—	—	1	1	1	1
in Rajapur	—	—	—	—	—	—	2	—
elsewhere in Nepal	—	41	15	8	49	77	94	6
in Jouljibi (Kumaon)	—	—	—	—	—	—	—	—
in the Indian plains	—	—	—	—	—	—	—	—
Grazing: Jumla area	—	—	—	—	—	3	27	—
Nepal midlands	—	—	—	5	1	3	23	—
Karnali highlands	—	2	—	—	3	12	62	1
Social: Jumla-Kalanga	12	58	59	135	154	127	125	38
elsewhere	—	29	10	33	63	113	393	15
Court case or government business:								
Kalanga	56	125	120	104	252	63	37	21
Kathmandu	—	—	—	—	—	—	2	—
elsewhere	—	—	1	6	—	2	36	1
Pilgrimage: Jumla	—	3	1	—	5	22	11	—
elsewhere in Karnali	—	5	—	—	3	26	45	1
Manasarowar	—	—	—	—	—	—	—	—
Muktinath	—	—	—	—	—	—	1	—
Kathmandu	—	—	—	—	—	—	—	1
India	—	—	—	—	—	—	—	—

)26 V.S. (1969-70).

Upper Mugu	Chaudhabisa/Upper Tila	West Dolpo	East Dolpo	Jajarkot District	Sallyan District	Dang Valley	Dailekh District	Surkhet Valley	Nepalganj	Seti and Mahakali zones	Kathmandu	Elsewhere in Nepal	India	Totals
184	596	90	28	354	4	2	96	10	5	32	27	52	—	4,982
139	418	55	18	291	4	2	73	4	4	30	19	31	—	3,229
76	285	25	7	106	1	1	16	2	1	12	4	13	—	2,152
412	623	232	56	959	7	4	368	42	18	59	94	167	—	10,190
37	78	20	5	26	1	1	1	—	—	—	—	1	—	632
—	6	5	2	41	—	1	7	11	7	3	27	39	—	1,476
—	6	42	—	464	2	—	30	—	—	8	3	5	—	2,257
176	456	162	18	337	4	4	219	26	8	43	42	82	—	5,829
216	143	8	9	—	—	—	—	—	—	—	—	—	—	383
47	224	28	—	163	—	—	96	4	—	17	—	16	—	1,957
—	40	8	30	60	1	—	24	—	—	—	2	2	—	177
—	20	3	2	—	—	—	3	3	—	—	—	3	—	53
—	—	—	2	—	—	—	1	—	—	—	20	—	—	64
—	—	—	—	—	1	—	4	—	4	—	—	1	—	19
49	11	1	—	—	—	—	—	—	—	—	4	7	—	97
—	2	—	—	—	—	—	—	—	—	—	—	25	—	30
91	553	89	27	317	4	1	86	9	3	27	10	16	—	4,569
1	32	4	3	29	1	3	27	38	1	13	5	77	—	697
19	190	18	9	66	1	—	14	11	24	12	1	8	—	852
110	158	14	5	230	1	—	39	1	1	3	—	—	—	1,100
2	—	—	—	—	—	—	—	—	—	—	—	—	—	6
—	—	—	—	—	—	—	—	—	—	—	—	—	—	2
22	38	4	4	29	—	—	7	2	—	—	1	1	—	398
—	—	—	—	—	—	—	—	—	—	—	—	—	—	0
1	—	—	—	—	—	—	—	—	—	—	—	—	—	1
2	12	10	1	1	—	—	—	—	—	—	—	—	—	56
—	21	—	—	1	—	—	—	—	—	—	—	1	—	55
—	9	—	—	6	—	—	—	—	—	—	—	1	—	96
9	170	25	10	54	2	1	22	1	1	15	3	6	—	1,027
6	66	9	5	17	—	—	8	—	—	1	2	8	—	778
14	38	6	2	1	1	1	9	2	2	5	16	22	—	897
1	—	—	—	—	—	—	—	—	—	—	—	2	—	5
5	5	—	—	—	—	—	5	—	1	7	5	5	—	79
—	21	10	—	6	—	—	1	—	—	—	—	1	—	81
—	6	8	—	8	—	—	12	3	—	1	—	3	—	121
—	—	—	—	—	—	—	—	—	—	—	—	—	—	0
—	1	—	—	—	—	—	—	1	—	—	—	—	—	3
4	—	—	—	—	—	—	—	—	—	—	—	—	—	5
—	—	1	—	—	—	—	—	—	—	—	—	—	—	1

(TABLE 36 *continued*)

				Home region				
	Trans-Karnali	Lower Tila	Palanta Dara	Lower Humla-Mugu	Sinja Dara	Pansaya Dara	Asi Dara–Kalanga	Upper Humla
Seasonal migration:								
Jumla	—	—	—	—	—	—	—	—
Midlands	—	—	—	6	3	3	29	—
Tarai	—	—	—	1	2	—	69	—
India	—	—	—	—	—	—	—	—
elsewhere	—	—	—	—	—	—	—	—
Permanent migration:								
Jumla	—	—	—	1	—	—	—	—
Midlands	—	—	—	—	—	—	1	—
elsewhere	—	—	—	—	—	—	1	—
Trip duration: 2-6 days	2	145	83	156	485	534	696	2
1-3 weeks	78	133	164	171	127	111	149	50
1-2 months	6	26	12	6	21	43	154	36
3-4 months	—	4	—	—	—	3	21	4
5-6 months	1	—	—	7	1	5	35	3
longer	1	1	1	3	6	—	15	1
Trip frequency: intermittent	32	116	120	180	224	262	228	58
1 per year	36	88	81	81	225	257	428	27
2 per year	9	55	30	40	71	53	96	4
3 per year	2	4	8	18	25	11	88	3
4 per year	—	—	2	8	10	3	16	1
5 per year	1	—	1	3	4	1	8	2
6 or more per year	8	46	18	13	81	109	206	1
Goods transported by travelers:								
Cattle: for sale	—	—	—	—	15	3	27	—
for grazing	—	—	—	—	7	29	356	—
Buffalo: for sale	—	—	—	—	—	—	7	—
for sacrifice	—	1	—	—	—	—	—	—
for grazing	—	—	—	—	1	—	3	2
Yaks and/or crossbreeds:								
for transport	—	—	—	—	—	—	4	—
for sale	—	—	—	—	—	—	—	—
for grazing	—	—	—	—	—	16	234	3
Horses and mules:								
for transport	45	1	—	7	—	34	3	—
for sale	—	—	—	—	12	—	21	—
for grazing	—	—	—	—	—	3	146	—
Sheep: for transport	—	358	32	526	839	5,151	3,029	133
for sale	12	476	174	—	30	90	59	—
for sacrifice	—	—	—	—	—	—	—	1
for grazing	—	83	—	1	20	103	3,657	—

Upper Mugu	Chaudhabisa/ Upper Tila	West Dolpo	East Dolpo	Jajarkot District	Sallyan District	Dang Valley	Dailekh District	Surkhet Valley	Nepalganj	Seti and Mahakali zones	Kathmandu	Elsewhere in Nepal	India	Totals
4	—	—	—	—	—	—	2	—	—	—	—	—	—	6
	18	1	—	1	—	—	1	—	—	—	—	—	—	62
2	32	2	—	—	—	—	—	—	—	—	—	—	—	108
—	1	—	—	—	—	—	—	—	—	—	—	—	—	1
—	—	—	—	—	—	—	—	—	—	—	—	—	—	—
2	—	—	—	—	—	—	—	—	—	—	—	2	—	5
—	—	—	—	—	—	—	—	—	—	—	—	—	—	1
—	—	—	—	—	—	—	—	—	—	—	—	—	—	1
24	485	37	1	42	1	—	2	—	—	4	—	4	—	2,703
92	38	45	21	271	2	—	76	6	1	17	4	8	—	1,564
46	35	4	5	34	—	1	8	3	1	8	7	15	—	471
11	8	3	—	1	—	—	1	—	3	—	3	4	—	66
6	17	—	—	5	—	1	4	—	—	—	1	4	—	89
5	13	1	1	1	1	—	5	1	—	3	12	17	—	88
51	103	20	11	141	2	1	71	8	5	25	24	36	—	1,718
86	232	56	13	156	2	—	23	1	—	5	3	12	—	1,509
24	53	12	2	33	—	1	1	—	—	1	—	3	—	488
6	24	1	1	4	—	—	—	—	—	1	—	—	—	196
3	14	—	—	7	—	—	—	—	—	—	—	1	—	65
—	4	—	—	2	—	—	—	—	—	—	—	—	—	26
14	166	1	1	11	—	—	1	1	—	—	—	—	—	677
8	28	—	—	16	—	—	—	—	—	—	—	—	—	97
5	49	26	1	56	—	—	—	—	—	—	—	—	—	529
—	—	—	—	22	1	—	—	—	—	—	—	1	—	31
—	17	—	—	—	—	—	—	—	—	—	—	—	—	18
—	2	—	—	78	—	—	—	—	—	—	—	—	—	86
85	9	13	28	—	—	—	—	—	—	—	—	—	—	139
—	—	—	—	—	—	—	—	—	—	—	—	—	—	0
—	12	1	—	—	—	—	—	—	—	—	—	—	—	266
8	184	17	—	—	—	—	1	—	—	—	—	6	—	306
1	1	—	—	2	—	—	—	—	—	—	—	—	—	37
—	207	—	—	—	—	—	—	—	—	—	—	—	—	356
43	1,953	—	—	—	—	—	—	—	—	—	—	—	—	12,064
—	—	8	60	—	—	—	—	—	—	—	—	—	—	909
1	—	—	—	—	—	—	—	—	—	—	—	—	—	2
—	1,506	77	—	50	—	—	—	—	—	—	—	—	—	5,497

(TABLE 36 *continued*)

	Trans-Karnali	Lower Tila	Palanta Dara	Lower Humla-Mugu	Sinja Dara	Pansaya Dara	Asi Dara–Kalanga	Upper Humla
Goats: for transport	—	45	140	136	110	1,568	446	—
for sale	19	658	219	6	64	38	12	92
for sacrifice	—	—	—	1	—	1	5	—
for grazing	—	—	1	—	6	5	1,030	1
Chickens: for sale	—	9	7	—	—	178	6	—
Trade items:								
Salt (kg)	—	1,806	—	1,803	1,568	1,504	4,076	896
Paddy (kg)	244	488	790	1,878	2,148	8,578	2,579	—
Wheat (kg)	480	160	—	—	24	9,112	4,600	—
Barley (kg)	—	—	—	68	2,232	16,335	1,649	—
Maize (kg)	—	—	—	—	—	129	1,817	—
Millets (kg)	—	—	—	82	—	—	20	—
Other grains (kg)	—	23	113	—	303	319	33	49
Pulses and lentils (kg)	—	370	374	—	127	383	7	—
Potatoes (kg)	—	—	—	—	—	2,410	—	—
Misc. vegetables (kg)	—	—	—	18	—	—	—	—
Tobacco (kg)	10	—	84	14	189	86	90	—
Peanuts (kg)	—	—	—	—	—	354	592	—
Walnuts (kg)	—	—	—	—	36	38	57	—
Fruits (kg)	12	28	120	780	780	3,290	1,762	—
Peppers (kg)	22	36	10	86	539	233	794	10
Onions, garlic, and betelnut (kg)	74	91	2	189	218	55	77	—
Oil seeds (kg)	28	96	28	—	82	359	155	—
Purified butter (ghee) (kg)	25	390	239	—	55	24	53	—
Honey (kg)	—	225	72	17	850	454	1,002	—
Musk (number of glands)	4	183	—	—	120	197	762	—
Medicinal herbs (kg)	—	—	—	—	120	—	—	168
Natural dyes (kg)	—	—	—	—	17	—	—	—
Lime (kg)	—	—	—	—	—	—	14	—
Homemade paper (sheets by gross)	—	—	—	—	—	9	—	—
Raw wool (kg)	—	—	10	17	5	—	26	—
Woolen homespun garments	29	93	19	4	27	6	128	—
Cotton homespun garments	50	—	103	15	12	355	109	1
Woolen and cotton homespun cloth (meters)	5	2,302	—	—	3,076	190	3,504	—
Ready-made garments	—	14	—	—	—	—	234	—
Iron (kg)	—	—	—	—	—	—	—	—
Metal pots (kg)	—	—	—	—	13	—	—	—
Clay pots	—	—	87	—	—	—	—	—
Bamboo products	—	—	—	—	35	13	—	—
Hides	—	—	—	—	—	—	—	—
Leather or canvas shoes (pairs)	—	8	—	63	130	—	218	—
Tibetan boots (pairs)	—	—	—	—	24	40	42	—

Upper Mugu	Chaudhabisa/ Upper Tila	West Dolpo	East Dolpo	Jajarkot District	Sallyan District	Dang Valley	Dailekh District	Surkhet Valley	Nepalganj	Seti and Mahakali zones	Kathmandu	Elsewhere in Nepal	India	Totals
81	908	—	13	—	—	—	—	—	—	—	—	—	—	3,447
—	—	90	20	22	—	—	—	—	—	—	—	—	—	1,240
—	10	—	—	1	—	—	—	—	—	—	—	—	—	18
20	806	—	—	—	—	—	—	—	—	—	—	—	—	1,869
—	28	—	—	—	—	—	—	—	—	—	—	—	—	228
5,591	8,577	593	467	108	—	—	—	—	—	—	—	—	—	26,989
739	5,085	18	—	1,709	—	—	939	—	—	—	—	—	—	25,195
—	339	255	—	1,341	—	—	—	—	—	—	—	—	—	16,311
109	1,870	8	—	—	—	—	—	—	—	—	—	—	—	22,271
425	886	—	—	34	—	—	—	—	—	—	—	—	—	3,291
—	480	—	—	—	—	—	—	—	—	—	—	—	—	582
102	128	—	—	82	—	—	66	—	—	—	—	—	—	1,218
—	—	—	—	145	—	—	—	—	—	—	—	—	—	1,406
—	2,168	342	—	—	—	—	—	—	—	—	—	—	—	4,920
—	30	—	—	6	—	—	—	—	—	—	—	—	—	54
—	—	—	—	38	—	—	—	—	—	12	—	—	—	523
—	174	—	—	4,054	—	—	—	—	—	—	—	—	—	5,174
—	—	—	—	—	—	—	10	—	—	—	—	—	—	141
36	225	24	—	603	—	—	134	—	—	—	—	—	—	7,794
48	129	—	—	141	—	—	—	—	—	12	—	—	—	1,460
413	17	—	—	326	—	—	416	—	—	—	—	—	—	1,878
227	39	—	—	1,233	—	—	851	298	—	—	—	—	—	3,396
—	36	—	—	1,328	—	—	—	—	—	26	—	—	—	2,176
—	8	—	—	249	—	—	309	—	—	—	—	—	—	3,186
—	4	—	—	—	—	—	414	—	—	—	—	—	—	1,684
120	—	—	—	302	—	—	—	—	—	—	—	—	—	710
—	—	—	—	—	—	—	—	—	—	—	—	—	—	17
—	4,437	—	—	—	—	—	—	—	—	—	—	—	—	4,451
—	38	—	—	151	—	—	—	10	—	—	—	—	—	208
1,174	1,256	65	19	—	—	—	—	—	—	—	—	—	—	2,572
201	89	11	—	3	—	—	—	—	—	5	—	—	—	615
—	2	—	—	14	—	—	—	—	—	—	—	—	—	508
197	168	219	—	442	—	—	—	1,820	—	—	—	910	—	12,833
—	—	—	—	—	—	—	210	—	—	—	—	—	—	458
—	—	—	—	694	—	—	—	—	—	—	—	—	—	694
5	43	—	—	—	—	—	—	—	—	—	—	—	—	61
55	—	—	—	—	—	—	60	—	—	—	—	—	—	202
—	245	—	—	700	—	—	—	—	—	—	—	—	—	993
—	1	26	—	—	—	—	22	—	—	—	—	—	—	49
—	—	—	—	—	—	—	664	—	—	—	—	—	—	1,083
2	7	—	—	—	—	—	6	—	—	—	—	—	—	121

(TABLE 36 *continued*)

	Home region							
	Trans-Karnali	Lower Tila	Palanta Dara	Lower Humla-Mugu	Sinja Dara	Pansaya Dara	Asi Dara–Kalanga	Upper Humla
Matches and cigarettes (boxes)	—	21	—	—	15	322	495	21
Kerosene (liters)	—	3	455	—	165	139	90	—
Informants always dealing with the same person	1	—	1	—	8	51	16	—
Informants dealing with anyone	19	87	68	52	146	271	196	18
Value of goods exchanged:								
for cash (rupees)	6,995	218,333	51,213	18,873	57,766	84,484	104,087	18,749
for paddy (rupee value)	—	—	—	160	—	85	78	1,080
for wheat (rupee value)	—	—	—	—	—	—	6,924	—
for barley (rupee value)	—	—	—	—	320	—	320	—
for other grain (rupee value)	—	60	—	—	—	—	—	—
for salt (rupee value)	—	—	—	—	267	9,773	2,481	—
for raw wool (rupee value)	—	—	—	—	168	—	—	—
for ghee and curds (rupee value)	—	—	—	—	—	—	125	—
for medicinal herbs (rupee value)	—	—	—	—	—	—	—	—
Total value of goods exchanged	6,995	218,393	51,213	19,033	58,521	94,342	114,015	19,829

Upper Mugu	Chaudhabisa/Upper Tila	West Dolpo	East Dolpo	Jajarkot District	Sallyan District	Dang Valley	Dailekh District	Surkhet Valley	Nepalganj	Seti and Mahakali zones	Kathmandu	Elsewhere in Nepal	India	Totals
—	38	—	28	100	—	—	1,424	—	—	—	—	—	—	2,464
—	34	—	—	—	—	—	281	—	—	—	—	—	—	1,167
—	2	4	—	21	—	—	4	1	—	1	—	—	—	110
135	194	14	9	238	1	—	42	2	1	2	1	1	—	1,497
30,410	49,434	14,569	7,124	92,585	500	—	48,050	9,410	—	1,368	—	6,000	—	819,950
4,786	23,023	186	960	—	—	—	—	—	—	—	—	—	—	30,358
131	—	104	—	—	—	—	—	—	—	—	—	—	—	7,158
—	—	—	—	—	—	—	—	—	—	—	—	—	—	640
—	—	—	—	—	—	—	—	—	—	—	—	—	—	60
—	51	—	—	—	—	—	—	—	—	—	—	—	—	12,572
—	—	—	—	—	—	—	—	—	—	—	—	—	—	168
—	—	—	—	—	—	—	—	—	—	—	—	—	—	125
—	—	—	—	9,040	—	—	—	—	—	—	—	—	—	9,040
35,327	82,508	14,859	8,084	101,625	500	—	48,050	9,410	—	1,368	—	6,000	—	880,072

Appendix I
Reorganization of Karnali Zone Administration, 1970 Onward

On April 5, 1970, the Ministry of Home and Panchayat expanded the number of panchayats in Tibrikot District from five to seventeen,[1] bringing the total number of panchayats in Karnali Zone to 106. Increase in population did not warrant this change. Instead it was an attempt by Kathmandu both to give the people of Tibrikot greater representation at the district panchayat level and to bring that district into better balance with the other districts of the zone.

On December 12, 1975, the Ministry of Home announced a number of changes in Nepal's zonal and district boundaries (Nepal 1975, *Nepal Gazette*). Karnali Zone was affected as follows:

1. Three panchayats along the north bank to the Mugu Karnali River in southern Humla District (i.e., old Soru Dara) were transferred to Mugu District (old Mugu, Karana, Gama, and Khatyad *dara*s). However, the panchayats of old Galpha Dara, the other southern area of Humla District, were not transferred.

2. The western part of Jumla District (i.e., the twenty-seven panchayats that constituted old Sanni, Raskot, Kalikot, Barabisa, Rakala, and Palanta *dara*s) became a separate district called Kalikot.

3. Tibrikot District (i.e., old Chaudhabisa Dara) was incorporated in what remained of Jumla District (i.e., old Sinja, Pansaya, and Asi *dara*s).

---

[1] Interview with the Zonal Commissioner on May 1, 1970.

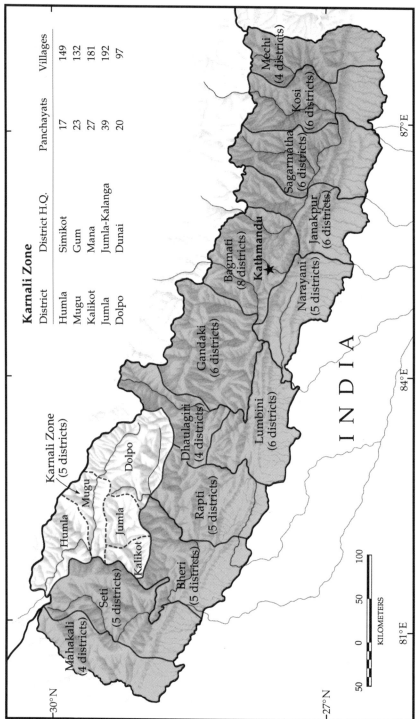

Karnali Zone			
District	District H.Q.	Panchayats	Villages
Humla	Simikot	17	149
Mugu	Gum	23	132
Kalikot	Mana	27	181
Jumla	Jumla-Kalanga	39	192
Dolpo	Dunai	20	97

Fig. 101. Map of the fourteen administrative zones of Nepal after 1975

4. Dolpo District (which included old Tibrikot Dara) was removed from Dhaulagiri Zone and included in Karnali Zone as its fifth district.

These moves (see map) were an attempt to better reflect the socio-economic and environmental realities of the region. It is significant that with the addition of Dolpo, Karnali Zone assumed the size and extent of the Kalyal kingdom of Jumla during the Baisi-Chaubisi period (ca. the fifteenth to eighteenth centuries).

Bibliography

Amatya, Soorya Lal. 1975. *Cash Crop Farming in Nepal*. Kathmandu: Tribhuvan University Press.

Andress, Joel M. 1966."Culture and Habitat in the Central Himalayas." Ph.D. diss., University of California, Berkeley.

Asimov, Isaac. 1977. "Salt of the Earth." *International Wildlife* 7 (2): 30-36.

Atkinson, Edwin T. 1882-86. *The Himalayan Districts of the North-Western Provinces of India*. Vols. 1-3 (comprising vols. 10-12 of the *Gazetteer of the North-Western Provinces and Oudh*). Allahabad: North-Western Provinces and Oudh Press.

Atlas Narodov Mira. 1964. Moscow: Academy of Sciences.

Bailey, F. G. 1957. *Caste and the Economic Frontier*. Manchester: Manchester University Press.

Barth, Fredrik. 1956. "Ecologic Relationships of Ethnic Groups in Swat, North Pakistan." *American Anthropologist* 58: 1079-89.

_____. 1969. *Ethnic Groups and Boundaries*. Boston: Little, Brown and Co.

Basham, A. L. 1963. *The Wonder That Was India*. New and rev. ed. New York: Hawthorn Books.

Bennett, John W. 1976. *The Ecological Transition: Cultural Anthropology and Human Adaptation*. Oxford: Pergamon Press.

Bennett, Lynn. 1977. "Mother's Milk and Mother's Blood: The Social and Symbolic Roles of Women among Brahmans and Chhetris in Nepal." Ph.D. diss., Columbia University.

_____. 1978. "*Maiti-ghar*: The Dual Role of High Caste Women in Nepal." In *Himalayan Anthropology: The Indo-Tibetan Interface*, edited by James F. Fisher, 121-40. The Hague: Mouton.

Berreman, Gerald D. 1960. "Cultural Variability and Drift in the Himalayan Hills." *American Anthropologist* 62: 774-94.

_____. 1972. *Hindus of the Himalayas: Ethnography and Change.* 2d ed., rev. and enl. Berkeley: University of California Press.

_____. 1978. "Scale and Social Relations." *Current Anthropology* 19 (2): 225-45.

Bhatt, D. D. 1970. *Natural History and Economic Botany of Nepal.* Kathmandu: Department of Information, Ministry of Information and Broadcasting, His Majesty's Government of Nepal.

Bishop, Barry C. 1962. "Wintering on Top of the World." *National Geographic* 122: 503-47.

_____. 1963. "How We Climbed Everest." *National Geographic* 124: 477-507.

Bishop, Barry C., with K. Angström, J. Drummond, and J. Roche. 1966. "Solar Radiation Measurements in the High Himalaya (Everest Region)." *Journal of Applied Meteorology* 5 (1): 94-104.

Bishop, Lila, and Barry C. Bishop. 1971. "Karnali: Roadless World of Western Nepal." *National Geographic* 140: 656-89.

Bista, Dor Bahadur. 1972. *People of Nepal.* 2d ed. Kathmandu: Ratna Pustak Bhandar.

Bobek, Hans. 1962. "The Main Stages in Socio-Economic Evolution from a Geographical Point of View." In *Readings in Cultural Geography,* edited by Philip L. Wagner and Marvin W. Mikesell, 218-47.

Borgström, Georg. 1973. *The Food and People Dilemma.* Belmont, Calif.: Duxbury Press.

Brar, Bharpur S. 1971. "Social Change and Marriage Patterns in the North-Western Himalayas." Ph.D. diss., University of London.

Brookfield, H. C. 1962. "Local Study and Comparative Method: An Example from Central New Guinea." *Annals, Association of American Geographers* 52 (3) 242-54.

Bunting, Brian T. 1965. *The Geography of Soil.* Chicago: Aldine.

Cadgil, D. R. 1964. *Women in the Working Force in India.* Bombay: Asia Publishing House.

Campbell, Gabriel. 1978. "Consultation with Himalayan Gods: Oracular Religion and Alternative Values in Jumla." Ph.D. diss., Columbia University.

Caplan, A. Patricia. 1972. *Priests and Cobblers.* San Francisco: Chandler.

Caplan, Lionel. 1970. *Land and Social Change in East Nepal.* London: Routledge and Kegan Paul.

Carrasco, Pedro. 1959. *Land and Polity in Tibet.* Seattle: University of Washington Press.

Center for Economic Development and Administration (CEDA). 1975. *Regional Development Study (Nepal).* Pt. 2a, "Far Western Development Region"; and 2b, "Rural Development Package Programme Dailekh." Kathmandu: Tribhuvan University.

Centre National de la Recherche Scientifique (CNRS). 1977. *Himalaya: Sciences de la Terre* and *Himalaya: Ecologie-Ethnologie.* Colloques Internationaux, Sèvres-Paris, Dec. 7-10, 1976. 2 vols. Paris: Centre National de la Recherche Scientifique.

Champion, H. G. 1936. *Indian Forest Records.* Vol. 1, no. 1. Delhi: Manager of Publications.

Chang, Jen-Hu. 1967. "The Indian Summer Monsoon." *Geographical Review* 57 (3): 373-96.

Chapagain, Devendra P. 1976. "Agricultural Productivity Pattern in Nepal." Master's thesis, University of the Philippines at Los Baños.

Chaudhary, Roop Lal. 1961. *Hindu Woman's Right to Property: Past and Present.* Calcutta: Temple Press.

Chayanov, A. V. 1966. *The Theory of Peasant Economy.* Homewood, Ill.: Richard D. Irwin.

Clark, Colin, and Margaret Haswell. 1970. *The Economics of Subsistence Agriculture.* London: Macmillan.

Cohn, Bernard S. 1971. *India: The Social Anthropology of a Civilization.* Englewood Cliffs, N.J.: Prentice-Hall.

Cool, John C. 1967. "The Far Western Hills: Some Longer Term Considerations." Kathmandu. (Mimeographed.)

Cormack, Margaret. 1953. *The Hindu Woman.* New York: Bureau of Publications, Teachers College, Columbia University.

Coulborn, Rushton, ed. 1956. *Feudalism in History.* Hamden, Conn.: Archon Books.

Dansereau, Pierre. 1966. "Ecological Impact and Human Ecology." In *Future Environments of North America,* edited by F. Fraser Darling and John P. Milton. Garden City, N.Y.: Natural History Press.

Das, P. K. 1972. *The Monsoons.* New York: St. Martin's Press.

Davis, Kingsley. 1951. *Population of India and Pakistan.* Princeton: Princeton University Press.

de Reuck, A., and J. Knight, eds. 1967. *Caste and Race: Comparative Approaches.* London: Churchill.

Dobremez, J. F. 1976. "Exploitation and Prospects of Medicinal Plants in Eastern Nepal." In *Mountain Environment and Development,* edited by S. P. Mauch. Kathmandu: Swiss Association for Technical Assistance in Nepal (SATA), Tribhuvan University Press.

Donner, Wolf von. 1972. *Nepal: Raum, Mensch und Wirtschaft.* Wiesbaden: Otto Harrassowitz.

Dumont, Louis. 1970. *Homo Hierarchicus: The Caste System and Its Implications.* Translated by Willard Sainsbury. Chicago: University of Chicago Press.

Eckholm, Erik P. 1976. *Losing Ground: Environmental Stress and World Food Prospects.* New York: W. W. Norton.

Energy Research and Development Group. 1976. *Nepal: The Energy Sector.* Kathmandu: Institute of Science, Tribhuvan University.

Field, A. R. 1959. "Himalayan Salt: A Political Barometer." *Modern Review* 105 (6): 460-65.

Fisher, James F. 1972. "Trans-Himalayan Traders: Economy, Society, and Culture in Northwest Nepal." Ph.D. diss., University of Chicago.

————. 1975. "Cannabis in Nepal: An Overview." In *Cannabis and Culture,* edited by Vera Rubin, 247-55. The Hague: Mouton Publishers.

Fisher, James F., ed. 1978. *Himalayan Anthropology: The Indo-Tibetan Interface.* The Hague: Mouton Publishers.

Fleming, Robert L., Sr., Robert L. Fleming, Jr., and Lain Singh Bangdel. 1976. *Birds of Nepal.* Kathmandu: Robert L. Fleming.

Flohn, Hermann. 1969. *Climate and Weather.* New York: McGraw-Hill.

Fürer-Haimendorf, Christoph von. 1964. *The Sherpas of Nepal.* Berkeley: University of California Press.

————. 1971. "Status and Interaction among the High Hindu Castes of Nepal." *Eastern Anthropologist* 24: 7-24.

————. 1975. *Himalayan Traders.* London: John Murray.

————., ed. 1966. *Caste and Kin in Nepal, India and Ceylon.* London: Asia Publishing House.

Gaborieau, Marc. 1969. "Note Preliminaire sur le Dieu Masta." *Objets et Mondes* 9 (1): 19-50.

Goetz, Hermann. 1955. *The Early Wooden Temples of Chamba.* Leiden: E. J. Brill.

Goldstein, Melvyn C. 1975. "A Report on Limi Panchayat, Humla District, Karnali Zone." *Contributions to Nepalese Studies* 2 (2): 89-101.

————. 1976. Review of *Himalayan Traders*, by Christoph von Fürer-Haimendorf. *American Anthropologist* 78 (4): 921.

Goldstein, Melvyn C., and Donald C. Messerschmidt. 1980. "The Significance of Latitudinality in Himalayan Mountain Ecosystems." *Human Ecology* 8 (2): 117-34.

Grierson, George A. [1916] 1968. *Linguistic Survey of India*. Vol. 9, pt. 4. Reprint. Delhi: Motilal Banarsidass.

Grigg, David. 1970. *The Harsh Lands: A Study in Agricultural Development*. London: Macmillan.

Grist, D. H. 1965. *Rice*. 4th ed. London: Longmans, Green and Co.

Gurung, Harka Bahadur. 1966. "Pokhara Valley, Nepal Himalaya: A Field Study in Regional Geography." Ph.D. diss., University of Edinburgh.

Hagen, Toni. 1961. *Nepal*. New Delhi: Oxford and IBH Publishing Co.

————. 1969. *Report on the Geological Survey of Nepal*. Vol. 1, *Preliminary Reconnaissance*. Zurich: Swiss Academy for Natural Sciences.

Halley, Edmund. 1686. "An Historical Account of the Trade-Winds and Monsoons, With an Attempt to Assign the Physical Cause of Said Winds." *Philo. Trans. Royal Soc. of London* 26: 153-68.

Halperin, Rhoda, and James Dow, eds. 1977. *Peasant Livelihood: Studies in Economic Anthropology and Cultural Ecology*. New York: St. Martin's Press.

Hamilton, Francis Buchanan. [1819] 1971. *An Account of the Kingdom of Nepal, and of the Territories Annexed to This Dominion by the House of Gorkha*. Reprint edition, series 1, vol. 10. New Delhi: Manjusri Publishing House.

Hamilton, M. G. 1976. "The South Asian Summer Monsoon." In *Progress in Geography*, vol. 9, edited by Christopher Board, Richard J. Chorley, Peter Haggett, and David R. Stoddart, 147-203. New York: St. Martin's Press.

Harris, Marvin. 1966. "The Cultural Ecology of India's Sacred Cattle." *Current Anthropology* 7: 51-66.

Hitchcock, John T. 1966. *The Magars of Banyan Hill*. New York: Holt, Rinehart and Winston.

————. 1978. "An Additional Perspective on the Nepalese Caste System." In *Himalayan Anthropology: The Indo-Tibetan Interface*, edited by James F. Fisher, 111-20. The Hague: Mouton Publishers.

Hoffpauir, Robert. 1974. "India's Other Bovine: A Cultural Geography of the Water Buffalo." Ph.D. diss., University of Wisconsin.

Holdridge, L. R. 1967. *Life Zone Ecology*. Rev. ed. San Jose, Costa Rica: Tropical Science Center.

Humboldt, Alexander von. 1817. *De Distributione Geographica Plantarum Secundum Coeli Temperiem et Altitudinem Montium*. Paris: Prolegomena.

Hutchinson, J., ed. 1974. *Evolutionary Studies in World Crops*. London: Cambridge University Press.

Hutton, J. H. 1963. *Caste in India*. 4th ed. Bombay: Oxford University Press.

Jackson, David P. 1976. "The Early History of Lo (Mustang) and Ngari." *Contributions to Nepalese Studies* 4 (1): 39-56.

————. 1978. "Notes on the History of Serib, and Nearby Places in the Upper Kali Gandaki." *Kailash* 6 (3): 195-227.

Jackson, Rodney. 1979. "Aboriginal Hunting in West Nepal with Reference to Musk Deer *Moscus moschiferus* and Snow Leopard *Pantera uncia*." *Biological Conservation* 16 (1): 63-72.

Jenny, Hans, and S. P. Raychaudhuri. 1960. *The Effects of Climate and Cultivation on Nitrogen and Organic Matter Reserves in Indian Soils.* New Delhi: Indian Council of Agricultural Research.

Jest, Corneille. 1974. *Tarap: Une Vallée dans l'Himalaya.* : Editions du Sevil.

_____. 1978. "Tibetan Communities of the High Valleys of Nepal: Life in an Exceptional Environment and Economy." In *Himalayan Anthropology: The Indo-Tibetan Interface,* edited by James F. Fisher, 360-64. The Hague: Mouton.

Joshi, Bhuwan L., and Leo E. Rose. 1966. *Democratic Innovations in Nepal.* Berkeley: University of California Press.

Karan, Pradyumna, with William M. Jenkins. 1960. *Nepal: A Cultural and Physical Geography.* Lexington: University of Kentucky Press.

Karan, P. P., and W. M. Jenkins, Jr. 1961. "Population, Land Utilisation and Possible Expansion of Cultivated Area in Nepal." *Pacific Viewpoint* 2: 41-58.

Kolenda, P. M. 1963. "Toward a Model of the Hindu *Jajmani* System." *Human Organization* 22 (1): 11-31.

Kumar, Satish. 1967. *Rana Polity in Nepal.* Bombay: Asia Publishing House.

Kurup, C. G. Raghava, ed. 1967. *Handbook of Animal Husbandry.* New Delhi: Indian Council of Agricultural Research.

Landon, Perceval. [1928] 1976. *Nepal.* Reprint edition, series 1, vol. 16, *Bibliotheca Himalayica.* Kathmandu: Ratna Pustak Bhandar.

Lattimore, Owen. 1962. *Studies in Frontier History: Collected Papers 1928-1958.* London: Oxford University Press.

Leach, E. R., ed. 1960. *Aspects of Caste in South India, Ceylon, and North-West Pakistan.* Cambridge: Cambridge University Press.

Levi, Sylvain. 1905-8. *Le Nepal: Etude Historique d'un Royaume Hindus.* 3 vols. Paris: Ernest Leroux.

McDougal, Charles. 1968. "Village and Household Economy in Far Western Nepal." Kirtipur, Nepal: Tribhuvan University.

McFarlane, Alan. 1976. *Resources and Population: A Study of the Gurungs of Nepal.* Cambridge: Cambridge University Press.

Majumdar, D. N. 1962. *Himalayan Polyandry.* Bombay: Asia Publishing House.

Majumdar, R. C., ed. 1971. *The History and Culture of the Indian Peoples.* Vol. 2. Bombay: Bharatiya Vidya Bhavan.

Mandal, Itihas Prakash. [V.S. 2012-13] 1955-56. *Itihas Prakash* [*Light on History*]. 4 vols. Kathmandu: The Mandal.

Mani, M. S., ed. 1974. *Ecology and Biogeography in India.* The Hague: Dr. W. Junk.

Manzardo, Andrew E. 1977. "Ecological Constraints on Trans-Himalayan Trade in Nepal." *Contributions to Nepalese Studies* 4 (2).

Manzardo, Andrew E., Dilli Ram Dahal, and Navin Kumar Rai. 1976. "The Byanshi: An Ethnographic Note on a Trading Group in Far Western Nepal." *Contributions to Nepalese Studies* 3 (2): 84-118.

Margalef, Ramón. 1968. *Perspectives in Ecological Theory.* Chicago: University of Chicago Press.

_____. 1969. "On Certain Unifying Principles in Ecology." In *Contemporary Readings in Ecology,* edited by A. S. Boughey, 374-90. Belmont, Calif.: Dickenson.

Marriott, McKim. 1960. *Caste Ranking and Community Structure in Five Regions of India and Pakistan.* Poona: Deccan College Postgraduate and Research Institute.

Mason, Kenneth. 1955. *Abode of Snow*. London: Rupert Hart-Davis.

Mauch, S. P. 1976. "The Energy Situation in the Hills: Imperative for Development Strategies." In *Mountain Environment and Development*, 123-47. Kathmandu: Swiss Association for Technical Assistance in Nepal (SATA), Tribhuvan University Press.

Mihaly, Eugene Bramer. 1965. *Foreign Aid and Politics in Nepal*. London: Oxford University Press.

Myrdal, Gunnar. 1968. *Asian Drama: An Inquiry into the Poverty of Nations*. 3 vols. Harmondsworth, Middlesex: Penguin Books.

Naraharinath, Yogi, ed. [V.S. 2022] 1966. *Itihas Prakashma Sandhipatra Sangraha* [A Collection of Treaties in *Light on History*]. Vol. 1. Kathmandu: The Editor.

Nash, Manning. 1966. *Primitive and Peasant Economic Systems*. San Francisco: Chandler Publishing Co.

Nepal, His Majesty's Government. 1958. *Census of Population 1952/54 A.D.* Kathmandu: Department of Statistics.

―――――. 1964. *Lands Act and Rules*. Kathmandu: Ministry of Law and Justice.

―――――. 1970. *Medicinal Plants of Nepal*. Bulletin no. 3. Department of Medical Plants, Ministry of Forests.

―――――. 1972. *Agricultural Statistics of Nepal*. Kathmandu: Ministry of Food and Agriculture, Economic Analysis and Planning Division.

―――――. 1975. *Statistical Pocket Book: Nepal*. Kathmandu: Central Bureau of Statistics.

―――――. 1975. *Population Census 1971: General Characteristic Tables*. Kathmandu: Central Bureau of Statistics.

―――――. 1975. *Nepal Gazette*, vol. 25, sect. 3, Dec. 12.

Nepal, His Majesty's Government, and Nippon Koei Co. 1970. *Master Plan for Power Developmet and Supply*. Kathmandu.

Nitzberg, Frances L. 1970. "Land, Labor, and Status: The Social Implications of Ecologic Adaptation in a Region of the Western Himalayas of India." Ph.D. diss., Harvard University.

―――――. 1972. "The Pahari Culture Area Reconsidered." Paper presented at the Seventy-first Annual Meeting of the American Anthropological Association, Toronto, Canada (Nov.)

―――――. 1978. "Changing Patterns of Multiethnic Interaction in the Western Himalayas." In *Himalayan Anthropology: The Indo-Tibetan Interface,* edited by James F. Fisher, 103-10. The Hague: Mouton Publishers.

Ohta, Yoshihide, and Chikara Akiba, eds. 1973. *Geology of the Nepal Himalayas*. Tokyo: Saikon Publishing Co.

Okada, Ferdinand S. 1957. "Ritual Brotherhood: A Cohesive Factor in Nepalese Society." *Southwestern Journal of Anthropology* 13 (3): 212-22.

Osmaston, A. E. 1927. *A Forest Flora for Kumaon*. Allahabad.

Palmieri, Richard Pietro. 1976. "Domestication and Exploitation of Livestock in the Nepal Himalaya and Tibet: An Ecological, Functional, and Culture Historical Study of Yak and Yak Hybrids in Society, Economy, and Culture." Ph.D. diss., University of California at Davis.

Pant, S. D. 1935. *The Social Economy of the Himalayans Based on a Survey in the Kumaon Himalayas*. London: George Allen and Unwin.

Pédelaborde, Pierre. 1963. *The Monsoon*. Translated by M. J. Clegg. London: Methuen and Co.

Prater, S. H. 1971. *The Book of Indian Animals.* 3d rev. ed. Bombay Natural History Society. Bombay: Leaders Press.

Purseglove, J. W. 1968. *Tropical Crops.* Vol. 2. London: Longmans.

Rahul, Ram. 1970. *The Himalaya Borderland.* Delhi: Vikas Publications.

Rajan, S. V. G., and H. G. G. Rao. 1971. *Soil and Crop Productivity.* New York: Asia Publishing House.

Rana, Pudma Jung Bahadur. [1909] 1974. *Life of Maharaja Sir Jung Bahadur of Nepal.* Reprint. Kathmandu: Ratna Pustak Bhandar.

Rana, Ratna S. 1971. *An Economic Study of the Area around the Alignment of the Dhanagadi-Dandedhura Road, Nepal.* CEDA Study Series no. 1. Kathmandu: Centre for Economic Development and Administration.

Redford, Robert. 1956. *Peasant Society and Culture.* Chicago: University of Chicago Press.

Reed, Horace B., and Mary Jane Reed. 1968. *Nepal in Transition: Educational Innovation.* Pittsburgh: University of Pittsburgh Press.

Regmi, Dilli Raman. 1958. *A Century of Family Autocracy in Nepal.* 2d ed. Nepal: Nepali National Congress.

_____. 1961. *Modern Nepal: Rise and Growth in the Eighteenth Century.* Calcutta: Firma K. L. Mukhopadhyay.

_____. 1965. *Medieval Nepal.* Pts. 1-4. Calcutta: Firma K. L. Mukhopadhyay.

_____. 1969. *Ancient Nepal.* 3d ed. Calcutta: Firma K. L. Mukhopadhyay.

Regmi, Mahesh C. 1963-68. *Land Tenure and Taxation in Nepal.* 4 vols. Berkeley: University of California Press.

_____. 1969. "Ban on Cow Slaughter." *Regmi Research Series* 1 (1): 15-19. (Mimeographed.)

_____. 1971. *A Study in Nepali Economic History, 1768-1846.* New Delhi: Manjusri Publishing House.

_____. 1976. *Landownership in Nepal.* Berkeley: University of California Press.

Rieger, H. C. 1977. "Deforestation in the Himalayas as a Social Problem." In *Himalaya: Ecologie-Ethnologie,* 539-47. Paris: Centre National de la Recherche Scientifique.

Rose, Leo E. 1971. *Nepal: Strategy for Survival.* Berkeley: University of California Press.

Rose, Leo E., and Margaret W. Fisher. 1970. *The Politics of Nepal.* Ithaca, N.Y.: Cornell University Press.

Rubin, Vera, ed. 1975. *Cannabis and Culture.* The Hague: Mouton.

Sahlins, Marshall D. 1968. *Tribesmen.* Englewood Cliffs, N.J.: Prentice-Hall.

Sandberg, Samuel Louis Graham. [1904] 1973. *The Exploration of Tibet: Its History and Particulars, 1623-1904.* Reprint. Delhi: Cosmos Publications.

Sanwal, Rami D. 1976. *Social Stratification in Rural Kumaon.* Oxford University Press.

Schroeder, Mark C. W., and Daniel G. Sisler. 1970. *The Impact of the Sonauli-Pokhara Highway on the Regional Income and Agricultural Production of Pokhara Valley, Nepal.* Occasional Paper no. 32, Cornell University, Department of Agricultural Economics.

Schwartzberg, Joseph E., ed. 1978. *A Historical Atlas of South Asia.* Chicago: University of Chicago Press.

Schweinfurth, Ulrich. 1957. "Die Horizontale und Vertikale Verbreitung der Vegetation im Himalaya." *Bonner Geographische Abhandlungen,* no. 20.

Shanin, Teodor. 1971. *Peasants and Peasant Societies.* Baltimore: Penguin Books.

Sharma, Prayag Raj. 1971. "The Matawali Chhetris of Western Nepal." *Himalayan Review* 4: 43-60.

———. 1972. "Preliminary Study of the Art and Architecture of the Karnali Basin, West Nepal." *Recherche Cooperative sur Programme 253 CNRS, Recherches sur l'Ecologie et la Geologie de l'Himalaya Central.* Paris: Centre National de la Recherche Scientifique.

Shrestha, Bhim Prasad, ed. [V.S. 2028] 1971. *Karnali Prades* [*Karnali Zone: One Piece of Study*]. Kathmandu: Association of Social Studies.

Shrestha, Tirtha Bahadur. 1977. "Le Nord: Quest du Nepal (Region Jumla-Saipal)." Recherches Ecologiques, Biogeographiques et Cartographiques. Ph.D. thèse, Université Scientifique et Medicale de Grenoble.

Singh, Jasbir. 1974. *An Agricultural Atlas of India: A Geographical Analysis.* Haryana, India: Vishal Publications.

Slusser, Mary. 1982. *Nepal Mandala: A Cultural History of the Kathmandu Valley.* 2 vols. Princeton: Princeton University Press.

Smith, Vincent A. 1923. *The Oxford History of India.* 2d ed. Revised by S. M. Edwardes. Oxford: Clarendon Press.

Snellgrove, D. L. 1961. *Himalayan Pilgrimage.* Oxford: Bruno Cassirer.

Snellgrove, David, and Hugh Richardson. 1968. *A Cultural History of Tibet.* Worcester: Trinity Press.

Sorre, Maximilien. 1961. *L'Homme sur la Terre.* Paris: Librairie Hachette.

Spate, O. H. K., and A. T. A. Learmonth. 1967. *India and Pakistan: A General and Regional Geography.* 3d ed. London: Methuen and Co.

Spencer, J. E., and G. A. Hale. 1961. "The Origin, Nature, and Distribution of Agricultural Terracing." *Pacific Viewpoint* 2 (1): 1-40.

Srinivas, M. N. 1962. *Caste in Modern India.* Bombay: Asia Publishing House.

———. 1967. "The Cohesive Role of Sanskritization." In *India and Ceylon: Unity and Diversity,* edited by Philip Mason, 67-82. London: Oxford University Press.

Srivastava, Ram P. 1966. "Tribe-Caste Mobility in India and the Case of Kumaon Bhotias." In *Caste and Kin in Nepal, India and Ceylon,* edited by Christoph von Fürer-Haimendorf, 161-212. London: Asia Publishing House.

Srivastava, S. K. 1958. *The Tharus: A Study in Cultural Dynamics.* Agra: Agra University Press.

Stainton, J. D. A. 1972. *Forests of Nepal.* London: John Murray.

Staszewski, J. 1957. *Vertical Distribution of World Population.* Warsaw: State Scientific Publishing House.

Stein, R. A. 1972. *Tibetan Civilization.* Translated by J. E. Stapleton Driver. Stanford: Stanford University Press.

Steward, Julian. 1963. *Theory of Culture Change.* 4th ed. Urbana: University of Illinois Press.

Stiller, Ludwig F. 1975. *The Rise of the House of Gorkha.* Kathmandu: Ratna Pustak Bhandar.

———. 1976. *The Silent Cry.* Kathmandu: Sahayogi Prakashan.

Stutley, Margaret, and James Stutley, eds. 1977. *Harper's Dictionary of Hinduism.* New York: Harper and Row.

Swiss Association for Technical Assistance in Nepal (SATA). 1976. *Mountain Environment and Development.* Kathmandu: Tribhuvan University Press.

Tabuchi, Hiroshi, and Kazuko Urushibara. 1971. "Climatic Change in the Quaternary in Asia: A Review." In *Water Balance in Monsoon Asia*, edited by M. M. Yoshino, 241-56. Honolulu: University of Hawaii Press.

Tamhane, R. V.; D. P. Motiramani; Y. P. Bali; and Roy L. Donahue. 1964. *Soils: Their Chemistry and Fertility in Tropical Asia*. New Delhi: Prentice Hall of India (Private).

Thomas, William L., ed. 1956. *Man's Role in Changing the Face of the Earth*. Chicago: University of Chicago Press.

Thorner, Daniel. 1956. "Feudalism in India." In *Feudalism in History*, edited by Rushton Coulborn, 133-50. Hamden, Conn.: Archon Books.

Thornthwaite, C. W. 1948. "An Approach toward a Rational Classification of Climate," *Geographical Review* 38: 55-94.

Thornthwaite, C. W., and J. R. Mather. 1955. "The Water Balance." In *Publications in Climatology* 8 (1). Centerton, N.J.: Drexel Institute.

————. 1957. "Instructions and Tables for Computing Potential Evapotranspiration and the Water Balance." In *Publications in Climatology* 9 (3). Centerton, N.J.: Drexel Institute.

Tod, James. 1914. *Annals and Antiquities of Rajasthan*. 2d ed., unabridged. 2 vols. London: George Routledge and Sons.

Traill, George W. 1828. "Statistical Sketch of Kamaon." *Asiatic Researches* 16: 137-234.

Troll, Carl. 1959. "Die tropischen Gebirge: Ihre dreidimensionale Klimatische und pflanzengeographische Zonierung." *Bonner Geographische Abhandlungen*, no. 25.

————. 1967. "Die klimatische und vegetations-geographische Gliederung des Himalaya-Sytems." In *Khumbu Himal*, edited by Walter Hellmich, 353-88. Berlin-Heidelberg: Springer-Verlag.

————. 1972. "The Three-Dimensional Zonation of the Himalayan System." In *Geoecology of the High Mountain Regions of Eurasia*, edited by Carl Troll, 264-75. Wiesbaden: Franz Steiner Verlag GMBH.

Tucci, Giuseppe. 1956. "Preliminary Report on Two Scientific Expeditions in Nepal." Rome: Instituto Italiano per il Medio ed Estremo Oriente.

————. 1962. *Nepal: The Discovery of the Malla*. New York: E. P. Dutton.

Tuladhar, Jayanti M., B. B. Gubhaju, and John Stoeckel. 1977. *The Population of Nepal: Structure and Change*. Research Monograph Series. Berkeley: University of California.

Turner, Ralph Lilley. [1931] 1965. *A Comparative and Etymological Dictionary of the Nepali Language*. Reprint, with corrections. London: Routledge and Kegan Paul.

Uhlig, Harald. 1969. "Hill Tribes and Rice Farmers in the Himalayas and Southeast Asia." *Transactions and Papers*, Institute of British Geographers, no. 47, pp. 1-23.

————. 1973. "Der Reisbau im Himalaya." In *Vergleichende Kulturgeographie der Hochgebirge des Sudlichen Asien*, vol. 5, edited by Carl Rathjens, Carl Troll, and Harald Uhlig, 77-104. Wiesbaden: Franz Steiner Verlag.

————. 1976. "Bergbauern und Hirten im Himalaya: Hohenschichtung und Staffelsysteme: Ein Beitrag zur Vergleichenden Kulturgeographie der Hochgebirge." In *40. Deutscher Geographentag Innsbruck, 1975*, 549-86. Wiesbaden: Franz Steiner Verlag.

————. 1978. "Geoecological Controls on High-Altitude Rice Cultivation in the Himalayas and Mountain Regions of Southeast Asia." *Arctic and Alpine Research* 10 (2).

United Nations. 1975. *Demographic Yearbook*. New York: United Nations.

Warriner, Doreen. 1969. *Land Reform in Principle and Practice*. Oxford: Clarendon Press.

Winich, Charles. 1956. *Dictionary of Anthropology*. New York: Philosophical Library.

Wiser, William and Charlotte Wiser. 1963. *Behind Mud Walls: 1930-1960*. Los Angeles: University of California Press.

Wolf, Eric R. 1966. *Peasants*. Englewood Cliffs, N.J.: Prentice-Hall.

Worth, Robert M., and Narayana K. Shah. 1969. *Nepal Health Survey, 1965-1966*. Honolulu: University of Hawaii Press.

Wright, Daniel, ed. 1877. *History of Nepal: Translated from the Parbatiya*. Cambridge: Cambridge University Press.

Yoshino, Masatoshi M., ed. 1971. *Water Balance of Monsoon Asia*. Honolulu: University of Hawaii Press.

Index

THE UNIVERSITY OF CHICAGO
GEOGRAPHY RESEARCH PAPERS
(Lithographed, 6 x 9 inches)

Titles in Print

127. GOHEEN, PETER G. *Victorian Toronto, 1850 to 1900: Pattern and Process of Growth.* 1970. xiii + 278 p.

130. GLADFELTER, BRUCE G. *Meseta and Campina Landforms in Central Spain: A Geomorphology of the Alto Henares Basin.* 1971. xii + 204 p.

131. NEILS, ELAINE M. *Reservation to City: Indian Migration and Federal Relocation.* 1971. x + 198 p.

132. MOLINE, NORMAN T. *Mobility and the Small Town, 1900-1930.* 1971. ix + 169 p.

133. SCHWIND, PAUL J. *Migration and Regional Development in the United States, 1950-1960.* 1971. x + 170 p.

134. PYLE, GERALD F. *Heart Disease, Cancer and Stroke in Chicago: A Geographical Analysis with Facilities, Plans for 1980.* 1971. ix + 292 p.

136. BUTZER, KARL W. *Recent History of an Ethiopian Delta: The Omo River and the Level of Lake Rudolf.* 1971. xvi + 184 p.

139. McMANIS, DOUGLAS R. *European Impressions of the New England Coast, 1497-1620.* 1972. viii + 147 p.

140. COHEN, YEHOSHUA S. *Diffusion of an Innovation in an Urban System: The Spread of Planned Regional Shopping Centers in the United States, 1949-1968.* 1972. ix + 136 p.

141. MITCHELL, NORA. *The Indian Hill-Station: Kodaikanal.* 1972. xii + 199 p.

142. PLATT, RUTHERFORD H. *The Open Space Decision Process: Spatial Allocation of Costs and Benefits.* 1972. xi + 189 p.

143. GOLANT, STEPHEN M. *The Residential Location and Spatial Behavior of the Elderly: A Canadian Example.* 1972. xv + 226 p.

144. PANNELL, CLIFTON W. *T'ai-Chung, T'ai-wan: Structure and Function.* 1973. xii + 200 p.

145. LANKFORD, PHILIP M. *Regional Incomes in the United States, 1929-1967: Level, Distribution, Stability, and Growth.* 1972. x + 137 p.

146. FREEMAN, DONALD B. *International Trade, Migration, and Capital Flows: A Quantitative Analysis of Spatial Economic Interaction.* 1973. xiv + 201 p.

147. MYERS, SARAH K. *Language Shift among Migrants to Lima, Peru.* 1973. xiii + 203 p.

148. JOHNSON, DOUGLAS L. *Jabal al-Akhdar, Cyrenaica: An Historical Geography of Settlement and Livelihood.* 1973. xii + 240 p.

149. YEUNG, YUE-MAN. *National Development Policy and Urban Transformation in Singapore: A Study of Public Housing and the Marketing System.* 1973. x + 204 p.

150. HALL, FRED L. *Location Criteria for High Schools: Student Transportation and Racial Integration.* 1973. xii + 156 p.

151. ROSENBERG, TERRY J. *Residence, Employment, and Mobility of Puerto Ricans in New York City.* 1974. xi + 230 p.

152. MIKESELL, MARVIN W., ed. *Geographers Abroad: Essays on the Problems and Prospects of Research in Foreign Areas.* 1973. ix + 296 p.

153. OSBORN, JAMES. *Area, Development Policy, and the Middle City in Malaysia.* 1974. x + 291 p.

154. WACHT, WALTER F. *The Domestic Air Transportation Network of the United States.* 1974. ix + 98 p.

155. BERRY, BRIAN J. L. et al. *Land Use, Urban Form and Environmental Quality.* 1974. xxiii + 440 p.

156. MITCHELL, JAMES K. *Community Response to Coastal Erosion: Individual and Collective Adjustments to Hazard on the Atlantic Shore.* 1974. xii + 209 p.

157. COOK, GILLIAN P. *Spatial Dynamics of Business Growth in the Witwatersrand.* 1975. x + 144 p.

160. MEYER, JUDITH W. *Diffusion of an American Montessori Education.* 1975. xi + 97 p.

162. LAMB, RICHARD F. *Metropolitan Impacts on Rural America.* 1975. xii + 196 p.

163. FEDOR, THOMAS STANLEY. *Patterns of Urban Growth in the Russian Empire during the Nineteenth Century.* 1975. xxv + 245 p.

164. HARRIS, CHAUNCY D. *Guide to Geographical Bibliographies and Reference Works in Russian or on the Soviet Union.* 1975. xviii + 478 p.

165. JONES, DONALD W. *Migration and Urban Unemployment in Dualistic Economic Development.* 1975. x + 174 p.

166. BEDNARZ, ROBERT S. *The Effect of Air Pollution on Property Value in Chicago.* 1975. viii + 111 p.

167. HANNEMANN, MANFRED. *The Diffusion of the Reformation in Southwestern Germany, 1518-1534.* 1975. ix + 235 p.

168. SUBLETT, MICHAEL D. *Farmers on the Road: Interfarm Migration and the Farming of Noncontiguous Lands in Three Midwestern Townships. 1939-1969.* 1975. xiii + 214 p.

169. STETZER, DONALD FOSTER. *Special Districts in Cook County: Toward a Geography of Local Government.* 1975. xi + 177 p.

171. SPODEK, HOWARD. *Urban-Rural Integration in Regional Development: A Case Study of Saurashtra, India—1800-1960.* 1976. xi + 144 p.

172. COHEN, YEHOSHUA S., and BRIAN J. L. BERRY. *Spatial Components of Manufacturing Change.* 1975. vi + 262 p.

173. HAYES, CHARLES R. *The Dispersed City: The Case of Piedmont, North Carolina.* 1976. ix + 157 p.

174. CARGO, DOUGLAS B. *Solid Wastes: Factors Influencing Generation Rates.* 1977. 100 p.

176. MORGAN, DAVID J. *Patterns of Population Distribution: A Residential Preference Model and Its Dynamic.* 1978. xiii + 200 p.

177. STOKES, HOUSTON H.; DONALD W. JONES; and HUGH M. NEUBURGER. *Unemployment and Adjustment in the Labor Market: A Comparison between the Regional and National Responses.* 1975. ix + 125 p.

180. CARR, CLAUDIA J. *Pastoralism in Crisis. The Dasanetch and Their Ethiopian Lands.* 1977. xx + 319 p.

181. GOODWIN, GARY C. *Cherokees in Transition: A Study of Changing Culture and Environment Prior to 1775.* 1977. ix + 207 p.

183. HAIGH, MARTIN J. *The Evolution of Slopes on Artificial Landforms, Blaenavon, U.K.* 1978. xiv + 293 p.

184. FINK, L. DEE. *Listening to the Learner: An Exploratory Study of Personal Meaning in College Geography Courses.* 1977. ix + 186 p.

185. HELGREN, DAVID M. *Rivers of Diamonds: An Alluvial History of the Lower Vaal Basin, South Africa.* 1979. xix + 389 p.

186. BUTZER, KARL W., ed. *Dimensions of Human Geography: Essays on Some Familiar and Neglected Themes.* 1978. vii + 190 p.

187. MITSUHASHI, SETSUKO. *Japanese Commodity Flows.* 1978. x + 172 p.

188. CARIS, SUSAN L. *Community Attitudes toward Pollution.* 1978. xii + 211 p.

189. REES, PHILIP M. *Residential Patterns in American Cities: 1960.* 1979. xvi + 405 p.

190. KANNE, EDWARD A. *Fresh Food for Nicosia.* 1979. x + 106 p.

192. KIRCHNER, JOHN A. *Sugar and Seasonal Labor Migration: The Case of Tucumán, Argentina.* 1980. xii + 174 p.

194. HARRIS, CHAUNCY D. *Annotated World List of Selected Current Geographical Serials, Fourth Edition. 1980.* 1980. iv + 165 p.

196. LEUNG, CHI-KEUNG, and NORTON S. GINSBURG, eds. *China: Urbanizations and National Development.* 1980. ix + 283 p.

197. DAICHES, SOL. *People in Distress: A Geographical Perspective on Psychological Well-being.* 1981. xiv + 199 p.

198. JOHNSON, JOSEPH T. *Location and Trade Theory: Industrial Location, Comparative Advantage, and the Geographic Pattern of Production in the United States.* 1981. xi + 107 p.

199-200. STEVENSON, ARTHUR J. *The New York–Newark Air Freight System.* 1982. xvi + 440 p.

201. LICATE, JACK A. *Creation of a Mexican Landscape: Territorial Organization and Settlement in the Eastern Puebla Basin, 1520-1605.* 1981. x + 143 p.

202. RUDZITIS, GUNDARS. *Residential Location Determinants of the Older Population.* 1982. x + 117 p.

203. LIANG, ERNEST P. *China: Railways and Agricultural Development, 1875-1935.* 1982. xi + 186 p.

204. DAHMANN, DONALD C. *Locals and Cosmopolitans: Patterns of Spatial Mobility during the Transition from Youth to Early Adulthood.* 1982. xiii + 146 p.

206. HARRIS, CHAUNCY D. *Bibliography of Geography. Part II: Regional. Volume 1. The United States of America.* 1984. viii + 178 p.

207-208. WHEATLEY, PAUL. *Nagara and Commandery: Origins of the Southeast Asian Urban Traditions.* 1983. xv + 472 p.

209. SAARINEN, THOMAS F.; DAVID SEAMON; and JAMES L. SELL, eds. *Environmental Perception and Behavior: An Inventory and Prospect.* 1984. x + 263 p.

210. WESCOAT, JAMES L., JR. *Integrated Water Development: Water Use and Conservation Practice in Western Colorado.* 1984. xi + 239 p.

211. DEMKO, GEORGE J., and ROLAND J. FUCHS, eds. *Geographical Studies on the Soviet Union: Essays in Honor of Chauncy D. Harris.* 1984. vii + 294 p.

212. HOLMES, ROLAND C. *Irrigation in Southern Peru: The Chili Basin.* 1986. ix + 199 p.

213. EDMONDS, RICHARD LOUIS. *Northern Frontiers of Qing China and Tokugawa Japan: A Comparative Study of Frontier Policy.* 1985. xi + 209 p.

214. FREEMAN, DONALD B., and GLEN B. NORCLIFFE. *Rural Enterprise in Kenya: Development and Spatial Organization of the Nonfarm Sector.* 1985. xiv + 180 p.

215. COHEN, YEHOSHUA S., and AMNON SHINAR. *Neighborhoods and Friendship Networks: A Study of Three Residential Neighborhoods in Jerusalem.* 1985. ix + 137 p.

216. OBERMEYER, NANCY J. *Bureaucrats, Clients, and Geography: The Bailly Nuclear Power Plant Battle in Northern Indiana.* 1989. x + 135 p.

217-218. CONZEN, MICHAEL P., ed. *World Patterns of Modern Urban Change: Essays in Honor of Chauncy D. Harris*. 1986. x + 479 p.

219.   KOMOGUCHI, YOSHIMI. *Agricultural Systems in the Tamil Nadu: A Case Study of Peruvalanallur Village*. 1986. xvi + 175 p.

220.   GINSBURG, NORTON; JAMES OSBORN; and GRANT BLANK. *Geographic Perspectives on the Wealth of Nations*. 1986. ix + 133 p.

221.   BAYLSON, JOSHUA C. *Territorial Allocation by Imperial Rivalry: The Human Legacy in the Near East*. 1987. xi + 138 p.

222.   DORN, MARILYN APRIL. *The Administrative Partitioning of Costa Rica: Politics and Planners in the 1970s*. 1989. xi + 126 p.

223.   ASTROTH, JOSEPH H., JR. *Understanding Peasant Agriculture: An Integrated Land-Use Model for the Punjab*. 1989. xiii + 173 p.

224.   PLATT, RUTHERFORD H.; SHEILA G. PELCZARSKI; and BARBARA K. BURBANK, eds. *Cities on the Beach: Management Issues of Developed Coastal Barriers*. 1987. vii + 324 p.

225.   LATZ, GIL. *Agricultural Development in Japan: The Land Improvement District in Concept and Practice*. 1989. viii + 135 p.

226.   GRITZNER, JEFFREY A. *The West African Sahel: Human Agency and Environmental Change*. 1988. xii + 170 p.

227.   MURPHY, ALEXANDER B. *The Regional Dynamics of Language Differentiation in Belgium: A Study in Cultural-Political Geography*. 1988. xiii + 249 p.

228-229. BISHOP, BARRY C. *Karnali under Stress: Livelihood Strategies and Seasonal Rhythms in a Changing Nepal Himalaya*. 1990. xviii + 460 p.